THE LONGEST CAMPAIGN

THE LONGEST CAMPAIGN

Britain's Maritime Struggle in the Atlantic and
Northwest Europe, 1939–1945

BRIAN E. WALTER

CASEMATE
Oxford & Philadelphia

Published in Great Britain and the United States of America in 2020 by
CASEMATE PUBLISHERS
The Old Music Hall, 106–108 Cowley Road, Oxford OX4 1JE, UK
and
1950 Lawrence Road, Havertown, PA 19083, US)

Hardback Edition: ISBN 978-1-61200-856-1
Digital Edition: ISBN 978-1-61200-857-8

A CIP record for this book is available from the British Library

Printed and bound in the Czech Republic by FINIDR, s.r.o.

Typeset by Versatile PreMedia Services (P) Ltd

For a complete list of Casemate titles, please contact:

CASEMATE PUBLISHERS (UK)
Telephone (01865) 241249
Email: casemate-uk@casematepublishers.co.uk
www.casematepublishers.co.uk

CASEMATE PUBLISHERS (US)
Telephone (610) 853-9131
Fax (610) 853-9146
Email: casemate@casematepublishers.com
www.casematepublishers.com

*To my daughters, Kaleigh and Ashley. You are my inspiration
and greatest source of pride.*

Contents

Introduction

Although often limited in its early applications, the origins of British naval power stretch back more than a millennium. As early as the waning stages of the Roman occupation, a Count of the Saxon Shore was established to defend the eastern and southern coasts of Roman Britain from maritime raiders. In the 9th century Alfred the Great created a small naval force to counter Viking marauders plaguing his Anglo-Saxon kingdom of Wessex. Later, in 1217 an English fleet of about 40 ships defeated a French force twice its size during the battle of Sandwich, thus helping to end a short-lived French occupation of southern England. Twelve decades later, England and France embarked upon a period of near perpetual warfare that later became known as the Hundred Years War. Early in this conflict, in 1340, an English fleet won a smashing victory over a larger French fleet off Sluys in Flanders, giving the English temporary control over the Channel and ensuring that the succeeding warfare would be waged on French soil. In the decades of combat that followed, fortunes waned back and forth, but England's maritime effort generally succeeded in providing adequate support for their forces in France.

The next major event in Britain's burgeoning naval heritage occurred in the latter half of the 16th century when England stood under the imminent threat of Spanish invasion. By this time numerous advances in nautical and navigational technology had been made, and naval combat was now dominated by multi-mast, cannon-armed, sailing ships. In 1587 a small English squadron launched a pre-emptive raid against Cadiz where it caused great destruction to the assembled Spanish ships and delayed Spain's invasion preparations. Sadly, this respite was short-lived. On 19 July 1588 a Spanish force of 130 ships, known as the Spanish Armada, entered the western English Channel and proceeded towards Calais where it planned to embark an invasion army for a subsequent assault against England. The English contested this incursion with an improvised fleet of roughly 200 ships that were generally smaller than their Spanish counterparts. After several days of inconsequential skirmishing, the English finally scored decisive victory during the battle of Gravelines on 29 July when they severely mauled the Armada and drove it out of the English Channel into the North Sea. Thereafter, the Spanish made a long circumvention around the British Isles which cost them several additional ships to storms and navigational hazards. When the survivors finally arrived back in Spain at the end of September, they did so with only about half of their original number.

England's victory over the Spanish Armada had momentous implications far exceeding the obvious result of saving the nation from invasion. In many respects, the battle served as a transitional point that saw England begin a long period of ascendancy while Spain began a concurrent period of decline. In the next three centuries, England, and later Great Britain following the union with Scotland in 1707, transformed itself from an unassuming island nation perched on the edge of the European continent to a premier world power with an empire spanning the globe. A number of factors contributed to this transformation, but none was more important than the effective exploitation of sea power to establish and maintain colonies, facilitate trade, fuel economic enterprise and exert national influence. This was by no means an easy process as England, and later Great Britain, engaged in an extensive series of wars against its European competitors. Generally speaking, these wars were waged to gain and hold economic and political power, and they rarely included a danger to national independence. Likewise, these conflicts often involved shifting alliances where allies and foes regularly changed depending upon the circumstances.

One factor that remained undeniably constant during this period was England's/Britain's dependency upon sea power as its primary instrument of war. As such, throughout these various conflicts the British engaged in hundreds of naval actions against their assorted maritime competitors, namely Spain, the Netherlands and France. These actions ranged in size from major fleet battles to combat between individual ships and occurred across the world's oceans as well as in European waters. The British were by no means universally successful in all of these actions, and many of the larger conflicts ended without decisive results. Still, the overriding trend throughout this period was one of growing British expansion and ascendancy. In keeping with this, the British won a number of noteworthy victories during this time including at Portland, Gabbard Bank and Scheveningen in 1653, Santa Cruz in 1657, Lowestoft in 1665, La Hogue in 1692, Vigo Bay in 1702, Cabrita Point in 1705, Cape Passero in 1718, Cape Finisterre in 1747, Lagos and Quiberon Bay in 1759, Cape St. Vincent in 1780 and the Saints in 1782.

By 1793 Great Britain had established itself as the world's premier naval power in terms of size, professionalism and capability, with France a close second and Spain and the Netherlands now relegated to the status of secondary powers. Over the next two decades this position was sorely tested as Britain began a long period of near-continuous warfare against France, fuelled by that nation's revolution and subsequent rise of Napoleon. Like so many earlier conflicts, this was coalition warfare with Britain forming a series of alliances with other European powers to confront France. While many of Britain's allies possessed sizable armies, none possessed any meaningful naval strength. By comparison, France was able to garner allies of its own, which throughout much of the conflict included both Spain and the Netherlands. As such, for at least part of the conflict the British found themselves outnumbered by a factor of more than two to one in terms of combined fleet sizes. Making matters worse, the French army proved to be a highly formidable adversary, and Britain's allies were repeatedly bested in a series of battles that left France the dominant military power on the continent. By the early turn of the century this dominance threatened to encompass Britain itself as the French made preparations to launch an invasion across the Channel. With an assembly of 130,000 French troops in the Boulogne area, this constituted Britain's most serious invasion threat since the Spanish Armada.

Fortunately, throughout this period the British Royal Navy effectively answered France's many triumphs on the battlefield with its own series of spectacular maritime victories and dozens of lesser successes. In terms of the former, the first major achievement occurred in the opening year of the war when British forces temporarily occupied Toulon and seized or destroyed a third of the French Mediterranean Fleet. Then on 1 June 1794 the British Channel Fleet scored a striking tactical victory over the French Atlantic Fleet some 400 nautical miles west of Ushant. Three years later disparate British squadrons scored noteworthy victories against Spanish and Dutch forces at Cape St. Vincent and Camperdown respectively. The next year a British squadron destroyed a larger French force off Aboukir Bay in the battle of the Nile, thus gaining Britain control over the Mediterranean and forcing France to abandon its ambitions in Egypt. In 1801 a British squadron destroyed a large portion of the Danish Fleet at Copenhagen, tightening Britain's blockade against France. Finally, in 1805 a British fleet won a decisive victory over a larger Franco-Spanish fleet off Cape Trafalgar in which the latter was largely destroyed. This spectacular victory solidified Britain's maritime dominance and irrevocably eliminated the threat of invasion to the British Isles. While the war continued on for another ten years, the remaining naval portion was limited to minor actions including follow-up British victories at Cape Ortegal in 1805, San Domingo in 1806, Basque Roads in 1809 and Lissa in 1811. Meanwhile, French fortunes on the battlefield eventually waned, culminating in their final defeat to an Anglo-Prussian army at Waterloo in 1815.

The conclusion of the Napoleonic Wars brought about a period of relative peace and stability to Europe that lasted almost a full century. Given this circumstance, the Royal Navy enjoyed a similar respite from hostilities. In fact, during the next 99 years it only participated in one major naval battle, which occurred in 1827 when a combined force of British, French and Russian warships destroyed a larger Turkish-Egyptian fleet at Navarino Bay in Greece. Devoid of significant European commitments, the navy turned most of its attention to consolidating, expanding and policing the British Empire while concurrently ensuring freedom of navigation for global British trade. Related to this, the British also made considerable efforts to suppress piracy and international slave trading. Meanwhile, the merchant fleet, which for centuries had played a significant role in facilitating Britain's maritime ascendancy, now enjoyed a period of unparalleled dominance as an ever-increasing number of British merchant ships staffed by the world's largest merchant marine of trained, commercial seaman traversed the world's oceans in pursuit of international commerce. In carrying out these various activities, the Royal Navy and British merchant marine played an essential role in bringing about a period known as Pax Britannica in which the British Empire became the global hegemonic power. This, in turn, brought immense prosperity to the British nation and served as an instrument of stability and advancement throughout the world.

The period also brought about great technical and industrial innovations that changed the face of naval warfare. In quick succession, the ships of the Napoleonic era became obsolete as the various navies built a series of new vessels in which steam propulsion replaced sails, iron and later steel construction replaced wood and rifled, breach-loading, turret-mounted guns replaced smooth-bore, muzzle-loading, deck guns. At points in time, this became a race between the various naval powers, and the pace of technical improvements was so great that ships were literally obsolete as soon as they were built. Yet, through this all, the Royal Navy maintained a level of overall superiority in terms of numbers and tradition, if not always in technology. Then, in 1906, the Royal Navy achieved a transitional milestone when it launched a new class of *Dreadnaught* super battleships that set the standard for all the world's navies to emulate. Soon the fleet hierarchy consisted of a whole series of heavy warships including battleships, battlecruisers, iron cruisers, light cruisers and destroyers. All of these vessels were immensely more powerful than anything imagined just a few generations before. Other technical innovations that came to the forefront during this period included submarines, mines, torpedoes, the fledgling airplane and radio.

In the opening decade of the 20th century, Britain retained its position as the world's premier naval power, but found itself increasingly challenged in this regard by the recently established state of Germany. During the same period economic and political rivalries and unrest in the Balkans threatened to unravel the stability that Pax Britannica had garnered over the previous century. As tensions mounted, the various European nations paired off in differing alliances to counter perceived adversaries. In 1914 war finally erupted and quickly escalated into a conflict of unprecedented proportions that eventually pitted the British Empire, France, Russia, Italy and the late-coming United States against the German, Austrian-Hungarian and Ottoman Empires. This was primarily a ground war with the naval contribution overwhelmingly focused on supply and blockade operations carried out by the two major naval antagonists, Britain and Germany. In this, there were only a handful of materially significant naval battles including Heligoland Bight and the Falkland

Islands in 1914, Dogger Bank in 1915 and most notably Jutland in 1916. Beyond this, the naval conflict primarily settled upon the execution of submarine and mine warfare. In many respects, this was gruelling and unspectacular duty, but in the end the Royal Navy and British merchant marine prevailed in all their objectives and performed an essential role in bringing about victory for the Allied powers in what eventually became known as World War I.

This conflict also saw the birth and rise of a new service that joined the navy and army in Britain's military establishment. In the 55 years prior, there had been some limited use of stationary balloons to perform reconnaissance, but World War I saw military aviation become an integral component in the execution of national warfare. The primary instrument in this new military revolution was the heavier-than-air airplane, which had only been in existence for 11 years prior to the start of the war. Not surprisingly, these early aircraft were extremely primitive and were initially only used in a reconnaissance role. However, within a matter of months the various combatants began incorporating a progressive series of technical improvements to their aircraft designs while expanding their uses into a variety of functions including tactical air support, strategic bombing, aerial combat and maritime support. In terms of the latter, on several occasions bomb- or torpedo-armed aircraft carried out successful attacks that sank or damaged both naval and commercial vessels thus establishing the airplane as a legitimate weapon in maritime combat. Meanwhile, the expansion of aerial operations continued, and by war's end all the major combatants possessed sizable 'air forces' to carry out this new form of warfare. Of these, none was larger than Britain's Royal Air Force, which was also the first such command to gain independent status from its naval and army counterparts.

With the cessation of hostilities in 1918, the world entered into an uneasy and turbulent peace. Much of Europe was engulfed in political disillusion and revolution while new global powers such as the United States and Japan came to the forefront of the world stage. This was also a period of economic turmoil, which ultimately morphed into a global depression by the end of the next decade. To manoeuvre through these difficult times, a war-weary Britain embarked upon a path of diplomacy, arms control and collective governance as a means to ensure peace and stability. In this regard, Britain was not alone in its diplomatic approach as a wave of pacifism spread across much of the world in response to the carnage of World War I. In the maritime realm, this manifested itself in the adoption of the Washington and London treaties, which curtailed the short-term prospect of a new naval arms race but put significant constraints upon the Royal Navy. Unfortunately, these noble sentiments and efforts quickly proved inadequate in preventing the rise of new adversaries, namely Imperial Japan, Fascist Italy and Nazi Germany, that once again threatened the world order. Of these, Germany was by far the greatest threat as it aggressively rebuilt its military, reoccupied the Rhineland, annexed Austria and Czechoslovakia and made territorial demands against Poland that finally prompted Britain and France to offer Poland defensive guarantees. Sadly, given its ill-placed faith in diplomacy and internationalism, Britain was initially slow in responding to these various provocations. As such, when the spectre of war finally engulfed Europe in the summer of 1939, Britain was only in the early stages of a belated rearmament programme.

Ready or not, Britain once again girded itself for war. In doing so, it depended upon its maritime forces like it had done so many times before to provide the backbone of its military effort. These forces consisted of the Royal Navy, British merchant marine and Royal Air Force (RAF) along with their counterparts from the Commonwealth nations. In considering the standing of the navy and merchant marine, the British could look back over the previous 400 years and take solace in a maritime heritage that was second to none. By comparison, the Royal Air Force was barely 20 years old, but what it lacked in longevity, it more than made up for in terms of enthusiasm, confidence and prior success. As had happened so many times in the past, the hour was once again at hand to put this legacy and esprit de corps to the test. This presented Britain's maritime forces with their greatest challenge to date as they confronted a collective enemy of unprecedented power and malevolence. At stake was not only the survival of the nation, but the prospect of a dark and sinister future for all freedom-loving people. With the world literally hanging in the balance, Britain's maritime services once again answered the call of history and went forth to do their duty.

Explanatory Notes

Main vessel categories

- Principal warships – major combat vessels ranging from battleships to large, purpose-built minesweepers broken down into 12 class groupings listed in Chapter 11.
- Merchant/commercial vessels – civilian vessels used for trade or other commercial purposes such as fishing.
- Minor warships/auxiliaries – small, coastal combatants of less than 500 tons, military support vessels and commercial vessels adopted/converted to perform military tasks.

Vessel sizes

The two primary means used to delineate vessel size are displacement and gross registered tonnage. Displacement refers to a vessel's actual weight as measured by the amount of water it displaces when afloat. Gross registered tonnage refers to a ship's internal volume measured as one ton equaling 100 cubic feet of capacity. In both cases, the resulting measurement is expressed in tons. All principal warship tonnage is an expression of displacement while that for merchant/commercial vessels is a calculation of gross registered tonnage. Minor warships and auxiliaries can reflect either. Finally, submarine displacement can be measured both surfaced and submerged. Unless otherwise specified, submarine tonnage reflects surface displacement.

Armament

- Other than light weapons, the size of most naval guns is expressed in inches reflecting the interior diameter of the barrel.
- Torpedoes are similarly measured in inches reflecting the diameter of the torpedo.

- Main armaments are expressed as guns for surface warships (reflecting the largest guns carried) torpedo tubes (TT) for submarines and aircraft capacity for aircraft carriers.
- At times in the text I will list the tonnage and main armament for certain vessels in the following manner: *T61* (1,931 tons, 4 × 5-inch guns).
- Aircraft bomb loads are expressed in pounds.

Loss presentation

Loss tallies are often presented showing the number of vessels lost and their corresponding tonnage. In terms of merchant/commercial vessels, these tonnage figures reflect gross registered tons. However, in the case of military vessels, tonnage figures can be a combination of both displacement and gross registered tons based upon the vessel types involved. While mixing these calculation methods is not ideal, I found it to be the most practical way to present the information reflecting the primary source data.

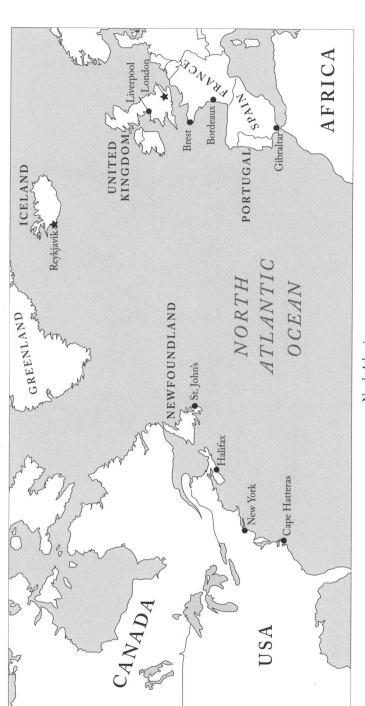

North Atlantic

Northern Europe

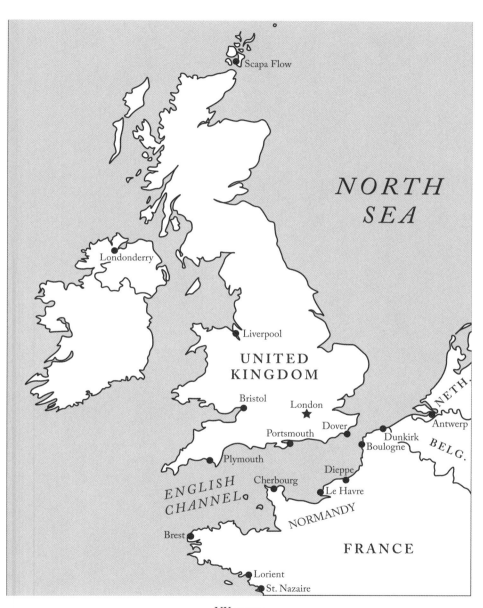

UK waters

CHAPTER I

A Not So Phoney War

Early on the morning of Friday, 1 September 1939, the German battleship *Schleswig-Holstein*, which was in Danzig under the guise of a ceremonial visit, slipped its moorings and commenced a point-blank bombardment of the Polish naval depot and garrison at Westerplatte. Soon, the sound of the battleship's booming guns was echoed a thousand times over as German forces launched a full-scale invasion across the length and breadth of the Polish frontier. With the coming dawn, waves of German aircraft attacked strategic targets throughout Western Poland including airfields, railway lines and other transportation and communication infrastructure. At the same time, five German field armies, containing over 1,500,000 men, crossed the border and attacked Poland from three different directions – out of the north from Prussia, out of the west from Germany and out of the south from Slovakia. Within hours, many of these thrusts were able to overcome or bypass ineffective Polish resistance and make strong advances into the interior of the country. This progress continued over the next few days as the Germans engulfed large tracks of Polish territory.

The Poles resisted this onslaught with bravery and perseverance, but it was quickly apparent that their forces were incapable of stopping the German juggernaut. Numerous factors and deficiencies degraded Poland's ability to offer effective resistance despite its sizable army of upwards of a million men. Foremost amongst these was the technical inferiority of its forces. The Polish army was largely armed with weapons dating back to a previous era and only possessed a fraction of the tanks, aircraft and artillery pieces available to the Germans. Likewise, what heavy weapons they did have were invariably inferior to those of their adversary, and the Polish army was dependent upon rail, horse and leg power for its mobility. As such, the Poles were extremely hard pressed to keep up with and counter the fast-moving armoured and mechanised thrusts of the German army. Adding to these woes, the Polish army was only partially mobilised when the war began. Despite months of tension, the Polish government had declined to fully mobilise its forces in an attempt to avoid provocation. Now, with the invasion wholly underway, many Polish reservists were still en route to their units and many units were still in their assembly areas.

Under these conditions, the Poles had no hope of stopping the German invasion without Allied intervention.

To this end, the British and French governments honoured the obligations they had made to Poland earlier in the year. On the evening of 1 September the British government issued an ultimatum to Germany demanding a suspension of offensive actions and a withdrawal from Polish territory. On the same day, they ordered a full mobilisation of the Royal Navy, army and Royal Air Force. Over the next 24 hours the British and French governments waited for a German response, but this response never came. In the meantime, some officials vainly groped for one last diplomatic solution to stave off a new European war, but these efforts went nowhere. Finally, on the evening of the 2nd, Prime Minister Neville Chamberlain, facing forceful calls for decisive action in the House of Commons, agreed to send one last ultimatum. At 0900 hours on the 3rd the British Ambassador in Berlin delivered a message to the German Foreign Secretary declaring that a state of war would exist between the two countries as of 1100 hours if Germany failed to issue an affirmative response to Britain's demand for a cessation of hostilities. Again, the British received no response, and shortly after the ultimatum's expiration time, Chamberlain informed parliament and the nation that Britain was at war. A few hours later, the French government also declared war on Germany.

Despite these declarations, the Allies did little or nothing to directly influence the fighting in Poland. At the time, Britain lacked the means to provide meaningful direct support to the Poles. The same was generally true of the French with one notable exception. Had the French, who possessed one of the largest armies in Europe, launched an immediate and massive offensive into Western Germany, the Poles might have received some relief. With the bulk of the German army deployed against Poland, Western Germany was thinly defended. Accordingly, a forceful French assault would have likely compelled the Germans to withdraw some of their Polish-engaged units to meet this new threat. This, in turn, may have given the Poles a chance to stabilise their situation; but even then, their long-term prospects would have remained grim. Unfortunately, this proved to be no more than idle conjecture as the French declined to take any significant action. Without this support, Poland's fate was sealed.

A key factor negating any effective Allied response was the speed of the German advance. The Germans employed a new tactical doctrine, referred to as blitzkrieg (lightning war), that emphasised speed and mobility to bypass and overcome less dynamic Polish formations. To the majority of military and political observers schooled in the static trench-style warfare of World War I, blitzkrieg came as a severe shock. With each succeeding day, the Polish situation became more desperate. On the 3rd, German forces cut the Polish Corridor at its base thus trapping sizable Polish formations within. At roughly the same time, the German Third Army, advancing out of Prussia, broke through formidable defences at Mlawa and forced the Poles to retreat. Meanwhile in the south, the German Tenth Army advanced 60 miles in the first five days of the war while the German Fourteenth Army captured the historic city of Krakow on the 6th. On 8 September units of the German Eighth Army reached the outskirts of the Polish capital of Warsaw. In the days that followed other German spearheads converged on Warsaw, and the Germans began a siege of the Polish capital. Meanwhile, on the 10th the Polish commander-in-chief, Marshal Edward Smigly-Rydz, ordered a general withdrawal to the southeast. Unfortunately, by this time many Polish formations were already cut-off and were incapable of making good their escape or offering coordinated resistance. Over the next several days the Germans destroyed many of these isolated units in a piecemeal fashion.

During this time, the naval portion of the campaign was much less pronounced. Early on, the Polish Naval Headquarters had recognised that their small navy was incapable of offering any significant resistance to a German invasion. Therefore, on 30 August the Poles dispatched the modern destroyers *Grom*, *Blyskawica* and *Burza*, to Britain. Of the surface units that remained behind, German aircraft sank most during the first few days of the war. These losses included the destroyer *Wicher*, the minelayer *Gryf*, the torpedo boat *Mazur* and the gunboat *General Haller*. Poland's small submarine force fared better in terms of its own survival, but was unable to score any significant successes against the Germans. On 11 September the Poles ordered their submarines to make for Britain or Sweden. Two submarines, *Wilk* and *Orzel*, eventually arrived in Britain while three others were interned by the Swedes. While this was underway, a number of German warships provided naval fire and logistical support to their forces assaulting Polish coastal positions. On 7 September, the Polish garrison at Westerplatte surrendered after enduring heavy shelling from German naval units including the battleship *Schleswig-Holstein*. In the days and weeks that followed, *Schleswig-Holstein*, its sister ship *Schlesien* and other German warships carried out numerous bombardments of Polish positions at Hochredlau, Oxhöft, Ostrowogrund, Hexengrund and Hela. On 1 October all Polish resistance along the Baltic coast ceased. On the same day the Germans suffered their only naval loss for the campaign when the minesweeper *M85* struck a Polish mine near Heisternest in Danzig Bay.

The cessation of Polish resistance in the Baltic reflected similar occurrences throughout the rest of the country. The coup de grace occurred on 17 September when the Soviet Union launched a major invasion into Eastern Poland. This action was in accordance with a recently signed non-aggression pact between Germany and the Soviet Union and signalled the end of the Polish nation. Over the next several days, the Germans eliminated the last major bastions of organised Polish resistance at Warsaw and Modlin while other German and Soviet forces partitioned the country. By 6 October all significant resistance ended thus culminating the Polish campaign. It had taken Germany just five weeks to conquer Poland. Total German casualties for the campaign amounted to 8,082 dead, 27,278 wounded and 5,029 missing.

Polish casualties were less precise, but may have numbered as high as 70,000 dead and 130,000 wounded.[1] Likewise, the Germans took upwards of 700,000 prisoners. Finally, between 70,000 and 90,000 Polish soldiers escaped to Hungary, Latvia, Lithuania and Romania, where many eventually made their way to the west.

For Poland, the war was over; for Britain, the war had just begun. From the onset, the Admiralty, under the leadership of Winston Churchill as First Lord and Admiral of the Fleet Dudley Pound as First Sea Lord, took stock of its situation and found reasons for cautious optimism. Despite two decades of shameful neglect, Britain still retained the largest navy in the world (with the United States a very close second). By the beginning of September 1939 the Royal Navy's principal warship fighting strength included twelve battleships, three battlecruisers, seven aircraft carriers, 13 heavy cruisers, 39 light cruisers, six anti-aircraft cruisers, 157 destroyers, 69 submarines and 51 sloops and escort vessels.[2] In addition, the Royal Navy had dozens of new warships under construction including five battleships, six aircraft carriers, 19 cruisers and 32 destroyers.[3] Some of these new vessels were just days or weeks away from completion while others would require years before they were ready to join the fleet. Adding to this, the British immediately placed an emergency wartime supplemental order for the procurement of six additional cruisers, 22 destroyers, 36 Hunt-class escort destroyers, 60 Flower-class corvettes, 24 submarines, 16 minesweepers and 38 anti-submarine trawlers.[4]

Nor was this the extent of British naval power. When Britain went to war, so too did its Empire and Commonwealth. In the hours and days immediately following Britain's declaration of war, Australia, New Zealand, South Africa and Canada each followed suit with their own declarations of war against Germany. Some of these nations maintained small naval contingents with close associations to the Royal Navy. Of these, the largest was the Royal Australian Navy, which maintained two heavy cruisers, four light cruisers, five destroyers and two escort vessels. This was followed by the Royal Canadian Navy, which possessed six destroyers. Likewise, the Royal Navy maintained a small Royal New Zealand division that included two light cruisers.[5] This latter division was still technically part of the Royal Navy (and would remain so until October 1941) and is thus already included in the previous strength totals listed above. Finally, the Royal Navy had a powerful ally in the form of the sizable French fleet, which contained five battleships, two battlecruisers, one aircraft carrier, seven heavy cruisers, 12 light cruisers, 70 assorted destroyers and 77 submarines.[6]

Against these powerful navies, the Germans could only muster a significantly smaller fleet. In maritime terms, Germany was unprepared for the war. Early on, Adolf Hitler had assured his naval commanders that war with Britain would not occur before 1944. The Germans had planned and executed their naval building programmes according to this premise, envisioning an eventual fleet consisting of six 56,000-ton super-battleships, seven lesser battleships, four aircraft carriers, dozens of cruisers and destroyers and upwards of 250 U-boats (submarines). Unfortunately for the Germans, the war had started five years earlier than Hitler's prediction, and most of their proposed construction was at the preliminary or planning stages. Adding to this, the Germans had hoped to confront Britain with the assistance of strong Axis partners, but both Italy and Japan were averse to entering the conflict at this time. Accordingly, the German Kriegsmarine (navy) would have to initially fight on its own. To do so, the Kriegsmarine possessed or was about to take possession of two old battleships, two battlecruisers, three pocket battleships, two heavy cruisers, six light cruisers, 22 destroyers, 11 torpedo boats (small destroyers) and 57 U-boats.[7] In addition to this, the Germans also had a number of vessels under construction, but their numbers still paled against that of the British building programme.

The picture was more mixed in terms of quality. Accompanying its immense size, the Royal Navy possessed a large number of older and less modernised ships. This was particularly true in the area of capital ships where 13 out of the 15 British battleships and battlecruisers were of a World War I design and construction. The status was much the same regarding aircraft carriers, with the majority of British carriers being of older and less capable designs. This situation improved markedly when reviewing other warship categories, but a third of Britain's cruisers and destroyers still originated out of the World War I era. Likewise, since the British had opted to maximise the highest number of vessels possible under the tonnage limitations set forth in the Washington and London treaties, many of their cruiser and destroyer classes were smaller and less heavily armed than counterparts in other navies. By comparison, since Germany had rebuilt its navy from almost nothing, the Kriegsmarine contained a significantly higher proportion of new and modern warships. In general, these warships were of excellent design and construction with some classes being larger and more heavily armed than their British counterparts. Therefore, despite the Royal Navy's numerical superiority over the Kriegsmarine, the qualitative position of both navies was more evenly matched.

Turning now to specific warship categories, the Admiralty still viewed the battleship as the main standard of naval power. Britain's two most modern battleships, *Nelson* and *Rodney*, had been completed in 1927. These ships were heavily armed with nine 16-inch guns and possessed good armour protection. However,

Table 1.1 Comparative Fleet Strengths for the Major Combatants in September 1939

	British Empire	France	Germany
Battleships/battlecruisers	15	7	7
Aircraft carriers	7	1	-
Cruisers	64	19	8
Destroyers and torpedo boats	168	70	33
Submarines	69	77	57
Escort vessels and sloops	53	24	10

British designers had compromised speed and some ship handling characteristics in order to attain these attributes while still complying with the tonnage limitations set forth in the Washington Treaty. The bulk of Britain's battle fleet consisted of the *Queen Elizabeth* and *Royal Sovereign* classes. These vessels had been the most powerful ships afloat in their day, but that had been over 20 years previous. Now, with the onset of World War II, more modern designs threatened to surpass these veterans. Nevertheless, despite their age, these were well-tested fighting ships still capable of providing much valued service. This was particularly true of *Warspite, Valiant, Queen Elizabeth, Barham* and *Malaya*, which had all undergone or were in the process of undergoing extensive or partial modernisation. Closing out the battle line were the five *King George V*-class battleships under construction. These were stoutly designed ships with excellent armour protection and reasonably good speed. Their ten 14-inch guns were capable of firing a 15,900-pound broadside some 38,560 yards. Unfortunately, the ship's quadruple 14-inch gun turrets were initially prone to technical problems, but these issues were largely resolved as the war progressed. The first *King George V*-class battleship was not scheduled to enter service until the latter part of 1940.

The greyhounds of the capital fleet were the three battlecruisers. Of these, *Hood* was the largest warship in the world weighing in at some 42,100 tons. It carried a main armament of eight 15-inch guns and was capable of speeds in excess of 30 knots. For two decades *Hood* had served as the pride of the Royal Navy and a global symbol of British maritime power. However, its imposing size and graceful lines concealed a ship with a dangerous deficiency. In order to attain its impressive speed, British designers had sacrificed armour protection. Accordingly, *Hood* was susceptible to enemy fire with particular vulnerability to high angle plunging shots. The remaining battlecruisers, *Renown* and *Repulse*, were capable of similar speeds, but only possessed three-quarters of *Hood*'s tonnage. Likewise, these latter battlecruisers were less heavily armed with a main armament consisting of only six 15-inch guns. Sadly, both vessels had similar deficiencies in armour protection. Of the three battlecruisers, only *Renown* had received significant modernisation during the inter-war years when it was extensively rebuilt from the hull up.

Table 1.2 Characteristics of British Battleships/Battlecruisers

	Number of vessels	Tonnage	Main armament (guns) (in)	Maximum speed (knots)
Nelson-class	2	33,900	9 × 16	23
Queen Elizabeth-class	5	30,600–32,700	8 × 15	24
Royal Sovereign-class	5	29,150	8 × 15	21.5
King George V-class (building)	5	36,700	10 × 14	28.5
Hood-class	1	42,100	8 × 15	31
Renown-class	2	32,000	6 × 15	29

The next major category in the fleet hierarchy was the aircraft carrier. The Royal Navy possessed a great deal of variety in the design and capabilities of its carrier force. Of the seven British carriers in use, five were one-off warships. Likewise, only two of these vessels were purpose build aircraft carriers with the rest being conversions from other warship types. The newest and most capable British carrier was *Ark Royal*. With a maximum speed of 31 knots and the ability to operate over 60 aircraft, *Ark Royal* was arguably one of the best aircraft carriers in the world and ideally suited for fleet operations. *Courageous* and *Glorious* followed this with similar speeds and the ability to carry up to 48 aircraft. *Furious*, *Eagle*, *Hermes* and *Argus* rounded out Britain's available carrier force, but these vessels had smaller aircraft capacities and tended to be less capable than their larger brethren. Of these, *Hermes* and *Argus* were ill-suited for anything other than trade protection and ferrying duties. Finally, the British had four *Illustrious*- and two *Implacable*-class aircraft carriers under construction. These vessels featured an armoured flight deck that afforded them a great deal of protection, but limited the number of aircraft they could carry as compared to contemporary American and Japanese designs. The first *Illustrious*-class aircraft carrier was not due to enter service until the summer of 1940.

Of course, these ships were only as effective as the aircraft they carried. At the onset of the war the Fleet Air Arm (FAA) possessed a mere 232 first-line aircraft with another 191 earmarked for training.[8] This was not even enough aircraft to fully provision each of the British carriers and still maintain necessary shore establishments. In fact, of the seven British carriers, only *Ark Royal* and *Glorious* had their full compliments of aircraft. The remaining carriers all maintained partial compliments with *Courageous* carrying half of its capacity and *Argus* assigned no aircraft at all. Nor was quantity the only factor limiting British naval aviation. The fleet also suffered from a lack of modern aircraft designs. The most prevalent aircraft in the navy's inventory was the Swordfish torpedo-bomber. This biplane equipped 13 squadrons, but looked more suited to World War I service than something you would find in a modern navy. Designed in 1934, the Swordfish was laboriously slow with a top speed of only 139 miles per hour and a limited range of only 546 miles. The aircraft could carry an 18-inch torpedo or an assorted 1,500-pound bomb load. The navy's other strike aircraft was the Blackburn Skua, a monoplane designed to serve as either a fighter or a dive-bomber. The Skua could carry a 500-pound bomb with a top speed of 225 miles per hour and a range of 761 miles. The last Fleet Air Arm aircraft worth mentioning was the Sea Gladiator, a naval version of the RAF's most recent biplane fighter. Although highly manoeuvrable, the Sea Gladiator was generally outclassed by more modern shore-based monoplane fighters.

The Fleet Air Arm's aviation partner in the maritime war was RAF Coastal Command. Unfortunately, just like its naval brethren, Coastal Command suffered from insufficient numbers and a lack of quality aircraft at the beginning of the war.

Table 1.3 Characteristics of British Aircraft Carriers

	Number of vessels	Tonnage	Normal aircraft capacity	Maximum speed (knots)
Ark Royal-class	1	22,000	60	31
Courageous-class	2	22,500	48	30
Furious-class	1	22,450	36	30
Eagle-class	1	22,600	21	24
Hermes-class	1	10,850	15	25
Argus-class	1	14,000	15	20
Illustrious-class (building)	4	23,000	55	30.5
Implacable-class (building)	2	23,450	81	32

Note: The *Illustrious* and *Implacable* classes only had design hanger capacities for 36 and 48 aircraft respectively, but were able to expand this to 55 and 81 aircraft using deck parking arrangements.

In September 1939, Coastal Command had 19 active squadrons. Half of these flew the Avro Anson, a small twin-engine aircraft. Unfortunately, the Anson's limited range of only 790 miles severely restricted its effectiveness as a maritime patrol aircraft and did not even allow it to fully cover the North Sea approaches to Germany. Likewise, the Anson's puny 360-pound bomb load rendered it fairly impotent to anything other than the smallest German vessels. Another obsolete aircraft was the Vickers Vildebeest torpedo-bomber. These comprised two squadrons, but were limited by poor speed and a lack of range. The command did have more capable aircraft coming into its ranks, but these were still few in numbers. One of these was the Lockheed Hudson, an American-built twin-engine reconnaissance bomber that possessed twice the range and bomb load of the Anson. Another was the Short Sunderland, a large four-engine flying boat that had a 2,980-mile range and 13½-hour endurance. This performance, coupled with a 2,000-pound bomb load, allowed the Sunderland to function as a credible mid-ocean patrol aircraft.

Returning now to the fleet, the Royal Navy possessed a variety of cruiser classes ranging from World War I-era designs to new ships still under construction. Amongst the navy's newest and most capable cruisers was the Town-class. These vessels displaced between 9,100 and 10,000 tons (depending upon their grouping) and vaunted a main armament of twelve 6-inch guns. The first Town-class cruiser, *Southampton*, entered service in 1937 and was followed by nine other vessels in the succeeding two years. Based upon this design, the British then introduced the Colony-class. These cruisers maintained the same armament as the 'Towns' but with a reduced displacement of only 8,800 tons. The British had nine such vessels under construction when the war broke out with another two started shortly thereafter. Another cruiser type under construction was the *Dido*-class. These were smaller cruisers primarily designed for air defence. They displaced between 5,450 and 5,770 tons and were armed with eight or ten 5.25-inch dual purpose guns.[9] The British produced a total of 16 '*Didos*' including six vessels started under the 1939 War Emergency

Table 1.4 Characteristics of British Cruisers

	Number of vessels	Tonnage	Main armament (guns) (in)	Maximum speed (knots)
York-class heavy cruisers	2	8,300	6 × 8	32
County-class heavy cruisers	13	9,750–10,000	8 × 8	31–32
Hawkins-class light cruisers	3	9,500–9,850	5-9 × 6 or 7.5	30.5
C-class light cruisers	7	4,180–4,200	5 × 6	29
D-class light cruisers	8	4,850	6 × 6	29
Adelaide-class light cruiser	1	5,100	8 × 6	25
E-class light cruisers	2	7,500	7 × 6	33
Leander-class light cruisers	8	6,980–7,270	8 × 6	32.5
Arethusa-class light cruisers	4	5,220–5,279	6 × 6	32
Town-class light cruisers	10	9,100–10,000	12 × 6	32
Colony-class light cruisers (building)	9 + 2	8,800	12 × 6	33
Dido-class light cruisers (building)	10 + 6	5,450–5,770	8-10 × 5.25	33
C-class anti-aircraft cruisers	6	4,200	6-8 × 4	29

Programme. Finally, in terms of heavy cruisers, the British and Commonwealth navies possessed two different classes, the *York*- and County-class, ranging in size from 8,300 tons to 10,000 tons. Thirteen of these vessels were armed with eight 8-inch guns and two with six 8-inch guns. All of these heavy cruisers were between nine and eleven years old when the war started.

The navy had similar diversity in the class, capability and age of its destroyers. The Empire's combined strength of 168 destroyers comprised no fewer than 17 different classes. The oldest of these were the R-, S-, V- and W-class destroyers built between 1917 and 1924. These classes numbered 54 vessels ranging from 905 to 1,120 tons and carrying main armaments of three to four 4-inch guns and three to six 21-inch torpedo tubes. As the war progressed the navy converted the majority of these older ships to escort destroyers. In fact, by the outbreak of the war the navy had already made 15 such conversions unrelated to the 54 vessels listed above. At the other end of the spectrum, the navy's newest and most capable destroyers were the Tribal, *Javelin*, *Kelly* and *Laforey* classes. These ships ranged in size from 1,690 to 1,920 tons and carried six to eight 4.7-inch guns and four to ten 21-inch torpedo tubes. A total of 40 destroyers, including some still under construction, fell under these classes.

An assortment of lesser warships complemented these fleet assets. Amongst these were the escort vessels earmarked for convoy protection and anti-submarine duties. Included in these numbers were the aforementioned 15 converted escort destroyers and a variety of purpose-built sloops. These latter vessels generally displaced between 990 and 1,350 tons and were armed with a variety of small calibre guns and depth charges. Representative of this was the *Black Swan*-class, the navy's newest sloop, which displaced 1,250 tons and carried a main armament of six 4-inch guns. Added to this were two new classes of escort vessels that were under construction at the beginning of the war. The first of these was the Hunt-class escort destroyer, which displaced 907 tons and carried a main armament of four 4-inch guns, but no torpedo tubes. Although lacking in sea endurance, these vessels were well suited for coastal operations. The second was the Flower-class corvette, which was a new type of anti-submarine escort based upon the design of a commercial whale catcher. Weighing in at 925 tons and armed with a single 4-inch gun as well as anti-aircraft guns and depth charges, the 'Flowers' were slow and lively seagoing ships, but they were cheap and easy to produce and had good endurance for convoy operations.

Closing out the navy's inventory were a variety of disparate vessels used for both offensive and defensive purposes. In terms of the former, the navy maintained 12 different submarine classes. The newest of these was the *Triton*-class, which had a surface displacement of 1,090 tons and an armament of ten 21-inch torpedo tubes and a single 4-inch deck gun. A second submarine type worth noting was the 1,520-ton *Grampus*-class. These boats were specially designed for minelaying and could carry 50 mines as well as six 21-inch torpedo tubes and one 4-inch deck gun. A new type of surface ship designed for the same purpose was the 2,650-ton *Abdiel*-class. These well-armed fast minelayers were capable of high-speed transits (34 knots) and could deliver 165 mines per sortie. Likewise, the British had three classes of minesweepers ranging in size from 656 to 835 tons. Finally, the British maintained two classes of monitors. These cruiser-sized vessels were armed with two 15-inch guns for shore bombardment duties.

Turning now to the Germans, the Kriegsmarine possessed seven capital ships with two more under construction. The oldest of these were *Schlesien* and *Schleswig-Holstein*. These were pre-dreadnought battleships dating back to 1908. Both warships had fought at Jutland where their presence had been more of a hindrance than a benefit to the German High Seas Fleet. Now twenty-three years later these veteran battleships were hopelessly obsolete and completely unsuitable for fleet operations. Accordingly, the Germans generally relegated them to training duties. Nevertheless, their performance in Poland had demonstrated that *Schlesien* and *Schleswig-Holstein* were still capable of some combat value if utilised in a shore bombardment, coastal defence or coastal escort role. The Kriegsmarine's next level of capital ships were the three armoured cruisers *Deutschland* (soon to be renamed *Lützow*), *Admiral Scheer* and *Admiral Graf Spee*. These vessels, referred to as pocket battleships by the British, were only slightly larger than most classes of heavy cruisers, but packed a heavier armament highlighted by six 11-inch and eight 5.9-inch guns. They also had a top speed of 26 knots, which gave them the ability to outrun most vessels they could not outfight. This formidable striking power, coupled with excellent range and endurance, made these pocket battleships highly effective surface raiders.

The remaining capital ships in the Kriegsmarine were significantly larger vessels. The first of these were the battlecruisers *Scharnhorst* and *Gneisenau*. In many respects these battlecruisers were larger extensions of the *Deutschland*-class with a displacement of 31,850 tons and a main armament of nine 11-inch guns. These were excellent fighting ships with a top speed of 31 knots and the ability to absorb heavy punishment. Their only significant deficiency was the small calibre of their main armament, but this was of little consequence if deployed against British commercial traffic. Closing out Germany's capital ship strength were two *Bismarck*-class battleships that were under construction at the outbreak of the war. These large battleships had a displacement of over 41,000 tons and a main armament of eight 15-inch guns. They were heavily armoured vessels, yet capable of speeds approaching 31 knots. Fortunately for the British, the first *Bismarck*-class battleship was not destined to enter service until 1941.

In terms of naval aviation, Germany's position was far less menacing. The Germans had an aircraft carrier, *Graf Zeppelin*, under construction with a projected completion set in 1940. Nevertheless, despite this fast approaching date, the Germans had no specialised naval aircraft ready to embark upon the ship, and the carrier's true operational status was thus far less certain. The Germans did maintain some 228 floatplanes for reconnaissance and torpedo-bomber duties, but the vast majority of these were low-performance shore-based aircraft. To augment this meagre force, the German Luftwaffe earmarked six wings of Heinkel 111 bombers to perform mine-laying and other naval duties. The Heinkel 111 could carry a 5,500-pound bomb load and had a maximum range of 1,280 miles. Likewise, the Luftwaffe had other aircraft that were capable of naval applications. This included the Junkers 87B dive-bomber, which had already earned a fearsome reputation in Poland. The

Table 1.5 Characteristics of Major German Warships

	Number of vessels	Tonnage	Main armament	Maximum speed (knots)
Schlesien-class battleships	2	13,200	4 × 11in guns	16
Deutschland-class pocket battleships	3	11,700–12,100	6 × 11in guns	26
Scharnhorst-class battlecruisers	2	31,850	9 × 11in guns	31
Bismarck-class battleships (building)	2	41,700–42,900	8 × 15in guns	31
Graf Zeppelin-class aircraft carrier (building)	1	23,200	42 aircraft	33.8
Hipper-class heavy cruisers	2 + 2	14,050	8 × 8in guns	32
Emden-class light cruiser	1	5,600	8 × 5.9in guns	29
Königsberg-class light cruisers	3	6,650	9 × 5.9in guns	32
Leipzig-class light cruiser	1	6,515	9 × 5.9in guns	32
Nurnberg-class light cruiser	1	6,980	9 × 5.9in guns	32

Junkers 87B, also known as the Stuka, had a top speed of 238 miles per hour and could carry a 1,100-pound bomb load. Another aircraft worth noting was the Junkers 88A medium bomber. This versatile aircraft had an impressive speed of 280 miles per hour and could carry a 3,960-pound bomb load. Although all of these aircraft were designed for use against land targets, they were capable of delivering heavy punishment against naval and merchant shipping if called upon to do so.

Rounding out the principal warships in the German surface fleet were 49 cruisers, destroyers, torpedo boats and escort destroyers. Included in these numbers were two *Hipper*-class heavy cruisers that were the largest warships of their type in the world weighing in at 14,050 tons. Yet, despite their unequalled size, the '*Hippers*' only carried a main armament equivalent to that of most British heavy cruisers. The Germans also tended to build large destroyers with all of their classes displacing over 2,000 tons. Likewise, the Germans armed their destroyers with 5- or 5.9-inch guns compared to the 4.7-inch guns carried on most British destroyer classes. To put this in perspective, these latter German destroyers with their 5.9-inch guns carried an armament equivalent to some light cruiser classes. The Germans augmented their destroyer force with torpedo boats. Although the British did not use this classification in the Royal Navy, torpedo boats were essentially small destroyers.[10] In this case, these torpedo boats displaced between 844 and 1,294 tons and carried a main armament consisting of one to four 4.1-inch guns and six 21-inch torpedo tubes depending upon the class. Finally, the Germans had ten F-class escort destroyers that weighed in at 712 tons and sported two 4.1-inch guns as their main armament.

As demonstrated in the previous conflict, the Kriegsmarine's most promising weapon was its U-boat force. Yet, despite its vast potential, this force was actually quite weak at the beginning of the war. From the onset, Commodore Karl Dönitz, the commander of Germany's U-boat arm, insisted that he needed 300 ocean-going U-boats to conduct a decisive and sustained campaign against Britain's vast merchant fleet. Nevertheless, in September 1939 Germany's total U-boat strength was only 57 boats or less than one-fifth of this required number. Of these, 30 were small coastal U-boats ranging in size from 250 to 300 tons. These small coastal boats lacked the range to operate in the Atlantic and could only carry a small complement of torpedoes. Accordingly, the Germans generally relegated them to training duties or local operations. Likewise, two of the larger U-boats, *U25* and *U26*, were experimental vessels that were ill suited for combat operations. Taking these factors into account, Donitz's effective ocean-going strength was only 25 boats or one-twelfth of his required number. To make matters worse, early U-boat operations were severely degraded by faulty torpedoes that often malfunctioned, detonated prematurely or failed to detonate altogether.

It is also prudent to briefly describe the technical limitations universal to all submarine classes (both Allied and Axis) at the time. A more accurate name to describe the era's submarines was submersibles, since these vessels were only capable of

Table 1.6 Comparative Characteristics of Selected British and German Destroyers and Escort Vessels

	Tonnage	Main armament	Maximum speed (knots)
British			
Laforey-class destroyers	1,920	6 × 4.7in guns, 8 × 21in TT	36
Javelin-class destroyers	1,690	6 × 4.7in guns, 10 × 21in TT	36
Tribal-class destroyers	1,870	8 × 4.7in guns, 4 × 21in TT	36
B-class destroyers	1,360	4 × 4.7in guns, 8 × 21in TT	35
V- and W-class destroyers	1,100	4 × 4in guns, 5–6 × 21in TT	34–35
R- and S-class destroyers	905	1–3 × 4in guns, 0–3 × 21in TT	34–36
Hunt-class escort destroyers	907–1,050	4–6 × 4in guns	27
Germans			
1934A-class destroyers	2,270	5 × 5in guns, 8 × 21in TT	38
1936-class destroyers	2,411	5 × 5in guns, 8 × 21in TT	38
1936A (Narvik)-class destroyers	2,603	5 × 5.9in guns, 8 × 21in TT	38.5
1923-class torpedo boats	924	3 × 4.1in guns, 6 × 21in TT	33
1935-class torpedo boats	844	1 × 4.1in gun, 6 × 21in TT	35
1939-class torpedo boats	1,294	4 × 4.1in guns, 6 × 21in TT	32.5
F-class escort destroyers	712	2 × 4.1in guns	28

operating submerged for finite periods of time. This was due to their limited battery capacity to power their electric motors and their inability to regenerate breathable air. Likewise, while submerged operations provided submarines with stealth, this came at a heavy cost including reduced handling and speed performance, severely restricted visibility and an inability to transmit and receive radio communications. As such, submarines spent most of their time operating on the surface using diesel engines for power and propulsion. This was particularly true when transiting across long distances. Likewise, these same diesel engines recharged the batteries used for underwater operations. Given these factors, most submarines only operated submerged sparingly as dictated by tactical circumstances.

Returning now to the competitive situation, in addition to the size and disposition of the opposing fleets, both Britain and Germany faced different strategic realities that impacted the way each nation conducted its maritime war. For Britain, access to the sea was a source of power and a necessary means to survival. In particular, Britain, as an island nation, depended upon maritime commerce to sustain its economy, population and ability to wage war. By 1939 Britain was no longer capable of feeding its entire population, and a significant portion of its foodstuffs had to come from overseas. Likewise, the British required large influxes of material imports to sustain their economy. These imports included some 11,000,000 tons of timber, 8,000,000 tons of iron ore and 12,000,000 tons of fuel oil on an annual basis. In all, pre-war British imports had amounted to an aggregated 68,000,000 tons in 1938.[11]

Of course, the British could reduce some of these import requirements through rationing and increased domestic production, but they were incapable of attaining anything close to full self-sufficiency. Accordingly, a significant disruption to British imports could immediately debilitate the nation, and a severe enough drop could result in a total economic and social collapse.

The Admiralty also had to consider the advantages and disadvantages associated with Britain's global empire. First of all, this empire and global position gave Britain access to all the world's resources including the vast industrial output of the United States and the rich oil fields of the Middle East. Likewise, it provided Britain with multiple bases from which the Royal Navy could operate and control the seas. However, Britain's global interest also presented obligations that required the Royal Navy to disperse its fighting strength across the world's oceans to confront threats both real and potential. Likewise, since Britain's overall position was essentially defensive, the Royal Navy surrendered some of the initiative to the Germans and had to maintain a presence everywhere in response to possible enemy incursions. This diversion of resources significantly negated Britain's numerical superiority over the Kriegsmarine since the latter could mass its forces at times and places of its choosing without being constrained by similar defensive considerations.

This latter point was true because of Germany's continental status and reduced reliance on maritime commerce. Positioned in the middle of Europe, Germany derived most of its economic needs from internal sources or its neighbours. Likewise, the Germans maintained no overseas possessions to defend or support. On the other hand, the 4,196,995-ton German merchant fleet was only a fraction the size of Britain's, and the Germans had to traverse British-controlled choke points to reach the open ocean. Accordingly, while the Germans were almost certain to lose their direct access to overseas trade, they were far better positioned to endure this likelihood than were the British. To this end, Germany's recent agreement with the Soviet Union provided for the importation of a number of materials including foodstuffs and oil. The Germans also hoped to receive some vital imports through the assistance of friendly European mediators such as Italy. On the other hand, despite these provisions, Germany still faced the prospect of a loss or reduction of many strategic imports. At the outbreak of the war, total German imports amounted to 56,500,000 tons of which 29,000,000 tons came from overseas sources. Paramount amongst these was 11,000,000 tons of iron ore imported annually from Northern Scandinavia.[12] Other important imports included nickel, molybdenum, copper, petroleum, timber, rubber, wool, tea, coffee, cocoa and citrus fruits. Thus, while not susceptible to an immediate collapse, the German economy was vulnerable to slow strangulation from a prolonged British blockade.

Under these conditions, the Royal Navy and Kriegsmarine went forth to wage war on each other. In many respects, each side adopted strategies that were identical to those used in World War I. For the Admiralty, the first order of business was to secure maritime lines of communication and ensure a steady flow of life-sustaining imports to the British nation. Concurrent with this, the British immediately initiated a maritime blockade of Germany to slowly debilitate that nation's will and ability to wage war. Finally, the Royal Navy resolved to support the needs of the army with the most immediate task being the transportation of the British Expeditionary Force to Europe and its subsequent maintenance. For their part, the Germans ceded the likelihood they would lose commercial access to the open oceans, but hoped for an early resolution of the war to mitigate the long-term impact of the British blockade. To this end, Hitler still hoped to arrange a negotiated settlement and initially restricted offensive naval actions to avoid further provocation. However, as it became clear that Britain was unwilling to negotiate, Hitler quickly loosened these restrictions, and the Kriegsmarine mounted an aggressive campaign to destroy British maritime commerce.

In response to this threat, the Admiralty immediately implemented a convoy system to shepherd Allied shipping to and from Britain and other strategic locations throughout the world. In 1939 the British merchant fleet contained some 3,000 deep-sea dry cargo ships and tankers and about 1,000 coastal vessels worth 21,000,000 tons. On average, 2,500 of these vessels were at sea at any given time.[13] Likewise,

The cornerstone in Britain's maritime defensive strategy was the convoy. Eventually, nearly all military and commercial traffic travelled in these protected groupings. Amongst these were 85,775 merchant ships that travelled to and from the United Kingdom in trade convoys as well as 175,608 ships that sailed in British coastal convoys during the duration of the war. (Priest, L. C. (Lt), Royal Navy official photographer, public domain)

the British employed hundreds of Allied and neutral merchant ships to support their commercial and military needs. Organising this large volume of traffic into a worldwide convoy network was a Herculean task, but the British persevered and quickly attained results. The first British convoy formed and sailed from Gibraltar to Cape Town on 2 September. In the days and weeks that followed, the British organised a comprehensive system of convoys to traverse British coastal waters and move shipping across the Atlantic. Early on, this coverage was far from complete, and large numbers of merchant vessels continued to sail independently. Nevertheless, during the first month of the war some 900 vessels sailed in these convoys with this increasing to 5,756 ships by the end of 1939.[14] Clearly, the Admiralty was committed to using escorted convoys as a cornerstone in its defensive strategy.

Of the various convoys involved, none were more important to Britain's long-term survival and war effort than those travelling between North America and the United Kingdom. The first of these were designated HX convoys, which assembled at Halifax, Nova Scotia and travelled across the Atlantic largely unescorted. It was only when they reached a longitude of between 12° and 15° west (about 200 miles west of Ireland) that British anti-submarine surface forces rendezvoused with these convoys to bring them the rest of the way into Liverpool or Southend depending upon their ultimate destination. Reverse convoys, designated OA if they originated from Southend or OB if they originated from Liverpool, followed similar patterns with escorts only proceeding with them as far as 12° to 15° west before breaking off to rendezvous with synchronised incoming convoys. The occasional presence of Coastal Command flying-boats provided a modicum of additional protection to these convoys, but this coverage was limited to a point of only 8° west.[15] Still, given the small size of the German U-boat force and the distances between German bases and the open Atlantic, these provisions were considered adequate.

While this was underway, the British implemented a series of measures to blockade Germany and sever its access to the Atlantic Ocean. This included periodic sorties by elements of the Home Fleet into the North Sea to search out German commercial and military traffic. At the same time the Admiralty dispatched ten cruisers to establish the Northern Patrol between the Shetland Islands and Iceland. In October the British sent additional cruisers and armed merchant cruisers[16] to reinforce this barrage and extend its patrol area to include the Denmark Strait. Meanwhile, British submarines established their own patrol lines between the Shetland Islands and Norway and off the north coast of Germany. Likewise, the British began laying defensive minefields to close off the English Channel to German U-boat traffic. Finally, the British deployed two hunting groups, built around the aircraft carriers *Ark Royal* and *Courageous*, to search for U-boats in the Western Approaches and Channel area.

Utilising these strategies, it did not take long before each side inflicted losses on the other. On 3 September 1939 the British destroyer *Somali* encountered and captured the 2,377-ton German merchant ship *Hannah Boge* some 350 miles south of Iceland. This was the first seaborne vessel to be captured during the war. At roughly the same time, the British cruiser *Ajax* intercepted the German merchant ships *Carl Fritzen* and *Olinda* (6,594 and 4,576 tons respectively) off the River Plate in the South Atlantic. In this case, the German ships scuttled themselves to avoid capture. Against this, the British merchant fleet also suffered its first loss on the evening of 3 September when the German U-boat *U30* torpedoed and sank the 13,581-ton passenger liner *Athenia* off Rockall Bank. This sinking, which cost 112 lives including 28 Americans, caused an immediate uproar in the West as many feared a return to unrestricted German submarine warfare. In fact, the attack was ostensibly the result of misidentification as the U-boat commander, Lieutenant Fritz-Julius Lemp, had reportedly mistaken *Athenia* for an armed merchant cruiser. In response to this, Hitler issued additional instructions further restricting mercantile rules of engagement.

Notwithstanding these restrictions, Germany's modest U-boat force continued to score a steady stream of successes against British and Allied shipping. One of the vessels almost included in this tally was the aircraft carrier *Ark Royal*. On 14 September *U39* fired a salvo of torpedoes at the carrier, which was patrolling west of the Hebrides. Fortunately for the British, the German torpedoes exploded prematurely, and the destroyers *Faulknor*, *Foxhound* and *Firedrake* immediately counterattacked and sank the offending U-boat. The situation had a different result three days later when *U29* torpedoed the British aircraft carrier *Courageous* southwest of Ireland. Hit by three torpedoes, *Courageous* sank in less than 15 minutes taking 518 officers and men with it. The loss of *Courageous* and near loss of *Ark Royal* persuaded the Admiralty to withdraw its aircraft carriers from anti-submarine operations. Meanwhile, the U-boats continued to operate around Britain and the eastern North Atlantic. Together, these boats sank a total of 41 merchant ships worth 153,879 tons during the month of September.[17] Most of these losses came from ships sailing independently and not under convoy protection.

In October the German U-boat arm scored its second spectacular success in as many months. On the night of 13/14 October *U47*, commanded by Lieutenant-Commander Gunther Prien, braved perilous tidal currents and shoals to penetrate through a gap in the British defences at Scapa Flow. Once inside the Home Fleet's main base, *U47* carried out a leisurely attack against the stationary battleship *Royal Oak*. Despite several torpedo failures, Prien succeeded in hitting *Royal Oak* with three torpedoes. In a matter of minutes the stricken battleship capsized and sank taking a heavy loss of life with it. In all, 833 members of the ship's company, including Rear-Admiral H. E. C. Blagrove, the commander of the Second Battle Squadron, lost their lives. In the melee that followed, *U47* was able to retrace its route and make good its escape. Lieutenant-Commander Prien and *U47* then returned to Germany and a well-deserved hero's welcome. Meanwhile, the British were left to contemplate their misfortune as they scurried to correct defensive deficiencies.

Yet, despite this dramatic success, the fortunes of Germany's U-boat arm actually declined during this period. Improved British defences, increased convoy usage and a lack of U-boat availability all combined to temper German successes. From October through December 1939 German U-boats sank 73 merchant ships worth a combined total of 267,277 tons. This averaged out to approximately 24 ships sunk per month compared to 41 lost in September. Losses increased in January and February as U-boats sank 85 merchant ships worth 280,829 tons. However, the vast majority of these losses came from Allied or neutral nations, and only a handful of British flag carriers were sunk. In March U-boat successes dropped to 23 ships worth 62,781 tons of which the majority were again Allied or neutral vessels. When added together, direct German U-boat attacks sank a total of 222 merchant ships worth 764,766 tons during the first seven months of the war.[18] Of these, only 91 ships worth between 364,683 and 369,700 tons (depending upon the source) were British.[19] Thus, given the size of the merchant fleets involved and the number of trips made during this period, these losses were not unduly heavy.

By comparison, the German U-boat arm paid a high price for these inconclusive results. During the first seven months of the war the Kriegsmarine lost a total of 17 U-boats through British action and accidents. In addition to *U39*, which was sunk following its unsuccessful attack against *Ark Royal*, British destroyers and escorts sank *U27, U42, U45, U16, U35, U55, U41, U33, U53* and *U63* from September 1939 through March 1940. Mines claimed the destruction of four more boats (*U12, U40, U54* and *U44*) during the same period. Finally, the British submarine *Salmon* and an accidental collision accounted for *U36* and *U15* respectively. In addition to these losses, a RAF Blenheim medium bomber severely damaged *U31* in shallow water in Schillig Roads thus contributing to a further erosion in German U-boat availability. Together, these losses represented an attrition rate exceeding the pace of replacement construction, and by April 1940 the Kriegsmarine's overall U-boat strength had declined to 52 boats.[20] Under these circumstances, the Royal Navy was clearly holding its own and making progress against Germany's vaunted U-boat arm.

Of course, U-boats were not the only weapons available to the Kriegsmarine. The Germans also employed large quantities of mines to interdict British coastal traffic. Of particular concern were German magnetic mines that could sit stealthily on the seabed until activated by the magnetic field of a ship passing overhead. The Germans used a number of means including submarines, destroyers and aircraft to deliver these mines. Principal targets included the Thames Estuary, Harwich, Cromer, the mouth of the Humber, the Tyne of Newcastle, the Firth of Forth and Loch Ewe. At first the British had no means to detect or counter magnetic mines, and shipping losses rose alarmingly. During the first two months of the war mines claimed 19 vessels worth 59,027 tons. In November these losses ballooned to 27 ships worth 120,958 tons, and the situation became so bad that only a single channel remained open in the Thames Estuary.

Despite two high-profile successes, the early German U-boat campaign was hampered by operational and technical deficiencies. Pictured here is *U39*, which was sunk by British destroyers following an unsuccessful attack against the aircraft carrier *Ark Royal*. (Public domain)

Fortunately for the British, relief was soon at hand. On 23 November the British discovered a German magnetic mine in the mud flats off Shoeburyness. This mine, dropped by a German aircraft, had landed in an area accessible to the British. A Royal Navy team led by Lieutenant-Commander J. G. D. Ouvry defused the mine and made it safe for transport to Portsmouth. Once there, British authorities studied the mine and learned its electromagnetic principles. With this knowledge, a research team under the direction of Rear-Admiral W. F. Wake-Walker quickly developed countermeasures to neutralise these mines. Paramount amongst these was a degaussing girdle attached to ships to demagnetise their hulls. The British also fitted degaussing girdles on RAF Wellington bombers to serve as aerial mine-sweepers. These specially modified aircraft would fly low over the sea to detonate any localised magnetic mines through the generation of an electromagnetic field. With the advent of these countermeasures and a dwindling of German magnetic mine stocks, the crisis soon eased. Nevertheless, during the first seven months of the war German mines claimed the destruction of 128 merchant ships worth 429,899 tons.[21] As in the case of U-boat attacks, only about half of this lost tonnage (220,100 tons) came from British flagged ships.[22] The remainder came from Allied or neutral vessels. In addition, the British destroyers *Blanche*, *Gipsy* and *Grenville* and six auxiliary warships all sank on German mines. Similarly, mine detonations severely damaged the cruiser *Belfast* and the battleship *Nelson* on 21 November and 4 December respectively.

Adding to British discomfort was the threat posed by German surface raiders. At the beginning of the war, the pocket battleships *Graf Spee* and *Deutschland* were both loose in the Atlantic. Although unaware of these specific movements, the Admiralty initially considered the threat of surface raiders as the greatest menace to their maritime communications. Yet, despite these concerns, both surface raiders remained idle during the first month of the war as Hitler hoped to entice the Allies back to the negotiating table after the demise of Poland. Finally, on 26 September Hitler gave the pocket battleships permission to begin offensive operations against British and Allied commercial traffic. *Deutschland*, which was operating in the North Atlantic, found it difficult to find undefended targets in lieu of the British convoy system and eventually returned to Germany on 15 November after sinking only two ships worth 6,962 tons. By comparison, *Graf Spee*, under the command of Captain Hans Langsdorff, found a plethora of targets in the South Atlantic where the vast majority of ships still sailed independently along established shipping routes. On 30 September *Graf Spee* claimed its first victim with the destruction of the 5,051-ton British merchant ship *Clement* off the coast of Brazil. Over the next several weeks, *Graf Spee* roamed the southern shipping lanes ranging from South America to the Indian Ocean and added another eight vessels worth 45,038 tons to this tally.

Fortunately, before its demise, *Clement* sent a distress signal informing the world of the surface raider's presence. Alerted to this threat, the Admiralty, in conjunction with the French navy, promptly dispatched eight hunting groups to search out and destroy the offending warship. Together, these hunting groups initially comprised the French battleships *Dunkerque* and *Strasbourg*, the British battlecruiser *Renown*, the aircraft carriers *Eagle*, *Ark Royal*, *Hermes* and *Bearn* (French) and 13 (later 16) cruisers of which eight (later 11) were British. The Admiralty also sent the battleships *Resolution* and *Revenge* and the cruisers *Emerald* and *Enterprise* to Halifax to escort homeward-bound convoys across the Atlantic. On 21 October the British learned that *Deutschland* was at sea, and they allotted additional warships to reinforce their North Atlantic convoy defences including the battleship *Warspite*, the battlecruiser *Repulse* and the aircraft carrier *Furious*. Despite this massive allocation of resources, the Allies were initially frustrated in their efforts to locate the elusive pocket battleships as they ranged the vast expanses of the Atlantic and Indian Oceans. On a more positive note, the various hunting groups did encounter and dispatch a number of German blockade-runners and other merchant ships during the course of their searches.

On 21 November German Vice-Admiral Wilhelm Marschall led the battlecruisers *Gneisenau* and *Scharnhorst* in a sortie against the British Northern Patrol.

The purpose of this operation was to further stretch already heavily committed Allied units and take some of the pressure off *Graf Spee* in the South Atlantic. On 23 November the German battlecruisers encountered the British armed merchant cruiser *Rawalpindi* in the Iceland-Faeroes gap. Despite being hopelessly outgunned, *Rawalpindi*, under the command of Captain E. C. Kennedy, put up a gallant fight against the two German capital ships. Unfortunately, there could only be one outcome to this uneven struggle, and the German warships quickly overwhelmed the valiant armed merchant cruiser. Nevertheless, the dying ship's radio messages had alerted the British to the presence of the two German warships (although both were misidentified as the pocket battleship *Deutschland* and a cruiser), and within minutes the British cruiser *Newcastle* charged upon the scene. The arrival of *Newcastle*, which wisely kept its distance from *Gneisenau* and *Scharnhorst*, convinced Vice-Admiral Marschall that his own ships were now endangered, and he promptly turned for home. Both German ships safely arrived back in Germany on 27 November despite an extensive search by the Home Fleet.

While the destruction of *Rawalpindi* was certainly a success, the Germans had failed to divert British attention away from the *Graf Spee*. With the coming of December, the Allies continued their relentless search for the marauding surface raider. One of the hunting groups involved with this search was Force G located off the east coast of South America. Commanded by Commodore Henry Harwood, Force G consisted of the heavy cruisers *Exeter* and *Cumberland* and the light cruisers *Ajax* and *Achilles*. On 2 December *Graf Spee* sank the British freighters *Doric Star* and *Tairoa* between St Helena and South America. During the course of the assault, *Doric Star* sent out a 'RRR' radio alert signifying that it was under attack by a surface raider. With this information, Commodore Harwood surmised that *Graf Spee* was ultimately heading for the rich shipping concentrations off Rio de Janeiro or the mouth of the River Plate between Uruguay and Argentina. He calculated that *Graf Spee* could arrive off Rio de Janeiro and the River Plate area by the 12th and 13th respectively. Accordingly, Harwood ordered *Exeter*, *Ajax* and *Achilles* to rendezvous some 150 miles off the entrance of the River Plate by 0700 hours on 12 December. In doing so, he left *Cumberland* to complete a minor refit at the Falkland Islands, but ordered the ship to be ready for sea at short notice.

At 0608 hours on the 13th, Harwood's insightful deployment paid off when his ships spotted *Graf Spee* coming over the horizon as if on schedule. Although outgunned by the pocket battleship's 11-inch guns, Harwood immediately ordered his cruisers to attack. Executing a prearranged plan, *Exeter* engaged *Graf Spee* from the south while *Ajax* and *Achilles* did the same from the east. By doing so, Harwood hoped to divide the pocket battleship's return fire. At first this tactic worked as *Graf Spee* initially engaged *Exeter* and then switched to *Ajax* and *Achilles*. However, Captain Langsdorff quickly recognised *Exeter* as the greater threat and immediately redirected *Graf Spee*'s main armament back to the heavy cruiser.

The German shooting was accurate, and soon *Exeter* was hit with dangerous regularity. By 0650 hours *Exeter* had lost two out of its three 8-inch gun turrets, was taking in water and had a heavy list to starboard. Recognising that *Exeter* was in imminent danger of destruction, Harwood, who was aboard *Ajax*, charged forward with his two light cruisers to engage *Graf Spee* at close range. The British cruisers scored a number of hits on *Graf Spee*, but their smaller calibre shells were far less capable of inflicting appreciable damage against the heavily armoured warship. Despite this, Langsdorff opted to make smoke and withdraw to the west. Harwood pursued *Graf Spee* with *Ajax* and *Achilles* while *Exeter* withdrew for repairs after an electrical failure silenced its last 8-inch gun turret. At 0725 hours an 11-inch shell hit *Ajax* and put its aft gun turrets out of action. With this and reports of dwindling ammunition supplies, Harwood disengaged from the fight, but continued to shadow the fleeing German raider.

Except for occasional flare-ups of long-range gunfire, the battle was now over. The British had clearly suffered the worst from *Graf Spee*'s 11-inch guns. *Exeter* was extensively damaged and was no longer capable of further action. The battered heavy cruiser departed the area and made its way to the Falkland Islands to undergo emergency repairs. Meanwhile, the light cruiser *Ajax* had lost half of its main armament, but was otherwise largely intact. Total British losses amounted to 72 dead and 28 wounded of which 61 dead and 23 wounded were from *Exeter*. Against this, *Graf Spee* had not escaped the battle unscathed. The British had scored at least 20 and possibly as many as 70 hits on the pocket battleship.[23] Much of *Graf Spee*'s superstructure was damaged. It had lost two guns from its secondary armament and one of its range finders was out of action. More urgently, *Graf Spee* had damage along its waterline and a 6-foot hole in its bow. Its water and oil purification plants, bakery and galley had all been wrecked thus severely impairing the long-term functionality of both ship and crew. German personnel losses amounted to 36 dead and 60 wounded. Although *Graf Spee*'s main systems and armament remained intact, the pocket battleship had suffered sufficient damage to convince Langsdorff to seek the safety of a neutral port to effect temporary repairs. Accordingly, at about midnight on the 13th, *Graf Spee* entered the Uruguayan port of Montevideo.

With this event, the focus of the encounter switched to the realm of diplomacy and psychological warfare. Under international law, *Graf Spee* was allowed 24 hours in the neutral port. Langsdorff realised that his repairs would take considerably longer to complete and requested an extension of at least 14 days. The British initially argued for enforcement of the 24-hour rule, but then quickly reversed themselves to give British reinforcements time to reach Harwood's depleted force. In any event, Uruguayan authorities only authorised Langsdorff 72 hours to make good his repairs. The British were able to extend this an additional 24 hours by sailing a British merchant ship from the harbour just prior to *Graf Spee*'s set departure time. Under the Hague Convention, Uruguay was compelled to delay *Graf Spee*'s sailing to allow the merchant ship time to make good its escape. Meanwhile, the Admiralty used this time to dispatch substantial reinforcements, including the battlecruiser *Renown* and the aircraft carrier *Ark Royal*, to the River Plate area. Unfortunately, it would take several days for these reinforcements to arrive. The only exception to this was the heavy cruiser *Cumberland,* which joined Harwood's force from the Falklands on the evening of the 14th. In the meantime, the British planted false reports through diplomatic and journalistic channels that these heavy units had already arrived.

This misinformation had a chilling effect upon German resolve and convinced Langsdorff that he faced an overwhelming force just outside of Uruguayan territorial waters. On the 15th, *Graf Spee*'s gunnery officer further reinforced this false belief when he erroneously reported that he could see *Renown* on the horizon from his control tower. On 16 December Langsdorff signalled Berlin regarding the perceived hopelessness of his situation and requested instructions. Among other things, he queried if it would be preferable to scuttle the ship or allow it to be interned if destruction was certain with no real opportunity to damage the enemy. Berlin's response was unequivocal: internment was out of the question. Therefore, on the evening of 17 December, *Graf Spee* departed Montevideo with a reduced crew. When the ship reached the four-mile limit, it stopped and transferred its remaining crew to the German tanker *Tacoma*. Then under the watchful eyes of Harwood's waiting cruisers, a series of scuttling charges erupted on *Graf Spee* promptly reducing the once proud warship into a twisted burning wreck. Over the next few days the hulk of *Graf Spee* slowly settled in the shallow waters of the estuary. Meanwhile, its crew travelled to Argentina for eventual internment while Captain Langsdorff committed one final act of perceived duty and shot himself in Buenos Aires on 20 December.

Although the scuttling of *Graf Spee* was arguably an anti-climactic outcome to the first major naval engagement of the war, the demise of the great warship nevertheless constituted a significant victory for the Royal Navy. In most obvious terms, *Graf Spee* represented the Kriegsmarine's first major warship loss. As such, the British were able to exploit this outcome to great public relations effect. During a time when good news was in short supply, the destruction of *Graf Spee* represented Britain's first appreciable wartime victory, and morale and confidence within the navy and nation rose accordingly. Nor was this point lost upon a number of neutral governments who viewed the scuttling as an affirmation of British sea power. Finally and most importantly in strategic terms, the loss of *Graf Spee* convinced the Germans to suspend future surface raider activity. Thus with the destruction of a single warship, the British had eliminated (at least on a temporary basis) the threat they had initially considered to be the gravest menace to their maritime communications.

The British could also take solace in the many successes achieved by their blockade. Beginning with the interception of German vessels on the first day of the war, the British commenced an aggressive campaign to eliminate German seaborne commerce.

The Royal Navy scored its first major success over the Kriegsmarine in December 1939 when the pocket battleship *Graf Spee* scuttled itself off Montevideo following an engagement with three British cruisers. (Royal Navy official photographer, public domain)

Despite pre-war warnings, some 400 German merchant ships worth nearly 2,000,000 tons were overseas at the beginning of hostilities. Fortunately for the Germans, the vast majority of these vessels were able to take shelter in neutral harbours before the British could intercept them. On a less positive note, these vessels were little more than prisoners as the British exercised control over the sea-lanes. During the next seven months a solid trickle of German merchant ships set out to return to Germany. In doing so, they had to run a gauntlet of British and (to a lesser extent) French warships. Despite the ominous nature of this task, Britain's blockade was far from complete during the early months of the war, and 82 German merchant ships worth some 480,000 tons were able to successfully complete this journey.[24] Still, even after arriving back in Germany, these ships remained virtual prisoners to the British blockade.

Many other German vessels were not as lucky as they encountered British and other factors that exacted a steady toll on their numbers. A key component to Britain's interdiction effort was the Northern Patrol guarding the Atlantic approach to Northern Europe. From September 1939 through March 1940 the cruisers and auxiliaries of the Northern Patrol captured or forced the scuttling of 23 German merchant ships worth 118,715 tons.[25] During the same period other British warships and affiliated authorities operating across the world's oceans and waterways added another 24 German merchant ships and three minor vessels worth 144,043 tons to this total.[26] Likewise, French warships captured or forced the scuttling of six German vessels worth 26,373 tons.[27] When combined together, the Allies captured 26 German commercial vessels worth 107,530 tons and sank or forced the scuttling of 30 more merchant ships worth 181,601 tons during the first seven months of the war.[28] Finally, neutral governments interned or sequestered at least six more German merchant ships worth 33,747 tons, while accidents and marine causes accounted for another 20 German commercial vessels and four naval auxiliaries totalling 53,986 tons lost during the same period.[29] The British blockade contributed to some of these latter losses as German merchant ships took avoidance measures that exposed them to heightened weather and navigational hazards.

Of course, the destruction of German shipping was not an end unto itself, but rather a means to accomplish the overriding goal of severing Germany's overseas commerce. A second major component to Britain's blockade was the interdiction of contraband bound for Germany in neutral shipping. Once again, the Northern Patrol played a leading role in this interdiction effort. During the period of 7 September 1939 through 9 April 1940 the Northern Patrol encountered 703 eastbound merchant ships of which 393 (including prizes) were sent to contraband control bases in the Orkneys and the Downs.[30] Once at these bases, British authorities searched the suspect merchant ships and removed any cargo deemed contraband. In this manner and in similar operations set-up in the Mediterranean, the British seized some 338,000 tons of contraband cargo during the first six weeks of the war.[31] This amount increased to 529,471 tons seized by 1 January 1940 and represented a greater volume of cargo lost to the Germans than they were able to inflict during their own interdiction efforts against the British.[32]

A far less successful component of the British blockade was the Royal Navy's submarine campaign. This campaign began on an unfortunate note when the British submarine *Triton* misidentified and sank its fellow submarine *Oxley* on 10 September 1939. Notwithstanding this tragedy, the main factors limiting the success of Britain's submarine force were a general lack of worthwhile targets, restrictive rules of engagement and a dangerous operating area that often favoured German defences. As such, the first British success did not occur until 20 November 1939 when the submarine *Sturgeon* sank the 428-ton German patrol vessel *V209* in the Heligoland Bight. Two weeks later the British submarine *Salmon* sank the outward-bound German U-boat *U36* in the same area. On 13–14 December the British submarines *Salmon* and *Ursula* teamed up to damage the German light cruisers *Leipzig* and *Nürnberg* and sink the German escort destroyer *F9*. Finally in March 1940 the submarines *Ursula* and *Truant* sank two German merchant ships worth 4,947 and 2,189 tons respectively.[33] Meanwhile, in a related event, the German minesweeper *M132* was lost in an accident during an anti-submarine hunt on 13 November. Unfortunately, the British paid a high price for these successes. In addition to the accidental sinking of

Oxley in September, the British lost three submarines (*Undine, Seahorse* and *Starfish*) to German escort vessels in January 1940.

The British enjoyed better results with their mine-laying campaign. From the earliest days of the war the Royal Navy conducted both defensive and offensive mine-laying operations to protect their own seaborne lines of communication while interdicting those of the enemy. In terms of the former, the British quickly established a mine barrage across the Dover Straits to deny direct U-boat access to the English Channel and Western Approaches. From September through October 1939 the Royal Navy laid two belts of mines across the Straits. The first stretched from the Goodwins to the Belgian coast and consisted of some 3,000 mines. The second contained 3,636 mines between Folkestone and Cape Gris Nez. The British then interspersed a double system of indicator loops to detect any U-boats attempting to pass between the two belts.[34] In October this barrage claimed the destruction of two U-boats (*U12* and *U40*) and was a factor in the demise of a third – *U16*. Based upon these losses, the Kriegsmarine suspended further attempts to traverse the Dover Straits, thus limiting their operations to the North Sea or forcing their U-boats to use the long and dangerous route around Scotland to gain access to the open Atlantic.

During the same time the Royal Navy conducted similar mining operations along suspected German transit routes in the Heligoland Bight and North Sea. In October these mines claimed the destruction of a 361-ton auxiliary patrol vessel off Borkum. The British continued their mining operations into the new year, and in February and March 1940 British mines claimed the destruction of two more U-boats (*U54* and *U44*) and the German destroyers *Leberecht Maass* and *Max Schultz*. In terms of the latter, these destroyers were part of a flotilla attempting to counter British mine-laying activities in the Heligoland Bight. On the evening of 22 February Luftwaffe bombers mistakenly attacked this flotilla causing the German ships to take violent evasive action. During the course of these manoeuvres the German destroyers strayed into a new British minefield and lost the vessels listed above. This action clearly demonstrated that the problems of misidentification and fratricide were applicable to both sides. For their part, the British suffered no losses during these early mine-laying operations and affirmed the mine as a cost-effective weapon in their maritime arsenal.

Less successful weapons in the early maritime war were aircraft. During the opening months of the war both the German Luftwaffe and RAF attempted to carry out a series of anti-shipping strikes against each other's maritime forces. In both cases, results were meagre. In terms of the former, the Luftwaffe did not enjoy any success until December 1939 and then only sank the minesweeper *Sphinx* and a total of 30 mostly minor vessels worth 36,189 tons through March 1940.[35] As for the British, the RAF carried out a series of bold daylight attacks against the major surface units of the Kriegsmarine. Sadly, these strikes were costly in terms of aircraft losses and only resulted in minor damage inflicted upon the pocket battleship *Admiral Scheer* and the cruiser *Emden* and the destruction of the 298-ton auxiliary minesweeper *M1407*.

A major factor in this lack of success was the unreliability of British bombs that often failed to explode when striking their targets. The RAF also suffered from a lack of suitable aircraft and ineffectual tactics in the prosecution of its anti-shipping role. Finally, initial government policy severely restricted the number of targets available to the RAF by limiting attacks to enemy warships, troopships and auxiliaries in direct attendance of the enemy fleet. As such, major changes were necessary to enhance the RAF's effectiveness in maritime strike operations, but at least this was a start.

Turning now to the third major tenet of British maritime strategy, from the opening days of the war the Royal Navy and merchant marine set about to support the needs of the army. The foremost task at hand was the safe transport of the British Expeditionary Force and affiliated RAF units to the continent. As such, on 9 September 1939 the first troopships departed Southampton for Cherbourg. In the days and weeks that followed the British repeated this process several times over as they deployed the initial four divisions of their expeditionary force to France. By 7 October this force numbered some 161,000 soldiers, 24,000 vehicles and 140,000 tons of stores all safely transported without a loss.[36] Despite the magnitude of this early success, these deployments only represented the beginning of a long and continuous process. Over the next seven months the British dispatched a steady stream of ships to reinforce and support their deployed formations. From December 1939 through April 1940 the British transported another nine divisions to France, bringing the total size of their expeditionary force to nearly a half million men and some 89,000 vehicles by June. This represented a major undertaking as Portsmouth Command alone administered the sailing of 731 transports and 304 laden convoys during the opening months of the war.[37]

Despite the size and success of this effort, the deployment of the British Expeditionary Force was generally anti-climactic in its initial outcome. During the first seven months of the war neither side took any serious opportunity to engage the other. Instead, both sides were content to sit behind their corresponding defensive lines and wait. A number of factors contributed to this inactivity. First, French strategic thinking was almost entirely defensive despite having a sizable and powerful army. Meanwhile, the small size and limited capability of the British army rendered independent British action impractical. As for the Germans, they initially needed time to reposition their forces at the conclusion of the Polish campaign and then were content to bide their time in preparation for a spring offensive. Under these conditions, the newly arrived British Expeditionary Force did little more than take up defensive positions alongside its French allies. In fact, the period was so devoid of action that the press dubbed it the 'Phoney War' or 'Twilight War'.

While this may have been an accurate characterisation regarding affairs in Europe, events at sea clearly indicated a different picture. For the Royal Navy and Kriegsmarine, the first seven months of the war were anything but phoney. This was a real shooting war with victories and losses sustained by both sides. With few exceptions, this fighting was not renowned, but still reflected a life and death struggle for those involved. At a

Table 1.7 British and German Maritime Losses due to Military Action during the Phoney War Period, September 1939–March 1940

	British			German		
	Number lost	Tonnage lost	Loss percentage*	Number lost	Tonnage lost	Loss percentage*
Capital ships	2	51,650	9.0	1	12,100	14.3
Destroyers/escorts	6	8,255	2.9	3	5,232	7.0
Submarines	4	3,174	5.8	17	11,619	29.8
Minesweepers	1	875	2.4	2	1,145	4.0
Merchant ships	190	683,800	3.2	74	341,069	8.1

Note: These figures are limited to losses sustained through military action. Warship tonnage losses reflect displacement while merchant tonnage losses reflect gross registered tons.
* Loss percentage measures the number of losses sustained compared to the corresponding fleet sizes by category in September 1939. This percentage is computed on a numerical basis for warships and a tonnage basis for merchant ships.

national level, this was a contest of overriding strategic objectives. In this regard, the British had attained real progress towards all three major tenants of their maritime strategy. First, the British had made great strides in securing their seaborne lines of communication. In doing so, they had suffered some shipping losses, but these losses were generally considered within acceptable levels. Against this, the British had once again driven the vast bulk of German shipping from the world's oceans and inflicted proportionally higher losses upon the Germans than they themselves had suffered. Finally, the British had attained complete success in the deployment and maintenance of their expeditionary force to France. In this light, the Admiralty had reason to be satisfied with these results. By any objective measure, this had been a solid start with a great deal of progress made. Now it remained to be seen if this good fortune would continue once the onslaught of total war was unleashed.

CHAPTER 2

Blitzkrieg

From the opening days of the war, authorities in both Germany and Britain contemplated the strategic implications that Scandinavia posed to their competing war efforts. For the Germans, this focus reflected the economic realities facing their nation. With the implementation of Britain's blockade and corresponding loss of overseas suppliers, Scandinavia became Germany's only remaining source for the importation of many essential raw materials. Paramount amongst these was phosphorus-rich Swedish iron ore, which was fundamental in the production of high-grade steel. While Germany did possess internal sources of iron ore, this domestically produced ore was generally of an inferior quality that rendered it incapable of meeting the demanding specification set forth by the German steel and armaments industries. By comparison, Sweden was the only country in Europe that could meet Germany's needs in terms of both quality and quantity of output. As such, in 1939 German imports of Swedish iron ore totalled 10,069,800 metric tons with another 1,071,800 tons coming from Norway.[1]

Scandinavia was also a primary or exclusive supplier of many other strategic resources. Amongst these was molybdenum, which was used in hardening steel. Prior to the war Germany had imported nearly all of its molybdenum, totalling over 100,000 ton per annum, from non-European sources. With the loss of these overseas imports, Norway became Germany's only supplier for this essential raw material. The same was true for nickel, which was used in the production of armoured plating and armour-piercing shells. With the loss of Canada as its primary supplier, Germany turned to Norway and Finland to fulfil its strategic needs, which amounted to an estimated 12,000 tons per year. Germany also turned to Norway to help meet its copper requirements, which in pre-war years had originated 77 percent from non-European sources. Other important imports from Scandinavia included iron pyrites, which accounted for 25 percent of German consumption, Lumber, wood pulp and paper products.[2] Finally, Norway was a primary supplier of fish and fish-related products. Prior to the war Norway and Britain had supplied 32 and 31 percent of Germany's fish requirements respectively. Likewise, Norway had fulfilled 69 percent of Germany's fish oil and whale oil needs. Now with the loss of

British exports and easy access to the sea, Norway became Germany's near-exclusive source for fish and fish-related products.[3]

The British were well aware of these dependencies and as early as September 1939 contemplated ways to sever or severely restrict German imports from Scandinavia. This was particularly true regarding the iron ore trade, which the British assessed as being critical to Germany's economic viability. Unfortunately for them, the geographical and political realities of the Baltic region made this a far more difficult undertaking than the curtailment of overseas trade. The vast bulk of Germany's imported iron ore came from mines located near Gällivare in northern Sweden. For most of the year this ore travelled from the Swedish port of Luleå through the Baltic to Germany, thus making it all but immune to British interference. However, during the winter months when Luleå became iced in, the Swedes transferred their export operations to the ice-free port of Narvik in Northern Norway. From there, German and neutral merchant ships transported the ore to Germany using the *Innereled* (inner leads), a narrow corridor of Norwegian territorial water stretching along the islands and waterways of the Norwegian coastline. By using this territorial water, the Germans and their neutral trading partners were able to largely circumvent the British blockade.

The British considered a number of options to counter this trade. The most prevalent of these was to mine the *Innereled*, forcing Germany's ore traffic into the open ocean where the Royal Navy could effectively interdict it. On 19 September 1939 First Lord of the Admiralty Winston Churchill officially proposed this mining option to the British Cabinet, but the Cabinet declined to take immediate action. In the weeks that followed the Allies continued to refine and consider this mining strategy as well as other more aggressive proposals to deal with the Scandinavian situation. The Allies devised plans to send an Anglo-French expeditionary force to occupy Narvik and even considered a follow-up proposal to advance across country and seize the Gällivare ore fields. Still, despite these many plans and proposals, the Allied leadership continued to vacillate in making a final decision. Influencing their considerations was a deep reluctance to violate Norwegian neutrality and thus incur the subsequent outcry in international opinion likely to follow.

Events in November and February added additional impetus to these Allied deliberations. The first occurred on 30 November when the Soviet Union launched a massive military assault against neighbouring Finland. The purpose of this was to seize Finnish territory and secure basing rights to improve the Soviet Union's defensive posture against Germany. Although heavily outnumbered, the gallant Finns put up a surprisingly effective defence that quickly ground the colossal Soviet juggernaut to an inglorious halt. Western reaction to this blatant aggression was overwhelmingly sympathetic to the Finnish cause. In Britain and the other Western democracies there was a great outpouring of public and governmental support to provide materiel assistance to the beleaguered Finns. While this sentiment was certainly sincere, the

British also saw this as an opportunity to gain a foothold in Scandinavia and thus impact Scandinavian trade with Germany. To this end, the Allies began sending diplomatic feelers to Norway and Sweden to gain logistical basing rights as a means to enhance Scandinavian security and provide materiel support to Finland. At the same time the Allies continued to develop plans and made preliminary preparations for the occupation of strategic locations in Norway and Sweden.

While this was underway, a second event occurred in Norwegian territorial waters that further enflamed British passions. In late January 1940 the German tanker *Altmark*, the former supply ship to the pocket battleship *Graf Spee*, made an attempt to return to Germany after spending several months in the South Atlantic. Aided by bad weather, *Altmark* successfully passed through the Denmark Strait and arrived in Norwegian territorial waters near Trondheim on 14 February. From there, *Altmark* began the final portion of its journey down the *Innereled* to Germany. At about this time the Admiralty learned of *Altmark's* presence and ordered British light forces to intercept it. The main impetus behind this action was to rescue captured British seamen reportedly held onboard *Altmark* after being transferred from merchant ships sunk by *Graf Spee*. On the 16th British destroyers sighted *Altmark* in Norwegian territorial waters near Egersund but were unable to intervene due to the presence of Norwegian torpedo boats travelling along side. In the verbal exchange that followed, the senior Norwegian officer stated that there were no prisoners onboard *Altmark* and denied the British access to the fleeing ship. Faced with a delicate diplomatic situation, the British destroyers withdrew to consult with the Admiralty.

Three hours later First See Lord Churchill directed the British commander on the scene, Captain Philip Vian, to propose a final compromise to the Norwegians, but if rejected, to use the minimum force necessary to secure the release of the British prisoners. At 2200 hours Vian took the destroyer *Cossack* into Jössingfjord and delivered his compromise proposal to the senior Norwegian officer. When this was refused, Vian manoeuvred *Cossack* alongside *Altmark* and dispatched an armed boarding party to rescue the prisoners. In the brief skirmish that followed, the British quickly overwhelmed and forced the German crew to flee after killing six of their number and wounding six more. Then proclaiming 'The Navy's here', the British proceeded to rescue 299 of their countrymen held within *Altmark's* holds. Throughout this process the Norwegians made no attempt to interfere, and by midnight the task was complete. With the last of the British prisoners safely onboard, *Cossack* slowly drew away from *Altmark* and began its journey back to Britain under the cover of the Home Fleet.

This action, soon to be referred to as the *Altmark* incident, impacted British thinking in two major ways beyond its immediate humanitarian result. On the positive side, the Royal Navy's decisive action in rescuing its countrymen proved to be highly popular within the navy and British public as a whole. Many construed the incident as a victory during a time when not much else was going on. As such, the matter provided a nice boost to confidence and morale in what was otherwise a drab and generally uneventful winter. On the other hand, many military and governmental officials recognised a more ominous lesson to be drawn from the matter. To them, the incident clearly demonstrated that the Norwegian government was either unwilling or incapable of ensuring Norwegian neutrality as it related to German use of its territorial waters. As such, the matter only served to emphasise the need for direct action if the Allies seriously intended to interdict Germany's Scandinavian trade.

Yet even as this realisation became increasingly apparent, consensus on a firm course of action remained frustratingly elusive. Despite months of diplomatic overtures, the Norwegian and Swedish governments continued to express vehement opposition to any Allied incursions into their territories. As such, the Allies were unable to provide any meaningful support to Finland, and the situation there slowly deteriorated. Finally, on 12 March the War Cabinet tentatively agreed to send a military force to occupy Narvik with follow-up landings proposed in Trondheim, Stavanger and Bergen. Ironically, on the very same day this decision was made, the Finns succumbed to the hopelessness of their situation and opted to make peace with the Soviet Union. In doing so, they eliminated the pretext for Allied intervention in Scandinavia, and two days later the War Cabinet reversed itself and cancelled its proposed landings.

Undeterred by this setback, Churchill promptly renewed his original proposal to mine the *Innereled*. With support from the new French premier, Paul Reynaud, the plan soon rose to prominent consideration. In addition to its obvious implications on German trade, many Allied planners surmised that the proposed mining operation would provoke an immediate German reaction against Norway. This belief was bolstered by a number of recent intelligence reports indicating German designs on Scandinavia. The British therefore devised a strong response to this anticipated German reaction. Adopting a dangerous strategy of move and counter-move, the British envisioned a German attack against Norway followed by their own immediate intervention on the smaller nation's behalf. In doing so, they hoped to draw the Kriegsmarine into open battle and gain access and influence over Scandinavian affairs. To this latter point, the British adopted a contingency plan, known as R4, to occupy key Norwegian locations as soon as the German threat materialised and hoped to be welcomed as allies against the common German aggressor.

On 28 March the Supreme War Council gave its approval for this mining option, designated Operation *Wilfred*, to be conducted on 5 April. To carry this out, the British dispatched the minelayer *Teviot Bank* and four destroyers to lay mines off Stadtlandet, four minelaying destroyers with four escorting destroyers to lay mines off Hovden in Vestfjord and two destroyers to simulate a mining operation off Bud. These forces departed on 5 April to perform their various missions now set to occur three days later. The British covered these operations with the battlecruiser *Renown* and four destroyers. Likewise, the British deployed 23 (later to be increased to 26) submarines from three British and one French flotillas to guard against possible German incursions south and southwest of Norway, in the Skagerrak and Kattegat and in the North Sea. Meanwhile, the British maintained the Home Fleet at Scapa Flow and the 2nd Cruiser Squadron at Rosyth to be ready for short-notice deployments if necessary. Finally, the British assembled an initial military force consisting of eight army battalions to be ready to occupy Stavanger, Bergen, Trondheim and Narvik once a pending German attack became apparent. Troops for the first two locations were embarked on the cruisers *Devonshire*, *Berwick*, *York* and *Glasgow* at Rosyth while those designated for Trondheim and Narvik awaited transport from the Clyde with the cruiser *Aurora* and six destroyers held as escorts. Despite this level of readiness, the British planned to hold these military forces in port until clear evidence of German aggression materialised.

Unfortunately for the British, German intentions towards Norway were farther along than they themselves realised. In October 1939 Grand-Admiral Erich Raeder, the Commander-in-Chief of the Kriegsmarine, had first advocated the strategic advantages associated with the occupation of Norway. In the weeks and months that followed, the Germans considered various strategies for bringing Norway within their sphere of influence. On 21 February 1940 the Germans began serious planning and preparations for an invasion of Norway. In doing so, they demonstrated a professional competence and thoroughness that far outpaced the planning efforts put forth by the Allies at the time. Likewise, the Germans allocated a significantly larger force than anything contemplated by the Allies for their Norwegian operation. This force included six army divisions, 290 bombers, 40 dive-bombers, 100 assorted fighters, 40 long-range reconnaissance aircraft, 30 coastal patrol aircraft and 500 transport aircraft.[4] For its part, the Kriegsmarine assigned nearly every major warship that was in an operational state along with numerous merchant ships to transport and support the assault forces. On 2 April Hitler gave the order directing the invasion of Norway as well as a concurrent operation aimed against Denmark to commence on 9 April.

In the days immediately following this directive, the Germans dispatched a steady stream of ships to carry out their invasion plans. Of particular importance were six naval groups assigned to conduct seaborne landings against seven strategic locations along the length of Norway ranging from Narvik in the north to Oslo in the south. Carrying a force of some 8,850 troops, these groups departed Germany at staggered intervals beginning on 7 April in order to arrive at their various target locations at the same time to launch a synchronised attack. The Germans followed the southernmost assault groups with 15 merchant ships carrying an additional 3,761 men, 672 horses, 1,377 vehicles and 5,935 tons of stores.[5] Meanwhile, to support the northernmost assaults, seven stores-laden merchant ships departed Hamburg on 3 April to travel along the normal trade routes to Narvik, Trondheim and Stavanger. Likewise, three tankers departed Wilhelmshaven and Murmansk

Table 2.1 Breakdown of the Initial German Naval Assault Groups against Norway and Denmark

Group 1	2,000 troops for Narvik. Ten destroyers supported by the battlecruisers *Scharnhorst* and *Gneisenau*.
Group 2	1,700 troops for Trondheim. Heavy cruiser *Admiral Hipper* and four destroyers.
Group 3	1,900 troops for Bergen. Light cruisers *Köln* and *Königsberg*, minelayer *Bremse*, two torpedo boats, depot ship *Karl Peters*, five E-boats (motor torpedo boats) and two auxiliary ships.
Group 4	1,100 troops for Kristiansand and Arendal. Light cruiser *Karlsruhe*, three torpedo boats, depot ship *Tsingtau* and seven E-boats.
Group 5	2,000 troops for Oslo. Pocket battleship *Lützow*, heavy cruiser *Blücher*, light cruiser *Emden*, three torpedo boats, eight R-boats (motor minesweepers) and two whalers.
Group 6	150 troops for cable station at Egersund. Four minesweepers.
Groups 7–11	3,390 troops for various locations in Denmark. Battleships *Schleswig-Holstein* and *Schlesien*, minelayer *Hansestadt Danzig*, an escort destroyer, 11 minesweepers and over 40 minor warships, auxiliary ships, coastal vessels and civilian transports.

to rendezvous with and replenish German warships involved in these northern operations. The Germans covered these movements with 31 U-boats positioned in strategic locations around Norway and the adjacent waters. Finally, the Germans rounded out their invasion plans by sending five naval groups to carry out assault operations against Denmark.

Despite German efforts to maintain stealth and surprise, these large shipping movements quickly attracted British attention. During the first week in April a number of reports reached British intelligence indicating a pending German operation. These reports were vindicated on 7 April when RAF aircraft spotted and unsuccessfully attacked the ships of Groups 1 and 2 in the Skagerrak while en route to Norway. Early the next morning the British destroyer *Glowworm*, detached from *Renown*'s screen to search for a lost seaman, had a chance encounter with the warships of Group 2 headed for Trondheim. Fighting in heavy seas and fog, *Glowworm* initially held its own against two German destroyers, but this quickly changed when the German heavy cruiser *Admiral Hipper* arrived on the scene. Hit by *Hipper*'s first salvo, the British destroyer soon found itself fatally damaged. Nevertheless, *Glowworm* managed to transmit a sighting report to the Admiralty. Then in a final act of defiance, *Glowworm* rammed *Hipper* tearing away 150 feet of the cruiser's armoured plating and wrenching its starboard torpedo tubes from their mountings. Shortly thereafter the broken destroyer exploded and sank taking most of its crew with it including the commanding officer, Lieutenant-Commander G. B. Roope. When the British government later learned the full details of this heroic action, they awarded Lieutenant-Commander Roope a posthumous Victoria Cross.

Unfortunately, on a more immediate note, the Admiralty failed to effectively respond to *Glowworm*'s sacrifice or the other reports reaching them. Instead, the unexpected discovery of German warships prior to their own minelaying activities prompted the British to abandon key provisions of Operation *Wilfred* and contingency plan R4. Of particular importance, the British initially ascribed these warship sightings as another German attempt to breakout into the Atlantic. Therefore, when the Home Fleet sortied out of Scapa Flow on the evening of 7 April, they initially took up positions to intercept a possible breakout attempt thus neglecting the most likely approaches to Norway. Likewise, the British cancelled their minelaying operation against Stadtlandet, although that against Hovden in Vestfjord still went forward. Meanwhile on the 8th the Admiralty effectively cancelled R4 by ordering their cruisers at Rosyth to disembark all army personnel and proceed to sea while the cruiser/destroyer escort force at the Clyde was ordered to join the Home Fleet.

While these actions were underway, the true magnitude of the situation became clearer. On the afternoon of the 8th the British-controlled Polish submarine *Orzel* sank the German transport *Rio de Janeiro* off Kristiansand on the southern coast of Norway. When Norwegian vessels later arrived to rescue the survivors, they were surprised to find that many were uniformed German soldiers who openly discussed the purpose of their mission. Based upon this and other submarine sightings, the Admiralty changed their assessment regarding German intentions and decided that an invasion was underway. To counter this, the British initiated a series of redeployments and manoeuvres in a last-minute attempt to impede the invasion. Of particular importance, on the evening of the 8th the Admiralty ordered Vice-Admiral William Whitworth to cover the approach to Narvik with the battlecruiser *Renown* and its accompanying destroyers. To support this effort, Admiral Charles Forbes, the Commander-in-Chief of the Home Fleet, sent the battlecruiser *Repulse*, the cruiser *Penelope* and four destroyers to reinforce Whitworth's command. Meanwhile, Forbes and the bulk of the Home Fleet, including the battleships *Rodney* and *Valiant*, turned south to counter potential invasion forces sighted in the Skagerrak and Kattegat. Unfortunately for the British, these actions were too little too late as severe weather and the advanced progress of the German forces made an effective interception nearly impossible.

Nevertheless, at 0337 hours on the 9th the battlecruiser *Renown* encountered *Gneisenau* and *Scharnhorst* some 50 miles off Vestfjord as they were making a diversionary run to the north. Disregarding his numerical inferiority, Admiral Whitworth promptly pressed forward to engage the German battlecruisers and immediately put them to flight. In the running artillery duel that followed, *Renown* hit *Gneisenau* with three 15-inch shells, wrecking its fire control system, putting one of its forward turrets out of action and causing serious damage to its superstructure. In return, *Renown* received two hits that caused no appreciable damage. Notwithstanding this difference in results, it was speed, and not gunnery, that proved to be the decisive factor in the engagement as the German battlecruisers gradually pulled away from their slower British adversary. By 0630 it was all over, with the German ships passing out of sight. Although Whitworth had inflicted some material damage and gained a moral victory over a superior enemy, the engagement was strategically insignificant and had no impact on the German invasion.

To this end, on the morning of 9 April the Germans launched their seaborne assaults against Norway. In most locations the Germans encountered non-existent or ineffectual resistance. One notable exception to this was at Dröbak on the approach to Oslo where Norwegian shore batteries and torpedo tubes pummelled the German heavy cruiser *Blücher* at pointblank range. Hit by several high-calibre shells and at least two torpedoes, *Blücher* capsized and sank taking about 1,000 men with it including many senior occupation personnel. The pocket battleship *Lützow* was also hit and forced to retire down the fjord thus prompting the Germans to disembark their assault troops far south of the capital. In the same fjord, defences at Bolaerne claimed the destruction of the German torpedo boat *Albatros* and the motor minesweeper *R17*. Meanwhile, in the north, Norwegian shore batteries hit and damaged the German cruiser *Königsberg* at Kvarven on the approach to Bergen. Finally, Norwegian naval units and shore defences sank or forced the scuttling of the German merchant ships *Main*, *Roda*, *Seattle* and *Kattegat* worth a combined total of 27,804 tons off Haugesund, Stavanger, Kristiansand and Aluangen respectively.[6] Despite these sporadic losses, the day was generally successful for the Germans, and by nightfall they had secured the majority of their initial Norwegian objectives as well as gained the capitulation of Denmark.

Things were not nearly as successful for the British. For the bulk of the Royal Navy, 9 April was another day of confusion, missed opportunities and frustration. Having failed to interdict the invasion, the British now refocused their efforts to counterattack exposed German forces, cut off return routes to Germany and disrupt re-supply and follow-up activities. Sadly, these British efforts suffered from incomplete intelligence, contradictory orders and untimely bouts of timidity. These shortfalls manifested themselves in a failure to carry out a proposed attack against German naval forces located in Bergen. Meanwhile, in the afternoon a new threat arose when the Home Fleet came under a prolonged air attack by 88 assorted German bombers. In a three-hour action the British shot down four of their attackers with anti-aircraft fire, but lost the destroyer *Gurkha* and suffered minor damage to the battleship *Rodney* and the cruisers *Devonshire, Southampton* and *Glasgow*. This aerial onslaught convinced Admiral Forbes to withdraw the Home Fleet westward thus temporarily ceding Norway's southern approaches to the Germans.

Fortunately, the British enjoyed better results with their submarine forces. Already mentioned was *Orzel's* success against the 5,261-ton *Rio de Janeiro* on the 8th. On the same day the British submarine *Trident* sank the 8,036-ton tanker *Posidonia* in the Skagerrak. On the afternoon of the 9th Vice-Admiral Max Horton, the Flag Officer Submarines, eased the rules of engagement governing his boats and allowed his commanders to engage German transports without warning. This easement garnered immediate results when minutes later the submarine *Sunfish* sank the 7,129-ton merchant ship *Amasis*.[7] That same evening the submarine *Truant* scored an even greater success when it torpedoed the light cruiser *Karlsruhe* off Kristiansand. Although only hit by a single torpedo, *Karlsruhe* was so severely damaged that the Germans were compelled to scuttle the stricken ship. Two days later the British almost repeated this success when the submarine *Spearfish* torpedoed the pocket battleship *Lützow* and damaged it so severely that it would be out of service for a year. Finally, in separate attacks on the 10th and 11th, the British submarines *Triton*, *Sunfish*, *Triad* and *Sealion* sank five German merchant ships and the patrol vessel *V1507* worth a combined total of 17,509 tons.[8]

While this was underway, equally important events transpired in the north. On the afternoon of 9 April the British 2nd Destroyer Flotilla, commanded by Captain B. A. W. Warburton-Lee, arrived at Vestfjord to reconnoitre Narvik and investigate a report of a minor German landing. Seeking information from the Norwegian pilot station at Tranöy, Warburton-Lee learned that six large German destroyers and a submarine had proceeded up the fjord earlier that morning. This was, in fact, an underestimation of the size of the German force, which actually included ten destroyers sheltering in Narvik and the adjacent fjords. Hoping to surprise his superior opponent, Warburton-Lee decided to proceed up Ofotfjord and attack the German force at dawn. After signalling the Admiralty of his intentions, he entered the fjord with the destroyers *Hardy*, *Hotspur*, *Havock*, *Hunter* and *Hostile*. Aided by mist and snowfall, this small British force exploited a gap in the German defences and arrived undetected off Narvik at 0400 hours on the 10th. Before them they found five German destroyers and a number of merchant ships slumbering in the small Norwegian harbour.

At 0430 hours the British launched their assault. Leaving *Hotspur* and *Hostile* behind to provide security against shore batteries, Warburton-Lee entered the harbour with his three remaining destroyers and commenced a devastating attack against his unsuspecting foes. With their first salvo of torpedoes, the British hit and fatally damaged the German destroyers *Wilhelm Heidkamp* and *Anton Schmitt*, tearing the bottom out of the former and blowing the latter in two. Warburton-Lee then swung his ships around, giving each destroyer an opportunity to engage the enemy with gunfire and torpedoes. *Hotspur* and *Hostile* quickly joined in when it became apparent that no shore battery threat existed. The British directed most of their assault against the destroyer *Diether von Roeder*, which was quickly reduced to a beached, burning wreck. The destroyer *Hans Lüdemann* was also heavily hit and set ablaze. Only the destroyer *Hermann Künne* escaped serious damage, but was nevertheless disabled when nearby torpedo concussions made its engines inoperable. As the threat from these German warships quickly subsided, the British increasingly turned their deadly fire against the eight German merchant ships sheltering in the harbour. In a series of sweeping attacks the British sank or otherwise wrecked six of these merchant ships worth 35,430 tons as well as a 4,292-ton Swedish merchant ship.[9]

After an hour of carnage, Warburton-Lee turned his ships to withdraw. As the British ships cleared the Narvik breakwaters they observed the German destroyers *Wolfgang Zenker*, *Erich Giese* and *Erich Koellner* emerging from Herjangsfjord. Increasing speed to 30 knots, the British tried to make their escape while engaging the German destroyers in a running fight. They almost succeeded in extricating themselves unscathed until two more German destroyers, *Georg Thiele* and *Bernd von Arnim*, appeared ahead of them coming out of Ballangenfjord. Blocked and outgunned by the larger German ships, the British were forced to fight their way through. In the desperate battle that followed, *Hardy* and *Hunter* were both sunk while *Hotspur* received heavy damage. In return, the British scored a number of hits on *Georg Thiele* and *Bernd von Arnim* compelling both ships to retire. Meanwhile, low fuel tanks forced *Wolfgang Zenker*, *Erich Giese* and *Erich Koellner* to break off their pursuit and turn back towards Narvik. These withdrawals allowed the battered *Hotspur* and the relatively undamaged *Havock* and *Hostile* to escape to the open sea. In doing so, the British scored a final parting-shot victory when they came across and sank the incoming 8,460-ton German merchant ship *Rauenfels*.

So ended what became known as the first battle of Narvik. By any measure, this was a clear British victory. For the loss of two destroyers sunk and one seriously damaged, the British sank two German destroyers, crippled a third, heavily damaged three more and temporarily rendered a fourth inoperable. Of the ten German destroyers present in and around Narvik on the morning of 10 April, only three remained fully operational at the close of the battle. Likewise, the British sank a total of seven German merchant ships including *Rauenfels*, which was carrying a re-supply of ammunition at the time of its demise. The loss of this ammunition, along with the battering their warships had taken, promised to put the Germans at a disadvantage during their next encounter with the British. As such, the battle wrested the local initiative away from the Germans and pushed their Narvik forces onto the defensive. Sadly, Warburton-Lee was unable to reap any personal accolades for his victory as he was one of the fatalities associated with the loss of *Hardy*. Nevertheless, his courage and decisive action against a superior enemy were amply recognised when the government awarded him a posthumous Victoria Cross.

10 April also saw the Fleet Air Arm join the fray in dramatic fashion. Early that morning 16 Skua fighter/dive-bombers from 800 and 803 Squadrons departed the Royal Navy Air Station of Hatston in the Orkneys to attack German naval forces reportedly located in Bergen. Operating at the limit of their range, the small force,

led by Royal Navy Lieutenant W. P. Lucy and Royal Marine Captain R. T. Partridge, made the 300-mile trek to Bergen. En route, one of their numbers was forced to turn back due to engine trouble. At 0715 hours the remaining 15 aircraft arrived over Bergen and commenced an attack against the only sizable target they could find, the damaged light cruiser *Königsberg* berthed along Skoltegrund Mole. In a well-executed attack using 500-pound bombs, the British scored three direct hits and many near misses against the stationary cruiser. Within minutes the heavily damaged *Königsberg* rolled over and sank, becoming the war's first major warship (above the size of destroyer) to be sunk by air attack. The British paid for this success with the loss of one Skua, which crashed on the return flight home.

Over the next few days the Fleet Air Arm carried out a number of follow-up strikes from both ship-borne and shore-based origins. Many of these were unsuccessful, and none attained results anywhere approaching those achieved on the 10th with the destruction of *Königsberg*. Still, the British did score a few notable successes during these operations. On 12 April 17 Swordfish from the aircraft carrier *Furious* attacked shipping at Narvik. Armed with mixed loads of 250-pound and 20-pound bombs, these lumbering strike aircraft inflicted minor damage on the German destroyers *Erich Giese* and *Erich Koellner* and sank three captured Norwegian naval auxiliaries that were under German control. These latter vessels consisted of the fishery protection sloops *Michael Sars* and *Heimdal* and the patrol vessel *Senja* worth a combined total of 1,132 tons. The next day a Swordfish floatplane from the battleship *Warspite* attacked and sank the German submarine *U64* off Bjerkvik near Narvik. Finally, on 14 April a force of 15 Skuas from Hatston returned to Bergen and sank the 7,569-ton German merchant ship *Bärenfels*, which was in the process of unloading a military cargo.[10]

Meanwhile, on the 13th Vice-Admiral Whitworth led a squadron, consisting of the battleship *Warspite* and nine destroyers, into Vestfiord to complete the destruction of German naval forces around Narvik. In doing so, the British were greatly assisted by *Warspite*'s Swordfish floatplane. In addition to destroying *U64*, the unassuming little aircraft provided valuable reconnaissance that allowed the British to locate and effectively engage various German destroyers lurking in the surrounding fjords and waterways. In a series of individual engagements, the British destroyers, assisted by *Warspite*'s 15-inch guns, sank or otherwise dispatched *Erich Koellner*, *Erich Giese*, *Hermann Künne* and *Diether von Roeder* and drove the remaining German destroyers into Rombaksfjord where they all eventually scuttled themselves. By mid-afternoon the major fighting was over with all eight German destroyers sunk or scuttled along with *U64* and the 11,776-ton German tanker *Jan Wellem*. For their part, the British did not lose any ships, but did suffer heavy damage to the destroyers *Eskimo* and *Cossack* and lesser damage to the destroyer *Punjabi*. In strategic terms, the battle effectively isolated the German garrison at Narvik, putting them squarely on the defensive and making them dangerously vulnerable to further British moves.

While this outcome represented a significant reversal for German ambitions in Narvik, developments in the rest of Norway generally favoured their cause. In the days immediately following the invasion, the Germans successfully consolidated and expanded their hold over the major population centres in Southern and Central Norway. They accomplished this despite the loss of several merchant ships employed in their initial reinforcement and re-supply efforts. Adding to the list of maritime casualties already mentioned, the Germans also lost the merchant ships *Alster* and *Skagerrak* (8,514 and 6,044 tons) to British warships, the 6,503-ton *Afrika* to shore artillery and the 4,977-ton *Sao Paulo* to mines during the period of 9–14 April.[11] Meanwhile, British submarines sank another three merchant ships worth 8,784 tons and the minelayer *Brummer* (2,410 tons, 4 × 4.1-inch guns) during the last three days of the same period.[12] The loss of many of these ships seriously disrupted Germany's original support plan. Nevertheless, neither the Norwegians nor the Allies were able to capitalise on these initial logistical shortfalls, and enough ships got through, coupled with an extensive airlift effort, to progressively improve Germany's manpower and materiel positions. With each passing day, the Germans continued to grow stronger as their hold on Southern and Central Norway increased.

In response to this, the British hastily organised a series of military expeditions to counter the German invaders. Realising that the Luftwaffe had all but rendered Southern Norway unapproachable, the British concentrated their counter-invasion efforts against Narvik and Trondheim in the northern and central parts of the country. In doing so, the British initially avoided direct assaults, but instead opted to envelop their targets with area landings. On 15 April the British 24th Guards Brigade landed at Harstad in Andfjord on the northern approach to Narvik. Meanwhile, during 14–18 April the British carried out a series of minor landings culminating in the deployments of the 146th and 148th Infantry Brigades at Namsos and Andalsnes on the northern and southern approaches to Trondheim. Over the next few weeks a steady flow of reinforcements, including French and Polish contingents, arrived at these locations. Although repeatedly attacked by German U-boats and aircraft, the majority of these operations occurred without loss. This was particularly true regarding the U-boats, which were almost universally unsuccessful in their attempted attacks, the sole exception being the destruction of the 5,139-ton transport *Cedarbank*. The Luftwaffe faired marginally better, sinking a handful of minor auxiliaries and damaging several larger ships. Still, they failed to sink any major vessels, and the Allies were able to successfully build-up their forces for follow-up operations.

Unfortunately, this success at sea was not matched by equal success on the ground. Despite an ultimate strength of some 12,000 and 30,000 men in the Trondheim and Narvik areas respectively, the Allies found themselves hampered by numerous problems ranging from the harsh terrain and weather to insufficient equipment and training. Almost immediately Allied efforts bogged down against the superior

German tactics, training and firepower. The Allies were particularly disadvantaged by the Luftwaffe's almost complete control of the air. Operating from captured Norwegian airfields, Luftwaffe fighters and bombers ranged freely across Southern and Central Norway attacking Allied positions at will. While these frequent attacks failed to curtail Allied maritime efforts, they nevertheless inflicted heavy damage upon shore installations at Namsos and Andalsnes and greatly imperilled large-scale ground movements or the ability to mass forces. This repeated aerial bombardment quickly eroded Allied morale and confidence at both the leadership and troop levels.

To counter this, the Royal Navy provided what little support it could. Since Luftwaffe activities were heaviest around Trondheim, the British concentrated most of their initial counter-air activities in this area. During the latter half of April the British rotated a number of anti-aircraft cruisers and sloops into Namsos and Andalsnes to provide air defence protection for their fledgling bases. This proved to be highly stressful duty as the ships involved often came under multiple German air attacks during the course of each day. Despite this, these ships, which often operated alone, all successfully held their stations and exacted a heavy toll on their German attackers. In addition to these defensive measures, the navy also took the offensive when the opportunity presented itself. On 17 April the British heavy cruiser *Suffolk* carried out a bombardment against the German seaplane base at Stavanger. This assault inflicted heavy damage including the destruction of four seaplanes, but prompted such a violent response from the Luftwaffe that *Suffolk* only made it back to Scapa Flow with great difficulty.

On 23 April the fleet received valuable reinforcements when the aircraft carriers *Ark Royal* and *Glorious* arrived from exercises in the Mediterranean. Immediately setting off for Norway, these ships carried 73 assorted Skua, Roc, Swordfish and Sea Gladiator aircraft. In addition, *Glorious* also ferried 18 RAF Gladiator fighters for use on a makeshift airstrip on the frozen surface of Lake Lesjaskog. Flying off *Glorious* on the 24th, these fighters immediately made their presence felt, claiming the destruction of at least six German aircraft in aerial combat. Sadly, this success was short-lived as heavy German air attacks quickly overwhelmed the small force and rendered the improvised airstrip unusable. Meanwhile, on 25 April the two British carriers launched 34 Skuas and Swordfish in strikes against the German airfield at Vaernes and shipping at Trondheim. Three days later *Ark Royal* dispatched another 18 aircraft against Vaernes airfield and the seaplane base at Ilsvika in Trondheim harbour. These attacks inflicted heavy damage on ground installations, damaged three merchant ships and destroyed or damaged upwards of 30 German aircraft. During this time the carriers also provided regular defensive fighter patrols that fought numerous engagements with German aircraft. The Fleet Air Arm's total claim for the period of 24 April through 1 May was 21 German aircraft destroyed with 20 more damaged. Their own losses amounted to 13 aircraft destroyed and two rendered unserviceable.[13]

Despite these and other efforts, the situation in Norway continued to deteriorate. On 27 April the Allied command realised that their positions around Trondheim were becoming increasingly untenable and therefore ordered the evacuation of Central Norway. During a series of operations beginning on 29 April and culminating on 3 May, the Royal Navy, with support from the French, successfully evacuated more than 11,000 Allied personnel from Namsos, Andalsnes and the surrounding areas. During this time the British also evacuated the Norwegian royal family, government and some 23 tons of Norwegian gold bullion. Personnel losses during these operations were thankfully light, although the navy did pay a materiel cost for its success. On 30 May the British sloop *Bittern*, which was on anti-aircraft duty off Namsos, lost its stern to an aerial bomb and had to be scuttled. Three days later the Allied destroyers *Bison* (French) and *Afridi* (British) were sunk in a heavy succession of German air attacks as the ships were en route home from Namsos.

Nor were these losses exclusive to the waters around Trondheim or the Allied navies. Despite their abandonment of Central Norway, the Allies still hoped to deny Narvik to the Germans. They continued to strengthen and provision their forces in Northern Norway as they slowly advanced towards this important strategic objective. While this was underway, naval and air operations continued in the waters around Norway with casualties sustained by both sides. On 30 April the German torpedo boat *Leopard* was lost when it accidentally collided with another German ship during a mining operation in the Skagerrak. Four days later German aircraft sank the Polish destroyer *Grom* in Ofotfjord, off Narvik. On 9 May the Allies reciprocated when FAA Skuas and RAF Blenheim bombers conducted a joint attack against shipping in Bergen Roads sinking the German minesweeper *M134*.[14] Finally, on 18 May the Royal Navy suffered its first cruiser casualty of the war when the light cruiser *Effingham* stranded on a rock pinnacle near Bodö and was rendered a total loss.

Meanwhile, submarine operations proceeded with varying degrees of success achieved by both sides. For the Allies, conventional attacks along with an increased use of submarine-laid mines continued to take a heavy toll on German shipping. During the period of 15 April through 10 June British submarines sank or captured nine merchant ships worth 33,191 tons, the minesweeper *M11*, seven auxiliaries and minor vessels worth 2,772 tons and seven Danish fishing vessels of unspecified tonnage. French submarines added another four vessels worth 2,247 tons during this time. When combined with earlier victories already listed, the total tally of Allied submarine successes during the Norwegian campaign amounted to 35 military and commercial vessels worth 94,671 tons sunk (excluding the aforementioned Danish fishing boats) and six vessels worth 25,869 tons damaged.[15] These successes did not come cheaply as the British lost the submarines *Thistle*, *Tarpon*, *Sterlet*, and *Seal* to enemy action while *Unity* was lost in an accidental collision. Meanwhile, the French submarine *Doris* and the Polish *Orzel* were also lost during this time frame.

A key factor in Germany's successful Norwegian campaign was its use of air power to impede Allied naval and ground operations. Pictured here is an Allied anchorage under the protection of a Bofors anti-aircraft gun in Norway. (Marshall Bishop H., War Office official photographer, public domain)

By comparison, this period was particularly frustrating for Germany's U-boat arm as time and again their attacks were plagued by torpedo malfunctions. As such, Germany's U-boats only succeeded in sinking 20 Allied or neutral merchant ships worth 92,562 tons during April and May. Of these, nine merchant ships worth 45,550 tons were British.[16] Against this, British mines, aircraft and destroyers sank *U50*, *U64*, *U49*, *U1* and *U22* while *U13* was lost to unknown causes.

Despite the lethality of these actions, events in the south soon overshadowed all activities in and around Norway. On 10 May the Germans launched their long-anticipated offensive against the West, shattering nine months of relative Phoney War calm. Employing the same blitzkrieg tactics used so successfully against Poland, the Germans unleashed 136 divisions consisting of some 2,350,000 men and 2,700 tanks in a massive assault designed to knock the Allies out of the war. Avoiding the strongest French defences along the formidable Maginot Line, the Germans instead opted to launch a sweeping attack through the neutral countries of Luxembourg, Belgium and the Netherlands. Spearheading these assaults were Army Groups A and B. The former, commanded by General Karl von Rundstedt and consisting of

44 divisions of which seven were armoured, attacked through the Ardennes into Luxembourg and Southern Belgium in a bid to advance to the coast and split the Allied defences. The latter, commanded by General Fedor von Bock and consisting of 28 divisions including three armoured divisions, attacked through the Netherlands and Northern Belgium to envelop the Allies' left flank.

Expecting an attack out of the Low Countries, the Allies immediately rushed their First Army Group, which included the bulk of the British Expeditionary Force, into Belgium to support the besieged Belgian army. At this time France possessed 94 divisions with Belgium, Britain and the Netherlands adding another 22, 10 and 10 divisions respectively.[17] This represented a combined total of some 2,862,000 men and 3,000 tanks. Yet, only a fraction of these forces were in position to counter the main thrusts of the German offensive, and the Germans were generally able to attain local superiority at selected points on the battlefield. The Germans also enjoyed other advantages that helped negate the Allies' overall parity in numbers.[18] Being a single nation, the Germans maintained a unity of purpose and command that was unmatched by the Allied coalition. With few exceptions, German leadership, training, operational execution and tactics were also superior to those of the Allies. As such, the Germans were able to attain an operational tempo far exceeding that of the less dynamic Allied formations or the antiquated French command and control system. Finally, the Germans were greatly assisted by the Luftwaffe, which maintained a nearly two-to-one numerical advantage in aircraft over the Allies (3,200 to 1,700) and an overall qualitative pre-eminence in aircraft performance, aircrew proficiency and tactical utilisation.

Fully exploiting these tactical and qualitative advantages, the Germans were able to make immediate and sustained progress against the Allied coalition. Picking off the weakest members first, the Germans overran Luxembourg in a single day while the Netherlands surrendered on 14 May. Meanwhile, powerful German spearheads smashed into Belgian and French forces sending them reeling back under a heavy onslaught of speed and firepower. On the 14th the British Expeditionary Force, which held positions along the Dyle River south of Brussels, came into its first substantial contact with the Germans and held its ground against a series of German attacks. Despite this initial success, the British were soon compelled to withdraw due to a growing disintegration of Belgian and French forces on their left and right flanks. Over the next several days the British made additional phased withdrawals as the overall Allied situation continued to worsen. This deterioration was particularly true on the right flank where Rundstedt's Army Group A broke through the French Ninth Army at Sedan and began a headlong drive to the coast against negligible opposition.

While these events were underway, the navy did what it could to lend support and respond to the quickly deteriorating situation. Although severely limited in its ability to directly influence the land battle, the navy took a number of actions to mitigate the looming calamity. Early in the campaign the British dispatched a number of naval and military teams to carry out clearing, blocking and demolition operations in Ijmuiden, Flushing, Antwerp and the Hook of Holland. As part of this undertaking, the British transferred a large number of ships and other assorted vessels to England. From Antwerp alone the British successfully extricated 26 merchant ships, 50 tugs and some 600 barges, dredgers and floating cranes.[19] During the same period the navy also evacuated the Dutch royal family and government along with the Dutch gold and diamond reserve. As the campaign progressed the British began evacuating non-essential and rear-echelon cadre from Belgium and Northern France culminating in the withdrawal of 27,936 such personnel by 26 May.[20] While generally successful, these operations did exact a heavy toll as German aircraft sank the British destroyers *Valentine* and *Whitley* and the French destroyer *L'Adroit* in the Schelde Estuary, off Nieuport and off Dunkirk on 15, 19 and 21 May respectively.

Meanwhile, on 19 May British authorities acknowledged the potential need for a full-scale evacuation and commenced planning and preparations for this contingency. As part of this process, the Admiralty assigned the Flag Officer Commanding Dover, Vice-Admiral Bertram Ramsay, as commander for this operation and earmarked a growing number of military and civilian vessels for his use. In viewing the situation, Ramsay immediately realised that the only suitable location for a large-scale evacuation was the French port of Dunkirk and its surrounding beaches. Unfortunately, while Dunkirk represented Ramsay's best alternative, it was far from ideal. Strong tidal currents made entering Dunkirk harbour a difficult undertaking that only promised to become more arduous under wartime conditions. German bombing had also rendered Dunkirk's extensive inner harbour with its seven dock basins unusable. The outer harbour featured two moles, but neither was designed for berthing ships. As for the beaches, the 16-mile coastline from Dunkirk to the Yset River formed the longest continuous stretch of sand in all of Europe. With its broad expanses of dunes, this area was well suited for staging large formations of men. However, the waterline's gradual slope and shallow shelf rendered the beaches inaccessible to anything other than small craft. Therefore, the British would have to shuttle their men to larger vessels waiting offshore in what promised to be a long and arduous task.

On 20 May the prospect of an evacuation became more likely as German forces reached the Channel coast near Abbeville thus isolating the British Expeditionary Force and other Allied formations from the bulk of the French army in the south. Despite this event, the British did not immediately retreat back towards the Channel. Instead, on 21 May the British launched a limited counterattack near Arras that achieved a fair degree of local success and threw the German command into a temporary panic. At the same time General Maxime Weygand, the French Commander-in-Chief, proposed a more ambitious counterattack against both sides of the German salient in an attempt to restore the situation. The British government under the new leadership of Winston Churchill, who had recently replaced Neville

Chamberlain as Prime Minister, also gave broad approval to this plan. Although highly sceptical about its prospects for success, General Lord Viscount Gort, the Commander-in-Chief of the British Expeditionary Force, dutifully supported the plan and made preparations for his portion of the attack.

While this was underway, British and French forces fought a series of delaying actions at Boulogne and Calais from 22 May through 26 May. During these engagements a number of British and French warships provided valuable assistance including the landing of reinforcements and supplies and the execution of numerous fire support missions against the oncoming Germans. As the fighting progressed to a decision point, these same warships then successfully evacuated 4,368 garrison troops from Boulogne. Unfortunately, the same was not true at Calais where only about 1,000 men escaped and the bulk of the garrison was forced to surrender after being ordered to fight to the last. Nor was this the full extent of the Allied losses. During the five-day period culminating on 26 May, German aircraft, artillery and E-boats inflicted heavy losses upon the Allied warships operating off the Channel ports. These losses included the British destroyer *Wessex* and three French destroyers sunk and several other destroyers damaged. Despite this sacrifice, the stout defence of Boulogne and Calais bought valuable time for the British Expeditionary Force to fall back upon and secure its potential escape route through Dunkirk.

During the last week in May the significance of this accomplishment became fully apparent. On the 25th General Gort determined that the French were hopelessly incapable of executing their portion of the Weygand counterattack and realised that his overriding priority must now be the salvation of the British Expeditionary Force. Accordingly, he cancelled all preparations for the counterattack and ordered his forces to begin a phased withdrawal back to the Dunkirk perimeter. On the evening of 26 May the British government finally acknowledged the reality of the situation and ordered the commencement of a full-scale evacuation, designated Operation *Dynamo*. At the time the Admiralty hoped to evacuate up to 45,000 men in what they envisioned would likely be no more than a two-day operation. However, on 27 May, the first full day of Operation *Dynamo*, the British only succeeded in lifting 7,669 men from Dunkirk.[21] Several factors contributed to this poor performance. First, although the Admiralty had earmarked an anti-aircraft cruiser, 39 destroyers, 38 minesweepers and hundreds of other military and civilian craft to the operation, many of these vessels had yet to arrive and only a small portion actually participated in the evacuation's first day. Likewise, heavy German fire from the recently captured Gravelines shore batteries had forced five British transports to abort their runs to Dunkirk. Finally, the process of loading troops had proved to be even slower and more laborious than previously anticipated due to a lack of minor craft and inadequate shore organisation.

Fortunately for the British, actions were already underway to correct these deficiencies. Already, the Admiralty was feverishly working to assemble additional shipping to participate in the evacuation. With each passing day, Ramsay hoped to supplement his command with additional vessels including large numbers of essential minor craft and contributions from the Dutch, Belgians and French. Regarding the German-controlled shore batteries at Gravelines, Ramsay's staff had already devised two routes to Dunkirk. When shore fire compromised the most direct route, the British simply switched their ships to the less direct route, designated Route Y. In doing so, they increased the passage time of their ships, but avoided the threat posed by the Gravelines batteries. Later the British adopted a third intermediate route, designated Route X, which reduced transit time but still avoided the deadly fire from Gravelines. Turning now to the slow process of loading troops, on the afternoon of 27 May Captain William G. Tennant arrived at Dunkirk with a party of 12 officers and 150 ratings to organise the embarkation arrangements. Tennant immediately set about making improvements to the shore organisation. Of particular importance, on the night of 27/28 May Tennant determined that the fragile east mole was indeed capable of berthing ships. With a length of 1,400 yards, the mole was capable of accommodating up to 16 vessels at a time thus significantly bolstering the lift capacity from the beaches.

These changes had an immediate and sustained impact upon Britain's evacuation effort. On the 28th the British successfully evacuated 17,804 men from Dunkirk, more than doubling their results from the previous day. On the 29th the British attained an even greater increase in output (2.66 times) when they safely delivered 47,310 men to Britain. They accomplished this latter feat despite a marked increase in German opposition. During the first two days of Operation *Dynamo*, weather and logistical factors combined to impede German air activity over Dunkirk, and British maritime losses were held to an acceptable level. On the morning of the 29th it looked like this trend might continue as rain and low clouds shrouded the evacuation area. However, the weather improved as the day wore on, and by the early afternoon the Luftwaffe descended upon the British evacuation fleet with a deadly vengeance. During the course of their attacks, the Luftwaffe sank the British destroyer *Grenade* and 15 assorted auxiliary and merchant ships worth 22,031 tons.[22] They further damaged a number of other ships including seven destroyers (one of which was French) and the British sloop *Bideford*. The Kriegsmarine added to the day's carnage when the E-boat *S30* and the U-boat *U62* sank the British destroyers *Wakeful* and *Grafton*.

Despite these losses and earlier Admiralty predictions regarding the likely duration of the evacuation, Operation *Dynamo* continued and actually accelerated during the succeeding days. On the 30th and 31st the British successfully evacuated 53,823 and 68,014 men respectively. In this, they were once again aided by inclement weather that helped hold the Luftwaffe at bay. Sadly, on 1 June the day dawned bright and clear, and the Luftwaffe reasserted itself with deadly proficiency. In the most effective series of attacks to date, the Luftwaffe sank 31 Allied vessels including the destroyers

Keith, Basilisk, Havant and *Foudroyant* (French), the minesweeper *Skipjack* and the gunboat *Mosquito*. They also damaged eleven other vessels including five British destroyers and two British sloops.[23] Despite these losses, the British still managed to evacuate 64,429 troops thus largely completing the evacuation of the British Expeditionary Force. By the 2nd fewer than 4,000 British personnel still remained in the Dunkirk perimeter along with upwards of 115,000 French troops. In order to rescue as many men as possible, the British continued the evacuation for two and a half more days. Operating mostly at night, the Allies avoided the worst of the German bombing and successfully evacuated another 79,177 men. On 4 June the remains of the Dunkirk garrison capitulated and the Admiralty announced the conclusion of Operation *Dynamo*.

For an undertaking that was only predicted to last two days with a hoped-for outcome of some 45,000 men rescued, *Dynamo* attained a scope and level of success far exceeding all expectations. During a nine-day period the British and their Allied partners successfully evacuated 338,226 soldiers from the Dunkirk perimeter. Of these, 308,888 were transported on British vessels.[24] When combined with the 27,936 rear echelon personnel evacuated during the week preceding *Dynamo*, the total number of rescued soldiers increased to 366,162. Of this total, roughly 224,000 were British representing almost the entirety of the trapped British Expeditionary Force.[25] The remainders were overwhelmingly French. In all, 848 Allied vessels participated in Operation *Dynamo* of which 72 were lost due to enemy action and 163 were lost to accidents, groundings and other maritime causes.[26] The vast majority of these losses came from the ranks of the minor vessels, but six British and three French destroyers were also included in these numbers. Likewise, at least 45 British vessels including the anti-aircraft cruiser *Calcutta* and 19 destroyers sustained damage. Nor was this entirely a maritime affair. The RAF, operating mostly from Britain, contributed 2,739 Fighter Command, 651 Bomber Command and 171 Coastal Command sorties in support of Operation *Dynamo*. This support cost the home-based RAF 145 aircraft including 99 fighters. Meanwhile, the Luftwaffe lost 132 aircraft in opposition to the evacuation.[27]

The successful completion of Operation *Dynamo* did not signal an end to the fighting in Europe. While the battle for the Low Countries was now over, the battle for France remained an open question. To support this battle, the British still possessed two divisions in France (51st Highland and 1st Armoured) with elements from two other divisions (52nd and 1st Canadian) earmarked for deployment. The British also still maintained some 150,000 support personnel on the continent. Even as the last evacuation vessels arrived in Britain to disembark their tired and dejected human cargoes from Dunkirk, the British contemplated plans to send further reinforcements to continue the fight in France. However, the rapid transpiring of events quickly rendered these plans obsolete. On 5 June the Germans launched a massive offensive with some 140 divisions against France's northern flank. The French, now

Table 2.2 Summary of Maritime Effort, Results and Losses for Operation *Dynamo*

Class of Ship	Number employed	Troops lifted	Lost through enemy action	Lost by other causes	Damaged (British only)
Anti-aircraft cruisers	1	1,856	-	-	1
Destroyers and torpedo boats	56	102,843	9	-	19
Sloops and dispatch vessels	6	1,436	-	-	1
Patrol vessels	7	2,504	-	-	-
Gunboats	2	3,512	1	-	-
Corvettes and chasseurs	11	1,303	-	-	-
Minesweepers	38	48,472	5	1	7
Trawlers and drifters	230	28,709	23	6	2
Special service vessels	3	4,408	-	-	-
Armed boarding vessels	3	4,848	1	-	2
Motor torpedo and anti-submarine boats	15	99	-	-	-
Schuyts	40	22,698	1	3	-
Yachts	27	4,895	1	2	-
Personnel vessels	45	87,810	9	-	8
Hospital carriers	8	3,006	1	-	5
Cargo ships	13	5,790	3	-	-
Tugs	40	3,164	6	1	-
Landing craft	13	118	1	7	-
Lighters, hoppers and barges	48	4,726	4	8	-
Small craft*	242	6,029	7	135	Unknown
Total	848	338,226	72	163	45

Source: S. W. Roskill, *The War at Sea 1939–1945, Volume I: The Defensive* (London: Her Majesty's Stationery Office, 1954), p. 603.
* Small craft include naval motor boats, war department launches, private motor boats and R.N.L.I. lifeboats. The number of small craft taking part and their losses was probably larger since the deployment of many such vessels went unreported.

largely devoid of Allied support and severely weakened by the previous four weeks of fighting, were unable to hold back this onslaught. Within a few days the French defences disintegrated, and the Germans were able to make rapid advances into the heart of the country. Meanwhile, on 10 June the Italian dictator Benito Mussolini opportunistically decided that the time was right to capitalise on Germany's success and declared war on Britain and France. Ten days later Italian forces launched a limited offensive across the Franco-Italian border.

As the situation in France progressively deteriorated, the British were once again compelled to consider the survival of their expeditionary units. This was particularly true regarding the 51st Highland Division, which soon found itself trapped along with lesser French forces in a defensive perimeter around St. Valéry-en-Caux.

On 10–13 June the Royal Navy launched Operation *Cycle* to rescue these entrapped forces as well as other endangered formations located at Le Havre. Unfortunately, fog severely hampered their efforts at St. Valéry-en-Caux and only 2,137 British and 1,184 French troops were successfully evacuated. The remainder of the 51st Division, including Major-General Victor Fortune, the division commander, and his headquarters staff, were forced to surrender. In all, some 6,000 British and 4,000 French prisoners were taken. Fortunately, operations at Le Havre went much better, and the navy successfully evacuated 11,059 men.[28] While this was underway, the situation in the rest of France became increasingly untenable. On 14 June the Germans captured Paris. That same evening the British government, after extensive consultations with the French leadership, realised that the battle was now hopeless and decided to withdraw the remainder of the British Expeditionary Force from France.

This final undertaking, designated Operation *Aerial*, took place on 16–23 June. During this time the Royal Navy and British merchant marine carried out a series of successful evacuations from Cherbourg, St Malo, Brest, St Nazaire, Nantes, La Pallice, Bayonne and St-Jean-de-Luz. The British were generally able to carry out these evacuations with minimal loss of life or maritime casualties. The only notable exception occurred on 17 June when Luftwaffe bombers sank the 16,243-ton British liner *Lancastria* off St Nazaire. Included in this loss were some 3,000 men out of the 5,800 men embarked on the stricken ship. Despite this single calamitous human tragedy, the balance of the operation proceeded with little meaningful disruption, and the British were able to evacuate the vast bulk of their remaining expeditionary force along with sizable contingents of Allied troops. When combined, Operations *Cycle* and *Aerial* resulted in the evacuation of 191,870 military personnel of which 144,171 were British, 24,352 were Poles, 18,246 were French, 4,938 were Czech and 163 were Belgian. Although the British were forced to abandon most of their equipment, they did manage to save at least 310 guns, 2,292 vehicles and 1,800 tons of stores.[29] Finally, in concurrent operations the British evacuated 22,656 civilians from the Channel Islands as they prepared to relinquish these outlying British territories to the Germans.

While the British were conducting these evacuations, the French succumbed to their German assailants. On 17 June the French government petitioned Germany for an armistice. Five days later the two parties signed an armistice agreement that formalised France's capitulation. In doing so, Britain suffered a strategic setback of the highest order. Total British losses during the fighting in France and the Low Countries had amounted to 68,111 casualties.[30] Of far greater importance, Germany's conquest of France, Belgium and the Netherlands had eliminated some 130 divisions from the Allied order of battle. This conquest had brought the Germans to the brink of Britain's doorstep as their forces occupied Europe's Atlantic coast from the Hook of Holland to the Bay of Biscay. The British did take solace in the fact that the bulk of their expeditionary force along with sizable contingents of Allied troops had been rescued. This came to a total of 558,032 military personnel of which 368,491 were British.[31] While this accomplishment was meaningful, it could only serve to lessen the calamity that had befallen Britain's strategic position.

Nor was this the extent of Britain's misfortune. Although overshadowed by events in the south, the conflict in Norway continued to an equally unsatisfactory result. On 23 May the British government decided that their position in Northern Norway was becoming insupportable given their overriding commitments in France and the Low Countries. The next day the Supreme Allied Command ordered the evacuation of Norway. As a precursor to this withdrawal, the Allies intended to first capture Narvik and demolish the port's ore loading installations. The British earmarked a number of cruisers and destroyers to support this assault. On 26 May German bombers sank the operation's proposed flagship, the British anti-aircraft cruiser *Curlew*, off Skaanland in Lavang Fjord. Despite this loss, the assault went forward on the night of 27/28 May with the support of the cruisers *Cairo*, *Coventry* and *Southampton*, five destroyers and a sloop, and the next day Allied forces completed the capture of Narvik and the surrounding peninsula. The Allies then began the process of destroying Narvik's port installations as they made preparations for their own withdrawal from Norway.

Although only a fraction of the size of Operation *Dynamo*, the Allied evacuation from Norway saddled the Royal Navy with another complex and difficult task to accomplish. It required the British to organise and evacuate some 30,000 men and large amounts of equipment from a wide area in Northern Norway. The main burden for this undertaking fell upon 15 large troopships and a handful of cruisers and destroyers. The aircraft carriers *Ark Royal* and *Glorious* provided air support for the operation along with two squadrons of RAF Hurricane and Gladiator fighters operating from a makeshift airstrip at Bardufoss. After a number of preliminary moves beginning with the abandonment of their advanced base at Bodo on 31 May, the British commenced their main evacuation efforts on the evening of 3 June. During this and the next four nights, the British successfully evacuated some 4,700, 4,900, 5,100, 5,200 and 4,600 men respectively.[32] They accomplished this with a minimal loss to the army personnel being evacuated.

Sadly, the same was not true for the Royal Navy. Unbeknown to the Admiralty, the German battlecruisers *Gneisenau* and *Scharnhorst*, the heavy cruiser *Admiral Hipper* and four destroyers had sortied into the waters off Norway. On the morning of 8 June this squadron, under the command of Vice-Admiral Wilhelm Marschall, encountered and sank the unloaded troop transport *Orama*, the tanker *Oil Pioneer* and the escort trawler *Juniper* (19,840, 5,666 and 505 tons respectively) some 300 miles off Bodo. Admiral Marschall then detached his lighter ships back to Norway while his battlecruisers continued their sortie. That afternoon *Gneisenau* and *Scharnhorst* encountered the British aircraft carrier *Glorious* and the destroyers *Ardent* and *Acasta* as these latter vessels were en route to Britain after evacuating

RAF fighters from Bardufoss. Caught by surprise and woefully unprepared for a surface action, *Glorious* frantically attempted to arm and launch an air strike while the two escorting destroyers charged forward in a desperate attempt to defend the endangered carrier. Unfortunately, the Germans pressed their advantage with great vigour, and in the lopsided battle that followed, *Gneisenau* and *Scharnhorst* quickly sank the three British ships. In doing so, some 1,515 British seamen perished along with their ill-fated vessels.

For their part, the Germans did not escape entirely unscathed from this action or its postscripts. Before its demise, the doomed *Acasta* first scored a single torpedo hit on *Scharnhorst* causing serious damage to the larger capital ship. Despite this damage and a belated British pursuit, the German battlecruisers then made good their escape and safely arrived back in Norway on the 9th. Unsatisfied with this result, the British set about to carry out further attacks against the German ships. On 13 June *Ark Royal* launched 15 Skuas in an air strike against the damaged *Scharnhorst* in Trondheim. During the course of this strike the British aircraft encountered strong German opposition and lost eight of their number. Against this, the British only succeeded in inflicting minor damage to the German battlecruiser with a single bomb hit that failed to explode. On 20 June *Gneisenau* and *Admiral Hipper* carried out a diversionary sortie into the Iceland-Faeroes gap to cover *Scharnhorst*'s withdrawal to Germany. At 2209 hours that evening the British submarine *Clyde* scored a single torpedo hit on *Gneisenau* some 40 nautical miles northwest of Halten. This hit forced *Gneisenau* to abandon its sortie and return to Germany for repairs. Thus, in a period of less than two weeks, both German battlecruisers were put out of action requiring several months to repair.

These events also signalled the conclusion of German naval operations in support of their spring offensives. Much of the Kriegsmarine now settled into a brief period of operational inactivity as its forces repaired battle damage, regrouped and prepared for follow-up operations – if indeed follow-up operations were necessary. For many Germans, including Hitler, the war was all but over. Dealing with Britain now seemed little more than an afterthought as Germany basked in the glow of its vastly successful blitzkrieg campaign. In a little more than ten weeks, Germany had conquered six European nations consisting of over 380,000 square miles of territory and a combined population of over 65 million people. In doing so, they had destroyed the powerful French army and made themselves masters over half of Europe. The butcher's bill for this accomplishment had been remarkably light. The conquest of France and the Low Countries had cost Germany 27,074 killed, 111,034 wounded and 18,384 missing.[33] Operations in Norway and Denmark had added another 5,660 military casualties to this total including 1,317 dead and 2,375 men lost at sea or missing.[34] German aircraft losses amounted to 1,284 and 242 machines respectively during the two campaigns.[35] When compared to the total forces committed and the results achieved, these losses were hardly prohibitive.

A British destroyer arriving at Dover with evacuees from Dunkirk. In May and June 1940 the Royal Navy and merchant marine along with Allied support evacuated nearly 600,000 Allied personnel from France and Norway, serving as a practical and psychological impetus in Britain's decision to fight on. (Puttnam and Malindine, War Office official photographer, public domain)

Indeed, the Germans still maintained some 160 divisions and over 3,000 combat aircraft in their order of battle.

Against this, Britain stood weak, but determined. For the first time in 135 years, Britain faced the very real prospect of invasion and conquest. With little more than a couple dozen ill-equipped divisions and a few hundred fighter aircraft, many observers openly wondered how the British could possibly prevail against their seemingly invincible opponents. Some even questioned the likelihood of further British resistance as they assumed the inevitable acceptance of a negotiated peace. Yet, under the indomitable leadership of Winston Churchill, the British resolved to defend their island nation. In a speech before parliament on 4 June 1940, Churchill clearly stated his unflinching determination to carry on the fight:

> We shall not flag or fail. We shall go on to the end, we shall fight in France, we shall fight on the seas and oceans, we shall fight with growing confidence and growing strength in the air, we shall defend our Island, whatever the cost may be, we shall fight on the beaches, we shall fight on the landing grounds, we shall fight in the fields and in the streets, we shall fight in the hills; we shall never surrender....[36]

During a subsequent speech before parliament on 18 June, Churchill illustrated the daunting challenge and burden placed before the British people:

> What General Weygand called the battle of France is over. I expect that the battle of Britain is about to begin. Upon this battle depends the survival of Christian civilization. Upon it depends our own British life, and the long continuity of our institutions and our Empire. The whole fury and might of the enemy must very soon be turned on us. Hitler knows that he will have to break us in this Island or lose the war. If we can stand up to him, all Europe may be free and the life of the world may move forward into broad, sunlit uplands. But if we fail, then the whole world, including the United States, including all that we have known and cared for, will sink into the abyss of a new Dark Age made more sinister, and perhaps more protracted, by the lights of perverted science. Let us therefore brace ourselves to our duties, and so bear ourselves that, if the British Empire and its Commonwealth last for a thousand years, men will still say, 'This was their finest hour.'[37]

So in the early summer of 1940, the British nation bravely braced itself to meet its destiny. It did so against the full potential of the German war machine. It did so devoid of European allies. It did so standing alone.

CHAPTER 3

Standing Alone

As British military authorities reviewed the state of homeland defences during the early summer of 1940, it was alarmingly clear that the British army maintained a substantially inferior position to that of the Germans. After two decades of peacetime neglect followed by defeat and expulsion from mainland Europe, the army now found itself scrambling to rearm and prepare itself for an expected German invasion. The British ostensibly possessed 29 divisions (including those recently evacuated from Europe and one stationed in Northern Ireland) for the defence of the United Kingdom. As such, the British were outnumbered by a factor of more than five to one when compared to the total number of divisions available to the Germans. To make matters worse, the majority of British divisions were under-strength in terms of manpower. Part of this deficit was due to casualties sustained during the recent fighting in Europe, but the main factor contributing to this staffing shortfall was the army's slow mobilisation and expansion. This latter dynamic was primarily due to materiel shortages that had prompted the government to implement an incremental mobilisation in order to balance the needs of industry and the military. As a result, the average strength of a home-based infantry division at the beginning of June 1940 was just under 11,000 men compared to an authorised establishment of 15,500.[1] Many of these divisions had only formed within the last nine months, and even with an accelerated expansion, it would still take time to make good these deficiencies.

Unfortunately, this was only the beginning of Britain's military disparity. During the first ten months of the war the army had generally deployed its best staffed, trained and armed formations to France as part of the British Expeditionary Force. In the debacle that followed, the British had successfully evacuated more than 85 percent of these men back to the United Kingdom. While most retained their individual weapons (a sign of good military discipline), nearly everything else had been lost or left behind. These materiel losses included 2,472 guns, 63,879 vehicles, 20,548 motorcycles and over 500,000 tons of stores and ammunition.[2] As such, the returning British Expeditionary Force was now almost totally devoid of the heavy weapons and equipment necessary for modern mechanised warfare. Many returning formations also suffered varying degrees of disorganisation, fatigue and attrition. The recently returned units of the British Expeditionary Force desperately needed time to rearm, reorganise and absorb casualty replacements before they could assume a reasonable level of combat readiness.

In many respects, the situation was even worse for Britain's home-based divisions. In addition to the staffing shortages already mentioned, the overwhelming majority of these formations were dangerously deficient in weapons and equipment ranging from machine guns to radios and artillery pieces to vehicles of all types. As of 1 June the total number of armoured vehicles in all of Britain (including those held in depots and training units) numbered just 963. Of these, only 213 were modern infantry or cruiser tanks with the remainder being light tanks or obsolete models of limited combat value.[3] Meanwhile, as of 8 June the British possessed just 2,300 Bren light machine guns, 54 2-pounder anti-tank guns, 420 field guns and 163 medium and heavy guns within their operational units.[4] This represented less than a third of the requirement for machine guns and one-sixth of the requirement for artillery pieces. Another major problem plaguing the army was a lack of sufficient training for many of its units. Much of this was due to the army's ongoing expansion during which tens of thousands of new recruits swelled military ranks and new units sprang up out of nowhere. This lack of training was evident at all levels of command, and was particularly prevalent in home-based units. For instance, of the army's 16 home-based divisions, two had done no divisional training whatsoever, five had done very little and nine were only rated as 'fair' in this regard.[5]

When combined together, these deficiencies represented a significant threat to Britain's national defence, the seriousness of which depended upon the timing of a potential German invasion. Regarding this latter factor, none of the problems plaguing the army were insurmountable given the passage of time. Already, efforts were underway to rearm and expand the army and strengthen homeland defences. The British could expect their defensive capabilities to improve with each passing week. Nevertheless, it would take several weeks or months before these deficiencies were corrected to a satisfactory level. In the meantime, the army's ability to repel a German invasion was severely degraded. This fact was clearly recognised by the Chiefs of Staff who reported at the end of May, 'Should the Germans succeed in establishing a force with its vehicles in this country, our Army forces have not got the offensive power to drive it out.'[6] Put another way, had Britain been physically connected to the European continent, it is almost assured that the army would have been incapable of withstanding a German invasion during the summer of 1940.

Fortunately for the British, this latter statement was purely hypothetical as geography and history combined to provide advantages that helped offset the army's many weaknesses. These mitigating factors all stemmed from the fact that Britain is an island and not physically connected to Europe. As such, the English Channel and North Sea provided a formidable natural barrier that helped shield the nation from

STANDING ALONE • 57

continental aggressors. Britain's island status had also played a major role in shaping the nation's history. Being surrounded by water, the British people had developed a natural connection to the sea that helped foster a great maritime heritage and eventually transformed the nation into a world-class naval power. In doing so, the Royal Navy, and not the army, became Britain's senior service and primary defender of the Realm. For centuries Britain's geographical separation along with the ships, seamen and guns of the Royal Navy had frustrated the plans of would-be invaders ranging from Philip II of Spain in 1588 to Napoleon Bonaparte in the early 1800s. Now in the summer of 1940 the British hoped that these same factors would prove equally decisive against Hitler and the German war machine.

To this end, the Royal Navy was once again thrust to the forefront of Britain's defensive posture. The British could take solace in the fact that the navy was in far better shape than the army. Still, the situation was far from ideal. Like their army counterparts, the Royal Navy had suffered heavy losses during the recent fighting off Norway, France and the Low Countries. From April through June 1940 these losses included the destruction of the aircraft carrier *Glorious*, the light cruiser *Effingham*, the anti-aircraft cruiser *Curlew*, 14 destroyers, three escort destroyers, five submarines, one sloop and two minesweepers. Of almost equal importance, dozens of additional ships had suffered varying degrees of damage requiring repair time in British dockyards. This damage fell particularly hard upon Britain's all-important destroyer/escort destroyer force, which could only muster 74 such vessels ready for duty in June 1940.[7] This shortage highlighted another factor burdening the navy. While the direct defence of Britain was of supreme importance, other obligations existed that were equally essential to the nation's long-term viability and war effort. Paramount amongst these was the continued maintenance of Britain's maritime trade and lines of communication. Thus, the navy had to distribute its reduced strength against a variety of competing priorities.

Taking this into account, the Royal Navy began marshalling and preparing its resources to meet the anticipated German invasion. Early on, the British anticipated that the Germans were likely to conduct their invasion across the English Channel to take advantage of the shorter crossing distances. With this in mind, the Admiralty positioned four destroyer flotillas with an assigned strength of 36 vessels in Humber, Harwich, Sheerness and Portsmouth to provide an immediate counter to this threat. They further called for additional destroyers, corvettes and escort vessels to reinforce these flotillas as circumstances and availability dictated. The British also provided cruisers to support this force. In July and August this included seven cruisers dispersed from the Home Fleet to various ports in and around the likely invasion area. The British retained the remainder of the Home Fleet at Scapa Flow, but held open the possibility of moving these ships south if the situation required. Finally, the Admiralty assembled an Auxiliary Patrol consisting of over 1,000 armed trawlers and drifters, of which approximately one-third were at sea at any given time, to provide early warning of German movements.

Against this, the British considered the probable composition of the invasion fleet likely to be arrayed against them. British Intelligence estimated that the Germans could potentially muster a maximum force consisting of the battlecruisers *Scharnhorst* and *Gneisenau*, the battleships *Schlesien* and *Schleswig-Holstein*, two heavy cruisers, at least two and possibly four light cruisers, seven to ten destroyers, 16 torpedo boats, eight escort vessels, 40 to 50 U-boats and a similar number of motor torpedo boats.[8] In addition, the British considered the possible contributions that other naval powers might make. The most obvious of these was Italy, which at the time of its declaration of war possessed a large fleet consisting of six battleships, one old armoured cruiser, seven heavy cruisers, 12 light cruisers, 61 destroyers, 69 torpedo boats and 115 submarines either on hand or nearing completion.[9] Although expected to retain the vast majority of their naval power in the Mediterranean, the British could not entirely discount the possibility that Italian ships might participate in a German invasion. If nothing else, Italy's presence and entry into the war forced the Royal Navy to maintain a sizable fleet in the Eastern Mediterranean to protect British interests there. Now with the collapse of France, the British were also compelled to send a battle squadron to Gibraltar to defend the Western Mediterranean and deny the Italians access to the Atlantic Ocean. This squadron, designated Force H, was commanded by Vice-Admiral James Somerville and initially consisted of the battlecruiser *Hood*, the battleships *Resolution* and *Valiant*, the aircraft carrier *Ark Royal*, two light cruisers and 11 destroyers.

The necessity of this latter action highlighted a second major concern confronting British officials. With the fall of France, the British feared that Germany might gain access to a sizable portion of the French fleet. At the time the French fleet was spread over a wide area. From a British point of view, the most secure portion of this fleet consisted of those vessels sheltering in British ports. This included the veteran battleships *Courbet* and *Paris*, four destroyers, six torpedo boats, seven submarines, 12 sloops, one minelayer and nearly 200 auxiliaries and minor vessels. Outside of Britain, the vast majority of the French fleet was stationed in a variety of African ports. This included the French capital ships *Dunkerque*, *Strasbourg*, *Bretagne* and *Provence* that were located in Mers-el-Kebir, *Lorraine* which was in Alexandria, *Richelieu* stationed in Dakar and the incomplete *Jean Bart* located in Casablanca. Beyond this, the French also maintained a number of cruisers, destroyers and submarines at these various locations. Finally, the aircraft carrier *Béarn* and two cruisers were located in the French West Indies.

Although French authorities repeatedly expressed a commitment to scuttle their ships before allowing them to fall under German control, the British remained rightfully concerned given the stakes involved. Under the provisions of the newly signed armistice agreement, German forces occupied Paris and the northern half of France while a semi-independent French government located in the spa town of Vichy administered the southern portion of the country and France's colonial possessions.

In light of these arrangements, the British were doubtful that the Vichy government would be willing or able to act contrary to German interests or withstand German pressure. Recent events seemed to bolster this concern. Already, the French had reneged upon a commitment made during a 12 June meeting of the Supreme War Council to withdraw their fleet to Canada. British appeals to the French president failed to change this decision. Meanwhile, reports from Algeria indicated that French morale was low and that the attitude within the navy was uncertain. An effort to persuade former French ministers to create an émigré government in North Africa failed when French authorities refused to meet with the British delegation sent to negotiate the matter. Finally and of the greatest concern, intelligence sources indicated that the Germans were in possible possession of the French naval codes thus giving them the ability to bypass the French naval leadership and directly communicate to the fleet in their name.

Fearing the erosion of naval superiority and degraded survival prospects sure to occur if Germany gained control over the French fleet, the British government felt compelled to take action before this threat could materialise. On 27 June the British War Cabinet authorised the execution of Operation *Catapult*, the simultaneous seizure, neutralisation or destruction of accessible French warships. This decision was made and received with great reluctance, and the overwhelming hope was that the mission could be carried out with a minimum of violence and casualties. This attitude was characterised by the instructions given to Admiral Somerville, whose Force H was tasked to deal with the main French fleet at Mers-el-Kebir. Before engaging in hostilities, Somerville offered Admiral Marcel-Bruno Gensoul, the French commander, four options regarding the disposition of his forces with a six-hour time limit for acceptance. First, the French could put to sea and join forces with the British. Second, they could sail to a French West Indian port and demilitarise their ships. Third, they could sail with reduced crews to any British port and be interned. Finally, they could scuttle all their ships in place. The British were resolved to carry out this mission, but would only open fire if forced to do so by French inaction or resistance.

Operation *Catapult* commenced on 3 July with simultaneous actions taken in Britain, Alexandria and Mers-el-Kebir. The former was a near complete success as British boarding parties successfully took control of over 220 French warships, including the battleships *Courbet* and *Paris*, with a minimum of violence and only a handful of casualties sustained on both sides. The British achieved a similar satisfactory outcome in Alexandria, where the French commander, Admiral René-Émile Godfroy, agreed to immobilise and demilitarise his squadron. Unfortunately, the situation at Mers-el-Kebir proved far more difficult, as the French refused to accede to the British ultimatum, and the British reluctantly opened fire on the French fleet. In a short engagement lasting only ten minutes, *Hood*, *Valiant* and *Resolution* rained down a heavy bombardment of 15-inch shells that destroyed the French battleship

Bretagne and disabled *Dunkerque*, *Provence* and a destroyer. In follow-up actions over the next few days, the British inflicted further damage to *Dunkerque*, rendering it truly immobile while attaining similar results against the battleship *Richelieu* at Dakar. Finally, the British were able to use diplomatic pressure and the denial of fuel oil to keep the aircraft carrier *Béarn* and other French warships stranded in the West Indies.

With the conclusion of these actions, the British halted their assault against the French fleet. In less than a week the British had accomplished their overriding objective by removing a sizable portion of the French navy from the potential clutches of the German enemy. This was particularly true regarding the main units of the French battle line. With the exception of *Strasbourg*, which had escaped from Mers-el-Kebir to safely arrive at Toulon, all of France's operational or near operational capital ships had either been seized, sunk or otherwise neutralised. The operation also had major political benefits in that it signalled to the world that Britain was fully committed to fighting on and would do whatever was necessary to act in its own defence. This demonstrated resolve reassured the United States, which also viewed Germany as a potential threat, that Britain was still a country worth supporting. As such, the United States, despite its official position of neutrality, increasingly implemented measures to assist the British war effort. Britain's bold action had an equally important impact upon Spain, which thereafter spurned German lobbying efforts for it to join the war on the side of the Axis. Still, the success of Operation *Catapult* came at a heavy price as Franco-British relations immediately deteriorated to a dangerous level following the attack. Fortunately, the Vichy government limited its response to this provocation to an ineffective retaliatory air strike against Gibraltar and the suspension of diplomatic relations. Nevertheless, the potential for further hostilities was always present with most French institutions now either apathetic or tacitly hostile towards British interests.

Of course, the British had more immediate matters to concern themselves with. Despite the neutralisation of the French fleet, the prospect of invasion still hung over the nation. To this end, the Admiralty adopted a three-prong strategy to combat this threat as it materialised. First, the British proposed to attack the German invasion forces in their assembly areas before they could depart. Second, they proposed to attack the enemy forces at their points of arrival. Finally, if intelligence and reconnaissance allowed, they hoped to intercept German invasion forces while en route to England. This latter tenet was considered most problematic since it required adequate early warning, ready pre-positioned forces and pinpoint timing. As a prerequisite for their strategy, the British also recognised the necessity of maintaining a viable air component to serve as an offensive weapon and provide at least minimal defensive coverage for their ships. This belief was clearly articulated on 26 May when the Chiefs of Staff reported that, 'While our Air Force is in being our Navy and Air Force together should be able to prevent a serious seaborne invasion of this country. But if Germany gained complete air superiority ... the Navy could hold up invasion for a time but not an indefinite period.'[10] As such, British authorities surmised that the Germans would strive to achieve air superiority before launching their invasion, but also held open the possibility of a no-notice surprise assault.

Had British defence planners known the true state of German readiness and capabilities, their fears would have been greatly allayed. Up to this point the Germans had only conducted rudimentary invasion planning, and no serious preparations were underway. Indeed, during the heady days following the collapse of France, many leading Germans believed that the war was all but over, and few seriously contemplated the potential need or requirements for an invasion. This was certainly true in the case of Hitler, who publicly anticipated that the British government would quickly recognise the hopelessness of its situation and agree to a negotiated peace. As such, Hitler did not order an invasion study until 2 July or the commencement of formal invasion planning and preparations until two weeks after this. Even then, inadequate resources and service disputes plagued the process, which was designated Operation *Seelöwe* (Sea lion). Much of this consternation stemmed from a lack of adequate seaborne lift. Despite their recent success against Norway, the Germans did not possess a readily available invasion fleet or specialised landing craft. Instead, they would have to depend upon an improvised fleet of civilian merchant ships, motorboats and barges to fulfil their lift requirements. It would take a number of weeks to assemble, modify and man this improvised fleet, which would then only be capable of handling a fraction of the initially proposed invasion force.

A second major problem plaguing German ambitions was the Kriegsmarine's questionable ability to provide adequate defence for the invasion fleet. While the German army and Luftwaffe had established themselves as premier fighting forces, the Kriegsmarine was in a markedly inferior position compared to that of the Royal Navy. Although smaller from the outset, this numerical weakness had been exacerbated by recent heavy losses suffered during the Norwegian campaign. From April through the first half of June these losses included the heavy cruiser *Blücher*, the light cruisers *Karlsruhe* and *Königsberg*, ten destroyers, two torpedo boats, one minelayer, six U-boats, two minesweepers, several auxiliary and minor vessels and at least 37 seagoing merchant ships worth 196,633 tons. The battlecruisers *Scharnhorst* and *Gneisenau*, the pocket battleships *Lützow* and *Admiral Sheer*, the heavy cruiser *Admiral Hipper* and a number of lesser warships were unavailable due to battle damage repairs or routine refits. This left the Germans with a markedly smaller force than British Intelligence had anticipated, centring upon the old battleships *Schlesien* and *Schleswig-Holstein* (which the Germans were disinclined to use due to their lack of adequate anti-aircraft defences), two light cruisers, a couple dozen destroyers and torpedo boats and 28 U-boats.

One of ten German destroyers sunk by the British at Narvik. Heavy Kriegsmarine losses during the Norwegian campaign proved to be a major impediment to subsequent German planning for the invasion of Britain. (Public domain)

When combined together, these two maritime weaknesses forced the Germans to scale back their invasion plans and seriously undermined the likelihood of success for the entire operation. The army's original proposal called for 13 divisions to carry out initial landings over a wide front between Ramsgate and Lyme Regis with 27 follow-up divisions to land shortly thereafter. Naval authorities immediately recognised the sheer impossibility of this plan given their limited resources and instead proposed more modest landings over a greatly reduced area. After much debate and study, military planners finally agreed to a first-wave seaborne assault of nine infantry divisions with two airborne divisions in support. However, even under this reduced plan, the navy still estimated that it would take 11 days to completely transport the nine initial assault divisions with further reinforcements arriving at a rate of two divisions every four days.[11] The navy would have to provide a continuous flow of rations, ammunition, fuel and other necessary supplies to sustain these deployed formations at a daily rate of approximately 300 tons per division.[12]

Of course, success in this endeavour depended upon the Kriegsmarine's ability to execute this tight schedule in the face of anticipated opposition from the Royal Navy and Royal Air Force. Even under ideal conditions, Operation *Seelöwe* represented an extremely difficult undertaking that promised to test the capabilities and endurance of the German ships and crews. If effective British opposition exacerbated these difficulties, the undertaking had the potential to become all but impossible. From the beginning, Grand-Admiral Raeder and the senior naval leadership realised that complete air supremacy was a necessary prerequisite for any invasion attempt. It was only under the protective umbrella of the Luftwaffe that the Kriegsmarine could possibly hope to contend with the Royal Navy's superior numbers. This realisation was acknowledged by Hitler, who stated in his 16 July invasion directive that, 'The Royal Air Force must be morally and operationally so reduced as to possess no further appreciable power to strike against the German crossing.'[13]

Thus in the summer of 1940, both sides came to the same conclusion that the struggle for air superiority, or at least air parity in the case of the British, represented a decisive component in the success or failure of any invasion attempt. The Battle of Britain would begin, and perhaps end, in the air. To conduct this aerial campaign, the Luftwaffe initially assembled a force of roughly 2,600 aircraft consisting of 1,200 bombers, 280 dive-bombers, 760 single-engine fighters, 220 twin-engine fighters and 140 reconnaissance aircraft.[14] The main force opposing this airborne armada was RAF Fighter Command, which on 7 July possessed a nominal strength of 644 aircraft and 1,259 pilots in 52 squadrons.[15] Thus, on the face of it, Fighter Command was outnumbered by a factor of approximately four to one. Of course, this only represented a portion of Britain's airborne strength, which also included Bomber Command, Coastal Command and the Fleet Air Arm, but it was Fighter Command that would have to deal with the brunt of the German onslaught as the latter tried to gain air superiority over the proposed invasion area.

Fortunately, the British enjoyed some advantages that helped redress this numerical disparity. First and foremost, the British possessed the best nation-wide air defence early warning and command and control system in the world at the time. This elaborate system used radar, ground observers, ground-based controllers and radio communications to acquire attacking Luftwaffe formations and direct RAF fighters to attain intercepts. In this manner, Fighter Command hoped to economise its limited resources and mount an enhanced defence. The British also benefitted from the fact that the battle would be primarily fought over their territory. As such, downed British pilots and damaged aircraft had a far greater likelihood of returning to active service than their German counterparts did. The same geographical factor restricted the effectiveness of the German fighter arm, which was hamstrung by the limited range of its top fighter, the Messerschmitt Bf 109E. Finally, although outnumbered, Fighter Command enjoyed a qualitative status that was at least comparable to that of the Luftwaffe. In particular, the British possessed two fighters, the Supermarine Spitfire and Hawker Hurricane, that were roughly equivalent in overall capability to the Messerschmitt Bf 109E and clearly superior to Germany's other primary fighter, the Messerschmitt 110.[16] Forty-four of Fighter Command's 52 squadrons were equipped with Spitfires or Hurricanes thus boosting the effectiveness of this force.

From the British point of view, the Battle of Britain started on 10 July 1940. Prior to this, the Germans had mounted minor incursions into British airspace, but the 10th marked a noticeable increase in Luftwaffe activities. It was during this time that the Luftwaffe launched a stepped-up series of attacks against British shipping, ports and military targets along the English Channel and eastern coast of England. The primary purpose of this strategy was to draw out and engage Fighter Command. In this, the Luftwaffe was successful, although the results achieved were contrary to their expectations. From 10 July to 11 August the Luftwaffe lost 255 aircraft in aerial combat compared to 128 lost to Fighter Command.[17] By comparison, British fighter production in July amounted to 496 aircraft.[18] As such, Fighter Command's position actually improved during this period, which became known as the Contact Phase. By 11 August the operational strength of Fighter Command stood at 704 aircraft (of which 620 were Spitfires and Hurricanes) with a further 289 aircraft held in reserve.[19] On the other hand, Britain's initial success in the air came at a cost beyond those directly involving the RAF. In particular, the German attacks in July destroyed 40 merchant ships worth 75,698 tons along with the destroyers *Brazen*, *Codrington*, *Wren* and *Delight*.[20]

On 12 August the Germans began the second phase of the battle, a direct all-out assault against Fighter Command and the RAF. Over the next four weeks the Luftwaffe carried out a series of daily raids (weather permitting) against British airfields, command and control sites and aircraft manufacturing facilities. By this time, German air strength allotted to the campaign had increased to over 3,000 aircraft, and the Luftwaffe was often able to launch over 1,000 sorties on many of their daily assaults.[21] Nevertheless, Fighter Command initially continued to hold its own against this onslaught. During a week of intense air combat (12–18 August) British defences and operational factors claimed the destruction of 289 Luftwaffe aircraft with hundreds more damaged to varying degrees. Fighter Command losses during the same period amounted to 125 aircraft destroyed in aerial combat with some 30 more destroyed on the ground. However, as time went on, the constant strain of these attacks took its toll. Although on most days the British continued to inflict heavier losses than they themselves suffered, the margin began to tighten. From 19 August to 6 September the Luftwaffe lost 412 aircraft in aerial combat compared to 297 for Fighter Command.

While this level of attrition was beyond either side's ability to sustain indefinitely, it was particularly distressing to the British, who increasingly worried that the tide of battle was slowly shifting against the fortunes of Fighter Command. For four consecutive weeks British fighter wastage had outstripped replacements. This trend was particularly apparent during the period of 24 August through 6 September when Fighter Command lost 466 Spitfires and Hurricanes destroyed or badly damaged against a replacement of only 269 such aircraft from new production or repair facilities.[22] Although transfers from British Aircraft Storage Units generally kept the front-line squadrons up to strength, reserve stocks were quickly depleting. Of even greater concern was the loss of trained pilots. During the same two-week period culminating on 6 September, Fighter Command lost 231 pilots killed, wounded or missing against a replacement of barely half this number. By early September Fighter Command's forward-deployed squadrons were down to an average of 19 pilots against an official compliment of 26, while squadrons in quieter sectors averaged fewer than 16.[23] These shortfalls were made worse by the fact that many replacement pilots were fresh out of training and lacked the skill and experience levels of the men they were replacing. When combined together, these factors, along with the debilitating impact of numerous raids against key command and control Sector Stations, threatened to bring Fighter Command to the brink of exhaustion.

Fortunately for the British, relief was soon at hand. During the initial portions of the air offensive, Hitler had forbidden attacks on London. Nevertheless, either by accident or design, a number of German bombers did attack the British capital on the night of 24/25 August. In response to this development, the British launched a series of reprisal raids against Berlin beginning on the night of 25/26 August. Although these British raids caused little materiel damage, they induced a German response that changed the entire direction of the battle. On 7 September the Luftwaffe launched an all-out assault against London with both day and night raids. This onslaught continued over the next several days and nights as weather permitted. In doing so, the Luftwaffe inflicted heavy human and materiel carnage upon the citizens of London, but inadvertently gave Fighter Command the respite it sorely needed by diverting pressure off the Sector Stations and airfields. This, plus a reduced scale of operations due to inclement weather, allowed Fighter Command time to rest and regroup as it waited for the ideal time to fully reassert itself.

While this was underway, the Germans continued their invasion preparations against a rapidly shrinking window of opportunity. German naval planners had estimated that the ideal time for launching Operation *Seelöwe* was between 19 and 26 September, given moon and tidal conditions. Although operations were still possible after this point, any such delay would significantly increase the likelihood of interference from adverse autumn weather. The Kriegsmarine required a ten-day notice prior to launch date in order to conduct essential preliminary operations. As such, a requisite decision point was only a matter of days away. In considering his options, Hitler was aware that the Luftwaffe had thus far failed to achieve the level of air supremacy thought necessary to carry out the operation. Nevertheless, reports from the Luftwaffe seemed to indicate that the RAF was weakening. The Germans hoped that given a few more days of good weather, they might still gain decisive ascendancy over Fighter Command. With this in mind, Hitler put off his invasion decision first to the 14th and then later to 17 September.

Meanwhile, the Kriegsmarine assembled its nominal invasion fleet in a number of prominent French and Belgian ports. Eventually this build-up included 170 transports, 1,918 barges, 386 tugs and 1,020 motorboats.[24] Not surprisingly, these moves were fully apparent to the British, whose reconnaissance aircraft were able to identify and track the growing concentration of shipping. On the night of 7/8 September the British initiated the first tenet of their anti-invasion strategy and dispatched bombers to attack German shipping in the port of Ostend. Over the next month aircraft from both Bomber and Coastal Command continued these attacks against various ports, assembly points and transiting shipping. The Royal Navy quickly followed suit and conducted a number of sweeps and nocturnal bombardments against selected enemy-held ports. This combined offensive exacted a modest, but growing toll against the would-be German invasion fleet. Likewise, these attacks caused considerable local damage to German points of embarkation and supply stocks. Finally, this aggressive defence effectively demonstrated just some of the potential dangers likely to befall the Germans if they attempted their invasion.

Of course, the degree to which these dangers might manifest themselves depended upon the Luftwaffe's ability to attain its air supremacy objectives. To this end, on 15 September the Luftwaffe took advantage of good flying weather and launched two massive attacks against London. The purpose of these attacks was to deliver, or at least advance, a final deathblow against what the Germans thought was a diminished Fighter Command. However, instead of encountering a spent British force, the attacking German formations found themselves continuously and heavily engaged by British fighters. The subsequent air battle cost the Luftwaffe 60 aircraft against 26 lost to Fighter Command. This result, along with the continuing anti-invasion activities of Bomber and Coastal Commands, made it undeniably clear that the Luftwaffe had failed in its effort to gain ascendancy over the RAF. Hitler now accepted the fact that he had run out of time. On 17 September Hitler postponed Operation *Seelöwe* indefinitely and ordered the invasion fleet to disperse. Although air attacks would continue against Britain on a diminished scale well into the next year, the invasion threat was over.

From the British point of view, the Battle of Britain ended on 31 October 1940. During the 114-day period that constituted the battle (from 10 July) the Luftwaffe lost 1,733 aircraft compared to 915 for Fighter Command. Adding to the British number were 118 and 130 aircraft from Bomber and Coastal Commands respectively that were lost from July through October in operations directly connected to the battle.[25] By comparison, aircraft from these two commands sank, through bombing or direct attacks, the torpedo boat *T3*, three merchant ships worth 8,007 tons, three minor auxiliary warships, five tugs, 106 barges, and 17 other minor craft from 7 September through 15 October.[26] During the same period British aircraft damaged a further two torpedo boats, 13 merchant ships worth 44,503 tons, five minor warships and 129 barges and other minor vessels. Finally, British warships added two tugs, three barges and two fishing vessels sunk and two auxiliary warships, one tug and one barge damaged during anti-invasion sweeps and bombardments.[27]

Of course, the true significance of the battle went far beyond the materiel losses sustained by both sides. For Britain, the battle had been a struggle for national survival. In prevailing over the Luftwaffe, the British had managed to do something that seven other European nations had failed to do – maintain their independence in the face of German aggression. Although the British still faced an exceedingly long and hard struggle against heavy odds, they could take solace in the fact that they were still in the fight. For the Germans, the battle represented the first significant check to their strategic ambitions. Although they remained masters over half of Europe, Germany's failure to subdue Britain would have monumental consequences as the war progressed. The Battle of Britain constituted the first major turning point of the war. It was also the first major conflict to be fought almost exclusively in the air. As such, the RAF deserves overwhelming credit for the victory. Nevertheless, it is also fair to distinguish the critical role played by the Royal Navy in securing Britain's survival. Indeed, it was the Royal Navy's superiority over the Kriegsmarine that posed the true deterrent to the German invasion. Had the German naval position

Notwithstanding the exemplary performance of the RAF during the Battle of Britain, it was British naval power and a demonstrated willingness to use this power that was the primary deterrent to a German invasion. Pictured here (prewar) is the battlecruiser *Hood*, which led the British assault against the French fleet at Mers-el-Kebir. (Allan C. Green and Adam Cuerden, public domain)

been stronger in relation to that of the British, the need for air supremacy would have been greatly reduced if not altogether eliminated.

Nor was the Royal Navy inactive during this period. Even as most observers remained focused on the invasion threat and related aerial combat over Britain, the maritime war continued at an unabated pace. The primary focus of this conflict remained the never-ending struggle to secure vital maritime lines of communication and seaborne commerce in the face of German opposition. This arduous task was made more difficult by the recent loss of Britain's European trading partners. Prior to the war, roughly a third of British imports came from European sources. Critical examples of this included timber products, iron ore and various foodstuffs. Now with Germany in control over much of Europe, access to these easily attainable commodities substantially vanished, and the British had to turn to more distant sources, most notably the Americas, to make up the difference. As such, almost everything imported into Britain now had to travel across the Atlantic Ocean either from the west or south, adding considerable time, cost and danger to the process. Given Britain's dependency upon seaborne trade for its social and economic survival, the successful execution of this ongoing commerce was indispensable and ultimately every bit as important as the need to deter and repel invasion.

Sadly, in carrying out this nation-sustaining task, the British had less reason for satisfaction compared to their recent success over the Luftwaffe. Although the British were able to maintain an acceptable level of seaborne imports (35,503,000 tons from June 1940 through February 1941[28]), they only accomplished this in the face of increasingly effective opposition and substantially higher shipping losses. In terms of the former, the British found their maritime traffic assaulted by a variety of means – both familiar and unfamiliar. This process was exacerbated on 17 August when Hitler declared a total blockade of Britain thus giving his forces greater freedom to attack vessels in the adjacent waters without warning. In terms of the latter, total British, Allied and neutral merchant shipping losses sustained during the nine-month period ending in February 1941 as a result of hostile actions in all theatres other than the Mediterranean amounted to 883 vessels worth 3,650,202 tons.[29] Of these, 592 were British-flagged merchant ships worth 2,561,800 tons.[30]

By a wide margin, the most effective weapon in Germany's anti-shipping arsenal was the U-boat. Although initially beset by technical problems, heavy losses and mediocre results during the first nine months of the war, Germany's U-boat arm enjoyed a remarkable renaissance during the latter half of 1940. Overcoming limited numbers that only allowed an average of six U-boats to be on patrol at any given time, these deadly vessels exacted a heavy toll against British and affiliated shipping. Indeed, during the second nine-month segment of the war (June 1940–February 1941) U-boats accounted for the destruction of 370 merchant ships worth 1,939,864 tons along with the British destroyer *Whirlwind*, the sloops *Penzance* and *Dundee*, the submarine *Spearfish*, eight armed merchant cruisers and a handful of minor vessels.[31] Against this, the Germans only lost eight U-boats of which at least five were sunk by British means. These latter losses included *U102, U32* and *U31* sunk by British warships, *U26* sunk by a Coastal Command Sunderland in conjunction with the corvette *Gladiolus* and *U51* sunk by the British submarine *Cachalot*. Two additional U-boats, *U57* and *U560*, were heavily damaged, but subsequently raised and put back into service. In comparing the results, even with the two damaged U-boats included, the Germans attained a victory to loss ratio during this period of slightly better than 38 to 1. In terms of tonnage, this amounted to some 210,000 tons of civilian and military shipping sunk for every U-boat casualty.

Two recent developments contributed to this deadly period, which German submariners dubbed the 'happy time'. First, with their recent conquest and occupation of the French Atlantic coast, the Germans possessed a far better base of operations from which to menace British maritime traffic. Beginning with the arrival of *U30* at Lorient on 7 July, the Germans quickly transferred the overwhelming majority of their U-boat replenishment and repair operations to the French Biscay ports. In doing so, they bypassed the choke points established by the British in the North Sea and English Channel and gained better access to the Atlantic Ocean. This move also brought the U-boats some 450 miles closer to their primary patrol areas, reducing transit time and increasing the amount of time U-boats could remain on station. Likewise, the small 250-ton coastal U-boats were now capable of operating within the eastern fringes of Britain's incoming ocean routes. Finally, dockyards in the Biscay area proved to be more efficient than their German counterparts, improving turnaround times and increasing the number of U-boats on operational sorties. This was demonstrated by the fact that in the first ten months of the war the proportion of U-boats on offensive sorties compared to the total number of operational U-boats was 1 to 2.35. In the year following Germany's occupation of the Biscay ports, July 1940 to July 1941, this ratio improved to 1 to 1.85.[32]

The second major development benefitting the Germans was the concurrent lack of British escort vessels available for convoy defence. This shortage was exacerbated by recent heavy losses sustained off Norway and Northwest Europe and the need to keep sizable forces in Britain to counter the expected German invasion. As a result, on 1 July 1940 the British could only muster nine anti-submarine escorts to support 16 separate convoys that were traversing the North Atlantic at the time.[33] While this was a one-off and perhaps extreme example, it still reflected the overall shortage of escort vessels plaguing the Royal Navy. In practical terms, this meant that in July the British were only capable of generally providing a single anti-submarine escort for their all-important North Atlantic convoys as far west as longitude 17°. In October, the easing of invasion fears and the establishment of new fuelling facilities allowed the British to increase this coverage to an average of two vessels out to 19° west, but this was still woefully inadequate to their needs. Meanwhile, Coastal Command's aerial coverage during this period only extended out to a longitude of 10° west.[34] Similar limited protection existed for convoys departing or returning to Canadian waters. In the vast area outside of these covered zones, a single ocean escort, often an armed merchant cruiser, was usually the only defence available for most convoys. Unfortunately, these vessels were invariably ill suited for anti-submarine operations, which was precarious since U-boats originating from the Biscay ports were now capable of operating out to 25° west, and this reach would quickly expand westward from there.[35]

The Germans enhanced these advantages by significantly expanding the use of two previously established tactical innovations. The first of these was the use of wolf pack tactics against the British convoy system. Under this practice, German U-boats ceased to function as individual hunters, but instead operated under centralised command to carry out joint, coordinated attacks against targeted convoys. In doing so, the Germans increased their ability to overcome British defences and engage the target-rich convoys with the maximum number of available U-boats. The Germans complemented this practice with the prevalent use of night surface attacks. By operating on the surface at night, the Germans accomplished three things. First, they rendered the British Asdic submarine underwater sound detection equipment all but useless. Second, since surfaced submarines were extremely difficult to visually detect at night given their low silhouettes, the German U-boats were able to stalk their victims with general impunity from British countermeasures. Finally, German U-boats enjoyed better speed and handling when on the surface.

When combined together, these tactical innovations quickly garnered results against the British convoy system. Although the majority of U-boat victims continued to be independently sailed or undefended merchant ships, an increased number of convoyed vessels also found themselves included in this tally. Of the 456 Allied merchant ships sunk by submarines during 1940, no fewer than 102 came to their demise while operating under convoy protection.[36] The vast majority of these occurred during the latter half of the year. This was particularly true in October when U-boats operating in wolf packs sank 38 ships from three different convoys in just three days (18–20 October). Thankfully for the British, these startling results proved to be an anomaly. Hindered by limited numbers and the onset of winter, the Germans were unable to sustain this same level of destruction into the succeeding months. Nevertheless, the advent of these tactics represented a long-term threat that jeopardised the very cornerstone of British trade defence.

Nor were the Germans alone in their anti-shipping efforts. In August 1940 Italian submarines also began operating in the Atlantic. Initially, these Italian boats conducted patrols between the Azores and Spain, but in subsequent weeks these patrols quickly ventured further north. By the end of November no fewer than 26 Italian submarines were present in the Atlantic. Operating under German control from the occupied French port of Bordeaux, this force constituted a larger number of boats than the Germans themselves could muster. Fortunately for the British, these Italian submarines and crews lacked the same level of technical capability and competence as their German counterparts. As such, their record of achievement was significantly less. From August 1940 through February 1941 Italian submarines operating in the Atlantic sank 26 Allied and neutral merchant ships worth 110,921 tons along with two minor vessels.[37] While not insignificant, these results represented a mere fraction of the sinkings accomplished by the less numerous German U-boats during the same period. By comparison, a total of four Italians submarines were lost in Atlantic waters during this time. Of these, British surface escorts sank *Faa di Bruno*, *Marcello* and *Nani* while the British submarine *Thunderbolt* accounted for *Tarantini*.

Of course, the British had to contend with more than just submarines. A variety of German surface raiders also menaced their maritime commerce. The first of these were armed merchant cruisers – fast merchant ships converted to naval use and armed with modern naval guns, torpedo tubes and reconnaissance floatplanes. By regularly changing their appearance through varied paint schemes and false upper works, armed merchant cruisers used deception to hunt unsuspecting merchant ships away from the normal convoy routes. These covert hunters used mid-ocean replenishment from pre-positioned supply ships to conduct extended patrols into the South Atlantic, Indian and Pacific Oceans. On 31 March 1940 the first armed merchant cruiser, *Atlantis*, departed Germany to begin its foray against British shipping. During the remainder of the year, six others – *Orion*, *Widder*, *Thor*, *Pinguin*, *Komet* and *Kormoran* – joined this vessel. Together, these raiders sank a total of 75 Allied and neutral merchant ships worth 452,159 tons through February 1941.[38] They accomplished this at no loss to themselves despite the costly diversion of various British warships to counter their activities.

The German supplemented these actions with the use of conventional surface raiders. From October 1940 through March 1941 the battlecruisers *Scharnhorst* and *Gneisenau*, the pocket battleship *Admiral Scheer* and the heavy cruiser *Admiral Hipper* conducted a series of offensive sorties into the Atlantic during which they sank a combined total of 51 merchant ships worth 257,381 tons.[39] Once again, the Royal Navy was ineffective in its efforts to interdict these elusive raiders despite a large drainage of assets earmarked to do so. Still, the navy did enjoy success of sorts in the form of a heroic sacrifice. On 5 November *Admiral Scheer* encountered convoy HX.84 with 37 merchant ships en route to Britain from Halifax. Captain E. S. F. Fegen in the convoy's sole escort, the armed merchant cruiser *Jervis Bay*, ordered the convoy to scatter under the cover of smoke while he moved forward to confront the immensely superior pocket battleship. In an outcome reminiscent of *Rawalpindi*'s loss the year before, *Admiral Scheer* quickly overwhelmed the hopelessly outgunned *Jervis Bay* and sent it to the bottom along with 191 crewmen including the indomitable Captain Fegen. Nevertheless, *Jervis Bay*'s brave sacrifice gave the bulk of the convoy time to escape, and *Admiral Scheer* was only able to sink five more merchant ships. This example of dutiful selflessness later earned Fegen a posthumous Victoria Cross.

The third component of Germany's anti-shipping surface assault was the use of E-boats against British coastal traffic. These vessels, designated as S-boats (short for *Schnellboot*) by the Germans but referred to as E-boats by the British, were highly capable, torpedo-armed, fast attack craft. Typically displacing around 100 tons, these stealthy boats were well suited for coastal interdiction operations given their two 21-inch torpedo tubes, 700-mile range and speeds in excess of 35 knots. With the capture and occupation of French ports, these boats were now ideally positioned to directly threaten Britain's coastal shipping routes. Operating almost exclusively at night, E-boat flotillas conducted regular sorties into the North Sea and English Channel to search for targets and carry out mining operations. In terms of conventional attacks, E-boats enjoyed a fair degree of success, sinking 24 merchant vessels worth 50,119 tons and the British escort destroyer *Exmoor* during the nine-month period ending in February 1941.[40] Against this, British mines and escorts claimed the destruction of four E-boats with a fifth heavily damaged.

The use of mines and aircraft rounded out the Axis' anti-shipping efforts. Together, these means sank 140 and 164 merchant ships worth 308,631 and 542,979 tons respectively during the nine-month period in question.[41] Meanwhile, excluding losses already mentioned, mines and air attacks accounted for the destruction of four destroyers, one escort destroyer, three submarines, one minesweeper and an auxiliary anti-aircraft vessel from June through February. While most of these losses were the result of established German weapons, a significant number succumbed to a new menace confronting the British. This new threat was the Focke-Wulf Fw 200 Kondor long-range reconnaissance bomber. Operating from bases in Bordeaux and Stavanger, these aircraft routinely ventured far to the west of Ireland in search of British convoys and independent ships. Although primarily tasked to provide reconnaissance for the U-boats, Kondors quickly established themselves as effective ship-killers in their own right and accounted for roughly two-thirds of the Luftwaffe's anti-shipping successes during this period. An overriding factor contributing to this success was the fact that Kondors could operate well beyond the range of British shore-based fighters thus rendering many British merchant ships all but defenceless in the face of their attacks. Sadly, this level of near defencelessness was an all too common experience for many British and Allied merchant ships braving the various threats arrayed against them.

Yet, as bad as it was, the situation could have been far worse. Given the inadequacy of British resources at the time, the British were fortunate not to have suffered even greater losses. This casualty mitigation was primarily due to the limited number of German naval combatants actually available for operations, the vastness of the contested oceans and the continued reliability problems associated with German torpedoes. This former point was particularly true regarding Germany's U-boat force. Even at this stage in the war, U-boat replacements had failed to keep up with losses. This problem was exacerbated by the long fitting out and training times required for new U-boats and crews. Accordingly, operational U-boat strength generally declined during the second

Although limited in its capabilities, the Flower-class corvette was inexpensive and easy to produce thus making it a regular fixture in British convoy defences for most of the war. Pictured here is the corvette HMS *Penstemon*. (Parnall, C. H. (Lt), Royal Navy official photographer, public domain)

nine-month period of the war culminating in an all-time low of just 21 operational boats in February 1941. When combined with the vastness of the waters involved, the German simply did not have enough U-boats or other maritime assets to do more than menace a minor percentage of the merchant ships traversing the world's oceans in support of the British war effort. This was even true in the relatively close waters of the North Atlantic where only 127 out of 17,882 merchant ships travelling in convoys to and from the United Kingdom and 68 out of 24,906 merchant ships travelling in British coastal convoys were actually lost due to hostile action in 1940.[42]

The British could also take solace in the fact that their own defensive position was progressively improving. This was particularly true regarding the increasing number of escort vessels becoming available. Three factors contributed to this increase. First, many of the destroyers undergoing repairs from damage sustained off France and the Low Countries were now coming back into service. Second, a growing number of destroyers, escort destroyers, corvettes and anti-submarine trawlers from the pre-war and emergency wartime supplemental building programmes were now completing construction and joining the fleet. Finally, in September 1940 Britain concluded an agreement with the United States in which the latter transferred 50 surplus destroyers and 10 coast guard cutters to the Royal Navy and associated Allied navies in exchange for basing rights in eight British possessions in the Caribbean and Western Atlantic. These Town-class destroyers (as the British referred to them) required considerable modernisation and maintenance before they were ready to assume operational status. Nevertheless, by the end of 1940 no fewer than ten of these transferred destroyers were in active service in the Royal Navy with the vast majority of the remainder becoming operational in the following year.[43]

In addition to these increasing numbers, the British also enjoyed other defensive improvements that promised to yield positive results. Of these, the most noteworthy was the organisation of various warships into collective units known as escort groups. By establishing these groups, the British transformed their normal escort scheme from random collections of warships into dedicated units that routinely trained and fought together as teams. The British also improved their tactical proficiency by establishing a number of schools charged with the development and training of anti-submarine tactics and methods. Likewise, the period saw the first introduction of rudimentary Sea Search and Air to Surface Vessel (ASV) radar systems on some British escorts and patrol aircraft. Although limited in range and prone to malfunctions and clutter interference, these early radar systems had the potential to ultimately eliminate one of the U-boats' key tactical advantages, the ability to stealthily operate on the surface at night or under conditions of poor visibility. Finally, on 7 February 1941 the British established a fully integrated headquarters for the navy's Western Approaches Command and Coastal Command's No. 15 Group in Derby House, Liverpool. Led by Admiral Percy Noble, this headquarters quickly honed Britain's collective anti-submarine effort and assumed a predominant role in what became known as the battle of the Atlantic.

So in the opening months of 1941 British authorities had reason to feel a combination of both relief and apprehension. This relief stemmed from the fact that the nation had survived an invasion threat and continued to prevail over German ambitions. Yet, despite this success, Britain was still very much on the defensive. On almost a nightly basis Luftwaffe bombers rained down death and destruction upon British cities. Meanwhile at sea, the British continued to fight an ongoing struggle to secure their vital lines of maritime communication against a growing tally of losses. The British lacked the resources to decisively take the war to the enemy thus putting them in the unenviable position of having to fight for their own survival without any immediate prospect of being capable of defeating Germany. This bleak situation surely warranted concern. Nevertheless, on at least a limited basis, the British had some reasons for hope. This was certainly true regarding the materiel, organisational and training improvements underway within Britain's maritime defence forces. Only time would tell if these enhancements would have a positive impact upon the all-important struggle in the Atlantic. In the meantime, the nation's survival hung in the balance.

CHAPTER 4

Respite in the Atlantic

In his memoirs of World War II, Winston Churchill wrote, 'The only thing that ever really frightened me during the war was the U-boat peril.'[1] This sentiment was never truer than in the latter half of 1940 and opening months of 1941. It was during this period, which the Germans referred to as the 'happy time', that a relative handful of U-boats exacted a heavy toll upon British and affiliated shipping for no equivalent loss to themselves. This was the era of the U-boat ace; a time when celebrated U-boat skippers were able to amass large tallies of ships and tonnage sunk. The highest scoring ace of them all was Lieutenant-Commander Otto Kretschmer who accounted for a combined total of 44 merchant ships worth 266,629 tons and one destroyer sunk. A number of lesser aces scored totals in excess of 100,000 tons. While skill and daring played a part in most of these successes, the U-boat aces also greatly benefitted from the inadequate defences arrayed against them. Often, U-boats were able to operate with near impunity from British countermeasures. This fact was clearly demonstrated by the small number of U-boats sunk during the period in question with no U-boats lost during the final three months of this phase, December through February.

In March 1941 the situation regarding German losses abruptly changed. On 7 March four U-boats descended upon convoy OB.293. During the battle that followed, one of these, *U70*, was engaged and sunk by the British corvettes *Arbutus* and *Camellia*. At about the same time *U47*, commanded by the accomplished ace Günther Prien, was lost in the corresponding area without a trace. Speculation as to the cause of this loss range from British escorts and drifting mines to a diving accident. In a subsequent convoy battle ten days later, two more German aces succumbed to British defences. The first of these was Lieutenant-Commander Joachim Schepke in *U100*. Early on the morning of 17 March the destroyer *Vanoc* located *U100* on the surface with its new search radar. Taking immediate action, the British destroyer rammed and sank the surprised U-boat killing most of its crew including the indomitable Schepke. Minutes later, the British destroyer *Walker* located Otto Kretschmer's *U99* with its Asdic and attacked the submerged U-boat with depth charges. This attack quickly forced *U99* to the surface where Kretschmer and most of his crew made good their escape before the stricken U-boat made its final plunge to the bottom. Kretschmer and his surviving crewmen were then picked up and made prisoners by the British. Six days later the German suffered their final loss of the month when the British trawler *Visenda* encountered and sank *U551* in the Iceland-Faeroes gap.

The loss of five U-boats, including three commanded by top-scoring aces, in a period of little more than two and a half weeks signalled an end to the German 'happy time'.[2] This did not mean that the U-boat threat had diminished to any significant degree. To the contrary, this threat remained as deadly as ever given the 41 merchant ships worth 243,020 tons sunk by German and Italian submarines in March.[3] Likewise, the British were only too aware that the German U-boat arm was finally poised to begin a sustained expansion in numbers thus actually increasing the threat. What was different was the fact that the Germans could no longer expect to operate in an environment of near impunity. Already, on 1 April the British had 49 anti-submarine escorts operating in the North Atlantic compared to just nine such vessels present there exactly nine months before.[4] As time passed, this number would only increase along with their technical and operational capabilities. Although fortunes in the Atlantic would continue to ebb and flow as conditions changed, the future indicated an increasingly widespread and difficult fight as both sides intensified their competing efforts. To this end, the period represented a transitional point in which the naval war transformed from a smaller, individualistic and somewhat amateurish struggle to a far larger, well-organised and technically complex battle of attrition. It was this contest, which Churchill officially dubbed the battle of the Atlantic on 6 March, that now became the overriding naval struggle of the war.

Both sides approached this battle with differing strategies and intensity. For the Germans, the battle represented their best opportunity to defeat Britain and protect their newly acquired European empire from western interference. In order to do this, the Germans adopted a long-term tonnage strategy against the British merchant fleet. The main tenet of this strategy was to sink British and affiliated merchant tonnage faster than it could be replaced. In doing so, the Germans sought to emasculate British shipping to the point where it was no longer capable of fulfilling the nation's import needs. Once this occurred, Britain would be starved into submission. The U-boat arm, under the command of Admiral Karl Dönitz, was the key protagonist in this campaign. In 1940 Dönitz and his staff calculated that it would take an average loss of 700,000 tons of shipping per month to attain the attrition rate necessary to wear down the British merchant fleet. Concurrent British estimates put this number at 600,000 tons per month.[5]

Dönitz further surmised that he required a force of 300 U-boats to achieve this level of attrition. Fortunately for the British, he only possessed a third of this number in the spring of 1941. Of these, only a fraction were operational with most of the rest undergoing maintenance, working up or carrying out training duties. Although the U-boat force was growing, it would take over a year to attain the numbers advocated by Dönitz. This stemmed from the fact that, despite assurances from Hitler to the contrary, U-boat production did not receive top priority. Instead, U-boat production shared manufacturing priority with a number of different weapon systems for the army and Luftwaffe. This was exacerbated by the fact that the Kriegsmarine generally maintained a subordinate position in relationship to the other services in the German hierarchy. This was certainly true with Hitler, who candidly acknowledged his own limited focus on naval affairs. Also, by this stage in the war, Hitler had largely lost interest in Britain and was instead focused upon new potential conquests in the East. As such, Admirals Raeder and Dönitz were largely on their own as they prosecuted the naval war against Britain.

By comparison, the British considered the battle of the Atlantic to be a top priority warranting direct involvement at the highest levels of the government and military. From the British perspective, the battle's overriding objective was to consistently maintain acceptable levels of imports to ensure the nation's survival and war-making ability. The British had to ensure the continued preservation of a viable merchant fleet to fulfil these needs. In March 1941 Winston Churchill established the War Cabinet Battle of the Atlantic Committee consisting of top ministers and high-ranking government and military officials. This committee met weekly with Churchill to address all matters related to the battle. During the same month Churchill sent a thirteen-point directive through the Ministry of Defence outlining a comprehensive strategy for securing British maritime trade. This directive made victory in the Atlantic a national priority requiring contributions from a variety of sources including the Royal Navy, merchant marine, RAF and Ministries of Labour, Transportation and Shipping. In keeping with this, the British invested considerable resources to build and maintain large numbers of new destroyers, escort vessels, merchant ships and other items related to the battle.

To this latter point, the British had to concern themselves with a potential shipping deficit. Despite the fact that total Allied and neutral merchant losses during the first 19 months of the war had averaged just 315,801 tons per month (of which 198,411 tons were British), the cumulative toll by the end of March 1941 amounted to 1,597 merchant ships worth 6,000,217 tons (of which 932 worth 3,769,800 tons were British).[6] Accidents, marine causes and normal wastage brought Britain's total loss for the period to some 4,109,000 tons. New construction during the same interval had only added 1,197,000 tons of additional merchant shipping to the British flag. The purchase, requisition and seizure of foreign vessels, including large numbers of German, Italian and French prizes, had added a further 2,138,000 tons for British use. As such, by the beginning of April the British merchant marine was operating under a deficit of some 774,000 tons.[7] Making matters worse, another million tons of damaged shipping lay immobilised in shipyards undergoing or waiting for repairs.

Fortunately for the British, these shortfalls were more than compensated for by the availability and use of foreign flagged merchant ships. Most of these foreign vessels came from conquered European nations. In particular, Norway, the Netherlands and Greece all possessed sizable merchant fleets that had largely escaped German seizure when their countries were overrun. Now many of these same vessels became available for British use on a time-charter basis. Belgian, Yugoslav, Danish and Polish merchant ships also contributed to this pool, as did vessels from various neutral nations. Yet despite these contributions, the British still had to concern themselves with the long-term viability of their overall shipping situation. With few exceptions, this infusion of foreign vessels, especially those from conquered nations, was a one-time augmentation that could not regenerate itself once the force was depleted. Without a reduction in losses and/or an increase in new shipping construction, the British faced the ultimate prospect of a dwindling merchant marine.

In the meantime, the strain on British shipping continued. In April a total of 90 British and affiliated merchant ships worth 395,383 tons were lost due to hostile action in all areas excluding the Mediterranean. In May and June this number increased to 120 and 106 ships worth 440,207 and 422,880 tons respectively. Of this total, German and Italian submarines sank 162 merchant ships worth 885,010 tons while aircraft, mines and surface raiders accounted for the vast majority of the rest.[8] Against this, British escort vessels during the period sank seven U-boats (*U76*, *U65*, *U110*, *U147*, *U138*, *U556*, and *U651*) and the Italian submarine *Glauco*. When combined together, total worldwide British, Allied and neutral merchant losses during the first six months of 1941 amounted to 760 vessels worth 2,884,307 tons.[9] When focusing on the increased rate of destruction experienced from March through May, the Joint Planning Staff in London projected a potential annual loss in shipping approaching 7,000,000 tons by year's end. They further estimated a potential shortfall in imports amounting to nearly 7,000,000 tons of raw materials and semi-manufactured goods, 2,000,000 tons of food and 318,000 tons of oil.[10]

If this were not bad enough, the British had to contend with a new and menacing threat. For months the Admiralty had awaited the pending emergence of the new German battleship *Bismarck* with great apprehension. In the third week in May the British received intelligence from diplomatic and SIGINT (Signal Intelligence) sources indicating that *Bismarck* and a second warship were proceeding out of the Baltic for a potential sortie into the North Atlantic. This fear was confirmed on the 21st when a photo-reconnaissance Spitfire photographed the two ships off Bergen. Indeed, the Germans were attempting a breakout into the Atlantic under the designation Operation *Rheinübung* (Rhine Exercise). This operation was commanded by Admiral Günther Lütjens and consisted of the battleship *Bismarck* and the new heavy cruiser *Prinz Eugen*. Initially Admiral Lütjens had advocated a concurrent breakout by the battlecruisers *Scharnhorst* and *Gneisenau* from Brest, but an extensive engine overhaul on the former and recent British torpedo damage on the latter had rendered both ships unavailable.[11] Despite these developments, Lütjens still possessed a formidable strike force capable of wreaking havoc against Britain's vulnerable convoy routes. This was particularly true of *Bismarck*, which, other than *Hood*, was the largest operational capital ship in the world.

In response to this threat, the new Home Fleet commander, Admiral John Tovey, gathered and positioned resources to interdict the expected German sortie. He immediately strengthened cruiser surveillance into the Atlantic's northern passages. He also dispatched Vice-Admiral L. E. Holland with the battlecruiser *Hood*, the newly completed battleship *Prince of Wales* and six destroyers from Scapa Flow to support these patrolling cruisers. Meanwhile, Tovey placed the battleship *King George V*, five cruisers and half a dozen destroyers on short notice for sea. He also acquired the use of the battlecruiser *Repulse* and the newly completed aircraft carrier *Victorious*, which were released from convoy escort duty. This seemed like an overwhelming force to engage a single capital ship and cruiser, but the British had a large volume of ocean to cover and many of their ships were not in fit fighting condition. Although as large and similarly armed, *Hood* was 21 years old and lacked *Bismarck*'s armour protection. *Repulse* was even older, less heavily armed and equally lacking in protection. Meanwhile, *Prince of Wales* was so new that it still had Vickers technicians onboard to make final adjustments to its 14-inch gun turrets when it departed Scapa Flow. A similar situation existed with the aircraft carrier *Victorious*, which only possessed a partial air group consisting of nine Swordfish and six Fulmar fighters.[12]

On 22 May a Maryland reconnaissance aircraft flew through stormy and overcast weather to determine that Bergen was empty. Taking this as a clear sign that the German breakout attempt was underway, Tovey sortied the remainder of his fleet into Icelandic waters to reinforce those ships already deployed. Tovey surmised that *Bismarck*'s most likely course of action was to proceed into the North Atlantic through the Denmark Strait or the Iceland-Faeroes gap. Accordingly, he had the cruisers *Suffolk* and *Norfolk* patrolling the former while the cruisers *Arethusa*, *Manchester* and *Birmingham* covered the latter. Behind these screens, Tovey positioned Vice-Admiral Holland's squadron to cover the Denmark Strait north of 62° while he and the main body of the Home Fleet covered the passage south of this line. At 1922 hours on 23 May this disposition paid off when the cruiser *Suffolk* sighted the German squadron proceeding on a southwesterly course at the northern entrance of the Denmark Strait. An hour later *Norfolk* also made contact. For the remainder of the night these two cruisers maintained sporadic surveillance and reported the progress of *Bismarck* and *Prinz Eugen* as they proceeded towards the guns of Admiral Holland's awaiting capital ships.

At 0537 hours on the 24th the opposing forces sighted each other at a range of 17 miles. At 0552 hours *Hood* opened fire with *Prince of Wales* following suit one minute later. The German ships immediately returned fire concentrating their efforts against *Hood*. The German shooting was excellent with hits scored on their second and third salvos. At 0600 hours Holland turned his ships to port in order to bring their full broadsides to bear. While executing this turn, a plunging salvo from *Bismarck* struck *Hood* penetrating the ship's thin deck armour and detonating one or more magazines. The resulting catastrophic explosion ripped the great battlecruiser apart killing all but three of its 1,419-man crew. The German ships then turned their fire against *Prince of Wales*, which quickly sustained four 15-inch and three 8-inch hits. One of these struck the bridge killing or wounding everyone there except the captain, J. C. Leach. Realizing that the odds had now turned dangerously against him, Leach ordered *Prince of Wales* to disengage under the cover of smoke.

Lütjens did not pursue the damaged British battleship as it made good its withdrawal. Rather, he was content to celebrate his victory over the vaunted *Hood* while preserving his own strength. This latter consideration was spurred by standing orders not to unduly endanger *Bismarck* and the fact that the just completed battle had not been an entirely one-sided affair. During the fighting *Prince of Wales* had scored three hits on *Bismarck*. One of these had passed through *Bismarck*'s forward hull causing heavy flooding and damage to two fuel tanks and pumping equipment thus rendering 1,000 tons of fuel oil unusable. This also caused *Bismarck* to trail a large oil slick. A second hit had disabled a boiler room thus reducing *Bismarck*'s speed to 28 knots, while the third hit had been inconsequential. Concerned about this damage and his diminished fuel status, Lütjens decided to abandon his sortie into the Atlantic and altered course for St Nazaire to enact repairs. As he did so, *Suffolk*, *Norfolk* and *Prince of Wales* continued to shadow his movements. Meanwhile, the Admiralty feverishly mobilised and diverted resources to join the pursuit. These resources included Force H from Gibraltar, the battleships *Rodney* and *Ramillies* from convoy escort duty and the battleship *Revenge* from Halifax. Unfortunately, these forces were spread over a wide area, and it would take time to get them into a favourable position to engage *Bismarck*.

Aware of this latter fact and concerned about his own fuel usage, Tovey, who was some 330 miles southeast of *Bismarck*'s location at the time of *Hood*'s demise, was becoming increasingly apprehensive regarding his prospects of catching the elusive German battleship. At 1440 hours he ordered *Victorious* to proceed ahead with four cruisers to a position where it could launch an air strike in an attempt to reduce *Bismarck*'s speed. At 2210 hours *Victorious* launched this air strike consisting of nine Swordfish and six Fulmars. Flying through atrocious weather, these aircraft succeeded in locating *Bismarck* some two hours later and scored a single torpedo hit against it. Unfortunately, this hit caused little damage and had no appreciable impact on *Bismarck*'s speed. Three hours later the situation significantly worsened when *Bismarck*, which had already detached *Prinz Eugen* to operate independently, executed an evasive manoeuvre and successfully broke contact with the shadowing British cruisers. For the next 31 hours the British frantically searched for the fugitive battleship, but all they encountered for their efforts were friendly ships and empty ocean. Making matters worse, British tracking stations were able to fix the location of *Bismarck*'s radio transmissions, but a plotting error actually sent Tovey searching in the wrong direction. By the time this error was realised and corrected, Tovey was 150 miles astern of *Bismarck* and badly out of position to catch the fleeing battleship.

At 1030 hours on the 26th a Coastal Command Catalina reconnaissance aircraft finally located *Bismarck* some 690 miles west of Brest. Tovey immediately realised that his only chance to catch the fleeing battleship now rested in his ability to impede its progress or reduce its speed. The only viable means to do this was through Admiral Somerville's Force H proceeding northward from Gibraltar. The main fighting strength of Force H consisted of the battlecruiser *Renown*, the aircraft carrier *Ark Royal* and the cruiser *Sheffield*. Shortly after learning of *Bismarck*'s location, Somerville ordered *Sheffield* to race forward and establish radar contact with the larger warship. At 1450 hours *Ark Royal*, which also now had reconnaissance aircraft in contact with *Bismarck*, launched a strike of 14 Swordfish torpedo-bombers to attack the formidable giant. Near-tragically, British authorities failed to brief the aircrews on *Sheffield*'s forward deployment, and when the aircraft encountered the light cruiser on ASV radar, they assumed it was *Bismarck* and attacked. Thankfully, through a combination of effective manoeuvring and faulty magnetic pistols on the torpedoes, *Sheffield* was able to escape damage. Nevertheless, precious time had been lost, and with each passing minute, the prospect of stopping *Bismarck* diminished.

At 1910 hours *Ark Royal* launched a second strike of 15 Swordfish. Upon these aircraft laid the hopes of the entire British operation as Tovey had already signalled Somerville stating that unless *Bismarck*'s speed was reduced, fuel constraints would force him to break off the pursuit by midnight. For the third time in as many days a strike of Swordfish torpedo-bombers flew into appalling weather to seek out and attack *Bismarck*. Unlike their previous outing, these aircraft were now armed with contact detonators on their torpedoes. Using *Sheffield* as a navigational aid, the strike, led by Lieutenant-Commander T. P. Coode, found and attacked *Bismarck*. Despite intense anti-aircraft fire and poor visibility that hindered a coordinated attack, Coode's Swordfish dropped 13 torpedoes of which two, and possibly three, hit *Bismarck*. The first of these exploded harmlessly against *Bismarck*'s armoured belt, but the second hit its stern causing extensive damage to steering gear and jamming both rudders 12° to port. Subsequent efforts to free the rudders or steer the ship using engines and propellers were unsuccessful. *Bismarck* was now incapable of manoeuvring. The best its crew could do was to maintain a moderate forward momentum into the wind to prevent *Bismarck* from wallowing and yawing in the heavy seas. Unfortunately for them, this movement took *Bismarck* directly into the path of Tovey's oncoming ships. Providence had finally dealt the British the break they needed.

The next morning Tovey arrived on the scene to deliver the coup de grace against *Bismarck*. By this time the composition of his force had significantly changed as many of his original ships had long since departed to refuel while a handful of newcomers had joined his flag or converged upon the area. These latter vessels included a destroyer flotilla, commanded by Captain Philip Vian, which had already engaged *Bismarck* during the night in a series of inconclusive torpedo attacks. Now with the rising sun, Tovey added *King George V* and *Rodney* as well as the cruisers *Norfolk* and *Dorsetshire* to this force. This gave him a main armament advantage of nine 16-inch guns, ten 14-inch guns and 16 8-inch guns compared to eight 15-inch guns for *Bismarck*. The British also benefitted from *Bismarck's* inability to manoeuvre thus making it a far easier target to hit. Yet, notwithstanding its inoperable steering, *Bismarck's* armament and critical systems were largely intact and still capable of fighting back. Also, the critical fuel status in many of his ships pressed Tovey to sink *Bismarck* quickly or lose key portions of his remaining fleet as major units were forced to turn back to refuel.

At 0847 hours Tovey's battleships opened fire on *Bismarck* thus beginning the final act of the seven-day drama. *Bismarck* quickly returned fire, but unlike the exceptional gunnery exhibited three days earlier, failed to score any hits on the British ships. By comparison, the British scored a steady succession of hits on the lumbering giant. One by one, *Bismarck's* main gun turrets fell silent as incoming shells savaged its upper decks. As *Bismarck's* return fire slackened, the British battleships and cruisers pressed forward to engage the stricken German warship at an ever-diminishing range until their firing became point-blank. Within minutes the once proud *Bismarck* was reduced to a blazing, twisted wreck. At 1020 hours Tovey ordered *Dorsetshire* to finish *Bismarck* off with torpedoes. The British cruiser quickly complied sending two torpedoes into *Bismarck's* starboard side and one into its port. At about the same time the Germans opened seacocks and set scuttling charges. At 1036 hours *Bismarck* rolled over and began its final plunge to the deep. The pride of the Kriegsmarine was gone, and with it, all but 115 men out of a crew of 2,200 perished.[13]

Although primarily used for shore bombardment duties, *Rodney's* massive 16-inch guns were instrumental in helping destroy the German battleship *Bismarck* in May 1941. (Public domain)

There were several postscripts to this battle. On 28 May Luftwaffe bombers sank the British destroyer *Mashona* some 100 miles west of Ireland as the vessel was returning from recent operations against *Bismarck*. Four days later *Prinz Eugen* arrived at Brest after failing to accomplish anything during its independent sortie in the Atlantic. For the rest of the year *Prinz Eugen* remained immobilised in the Biscay ports along with *Scharnhorst* and *Gneisenau*. During this time Bomber Command aircraft carried out a series of raids against these ships, and all three suffered varying degrees of debilitating damage. Meanwhile, on 12 June a RAF reconnaissance aircraft sighted the pocket battleship *Lützow* off Lindesnes as the latter was attempting a breakout into the North Atlantic. Shortly before midnight 14 Coastal Command Beaufort torpedo-bombers departed Scotland to seek out and attack *Lützow*. Nocturnal darkness frustrated most of their efforts, but a single aircraft, commanded by Flight Sergeant Ray Loveitt, did locate and torpedo the transiting warship. The resulting damage forced *Lützow* to abandon its sortie and return to Kiel for six months of repairs.

Perhaps of even greater consequence, in May, June and July British forces carried out a series of successful interdiction operations that dealt a serious blow to Germany's maritime logistical network. Prior to the battle the Germans had pre-positioned several tankers, supply ships and support vessels in the Atlantic to support Operation *Rheinübung* and other offensive activities. During this time the Germans also had various blockade-runners attempting to transit through the area. Using SIGINT information (which will be described in greater detail later), the British systematically located and eliminated many of these ships. From 28 May through 25 July British forces captured, sank or forced the scuttling of 13 German merchant ships, of which six were tankers, worth a combined total of 93,320 tons.[14] Of these, Swordfish aircraft from *Eagle* sank the 9,179-ton blockade-runner *Elba* while the rest were lost to British warships. During the same period the British also sank two German weather reporting trawlers and seized four Vichy French blockade-runners worth 27,312 tons.[15] By inflicting these losses, the British markedly reduced Germany's ability to logistically support further surface raider or long-range U-boat operations.

The destruction of *Bismarck* had immediate and long-term results far exceeding the loss of a single capital ship. When coupled with the damage and wastage inflicted upon other German warships and support vessels, *Bismarck*'s demise effectively signalled the end of Germany's North Atlantic surface raider campaign. Hitler had never had much interest in naval affairs or faith in the usefulness of German capital ships. *Bismarck*'s loss only reinforced this scepticism. Hitler viewed this destruction as an affront to German morale and prestige. As such, he resolved to never again allow a major German warship to expose itself to the potential risks of a North Atlantic sortie. Of course, this long-term development was unknown to the British at the time. For them, the destruction of *Bismarck* represented an essential victory during a time when victories were hard to come by. This was particularly true after the loss of *Hood*, when *Bismarck*'s destruction became a national priority. By accomplishing this, the British prevented the potential carnage that *Bismarck* might have inflicted upon their shipping and restored a degree of morale and confidence to the national psyche.

On 22 June Britain received more good news of far greater importance when Germany launched a full-scale invasion against the Soviet Union. In doing so, Germany dramatically altered the strategic realities of the war and gave Britain a new and powerful ally in the form of the colossal continental nation. No longer would Britain have to stand alone or bear the brunt of Germany's military effort. It was now time for the Soviet Union to experience the destructive power of the German blitzkrieg. And like so many nations before it, the Soviets quickly found themselves reeling before the massive German onslaught. In the weeks and months that followed, the invading German forces won spectacular victories, seized large tracks of territory, destroyed whole Soviet armies and took prisoners by the hundreds of thousands. Nevertheless, the immense territorial and population size of the Soviet Union gave the Russians staying power far exceeding that of previous German victims, and the campaign eventually became protracted. For the rest of the war, Britain benefitted from the tremendous diversion of resources the Germans were required to expend in this struggle. In the summer of 1941 this included the overwhelming majority of the German army and Luftwaffe as only the Kriegsmarine continued to focus its main war effort against Britain.

To this end, the battle of the Atlantic remained the decisive campaign in the West. As previously stated, recent heavy shipping losses from March through June seemed to foretell a degraded shipping and imports situation for Britain by year's end. Yet, despite these dire predictions, there were a number of developments recently passed or currently in the works that promised to offer the British some needed relief. First and foremost amongst these were significant breakthroughs in the SIGINT area. From the beginning of the war both sides had operated tracking stations to monitor the other's radio traffic. By correlating signal bearings from two or more tracking stations, officials could determine the general locations of ships, submarines or aircraft originating radio messages. While this information had obvious intelligence value, this value increased exponentially with the ability to actually read the encrypted messages. To this end, both sides pursued efforts to break the other's encryption codes. The German Navy's Intelligence Division, known as B-Dienst, provided this service for the Kriegsmarine while the Government Code and Cypher School (GC and CS) at Bletchley Park did the same for the British. During the first 18 months of the war B-Dienst attained considerable success in breaking portions of the various Royal Navy and merchant shipping codes. By comparison, GC and CS achieved similar success against selected German air force and army codes, but generally failed to make meaningful progress in breaking Germany's more complex naval encryptions.

For the British, this was no simple task. Confronting their efforts was the highly capable German Enigma electromechanical cypher machine. The Germans used Enigma as their primary encryption and decryption system for long-range radio communications. Each service used a variety of different keys depending upon the purpose. Eventually, GC and CS identified nearly 200 keys of which as many as 50 were in concurrent use. Of the various keys used by the Kriegsmarine, the most prolific in terms of operational traffic was the Home Waters key. This key utilised an eight-rotor system of which three rotors were in use at any given time. By altering the selection and placement of these rotors and the arrangement of interconnecting plugs, the key was capable of producing millions of different settings. The Germans changed these settings on a daily basis and used the Home Waters key to transmit more than 95 percent of their encrypted naval messages. So formidable was this key that during the first 18 months of the war GC and CS only succeeded in breaking it for a total of 11 days.

In the late winter and spring of 1941 the British orchestrated a series of events that decisively improved this situation. The first of these occurred on 4 March when the British seized the armed German trawler *Krebs* during a raid on Norway's Lofoten Islands. From this capture the British gained rotors and settings that allowed them to read portions of German naval traffic for February and March. Based upon this and further cryptanalytical breakthroughs in April, GC and CS learned that the Germans maintained a force of eight weather reporting trawlers of which at least two were on station at any given time in the mid-Atlantic and north of Iceland. Capitalising on this information, the Admiralty launched two specialised operations to seize Enigma material from these vessels. On 7 May and 28 June British naval units captured the weather reporting trawlers *München* and *Lauenburg* thus acquiring the Enigma settings for June and July. Meanwhile, on 9 May a chance seizure from *U110* yielded further valuable materials. British escorts from convoy OB.318 forced *U110* to the surface with depth charges. An armed boarding party from the destroyer *Bulldog* then promptly captured the German U-boat after the latter's crew had abandoned ship. Although *U110* subsequently sank two days later while under tow, this was only after the British had removed everything of intelligence value including a complete Enigma machine, special settings for 'officer-only' signals, the codebook for short-range U-boat sighting reports, the vessel's signal log and various other charts and documents.

The cumulative value of these seizures was enormous. The most immediate impact was to allow the British to read the bulk of German naval traffic for June and July as well as part of the traffic for May. This provided the British with valuable operational intelligence and important insights into German signal procedures and formats. This technical knowledge coupled with expanded and improved cryptanalytical methods soon allowed GC and CS to break the Home Waters key without the benefit of additional captured codes. From August through the end of the war GC and CS was able to read nearly all Home Waters encrypted messages with a typical delay ranging from a few hours to a few days. In practical terms, this meant that from June onwards the overwhelming majority of signals transmitted to or from U-boats and other German ships operating in the Atlantic were accessible to British decryption. Based upon this, the British were able to develop and maintain a virtually complete picture of all U-boat movements, locations and statuses on a continuous running basis. This invaluable intelligence, which the British referred to as Ultra, allowed Western Approaches Command to route numerous convoys away from U-boat concentrations and/or reinforce threatened convoys with additional escort coverage.

This latter ability was also the result of an immensely improved escort situation. Throughout 1941 new construction, along with transfers from the United States, produced sizable additions to the British escort fleet. This process was assisted by an increased role played by the Royal Canadian Navy and Canadian shipyards. By June 1941 the British could muster a force of 248 destroyers and escort destroyers, 48 sloops and cutters, 99 corvettes and 300 trawlers and anti-submarine yachts. They had another 157 destroyers and escort destroyers, three sloops, 96 corvettes and 47 trawlers under construction.[16] Of course, only a portion of these escorts were actually at sea at any given time, but this number also increased as demonstrated by the 65 and 94 such vessels on duty in the North Atlantic on 1 July and 1 October respectively.[17] The British enhanced their increased numbers by the establishment of new bases around the battle area. The most important of these was on the Danish-controlled island of Iceland. In May 1940 British and Canadian troops had occupied Iceland in response to Germany's conquest of Denmark. Now in April 1941 the British opened an advanced fuelling station at Hvalfjord, north of Reykjavik. By routing their convoys nearer to Iceland and taking advantage of this fuelling station, the British increased the amount of time their escorts could remain on duty thus immediately extending convoy coverage out to 35° west.[18] The Allies also established a major escort base at St. John's, Newfoundland, where by June 1941 they maintained a force of 30 destroyers, nine sloops and 24 corvettes.[19]

With this enlarged escort fleet and improved basing situation, the British were finally able to provide convoys with continuous protection across the Atlantic. They accomplished this through a series of escort zones. Canadian groups from St. John's, which often included British as well as Canadian ships, escorted inbound (eastbound) North Atlantic convoys to a Mid-Ocean Meeting Point at approximately 35° west. Once there, British groups from Iceland met the convoys and escorted them to the Eastern Ocean Meeting Point at about 18° west. Escort groups from Western Approaches Command then took charge of the convoys and covered them for the final portions of their journeys.[20] The first such convoy occurred on 27 May when convoy HX.129 proceeded from Halifax to the British Isles. Over the next two months the British extended this continuous coverage to include outbound

North Atlantic convoys and convoys travelling the Southern Atlantic route to and from Sierra Leone. They accomplished the latter through the use of escort groups operating out of Freetown and Londonderry with a meeting point located in the vicinity of latitude 19° north. This arrangement was made possible by the use of Bathurst, Gambia as an intermediate fuelling station.[21] When combined together, the above-mentioned system provided end-to-end coverage for most overseas commerce coming into and out of the United Kingdom. While much of this coverage was limited or periodically incomplete, it represented a monumental improvement over the escort situation of the year before.

The British could also take note of tangible improvements in Coastal Command. By July 1941 Coastal Command possessed 13 medium and long-range squadrons with a nominal strength of 242 aircraft compared to just five such squadrons with 105 aircraft the year before.[22] These squadrons were generally armed with improved aircraft types including the Lockheed Hudson reconnaissance bomber, the Short Sunderland flying boat, the Vickers Wellington medium bomber and the new American-built Catalina flying boat. June also saw the establishment of Coastal Command's first very long-range squadron armed with the exceptional American-built Consolidated B-24 Liberator four-engine bomber. Whereas Hudsons and Wellingtons could operate some 500 miles from base while Sunderlands and Catalinas could spend two hours patrolling at ranges of 600 to 800 miles, the Liberator, with its maximum fuel load of 2,500 gallons, could spend three hours patrolling over 1,100 miles from home station.[23] When coupled with new bases, the British were able to extend their general air coverage into the Atlantic to a distance of 700 miles from the British Isles, 600 miles from Canada and 400 miles from Iceland.[24]

Table 4.1 Principal British Convoy Routes to and from the United Kingdom in 1941

Type	Code Letters	Route	Notes
Ocean inbound	HX	Halifax to the United Kingdom (fast)	Started 16 Sep 39
Ocean inbound	SC	Halifax to the United Kingdom (slow)	Started 15 Aug 40
Ocean inbound	HG	Gibraltar to the United Kingdom	Started 26 Sep 39
Ocean inbound	SL	Freetown, Sierra Leone to the United Kingdom	Started 14 Sep 39
Ocean inbound	QP	Russia to the United Kingdom	Started 28 Sep 41
Ocean outbound	OB	Liverpool Outwards	Started 7 Sep 39 Replaced by ON convoys in 1941
Ocean outbound	ON	United Kingdom to Halifax (fast)	Started 27 Jul 41
Ocean outbound	ONS	United Kingdom to Halifax (slow)	Started 26 Jul 41
Ocean outbound	OG	United Kingdom to Gibraltar	Started 1 Oct 39
Ocean outbound	OS	United Kingdom to Freetown, Sierra Leone	Started 24 Jul 41
Ocean outbound	PQ	United Kingdom to Russia	Started 29 Sep 41

While Coastal Command still lacked sufficient aircraft to truly saturate these areas, especially given the poor serviceability rates present in many of their squadrons at the time, the situation was clearly improving.

The British also had plans in the works to counter the German Kondor threat. The first of these was the development of Fighter Catapult (FC) ships and Catapult Aircraft Merchantmen (CAM). These were merchant ships fitted with catapults that were capable of launching a single fighter, either a Fulmar or a Hurricane, for immediate convoy defence. This was a single use system since once the fighter was launched, it was impossible to recover. Instead, the pilot would have to fly on to a nearby land-based airfield or bail out/ditch in the vicinity of a British ship for retrieval from the sea. The distinction between FC and CAM ships was that the former were auxiliary naval vessels while the latter were still merchant ships capable of carrying normal cargo. The British eventually acquired four FC and 35 CAM ships with the first coming into service during the late spring and early summer of 1941. Their first combat success came on 3 August when a Hurricane from the FC ship *Maplin* shot down a Kondor reconnaissance bomber some 400 miles off the Iberian coast. In the weeks and months that followed catapult fighters only succeeded in shooting down another four Kondors, but the mere presence of these ships proved to be an important deterrent to Kondor operations.

A solution of a more practical nature was the development of merchant-converted and purpose-built escort carriers. The first of these was the 5,540-ton auxiliary escort carrier *Audacity*, which was a conversion from the captured German merchant ship *Hannover*. Rebuilt with a simple 463-foot flight deck, *Audacity* did not possess a hanger, but was capable of repeated flight operations with a small compliment of aircraft. Obtaining operational status in August 1941, *Audacity* performed convoy defence duties along the dangerous Gibraltar route with a compliment of six American-built Martlet fighters.[25] During the next three months these fighters claimed the destruction of three Kondor reconnaissance bombers thus proving the value of the escort carrier. Yet, this was only the beginning. Already the British had another five escort carriers under conversion in the United Kingdom with six more ordered from the United States under Lend-Lease. These new carriers were larger, had built-in hangers and were capable of operating upwards of 20 aircraft. As such, they could perform both air defence and anti-submarine duties and thus held the promise of not only defeating the Kondor threat, but also closing the 300-mile gap that was still devoid of land-based aerial coverage in the central North Atlantic. The first of these new escort carriers would become operational in March 1942, but it would take several additional months before these promising warships were ready and available for widespread Atlantic use.

The British complimented their naval and aerial strength increases with a number of technical innovations and an important operational change. The first of these was an improved centimetric surface search radar, the Type 271, which could acquire surfaced U-boats at ranges of 4,000 to 5,000 yards and periscopes from submerged U-boats at ranges of 1,100 to 1,500 yards. By July 1941 the British had 25 corvettes equipped with Type 271 radars with a further 25 installed by year's end. During the same period the British also began deployment of ship-borne High Frequency Direction Finders (HF/DF). These devices were capable of determining the presence, bearing and general proximity of nearby U-boats based upon their radio transmissions. The British supplemented these enhanced acquisition systems with the Snowflake pyrotechnic flare, a significant improvement over the then existing star-shell for nocturnal illumination. Other promising weapon systems that were either entering service or under development included improved ASV radar, the Leigh Light airborne-mounted spotlight, air dropped depth charges and the ship-based Hedgehog forward-firing mortar system.

Regarding the operational change, in June the Admiralty raised the minimum speed requirement for independently sailed merchant ships from 13 to 15 knots. In doing so, they significantly reduced the number of ships sailing devoid of convoy protection and enhanced the survivability of those sailing independently. This, in turn, did three things. It improved the security for the transiting merchant ships, increased the dangers confronting the U-boats and made it more difficult for the U-boats to find targets. This latter point was true because in the vastness of the Atlantic Ocean, the detectability of a convoy was only marginally greater than that of an independently sailed ship. Thus, with the vast bulk of ships massed in these transiting convoys, this presented a much smaller area of potential detection than a similar number of ships sailing independently. As a result, the majority of U-boats spent most of their time searching empty ocean. Soon, nearly all Allied shipping traversing the North Atlantic did so under the protection of these escorted convoys. This included 85,775 merchant ships that travelled to and from the United Kingdom in trade convoys as well as 175,608 ships that sailed in British coastal convoys during the duration of the war.[26]

The final factor benefitting the British in their Atlantic struggle was the substantial and ever-increasing assistance provided by the United States. On 11 March 1941 the United States passed the Lend-Lease law authorising the transfer of weapons, munitions, food and equipment to any nation whose fight against the Axis powers aided the defence of the United States. Under this act, the United States provided Britain with billions of dollars' worth of materiel support on an essentially no-charge basis, significantly reducing Britain's financial burden. Included in this support was the eventual construction of dozens of military and commercial ships as well as the repair and refitting of numerous British vessels in American shipyards. In addition to materiel support, the United States also provided varying degrees of direct assistance. In April the United States extended its self-declared security zone from 60° to 26° west. Within this zone, American forces were inclined to report the position of sighted U-boats or other German ships to the British, but did not engage them directly. To help accomplish this, the Americans established naval and air installations in a number of strategic locations including Greenland, Bermuda and Newfoundland. Finally, in July the United States assumed responsibility for the defence of Iceland, thus relieving British forces of this burden.

When combined together, this series of factors had an immediate and profound impact upon British merchant shipping losses. Whereas total British, Allied and neutral shipping losses, due to submarine attacks in April, May and June, had averaged 54 vessels worth 295,003 tons per month, these losses fell to 22 ships worth 94,209 tons and 23 ships worth 80,310 tons in July and August respectively. The primary factor contributing to this reduction was the U-boats' inability to find British convoys or independently sailed ships. This was largely the result of successful Admiralty efforts to route convoys away from U-boat concentrations and the reduced number of independently sailed ships travelling to and from the United Kingdom. For periods of days or even weeks, the U-boats searched in vain as British convoys successfully transited around their patrol lines. The situation partially reversed itself in September and October when submarine-induced losses increased to 53 ships worth 202,820 tons and 32 ships worth 156,554 tons respectively. This jump was largely due to the increased numbers of U-boats on patrol and improved German SIGINT procedures that temporarily reduced Enigma intelligence from GC and CS. Nevertheless, in November submarine-induced losses once again dropped to an 18-month low of just 13 ships worth 62,196 tons.[27] When combined together, these results represented a 55 percent reduction in merchant tonnage losses due to submarine attacks from July through November as compared to the previous five-month period.

Nor was this trend limited to losses incurred from submarines. During the same five month period culminating in November 1941, there was an 82 percent reduction in tonnage loss due to air attacks, a 55 percent reduction in loss due to mines and a 76 percent reduction in loss due to all forms of surface raider attacks.[28] A number of factors contributed to this pronounced decline including improved British defences, a major shift in German resources to support their invasion of Russia and a significant curtailment of German surface raider activity. This latter factor was precipitated by the destruction of three German armed merchant cruisers. The first of these was the 7,766-ton *Pinguin*, which was sunk by the British cruiser *Cornwall* in the Indian Ocean on 8 May. The second was the 8,736-ton *Kormoran*, which was sunk on 19 November by the Australian cruiser *Sydney* some 170 miles west of Shark Bay off Western Australia. The third was the 7,862-ton *Atlantis*, which was sunk three days later by the British cruiser *Devonshire* some 300 miles northeast of Ascension Island.

Sadly, these successes did not come without cost. During the same engagement that resulted in the destruction of the armed merchant cruiser *Kormoran*, the Australian cruiser *Sydney* sustained fatal damage and was lost with all hands. Meanwhile, two days after the destruction of *Atlantis*, the German submarine *U124*, which was en route to the area to assist the survivors from the stricken German raider, encountered and sank the British cruiser *Dunedin* some 900 miles west of Freetown. Likewise, a number of lesser British and affiliated warships were lost to U-boats while engaged in trade defence operations in the Atlantic. In August this toll included the Norwegian-manned escort destroyer *Bath* and the corvettes *Picotee* and *Zinnia*. In September U-boats sank the Canadian corvette *Levis* and the auxiliary anti-aircraft ship *Springbank*. Finally, in October U-boats accounted for the destroyer *Cossack*, the escort destroyer *Broadwater* and the corvettes *Fleur de Lys* and *Gladiolus*.

By comparison, from July through November 1941, no fewer than 13 German U-boats and five Atlantic-based Italian submarines were lost to all causes including at least 14 to British or affiliated means. Of this latter number, British and Canadian surface escorts accounted for *U401*, *U501*, *Maggiori Baracca*, *U207*, *Alessandro Malaspina*, *U111*, *U204*, *Galileo Ferraris* and *U433*. Meanwhile, the British submarine *Severn* and Dutch submarine *O21* sank *Michele Bianchi* and *U95* respectively. Finally, Coastal Command aircraft accounted for *U452*, *U570* and *U206*. Two of these latter boats were sunk outright while the third, *U570*, met a far stranger end. Damaged and badly shaken by air dropped depth charges, *U570* actually surrendered to the offending Hudson aircraft. For the next 12 hours a series of Coastal Command aircraft maintained vigilance over the damaged U-boat until surface vessels finally arrived on the scene to take charge of the situation. With some difficulty, the British towed *U570* to Iceland and then later sailed it to England where it was renamed HMS *Graph* and used for experimental research.

The fact that two of the above listed U-boats were actually sunk in the Mediterranean indicated another problem facing Dönitz and his command. By the autumn of 1941 a number of factors forced Dönitz to divert a large percentage of his U-boats from the Atlantic to secondary theatres. At one end, Hitler ordered the dispatch of a number of U-boats to Norwegian waters as a defensive measure against potential Allied incursions. At the same time, he also compelled Dönitz to send several U-boats to the Mediterranean to help remedy the flagging logistical situation facing the Axis forces in North Africa. By December the Germans had six U-boats assigned to operate in Norwegian waters with a further 28 stationed in or earmarked for service in the Mediterranean. Of these, the Norwegian boats accomplished virtually nothing while those in the Mediterranean scored a few notable successes against British warships and a handful of victories against merchant shipping. On the other hand, these diversions seriously undermined the Kriegsmarine's ability to menace critical British convoy routes or engage the maximum amount of British shipping. This deficiency was demonstrated by the fact that on 8 December the Germans only had 27 U-boats available to cover the entire Atlantic. Both Raeder and Dönitz considered these deployments a significant detriment to their long-term strategic goals, but they were powerless to contradict Hitler's orders.

Making matters worse for the Germans, the United States continued to play an ever-increasing role in the North Atlantic. On 10 August 1941 Churchill met with America's President Roosevelt in Argentia, Newfoundland to discuss various issues including the situation in the Atlantic. As a result of this meeting, on 4 September the United States implemented 'Western Hemisphere Defense Plan Number 4' by which American warships began taking an active escort role for certain Atlantic convoys. Under these new provisions, the Canadian navy continued to escort eastbound convoys from their departure ports to the Western Ocean Meeting Point south of Newfoundland. From there the United States assumed escort responsibility for the faster HX convoys to the Mid-Ocean Meeting Point (now located at about 58° north and 22° west) while the Canadians, with British support, continued to escort the slower SC convoys. Britain's Western Approaches Command assumed coverage for the final portion of the journey.[29] By adopting these arrangements, the British were able to release three escort groups to reinforce their inadequately protected Gibraltar and Freetown routes. The British also benefitted from American aircraft support operating in conjunction with the RCAF and RAF Coastal Command out of Argentia and Iceland.

Although still technically neutral, the United States was now effectively an active participant in the naval war. As if to emphasise this point, on 4 September the American destroyer *Greer* and *U652* exchanged fire in an accidental and ultimately indecisive engagement. A month and a half later an American task unit of five destroyers was diverted to reinforce the embattled convoy SC.48 southwest of Iceland. On 16 October these destroyers joined British, Canadian and Free French warships already in defence of the convoy thus making the operation a true Allied affair. Early the next morning the United States Navy suffered its first combat casualty of the war when *U568* torpedoed and damaged the American destroyer *Kearny* in a nocturnal attack. Two weeks later on 31 October the Americans suffered their first warship loss when *U552* torpedoed and sank the destroyer *Reuben James* while it was operating in defence of Convoy HX.156 some 600 miles west of Ireland. This destruction caused the loss of 115 officers and men, giving the United States a harsh exposure to the human costs of war. Nevertheless, the United States continued its immense support for Britain and the British war effort.

While this help was sorely needed, the British were quick to learn that having allies also required commitments on their own part. In the summer of 1941 Churchill pledged to provide materiel support to the hard-pressed Soviet Union. The most direct route for delivering this aid was by sea through the Arctic to the ports of Murmansk and Archangel. On 21 August 1941 the first of these convoys, code-named 'Dervish', departed Iceland with six merchant ships carrying stores and aircraft along with a Royal Fleet Auxiliary (RFA) tanker destine for Archangel. The British conducted a concurrent operation with the aircraft carrier *Argus* to ferry 24 Hurricane fighters to Murmansk. The aircraft carrier *Victorious*, the cruisers *Devonshire*, *Suffolk* and

Shropshire, nine destroyers and three minesweepers provided the combined escort for these twin operations. The mission was a complete success with all ships and aircraft arriving at their prescribed destinations on 31 August and 7 September respectively.

This was only the beginning of what would become a long and difficult effort. In September the British formalised their Arctic convoy operations with Russia-bound convoys given the letter designator PQ and returning convoys referred to as QP. The first PQ convoy sailed from Iceland with ten merchant ships, the heavy cruiser *Suffolk* and two destroyers on 29 September. At the same time, a returning QP convoy departed Archangel with the six original 'Dervish' merchant ships and eight Soviet vessels sailing in ballast to collect cargo from the West. By year's end, a total of six PQ convoys successfully made the trip to Russia with 45 merchant ships while a further three QP convoys consisting of 34 merchant ships made the return journey back to the United Kingdom or Iceland.[30] These operations delivered 750 tanks, 800 fighter aircraft, 1,400 trucks and other military vehicles and more than 100,000 tons of ammunition and general stores to the Soviets.[31] The Germans failed to take any serious actions against these convoys, and all passages were made without loss. Nevertheless, the Admiralty was well aware of the vast potential dangers that likely awaited their convoys in the future.

In addition to this materiel support, the British took other actions to assist their Russian allies. In August the British conducted Operation *Gauntlet* to evacuate the Russian and Norwegian coal mining settlements located on Spitzbergen. Utilising the transport *Empress of Canada* along with cruisers and destroyers, the British successfully evacuated the settlements and carried out demolition operations to deny the mines to the Germans. While en route back to Britain, the cruisers *Nigeria* and *Aurora* intercepted a small German convoy off Porsangerfjord and sank the gunnery training ship/minelayer *Bremse* (1,460 tons, 4 × 5-inch guns). At about the same time, the aircraft carriers *Victorious* and *Furious* with elements of the Home Fleet launched a series of air strikes against German controlled shipping in various Norwegian ports and waterways to hamper German troop movements in support of the Russia invasion. During these operations British carrier aircraft sank two merchant ships and two minor vessels worth 4,474 tons and damaged a further five vessels worth 4,764 tons.[32]

While these operations involved key elements of the Home Fleet, the main focus of Britain's Atlantic-based naval effort remained the U-boat war. In this, the British continued to enjoy significant progress against their German opponents. This point was emphasised in December when a reinforced British escort group fought a momentous battle in defence of convoy HG.76 en route from Gibraltar to the United Kingdom. During an eight-day period culminating on 23 December, this British force under the leadership of Commander Johnny Walker and consisting of three destroyers, two sloops, seven corvettes and the auxiliary escort carrier *Audacity* repelled a series of probes and attacks from ten different U-boats. Of particular service was *Audacity*, whose aircraft participated in the destruction of *U131*, made sightings on seven other U-boats, destroyed two Kondor reconnaissance bombers, damaged three more and chased off a further three. Meanwhile, the British surface escorts shared in the destruction of *U131* and destroyed three other U-boats (*U434*, *U574* and *U567*). Against this, the convoy only lost two merchant ships along with the escort destroyer *Stanley* and the brave *Audacity*, which was torpedoed on the night of 21/22 December. Despite these casualties, both sides considered the battle to be a major victory for the escorts and an unacceptable exchange rate for the U-boats. The battle further demonstrated the value of the escort carrier and that a well-defended convoy was capable of holding its own against persistent attack.

The Germans suffered other misfortunes during December. In addition to their casualties sustained against convoy HG.76, the Germans lost six U-boats in other operations during the month. Of these, British surface escorts destroyed *U208*, *U127*, *U79* and *U75*. A FAA Swordfish patrol aircraft operating out of Gibraltar accounted for a fifth, *U451*, off Cape Spartel. Finally, *U557* was lost as a result of an accidental collision with the Italian torpedo boat *Orione*. It is interesting to note

A British destroyer on escort duty in the Atlantic. With the procurement of additional escorts along with technical innovations such as Ultra, surface search radar and HF/DF, the British ended the German 'happy time' in March 1941 and then facilitated a temporary reversal of fortunes against the U-boats during the latter half of the year. (Royal Navy official photographer, Tomlin, H. W. (Lt), public domain)

that all of these losses occurred in the Mediterranean or near Gibraltar, indicating the degree to which Germany's U-boat effort had shifted away from the North Atlantic. By comparison, British, Allied and neutral merchant losses due to submarine attacks in December amounted to 26 ships worth 124,070 tons of which only nine ships worth 45,931 tons were lost in the Atlantic.[33] While this represented an increase from November's 18-month low, these shipping losses were still less than half of those sustained six months before. On the other hand, December's toll of ten U-boats sunk constituted the deadliest month for U-boat losses so far in the war.

December also represented a fitting conclusion to a critical period of the Atlantic conflict. In June British defence planners had lamented over the potential loss of some 7,000,000 tons of commercial shipping for the year. Had this occurred, Britain's strategic situation would have undoubtedly declined. Fortunately, June proved to be a transitional month with losses dropping sharply thereafter. From July through December total British, Allied and neutral merchant losses as a result of German, Italian or other European-based adversarial actions amounted to 298 ships worth 1,012,578 tons.[34] When combined together, total worldwide losses for the year amounted to 1,299 merchant ships worth 4,328,558 tons of which Britain's portion amounted to 833 vessels worth some 2,863,800 tons.[35] While this was certainly a large number, it was a far cry from the 7,000,000 tons that British defence planners had feared might be lost. Instead, Britain's shipping situation actually improved as new construction and inputs from foreign sources added another 1,109,000 tons to the British flag during the latter half of 1941. This influx provided the British with a net gain of some 249,000 tons from July through December.[36] When combined with foreign flagged time-charters, the British actually had more ocean-going merchant tonnage available for their use at the end of 1941 than they did at the beginning of the war.

Of course the ultimate measure in the battle of the Atlantic revolved around British import levels and not the state of the British merchant fleet. For the year of 1941, total imports into the United Kingdom numbered some 44,586,000 tons. Of these, 14,654,000 tons were foodstuffs, 15,046,000 tons were raw materials, 13,603,000 tons were tanker commodities (petroleum products, molasses, unrefined whale oil and industrial alcohol), 778,000 tons were munitions and manufactured goods and 505,000 tons were various items from Ireland.[37] While this level satisfied basic British requirements and was an improvement over earlier forecasts, it still represented a marked decline compared to pre-war import levels. A number of factors contributed to this reduction including the diversion of merchant shipping to military service, delays associated with the assembly and execution of convoys, the loss of shipping routes through the Mediterranean and slow turnaround times due to inefficiencies in the British port and distribution system. As such, the British government was compelled to implement rationing on a variety of commodities, and efforts were intensified to increase domestic food production. Yet while these results were a nuisance, the Germans had thus far failed to reduce imports to a truly prohibitive level.

Table 4.2 Merchant Shipping under British Control

Date	British flag* ships/tonnage	Foreign flag time chartered to the United Kingdom ships/tonnage	Total ships/tonnage
3 Sep 39	2,965/17,524,000	34/260,000	2,999/17,784,000
31 Dec 39	2,952/17,391,000	55/381,000	3,007/17,772,000
30 Jun 40	3,049/17,736,000	486/2,741,000	3,535/20,477,000
31 Dec 40	2,991/17,154,000	681/3,700,000	3,672/20,854,000
30 Jun 41	2,790/16,025,000	777/4,106,000	3,567/20,131,000
31 Dec 41	2,787/16,284,000	829/4,409,000	3,616/20,693,000

Source: The Central Statistical Office, *Statistical Digest of the War* (London: Her Majesty's Stationery Office, 1975), pp. 173–174.
Note: This data only covers merchant ships of 1,600 gross tons or greater.
* British flagged vessels constitute ships registered to the United Kingdom, Dominions and colonies as well as foreign vessels requisitioned or operating under bareboat charter.

Nor was this the extent of British good fortunes, as the close of this period also saw the United States formally enter the war. This was brought about in early December by a series of surprise Japanese attacks against American and British interests in the Pacific, which prompted the United States to declare war on Japan. A few days later Germany and Italy came to the support of their Tripartite ally and declared war on the United States.[38] The Americans promptly reciprocated and expanded the war into a truly global conflict with the British Empire, the United States and the Soviet Union in one camp and Germany, Italy and Japan in the other. From the British perspective, this constituted an overwhelmingly positive result since the United States was an immensely more powerful ally than Japan was an adversary. On this point, Churchill wrote:

> Hitler's fate was sealed. Mussolini's fate was sealed. As for the Japanese, they would be ground to powder. All the rest was merely the proper application of overwhelming force. The British Empire, the Soviet Union and now the United States, bound together with every scrap of their life and strength, were, according to my lights, twice or even thrice the force of their antagonists. No doubt it would take a long time. I expected terrible forfeits in the East; but all this would be merely a passing phase. United we could subdue everybody else in the world. Many disasters, immeasurable cost and tribulation lay ahead, but there was no more doubt about the end.[39]

So as 1941 drew to a close, the British could rightly feel a sense of relief and guarded optimism regarding their position in the Atlantic as well as the overall war. In terms of the former, they had begun the year during a period of severe uncertainty as their maritime lines of communication were assaulted by a variety of sources including mines, aircraft, surface raiders, armed merchant cruisers and most importantly U-boats. The Germans had referred to this period as the 'happy time', a reference to their U-boat fortunes, but equally applicable to all aspects of their maritime assault. As the year developed, these fortunes began to disappear, but Allied shipping losses remained persistently high. Then, in July, a number of factors finally came to fruition to drastically alter the situation. During the latter half of the year shipping losses dropped by two-thirds while German/Italian submarine losses more than doubled and other German threats all but disappeared or were significantly curtailed. This is not to say that the battle was over. Indeed, despite the loss of 35 U-boats throughout the year, the German U-boat arm continued to grow in size and capability. It was undoubtedly clear that considerable fighting remained ahead. Nevertheless, on at least a temporary basis, the British had gained themselves a vital respite, and with the United States now in the war, their long-term outlook was exceedingly positive.

Table 4.3 Key Performance Indices from the Battle of the Atlantic

	Total Allied tonnage lost due to submarine attack	Total Allied tonnage lost due to other military means*	Total British tonnage lost due to submarine attack	Total British tonnage lost due to other military means*	Additional merchant tonnage added to the British flag**	Total import tonnage delivered to the United Kingdom***	German U-boats sunk****
Sep–Dec 39	421,156	334,081	266,300	164,000	397,000	16,234,000	9
Jan–Mar 40	343,610	204,825	103,400	150,100	295,000	14,545,000	8
Apr–Jun 40	372,160	660,015	174,500	266,300	901,000	16,345,000	7
Jul–Sep 40	758,778	473,985	550,400	329,200	717,000	13,021,000	4
Oct–Dec 40	711,610	466,658	531,400	341,500	467,000	11,098,000	3
Jan–Mar 41	566,585	686,754	451,100	441,600	558,000	9,380,000	5
Apr–Jun 41	885,010	745,958	626,400	392,500	429,000	11,266,000	7
Jul–Sep 41	377,339	160,277	289,200	118,500	606,000	12,646,000	6
Oct–Dec 41	342,820	563,815	196,000	348,500	503,000	11,958,000	17

Source: The Central Statistical Office, *Statistical Digest of the War* (London: Her Majesty's Stationery Office, 1975), pp. 177–181, 184–185 and S. W. Roskill, *The War at Sea 1939–1945, Volume 1: The Defensive* (London: Her Majesty's Stationery Office, 1954), pp. 615–616.
Note: Loss figures are compiled from all theatres of the war. The total Allied tonnage columns cover all British, Allied and neutral merchant shipping sunk by Axis submarines or other military means. The total British tonnage columns cover the British portions of those losses.
* The tonnage figures for merchant shipping sunk by other military means include a large influx of vessels sunk in the Mediterranean in April 1941 and the Pacific in December 1941.
** Only covers ships of 1,600 gross tons or greater added to the British merchant fleet through new construction, requisition or other means. It does not include foreign flagged time-charters.
*** These import figures are based upon estimated weights included in the Trade and Navigation Accounts for each month and are unadjusted for subsequent minor revisions. All annual import figures listed in the text have been adjusted and are a more accurate accounting.
**** Only covers German U-boat losses. Italian submarine losses are not included due to the limited role these Italian boats played in the overall tonnage battle.

CHAPTER 5

Offensive Operations

On the early morning of 1 March 1941, a small British force consisting of the converted assault ships *Queen Emma* and *Princess Beatrix* and the destroyers *Somali*, *Eskimo*, *Tartar*, *Legion* and *Bedouin* departed Scapa Flow and began a northward journey towards the Arctic Circle. Embarked upon these vessels were 500 elite troops from the 3rd and 4th Commando units, a detachment of Royal Engineers and a platoon of 52 Norwegian volunteers. Proceeding under the protection of the light cruisers *Edinburgh* and *Nigeria*, this force made an uneventful three-day passage through heavy seas to arrive at its target destination of the Lofoten Islands in German-occupied Northern Norway on the morning of the 4th. From there, the British discharged their assault personnel into landing craft and carried out demolition raids against specified industrial and maritime targets within the area. Of particular importance were a number of local factories that processed herring and cod oil into glycerine, which, in turn, was used by the Germans to manufacture munitions. Attaining complete surprise, the British easily subdued the local German authorities and carried out their demolition activities with great precision and efficiency.

Within a matter of hours, the operation was complete, and the assault parties re-embarked upon their ships to begin an uneventful journey back to Britain. In their wake, the British left behind a scene of large-scale destruction, which included the demolition of 11 fish-oil factories, a power station and storage tanks containing 800,000 gallons of oil, glycerine and petroleum products. They also destroyed seven merchant ships and five minor vessels worth a combined 15,641 tons.[1] Included in this toll of minor vessels was the armed German trawler *Krebs*, which yielded valuable encryption materials as previously described in Chapter 4. Finally, the British seized 216 German prisoners as well as 60 Norwegian collaborators and evacuated 314 volunteers for the fledgling Free-Norwegian forces.[2] The raid, which fell under the designation of Operation *Claymore*, also provided a morale boost to the British people and armed forces and demonstrated a welcome example of offensive action during a time more commonly characterised by defensive thinking and activities.

The British attained these many accomplishments at the cost of a single, non-fatal casualty when an accidental weapon's discharge wounded an officer in the thigh.

While noteworthy in its scope and public exposure, Operation *Claymore* was not unique in its overriding function. To the contrary, Operation *Claymore* represented a single action out of thousands that made up a continuous campaign lasting for the duration of the war. During a time when the main focus of Britain's maritime effort was centred on the defensive struggle in the Atlantic or the ongoing conflict in the Mediterranean, a concurrent, although much less publicised, campaign was also underway in the waters off Northwest Europe. Unlike its more predominant counterparts, this was an offensive campaign, the purpose of which was to diminish the German war effort through attacks on German-controlled shipping and seaborne commerce. By doing this, the British hoped to disrupt the importation of essential raw materials for the German economy, put strain upon the German transportation system, which, in turn, would impair German manufacturing and military support, and force the Germans to divert resources from offensive to defensive applications.

As already discussed in previous chapters, Germany, being a continental power, enjoyed significantly less dependency upon overseas trade for the subsistence of its economy and population than did Britain. Nevertheless, it did require the importation of certain essential raw materials including iron ore and other key minerals from Scandinavia to support its war effort. Scandinavia also provided Germany with other useful products such as lumber, wood pulp, fish and fish oil that helped satisfy the Reich's consumer and industrial needs. In 1940 the Germans seized Norway and Denmark thus enhancing their access to these vital resources. Yet, even with this increased control and influence (in the case of Sweden), the Germans still depended upon maritime transport to deliver these critical imports to Germany. If the British could impede or seriously disrupt the flow of these vital materials, it would have a debilitating effect upon Germany's long-term ability to wage war.

Maritime transport also provided direct support to the German military and helped facilitate other economic benefits beyond the importation of essential raw materials. In terms of the former, this was nowhere more evident than in the case of Norway where the German garrison was almost entirely dependent upon seaborne commerce to provide all manner of sustenance not attained locally. German garrisons in Poland, Denmark, France and the Low Countries were not similarly dependent, but these too used coastal shipping to fulfil many of their logistical needs. Later when the Germans invaded the Soviet Union, they supported part of their effort through the use of maritime transport in the Baltic. This requirement continued once the fighting there became protracted. Finally, in addition to military applications, the Germans used commercial shipping to transport goods and materials as part of their normal economic exchange. The reason for this was simple; in many cases maritime transport was the fastest and/or most economical way to move materials and products from one point to another. Of course, there was also rail transport, but this had limited capacity and lacked the versatility available to shipping in coastal areas. Thus, if the British could seriously disrupt German seaborne commerce, it would have a corresponding negative impact upon various German military and economic activities.

In terms of diverting men and resources from offensive to defensive applications, this also had tangible benefits. Given its finite resources, if the Kriegsmarine was compelled to acquire and operate increasing numbers of escort and mine-clearing vessels to defend German seaborne commerce and keep transit routes open to the Atlantic, fewer resources would be available to prosecute the U-boat campaign and other offensive operations. If German shipyards were compelled to produce or repair merchant/escort ships, less capacity would be available to produce or repair U-boats and other offensive warships. If steel plating that could be used to manufacture tanks or guns was instead diverted to build or repair merchant/escort ships, armament production might suffer. Likewise, if guns that were produced were mounted on merchant/escort ships or assigned to coastal defence batteries, less armament would be available to support operations in Russia and North Africa. Finally, if the Germans were compelled to increase garrison staffing in coastal areas to defend against British incursions, both real and potential, less manpower would be available to serve on more active fronts. By waging an aggressive anti-shipping campaign, the British could make a vast coastline stretching from Norway to Spain a potential target thus forcing the Germans to respond in kind with defensive measures.

In addition to these tangible objectives, the anti-shipping campaign provided the British with psychological benefits. During a period when most British activities were defensive in nature, the anti-shipping campaign gave them an avenue to think and operate in an offensive manner. With few exceptions, wars are not won by defensive action alone. In most cases, offensive action is needed to take the war to the enemy and destroy his willingness and/or ability to resist. During the first half of World War II, Britain lacked the ability to do this in a decisive manner. This was particularly true after the fall of France when Britain faced the prospect of invasion and economic strangulation. It was only through occasional commando raids, anti-shipping operations and the fledgling strategic bombing campaign that the British were able to strike back at the Germans and maintain a semblance of offensive action. In the beginning, these activities were little more than pinpricks, but it allowed the British the means to maintain an offensive spirit that would later translate into more decisive action. It also gave them minor victories that provided morale and confidence boosts during a time when good news was often in short supply.

While these objectives were clear enough, attaining them was no simple task. The British faced a number of challenges, many of which will be discussed in greater detail later. For consideration now was the fact that the British faced an elusive adversary in their anti-shipping campaign. This was primarily true for two reasons.

First, due to the coastal nature of most German seaborne commerce, German-controlled convoys and ships were able to hug the coasts using harbours, fjords and the *Innereled* as cover. Often, these convoys and ships proceeded to their destinations using intermediate jumps that allowed them to travel at night and shelter in safe harbours during the day. This made detection difficult, and often gave the Germans proximity to safety when attacks were made. A second and even more significant reason for this elusiveness was the fact that much of the most important commerce, such as the Swedish ore trade, took place in the Baltic, and was thus more difficult to interdict due to its distance and geographical isolation from Britain. Under these conditions, British warships and submarines were prohibited from operating in the Baltic while aircraft could only reach the extreme western portion after crossing German-controlled territory. Fortunately for the British, this limited accessibility to the Baltic was partially mitigated by the seasonal need to divert Swedish ore through Narvik and the fact that many ore shipments culminated in Rotterdam, exposing them to increased threats of attack.

Faced with these geographical difficulties, the British adopted a tonnage strategy to help attain their overall objectives. Where they could, the British would take whatever limited actions were available to directly interdict German traffic in the Baltic. Beyond this, they would attack German-controlled shipping in more accessible areas with the goal of causing continuous attrition that would strain the overall German shipping situation and eventually degrade operations everywhere. At the beginning of the war the Germans possessed 4,196,995 tons of merchant shipping.[3] By the early summer of 1940 over 1,700,000 tons of this shipping had been lost through Allied actions or stranding in foreign ports. Against this, the Germans had gained access to 1,395,872 tons of captured shipping from Norway, Holland, Denmark and Belgium.[4] When combined with new construction, this gave the Germans about 4,000,000 tons of shipping available for all applications during the summer of 1940. Of this, the Kriegsmarine requisitioned over 2,100,000 tons to serve as auxiliary warships, military transports and other various support vessels. Much of what remained was ill suited for large-scale trade operations due to size, design and mechanical issues. As such, the Germans were only able to generally employ between 1,100,000 to 1,200,000 tons of shipping to carry out their commercial trade in the North Sea and Baltic, which included the all-important importation of ore and minerals from Scandinavia.[5]

Britain's offensive campaign against these shipping and other economic targets took many forms. At one end of the spectrum were large-scale raids such as Operation *Claymore*. In the latter part of December 1941 the British launched a follow-up to *Claymore* with two concurrent raids on the Lofoten and Vaagsö Islands. The first of these, designated Operation *Anklet*, began on 22 December when a force, consisting of the cruiser *Arethusa*, the landing ships *Prince Albert* and *Princess Charlotte*, eight assorted destroyers, two corvettes, three minesweepers and five support vessels, departed Scapa Flow. Four days later this force arrived off Lofoten where 260 commandos captured the local garrison and destroyed the fish-oil factory at Moskenesöy and the wireless station at Tind. While this was underway, the destroyer *Bedouin* destroyed the wireless station at Flakstadöy while *Arethusa* and the destroyers *Somali*, *Ashanti* and *Eskimo* entered Vestfjord to seize and subsequently disable the Norwegian merchant ships *Kong Harald* and *Nordland* (1,151 and 725 tons respectively) and sink the 163-ton German patrol vessel *V5907/Geier*. On 28 December the force departed Lofoten with a number of prisoners and Norwegian volunteers and safely returned to Britain despite bomb damage to *Arethusa*.

While Operation *Anklet* attained a degree of success on its own, its primary purpose was to divert German attention away from the subsequent British raid that was launched against industrial and maritime targets in Central Norway. This endeavour, designated Operation *Archery*, commenced on the evening of 24 December when the cruiser *Kenya*, the landing ships *Prince Charles* and *Prince Leopold* and four destroyers departed Scapa Flow and proceeded towards Vaagsö Island. On the morning of the 27th this force entered into Vaagsfjord and landed 585 commandos in five groups around Vaagsö and Maalöy. Supported by naval gunfire and RAF aircraft, the British commandos subdued the sizable German garrison after heavy fighting and proceeded to destroy the local fish-oil and telecommunication installations. Meanwhile, in the adjacent waters British warships destroyed four merchant ships and four minor vessels worth 13,604 tons and damaged two additional ships worth 1,112 tons.[6] From one of these minor vessels, the auxiliary *V5108/Föhn*, the British gained a major intelligence find when they recovered codebooks containing the radio call signs for every German vessel in Norway and France, along with challenges, countersigns and emergency signals.

By the afternoon of the 27th the raid was over, and the commandos returned to their ships to begin their journey back to Britain. Accompanying them were 98 German prisoners, four Norwegian collaborators and 77 Norwegian volunteers. They left behind an estimated 150 Germans dead and widespread materiel destruction.[7] Their own casualties amounted to 20 killed and 57 wounded.[8] In addition to these immediate human and materiel results, Operation *Archery* had a long-term effect that advanced Britain's overall strategic objective. Alarmed by the growing threat these raids seemed to indicate, Hitler ordered sizable reinforcements to Norway. Within a matter of weeks the Germans dispatched 30,000 additional soldiers to Norway to fill in personnel shortages and create a number of 'fortress' battalions. Later in 1942 the Germans established three additional divisions in Norway and constructed extensive shore installations and gun emplacements. Finally, Hitler ordered the main units of the German surface fleet to assemble in Norway to defend against a possible British invasion. In carrying this out, the Germans significantly reduced the potential threat their surface fleet posed against Britain's Atlantic convoy routes, and this move would ultimately cost them one of their remaining capital ships (as will be covered later in Chapter 6).

Bolstered by these results, the British embarked upon an even more aggressive raid, designated Operation *Chariot*, at the end of March 1942. Unlike its celebrated predecessors, this raid culminated in the French Biscay port of St. Nazaire and had a military application instead of one that was predominantly economic in nature. The target for this raid was the immense Normandie dry dock, which was the only available dock outside of Germany capable of handling the battleship *Tirpitz*. The British believed that by disabling this dry dock, they would further discourage the Germans from dispatching *Tirpitz* into the Atlantic. This was because if *Tirpitz* was damaged, it would have to return to Germany to enact repairs and would not have the option to berth in occupied France. The device by which the British proposed to deliver this outcome was the ex-American Town-class destroyer *Campbeltown*. In particular, the British planned to ram *Campbeltown* into the dock's main lock gates and detonate explosives packed in the ship's bow using a time fuse. Commandos from *Campbeltown* and accompanying coastal vessels would disembark and destroy the pumping and mechanical stations that operated the dock as well as other port installations. Naval and military personnel would then make good their escape on these same coastal vessels while *Campbeltown* was left behind to deliver the main destruction against the dock's lock gates.

On the afternoon of 26 March the British raiding force departed Falmouth. In addition to the explosive-laden *Campbeltown*, which had been modified to appear as a German torpedo boat, this force consisted of a motor gunboat, a motor torpedo boat and 16 motor launches. Embarked upon these vessels were 268 commandos and 353 naval personnel. Likewise, the destroyers *Atherstone* and *Tynedale* escorted the force while *Cleveland* and *Brocklesby* were later dispatched as further support. Initially, the force proceeded southwest into the Atlantic before turning back towards the Biscay coast. While en route, *Tynedale* sighted and attacked a U-boat that was forced to crash-dive but was not destroyed, and later the force encountered two French trawlers that were sunk after their crews were taken off. After proceeding on a decoy route across the Bay of Biscay towards La Pallice and La Rochelle, the assault force turned northeast and made a 15-knot dash towards St. Nazaire while the escorting destroyers detached seaward to wait for their return.

Shortly after midnight on the 28th the assault force entered the Loire and proceeded on its final approach to St. Nazaire. Aided by a diversionary RAF raid, the British initially proceeded unchallenged. Finally, at Les Morées Tower some three miles from St. Nazaire a German shore station signalled a challenge to the British warships. The British responded with a false identification and message designed to deceive the Germans into thinking they were friendly vessels. They were able to do this due to the captured codebooks taken from *V5108/Föhn* during Operation *Archery* some three months earlier. The bluff worked for a while, but two miles from target the Germans blanketed *Campbeltown* in searchlights and opened fire. The British responded in kind and increased speed. Despite withering fire, *Campbeltown* forged on and at 0134 hours ran itself up on the lock gates. From there, British commandos streamed off the stricken destroyer to carry out their demolition duties while key naval personnel flooded *Campbeltown* to affix it in place. Meanwhile, the various coastal craft launched torpedoes against submarine pens and attempted to land their own commando charges. In terms of the latter, they found themselves heavily engaged and were generally unsuccessful.

After an hour of fighting the British attempted to withdraw. This was no simple task given the heavy casualties they had already sustained including several coastal craft sunk or damaged. Returning torpedo boats from the German 5th Flotilla soon blocked their route of departure. Nevertheless, a severely reduced force was able to fight its way out of the Loire estuary and rendezvous with the escorting destroyers. Of the 18 coastal craft and 621 men that had originally left England, a mere four motor launches and 224 men returned. Of those men left behind, 169 were killed or missing, five made it to Spain and the balance ended up as German prisoners.[9] Yet, despite this heavy loss, the British considered the raid to be a great success. Shortly before noon on the 28th *Campbeltown's* demolition charges exploded, causing severe damage to the lock gates and putting the dry dock out of service for the remainder of the war. In addition to this, two tugs and a minesweeper were sunk and various harbour installations destroyed or damaged by the accompanying commando assault. Meanwhile, German casualties included 42 killed and 127 wounded during the initial fighting and between 100 and 380 killed when *Campbeltown* exploded.[10] In recognition for their success and gallantry, the British government awarded the participants of Operation *Chariot* 85 decorations including five Victoria Crosses.[11]

While raids such as Operations *Claymore*, *Archery* and *Chariot* represented spectacular successes for the British, the vast majority of actions related to the anti-shipping campaign were far more mundane. In fact, during this period the greatest source of success against enemy shipping, at least in terms of tonnage, was the seizure or forced scuttling of Italian, Vichy French, Finnish and Romanian merchant ships that were located in Britain or the surrounding area when those nations joined or became affiliated with the Axis cause. In terms of the former, in June 1940 the British seized 13 Italian merchant ships that were sheltering in Britain worth 72,363 tons and forced the scuttling of another eight vessels worth 42,505 tons upon Italy's entry into the war. During the same period and extending into 1941, the British seized 11 Vichy French merchant ships worth 46,666 tons in the same area. Then, in the latter half of 1941 the British seized 17 Finnish and two Romanian merchant ships worth a combined 55,775 tons as those nations joined the Axis in support of Germany's invasion of the Soviet Union. When combined together, this deprived the Axis of 217,309 tons of merchant shipping of which the majority ended up in active Allied service.[12]

Turning now to the conventional campaign against Germany's local shipping, the British employed a number of weapons of which the mine was most effective. This was particularly true regarding aerial mines, but also included those laid by ships and submarines. Aerial mines provided the British with numerous advantages. First, they were highly versatile weapons that could impact shipping in locations that were generally inaccessible to other forms of attack. In particular, when utilising long-range aircraft, the British were capable of planting mines in the Kattegat, Kiel Bay and the Western Baltic. Second, aerial mining was highly efficient in that it avoided large-scale expenditures of time, effort and resources in seeking out illusive targets. As such, a significantly higher portion of minelaying sorties resulted in the delivery of offensive weapons than other forms of attack did. Conversely, because of its concentrated, yet indirect nature, mine warfare was less dangerous than other offensive actions. Finally, mines were very potent weapons capable of sinking or causing serious damage to every category of ship. The mere presence of mines often caused disruption to enemy sea communications. Thus, when combined together, these factors gave mines the means to cause significant damage and interference to Axis seaborne activities for a minimal outlay of effort and cost.

On the night of 13/14 April 1940 a force of 15 Handley Page Hampden bombers set out from Britain, and for the loss of one aircraft, successfully laid mines in the sea routes off Denmark. This was the RAF's first minelaying operation of the war. It would soon be followed by many more as the RAF, and to a far lesser extent the Fleet Air Arm, eventually laid some 53,000 mines in the waters around Europe, constituting 72 percent of Britain's offensive minelaying effort.[13] Targets

The Royal Air Force was a major participant in the maritime conflict. Pictured here is the Vickers Wellington, which fulfilled a variety of roles including submarine-hunter, minelayer, general purpose bomber and torpedo-bomber. (Royal Air Force, public domain)

for this onslaught included the Norwegian and Western European coastlines, Bay of Biscay and Western Baltic. Early on, the frequency and scale of these operations were often limited as the RAF diverted suitable aircraft to perform other duties such as anti-invasion reconnaissance, anti-submarine patrols and conventional bombing raids. Nevertheless, by the end of 1941 the RAF had flown 3,226 minelaying sorties during which they laid 2,562 mines.[14] During the same period British warships and submarines added large numbers of additional mines to this effort. Many of these latter mines were laid in defensive belts as Britain prepared to meet a potential invasion, but as this threat subsided, a larger percentage of this enterprise was devoted to offensive applications.

The results of this early mining campaign were generally favourable. During the period of April 1940 through December 1941 British and Allied mines claimed the destruction of 155 German and German-affiliated merchant ships and commercial craft worth a combined 147,271 tons.[15] Likewise, these same mines destroyed 38 German warships and auxiliary vessels worth 26,551 tons.[16] Included in these military losses were the torpedo boats *T6* and *Wolf* and the fleet minesweepers *M11*, *M5*, *M61*, *M89*, *M136*, *M6*, *M511* and *M529*. Finally, mine strikes during this period damaged 21 German or German-affiliated merchant ships, two minesweepers and an E-boat worth an additional 53,585 tons.[17] Of these various totals, British air-laid mines accounted for the destruction of at least 142 vessels worth 134,611 tons and damage to a further 22 vessels worth 36,746 tons.[18] This amounted to over 75 percent of the tonnage sunk or damaged by Allied mines during this period. Of the remainder, Norwegian mines claimed a handful while mines laid by ships and submarines accounted for the rest. The cost the British paid for these results were 94 aircraft and the destroyers *Esk* and *Ivanhoe* lost during minelaying operations.[19]

The RAF's other major contribution to the initial anti-shipping campaign was direct attacks at sea. Unfortunately, during the early years of the war this method was beset by numerous problems that limited its overall effectiveness. Paramount amongst these was the quality and quantity of aircraft assigned to perform this role. At the beginning of the war RAF Coastal Command possessed two squadrons of obsolete Vickers Vildebeest torpedo-bombers as its sole dedicated strike force. During much of 1940 Coastal Command still lacked an adequate purpose-built aircraft to perform anti-shipping operations. The exception to this was the Bristol Beaufort torpedo-bomber which, with a speed of 265 miles per hour and a range of 1,600 miles, constituted the RAF's first modern maritime strike aircraft. Unfortunately, technical and operational difficulties delayed the Beaufort's introduction, and it wasn't until September 1940 that the Beaufort first performed its intended function. Thereafter, competing production priorities and the need to send strike aircraft to the Mediterranean limited the number of Beauforts available to Coastal Command. To make up the difference, the RAF had to depend upon other aircraft types, such as the Avro Anson, Bristol Blenheim and Lockheed Hudson, to perform the majority of its maritime strike operations. This dependency upon improvised aircraft remained well into 1942.

In addition to these aircraft limitations, Coastal Command also suffered from other materiel deficiencies. First, at the beginning of the campaign the RAF lacked a suitable bombsight for anti-shipping operations. As such, RAF aircraft had great difficulty in scoring hits against Axis ships. To compensate for this, strike aircraft often performed low-level attacks that exposed them to increased danger from return anti-aircraft fire. In those rare cases when hits were scored, ineffective British bombs often failed to cause significant damage. This was because during the first year of the anti-shipping campaign Coastal Command had to depend upon old stocks of general purpose and semi-armour piercing bombs. Many of these bombs had faulty fusing mechanisms and/or insufficient explosive to weight ratios that limited their destructive power. In many cases, these bombs either failed to explode or were only capable of causing superficial damage. Finally, early Coastal Command aircraft lacked advanced navigational aids and Air to Surface Vessel (ASV) radar, which limited their ability to find targets. Later when these items became available, Coastal Command's strike components often received low priority for their acquisition. As an example of this, the British prioritised early ASV radar technology towards the anti-submarine effort, and it would be 1943 before ASV radar became readily available for strike applications.

Coinciding with these qualitative shortfalls, Britain's maritime strike effort also suffered from a number of structural and operational difficulties. First, this strike function was initially hamstrung by onerous rules of engagement that severely restricted the command's freedom of action. Over time British authorities progressively relaxed these rules of engagement, but it would still take until March 1941 before British aircraft were given full permission to attack German-affiliated shipping whenever and wherever it was located. Unfortunately, the ability to do this was hindered by a second major barrier. During the opening stages of the war Britain lacked an adequate intelligence network to provide timely information regarding German shipping movements. As such, the British spent considerable time and effort trying to locate German ships and convoys in what was often a needle in a haystack-type affair. Finally, many British aircrews lacked sufficient operational training due to the RAF's precipitous expansion and inefficiencies within Coastal Command's maintenance organisation resulting in low serviceability rates.

Despite these many difficulties, the British persevered in their aerial campaign of direct attacks against German-controlled shipping. To carry this out, Coastal Command assigned three groups with different areas of responsibility. No. 18 Group covered the northern North Sea, No. 16 Group covered the southern North Sea and English Channel and No. 15 Group covered the Bay of Biscay. While this was overwhelmingly a Coastal Command undertaking, aircraft from Fighter Command, Bomber Command and the FAA also participated in this effort. Not surprisingly, given the conditions in which they were operating, the British failed to attain optimum results for the amount of effort expended. From May 1940 through December 1941 the RAF flew 11,737 direct attack sorties along with a smaller number of FAA sorties.[20] Together, these aircraft sank 57 German and German-affiliated merchant ships and 14 warships/auxiliaries worth a combined 90,429 tons. They damaged a further 54 commercial vessels and three auxiliary warships worth a combined 127,022 tons along with three German capital ships.[21] These results, while not insignificant, came at a heavy cost as the RAF lost 373 aircraft during regional anti-shipping strikes from April 1940 through December 1941.[22]

The Royal Navy's main contribution to the anti-shipping campaign, beyond minelaying and the actions of the FAA, came in the form of submarine operations. Unfortunately, like their RAF comrades, British submarines faced a number of challenges that plagued them through the duration of the campaign. First, due to the limited and predominately coastal nature of German seaborne commerce, British submarines had great difficulty in finding worthwhile targets to attack. After the relative abundance of German merchant ships encountered during the Norwegian campaign, sightings fell off progressively during the succeeding months, and by 1941 it was not uncommon for British submarines to carry out multiple patrols without ever sighting a suitable target. Admiralty directives that diverted much of Britain's local submarine effort to defend against German surface raiders only served to exacerbate this problem. Likewise, since British submarines had to operate in German-controlled coastal waters in order to effectively engage enemy shipping, these submarines were exposed to great dangers from mines, aircraft and a variety of escort vessels. Periods of extended sunlight in the northern latitudes worsened these dangers. Finally, the priority given to British submarine operations in the Mediterranean often limited the number of boats available for patrols in northern waters.

In addition to these submarine efforts, the Royal Navy utilised a variety of surface warships to carry out offensive operations against local German maritime traffic. While cruisers and destroyers occasionally participated in these actions, it was primarily coastal craft that conducted the bulk of this effort. These coastal craft generally came in two types. The first was the motor torpedo boat, which was the British equivalent to the German E-boat. Typically weighing in at between 30 and 100 tons and armed with two or four torpedoes (depending upon the model), these fast attack craft generally operated at night where they used stealth to stalk and engage their targets. While torpedoes constituted their primary striking power, these boats were also armed with machine guns and other small-calibre weapons for self-defence. The second major coastal vessel associated with this campaign was the motor gunboat. Similar in basic design and performance to the motor torpedo boat, motor gunboats were primarily earmarked to engage E-boats and other minor vessels. As such, motor gunboats lacked torpedoes, but were armed with heavier-calibre guns. When combined together, these small, but potent, warships constituted a growing threat to German shipping in the English Channel and North Sea from the summer of 1940 on.

During this period British submarines and surface warships took a steady, if less than substantial, toll on German military and commercial vessels. From 10 June 1940 through 31 December 1941 British and British-controlled Allied submarines sank 23 merchant ships and 12 minor vessels worth a combined 78,654 tons in Northern European waters and the Bay of Biscay. Likewise, these same submarines also sank the German torpedo boat *Luchs*, three submarines (one German and two Italian) and five auxiliary warships.[23] Finally, British submarines may have been responsible for the destruction of four additional vessels worth 12,591 tons, but these claims remain in dispute.[24] Sadly, these results came at a heavy cost as the British lost 12 submarines in Northern European waters during this period. Of these, mines accounted for *Salmon*, *Thames*, *Swordfish* and *O13* (Dutch); surface warships sank *Shark*, *H49* and *O22* (Dutch); *U34* sank *Spearfish*; aircraft sank *Narwhal* and unknown or accidental causes accounted for *Snapper*, *Umpire* and *H31*. Meanwhile,

Despite their seemingly modest appearance, British motor torpedo boats and motor gunboats played a significant role in the navy's interdiction effort and eventually accounted for the destruction of dozens of German vessels in the English Channel and North Sea. (Priest, L. C. (Lt), Royal Navy official photographer, public domain)

from May 1940 through December 1941 British home-based surface warships sank 25 military and commercial vessels worth 28,319 tons excluding the battleship *Bismarck* and vessels sunk during the Lofoten and Vaagsö Island raids.[25]

When combined together, these losses began taking a toll on the German shipping situation. In April and May 1940, the period covering the Norwegian campaign, total German and German-affiliated merchant losses amounted to 98 vessels worth 296,673 tons. During the subsequent 19 months (through December 1941) a further 287 German and German-affiliated merchant ships worth a combined 753,457 tons were lost in Northern and Western European waters from all causes including seizures, Soviet action and non-combat related factors.[26] Added to this was the destruction of at least another 135 barges and minor craft of unknown tonnage. Beyond direct losses, many additional ships were laid up for repairs or maintenance due to combat damage or normal operational wear. New construction and additional shipping attained from the occupied nations had failed to keep pace with this attrition. By January 1942 the amount of merchant tonnage readily available to Germany for trade and military maintenance purposes in Northwest European waters had dropped to 975,000 tons. Three months later this total dropped further to 882,000 tons.[27] When considering these shortfalls along with delays and increased turnaround times due to the threat of Allied attacks, Germany's cargo-carrying efficiency had declined by an estimated 19 percent from 1940 to 1942.[28]

In response to this deteriorating situation, the Germans created a Commissioner of Shipping in May 1942. Reporting directly to Hitler, this commissioner had extra-departmental powers for the oversight of Germany's merchant shipping administration and related shipbuilding industries. The man chosen to fill this position was Karl Kaufmann, a high-ranking Nazi official and the regional governor of Hamburg. Almost immediately, Kaufmann enacted a number of actions to increase shipping capacity. Paramount amongst these, he launched an initiative to comb through the Kriegsmarine to identify underutilised ships that could be returned to the merchant marine for trade duties. He likewise initiated a comparable exercise within Germany's deep-sea fishing fleet to find ships that were similarly suitable. Finally, he adopted a number of operational and administrative changes designed to enhance the existing fleet's efficiency including better space utilisation, streamlined shipping schedules, quicker turn-around times, expanded port facilities and support transportation, more port labour and reduced repair times.

To address the long-term problem, Kaufmann initiated a new building programme to expand the German merchant marine. Devised in two parts, this undertaking, which eventually became known as the *Hansa* Programme, called for the initial construction of 100 3,000-ton merchant ships followed by another 100 vessels weighing in at between 3,000 and 9,000 tons. Utilising simple designs to hasten the manufacturing process, the Germans placed the bulk of their new shipping orders with various Dutch and Danish yards, although a small portion of this construction was earmarked to be done in Germany. Operating with the full support of the Ministry of Armaments, the Germans allocated an additional quota of 15,000 tons of steel per quarter to implement this programme. Likewise, the Germans diverted labour and resources from naval to civilian construction. If all went according to plan, the Germans hoped to complete at least half of their initial order of *Hansa* ships by the end of 1943 with the programme fully concluded in 1945.

In addition to these commercial actions, the Kriegsmarine also stepped up efforts to defend German seaborne commerce with an increasing number of minesweepers and escort vessels. While the Germans rarely used destroyers or torpedo boats for defensive purposes, the use of M-class minesweepers was quite common. In addition to their prescribed purpose, these minesweepers were extensively used in an escort role. The Germans also used a smaller class of motor minesweepers referred to as R-boats. About the same size as E-boats, these R-boats performed a variety of duties beyond their minesweeping function. Augmenting these purpose-build combatants, the Germans also utilised a variety of auxiliary warships. These were civilian vessels converted to perform military applications. The most formidable of these were the *sperrbrechers*. Weighing in at several hundred to several thousand tons, these specially strengthened and heavily armed auxiliaries were earmarked to perform mine clearance and escort duties. The Germans augmented these *sperrbrechers* with

Table 5.1 Selected German Warships and Auxiliaries used for Defensive Purposes

Designation	Description
Minensuchboot M-class	Minesweeper/escort vessel. 550–700 tons. 1–2 × 4.1in guns and various light weapons.
Räumboot R-boat	Small motor minesweeper/escort vessel. 100–125 tons. Armed with various light weapons.
Sperrbrecher	Ex-merchant ships specially strengthened to serve as mine clearance/escort vessels. 500–8,000 tons. Armed with 88mm and smaller caliber guns.
KriegsUjäger UJ-boat	Ex-trawlers converted for anti-submarine use. 150–750 tons. Armed with light weapons and depth charges.
Vorpostenboot Vp-boat	Ex-trawlers converted for convoy escort duties. 150–750 tons. Armed with various caliber guns up to 88mm in size.
Artillerieträger A-boat	Gun barge. 300–400 tons. Armed with various caliber guns up to 88mm in size.
Kriegsfischkutter KFK-boat	Ex-drifters converted to serve as auxiliary minesweepers, harbor defense and local escort vessels. Up to 150 tons. Armed with various light weapons.

hundreds of lesser vessels that fell under numerous designations including UJ-boats (sub-chasers), Vp-boats (patrol boats), A-boats (artillery barges) and KFK-boats (harbour and local defence).

Against these various actions, the British continued their anti-shipping campaign. As had been the case during the previous year and a half, mines remained the most potent weapon in the British arsenal. In 1942 British mines sank 160 German-affiliated merchant ships worth 179,253 tons in Northern European waters. Additionally, these mines claimed 48 minor and auxiliary warships worth 27,455 tons, the destroyer *Bruno Heinemann* and the submarines *U253, U165, U446* and *U171*. Fifteen of these auxiliary vessels were *sperrbrechers*, reflecting the growing emphasis the Germans were putting on defence. Finally, these mines damaged 30 merchant ships and 33 military vessels worth a combined 198,047 tons.[29] Once again, air-laid mines were the primary perpetrators of these results accounting for over 90 percent of the total vessels sunk and damaged by Allied mines during this period. The cost in attaining these results amounted to 174 aircraft destroyed during minelaying operations.[30]

British successes by other means were less pronounced, but still significant. RAF action through direct attacks at sea and raids against ports accounted for the destruction of 44 merchant ships and 19 military vessels worth a combined 126,336 tons. Included in this total were the battlecruiser *Gneisenau* (the fate of which will be covered in Chapter 6) and the minesweeper *M26*. In addition, RAF/Allied aircraft destroyed 20 barges and a lighter of unspecified tonnage and damaged a further 38 merchant ships and military vessels worth 112,349 tons.[31] Meanwhile British/Allied submarines and surface warships added a further 61 naval and merchant vessels worth an estimated 62,792 tons sunk or captured during this period.[32] British motor torpedo boats accounted for many of these successes including the destruction of the German torpedo boats *Iltis* and *Seeadler* and the auxiliary cruiser *Komet*. Against these victories, the British paid a heavy cost which included 259 RAF aircraft lost during direct attack operations and the submarines *Jastrzab* (Polish), *P514*, *Unique*, and *Unbeaten* that were sunk in Northern or Western European waters in 1942.[33]

When combined together, the results of these various efforts continued to pressure Germany's overstretched shipping situation. In 1942 total German and German-affiliated merchant losses from all causes amounted to 196 cargo vessels worth a combined 441,708 tons along with 144 minor vessels worth 19,270 tons in European waters outside of the Mediterranean and Black Sea.[34] New construction under the *Hansa* Programme added only 17,282 tons of additional shipping from June through December of that year. Fortunately for the Germans, efforts to comb through the Kriegsmarine and deep-sea fishing fleet were more successful, netting a further 300,120 tons of shipping that could be used for trade purposes.[35] Likewise, other initiatives instituted by the German commissioner of shipping, Karl Kaufmann, attained positive results that improved operational efficiency and reduced the number of ships awaiting repairs. As a result, despite their losses, the Germans were able to increase the amount of merchant tonnage available for trade purposes to 1,051,000 tons by February 1943.[36] Still, because many of the actions that facilitated this recovery were one-time affairs or finite in their effectiveness, the Germans could expect their shipping availability to drop again unless they attained a reduction in losses and/or a meaningful influx of new construction.

Of course, the primary significance of this shipping situation was the extent to which it impacted Germany's overall trade volume and industrial output. In this, Germany suffered a 19.72 percent decrease in imports from Sweden and Norway from 1941 to 1942 (13,711,900 tons to 11,007,500 tons). Of the various commodities making up this shortfall, none was more important than iron ore, which experienced an 11.91 percent import reduction from 9,747,000 tons in 1941 to 8,586,100 tons in 1942. When compared to the beginning of the war, this decrease in Scandinavian iron ore was even more dramatic constituting a 22.94 percent decline since 1939. Other significant import shortfalls from 1941 to 1942 included a 43.23 percent reduction in timber, a 58.07 percent reduction in wood pulp, a 15.63 percent reduction in pyrites and a 31.72 percent reduction in non-ferrous metals.[37] The direct impact these various shortfalls had on German industrial output is difficult to measure, but one area that clearly suffered was crude steel production in the Ruhr, which decreased from a monthly average of 1,370,000 metric tons in 1939 to 1,150,000 metric tons in 1942 (a 16.06 percent reduction).[38]

In addition to Scandinavian imports, the Germans also made efforts to acquire certain essential resources not readily available in Europe. The primary means by which they attempted to do this was through the use of blockade-runners, which were generally merchant ships stranded in the Far East at the beginning of the war. Assisted by the Japanese and using deception and the vastness of the oceans to avoid detection, these blockade-runners attempted to return to the French Biscay ports with valuable cargoes of rubber, tin, tungsten, tea and other prized commodities. Excluding five vessels that turned back, a total of 26 blockade-runners attempted to journey from the Far East to Europe from January 1941 through April 1943. Of these, British warships and aircraft sank or forced the scuttling of six worth 44,663 tons, American warships captured one and sank one worth a combined 12,331 tons and German U-boats inadvertently sank two worth 10,237 tons. Those ships that did arrive delivered 104,600 tons of cargo out of 224,675 tons dispatched.[39] Thus, in terms of attrition, 38.46 percent of the ships and 53.44 percent of the cargo failed to arrive. During roughly the same period the Germans dispatched 20 blockade-runners (excluding three that turned back) from occupied France to the Far East carrying manufactured goods, chemicals and oil. Of these, British warships forced the scuttling of two worth 15,143 tons, Allied warships accounted for two more worth 12,305 tons and one worth 7,021 tons was destroyed in an accidental explosion thus resulting in the delivery of 56,987 tons of cargo out of 66,369 tons dispatched.[40]

Of course, these vessels represented a mere fraction of the Axis merchant ships that were located in the waters outside of Europe. Most of these vessels were outcasts from the beginning of hostilities, although some were purposely dispatched to serve as blockade-runners and support vessels for German raiders. From April 1940 through the end of the war at least 111 of these displaced merchant ships (both German and Italian) worth 724,051 tons came under Allied control as the various neutral nations they had taken refuge in progressively joined the Allied cause. Of those vessels that remained at large, the British and their Allied partners inflicted a steady stream of attrition. Including the Axis merchant ships already described as lost in this and previous chapters, British forces sank, captured or forced the scuttling of at least 41 German and 55 Italian merchant ships worth a combined 600,323 tons in the waters outside of Europe and the Mediterranean from May 1940 through December 1942. During the same period Allied warships accounted for another five German merchant ships worth 29,518 tons. Meanwhile, from 1940 through 1943 12 German and six Italian merchant ships worth 103,442 tons scuttled themselves to avoid seizure by Allied and neutral authorities in these outer areas. Finally, beyond these German and Italian vessels, British and Allied forces seized at least 34 Vichy French merchant ships worth 221,024 tons and sank or forced the scuttling of 14 more worth 63,469 tons while further seizing 18 Finnish and Romanian ships worth 57,545 tons (as the latter nations joined the Axis cause) in these same waters.[41]

Returning now to Europe, by the summer of 1942 Britain's offensive aspirations were growing in scope and showing signs of success. Still, British authorities realised that ultimate victory depended upon Britain and America's ability to return to occupied Europe and decisively defeat the German army in direct combat. In 1942 the Allies were far too weak to do this, but they still needed to make progress towards this end. As such, in August the Allies launched the largest raid yet attempted against occupied Europe. Under the designation of Operation *Jubilee*, the objective of this raid was to seize and hold the French port of Dieppe for a short duration of time. The purpose behind this was to assess the feasibility of such actions, gather intelligence from prisoners and captured materiel and test the German response to this intrusion. To carry this out, the British assembled an assault force ten times larger than that used in earlier raids consisting of 4,963 Canadian troops from the 2nd Canadian Division, 1,075 British commandos and 50 American rangers.[42] The naval contingent transporting this force consisted of 252 vessels centred upon the landing ships *Prince Albert, Princess Beatrix, Invicta, Queen Emma, Princess Astrid, Glengyle, Prince Charles, Prince Leopold* and *Duke of Wellington* along with 179 assorted landing craft. The destroyers *Calpe, Garth, Berkeley, Albrighton, Bleasdale, Brocklesby, Slazak* (Polish) and *Fernie* made up the primary escort while 15 minesweepers, 39 coastal craft and two miscellaneous vessels rounded out the force.[43] Finally, 74 squadrons of aircraft, mostly from the RAF, supported the undertaking.

On the evening of 18 August these various forces departed Britain from five different ports between Southampton and Newhaven to begin their trek to Dieppe. At 0348 hours the next morning the vessels on the eastern flank inadvertently encountered a German convoy, and a brief battle ensued during which the German escort *UJ1404* was sunk. Unfortunately, this encounter delayed and disorganised the British assault and gave the Germans warning of their approach. When the Allied forces landed within the next hour and a half, they encountered withering fire from the 1,500 German defenders of the 571st Infantry regiment. While the landings on the flanks achieved varying degrees of success, the main assault against the centre stalled as heavy enfilading fire pinned the troops down on the beach and prevented the supporting tanks from penetrating into the town. The accompanying naval forces did what they could to provide fire support, but since destroyers constituted their most powerful warships, their gunfire was generally ineffective against the built-up German defences. Despite their best efforts, the assault forces were unable to make appreciable progress, and at 1050 hours a withdrawal was ordered. This proved to be a difficult undertaking given the heavy German fire, and large numbers of men had to be abandoned.

Upon their return to Britain, the Allies assessed the results of the raid. In human and materiel terms, Operation *Jubilee* had been a costly failure. Allied casualties for the operation numbered 4,250 men including 1,181 killed and 2,144 taken prisoner. Materiel losses included the destroyer *Berkeley*, which was crippled by German bombers and subsequently scuttled, 33 landing craft and small vessels, 29 tanks and 106 aircraft. Against this, the Germans suffered 591 casualties including 311 killed and missing and three small vessels and 48 aircraft destroyed.[44] Beyond these tangible results, the long-term legacy for the raid was more beneficial. In particular, the British learned a number of valuable lessons that would pay dividends during subsequent operations. This included the need for far heavier fire support, improved shore-to-sea communications and specialised equipment for overcoming defensive obstacles. The Allies also learned the folly of directly assaulting strongly defended built-up areas. Finally, the raid exposed Allied inadequacies and faulty thinking that would help them adopt more realistic strategies for the conduct of the war.

Looking at the bigger picture, raids like Operation *Jubilee* and other related actions transformed the Allied war effort from one that was predominately defensive in nature to one that was increasingly offensive in its purpose and application. Through a variety of means, the British were exacting a steady stream of attrition against the Germans that was slowly debilitating their maritime and industrial capabilities and forcing them to expend greater resources on their own defence. In the same light, these actions helped instil an offensive spirit within the Allied ranks that was destined to grow into a torrent. Finally, these actions provided a modicum of relief to the hard-pressed Soviets during a time when more substantial support was impractical. Ever so slowly, the tide of the war was changing, and it was only a matter of time before the Allies once again returned to Europe in a much more forceful and permanent manner. This would first occur in the Mediterranean and then later in Northwest Europe. Until then, Britain would continue its ongoing assault against Germany's maritime assets and commercial trade with increasing effectiveness and vigour.

Table 5.2 Axis Military and Commercial Surface Ships sunk, captured or destroyed in European Waters outside of the Mediterranean and Black Sea (Number of Ships / Tonnage)

	Mines laid by Allied aircraft and naval vessels	Allied air attacks against ships and ports	Allied naval/ submarine actions and seizures	Soviet actions, scuttlings, accidents and other causes	Total
Military					
1939	1/361	1/248	2/1,196	5/2,432	9/4,237
1940	27/19,310	7/8,669	25/53,628	12/10,643	71/92,250
1941	13/11,705	15/4,206	13/45,234	34/13,071	75/74,216
1942	49/29,725	19/40,345	19/22,309	43/12,090	130/104,469
Commercial					
1939	-	-	22/98,508	16/24,496	38/123,004
1940	104/96,619	146/22,996	121/466,762	46/90,171	417/676,548
1941	51/50,652	56/86,402	69/156,472	69/159,437	245/452,963
1942	160/179,253	65/85,991	43/41,106	72/154,628	340/460,978

Note: The geographical area covered in this table consists of the waters from Archangel in the north to Gibraltar in the south, including the Baltic, and stretching out 350 miles to the west of the European coastline. Military losses include surface warships and naval auxiliary vessels. Commercial losses include civilian merchant ships and minor vessels such as tugs, fishing trawlers, harbor craft and barges. Included in these figures are a number of minor vessels of unknown, but presumably minimal tonnage.

CHAPTER 6

The Battle Intensifies

Hitler's abrupt declaration of war against the United States in December 1941 came as an unwanted surprise for most of Germany's senior leadership. Already heavily engaged with the various forces of the Soviet Union and British Commonwealth, the Germans now found themselves confronted by a new and powerful adversary. It would take time before America's substantial power could be brought to bear, but the long-term ramifications were clearly worrisome. While this reality was understood in the Kriegsmarine, naval authorities took some satisfaction in knowing that they were finally free to strike back against the Americans. Although technically neutral, from almost the beginning of the war the United States had tilted its moral and materiel support towards the Allied cause. As time went on, this support became increasingly tangible, and in the last few months of 1941 the United States had become an active partner in Allied convoy operations. Yet, despite these belligerent actions, the United States had enjoyed relative immunity from German retaliation. Now with the declaration of war, the facade of American neutrality was lifted, and the Kriegsmarine was finally free to fight back.

A key beneficiary of this was Admiral Dönitz, who had long considered the prospect of attacking the vast concentrations of shipping present in the waters off America's eastern seaboard. Along the entire length of the North American coastline and stretching into the Gulf of Mexico and Caribbean, ships of all applications and sizes travelled in support of the local economies or in conjunction with the assembly and dispersion of transatlantic convoys. Paramount amongst these were tankers transporting oil from production fields in the Southern United States, Venezuela and the Netherlands West Indies. The vast majority of these vessels sailed independently thus making them vulnerable targets. Until now, Hitler had denied authority to dispatch U-boats to this rich hunting ground for fear of giving the United States provocation for even greater involvement in the war. Now the opportunity was finally at hand for Dönitz to exploit this fertile area, assuming he could find the assets to do so.

This latter point was no small matter. The backbone of the U-boat fleet was the Type VII. This medium-sized submarine came in a number of variants, but typically weighed in at 740–749 tons, had a cruising range of 6,500 miles at 12 knots or 8,500 miles at 10 knots and carried 12–14 torpedoes. With the closest German bases in the French Biscay ports located some 3,000 miles from New York and 4,000 miles from Florida, these boats simply lacked the range to effectively operate off the American coastline without the benefit of mid-ocean refuelling. The Germans did possess a larger U-boat, the Type IX, which had a cruising range of 11,000 miles at 12 knots or 13,450 miles at 10 knots thus making it a viable option for operations off the United States, but these boats only existed in limited numbers. To this end, at the close of 1941 Dönitz possessed a total of 91 operational U-boats of which only a handful were Type IX variants. Of these, 33 were in dockyards undergoing maintenance or repairs while 33 more were assigned to service within the Mediterranean, west of Gibraltar or off the coast of Norway. Many of the boats that remained were already dispatched in the Atlantic or traversing to and from their patrol areas.[1] As such, Dönitz could only find five U-boats immediately available for service off the Americas. Fortunately for him, these all happened to be Type IXs.

Utilising these five boats, Dönitz commenced Operation *Paukenschlag* (Drumroll) during the latter half of December 1941. Proceeding from the French Biscay ports, *U123*, *U130*, *U66*, *U109* and *U125* began individual treks across the Atlantic to take up patrol stations on America's eastern seaboard. After largely uneventful crossings, these boats arrived in American waters by mid-January to encounter an abundance of targets operating under peacetime conditions with virtually no protection. After months of chasing elusive convoys in the face of growing British defences, the Germans wasted little time in exploiting these newfound fortunes. Within a matter of days, Operation *Paukenschlag*'s original five Type IX U-boats sank 23 merchant ships worth 150,505 tons. Meanwhile, during the same period a number of Type VII U-boats added a further 18 merchant ships worth 85,374 tons sunk in the waters around Newfoundland and Nova Scotia.[2] The Germans attained these successes for no losses to themselves.

While these initial results were impressive, they only represented the beginning of a long and productive campaign. Even before the first wave of U-boats arrived in American waters, Dönitz deployed additional U-boats to follow-up this initial assault. Thereafter, bolstered by the subsequent flood of positive reports, Dönitz dispatched a steady succession of submarines to operate in these fertile hunting grounds. He did this by diverting nearly all offensive U-boat activity in the Atlantic to operations off the North American coastline. From January through March a total of 70 attack boats departed for these waters. Of these, the Type IXs operated as far south as the Caribbean while the shorter-range Type VIIs generally limited their patrols to the sea-lanes off Newfoundland and Nova Scotia. Despite the passage of time, each successive wave found favourable conditions similar to those encountered in January, and the tally of Allied shipping losses continued to rise. Together, the January through March boats sank a total of 203 merchant ships worth 1,151,506

Among the numerous threats arrayed against the British in the maritime struggle, none was more daunting than the German U-boat arm. The Type VII (left) and Type IX (right) models pictured here were the mainstays of the German U-boat fleet. (No 5 Army Film; Photographic Unit, Tanner (Lt), public domain)

tons.[3] Against this, only four of the involved U-boats were sunk through March (*U82* and *U587* by British destroyers and *U656* and *U503* by American aircraft), constituting an exchange rate of 51 merchant ships sunk for each U-boat casualty.[4] Not surprisingly, German submariners quickly dubbed this period the 'second happy time'.

A number of factors contributed to this Allied calamity, nearly all of which fell squarely upon the shoulders of the United States. Despite nearly two and a half years of conflict during which the United States had played an increasingly active role, the Americans were surprisingly unprepared when the war finally came to their shores. First, despite the abundant lessons learned during World War I and by British experiences in the current conflict, the Americans had no provisions in place to establish a coastal convoy system. As such, nearly all merchant traffic travelling along America's eastern seaboard did so in an independent manner. With the advent of war, these vessels continued to use peacetime transit routes, display navigation lights and practice open radio procedures that increased their stature for detection. Likewise, American authorities failed to enact a coastal blackout thus assisting U-boat navigation and target location. Regarding this latter point, a favourite nocturnal tactic used by U-boat commanders was to silhouette their targets against the glow of cities, lighthouses and other coastal light sources.

An equally important factor contributing to Germany's 'second happy time' was the inadequate defence put forth by America's naval and airborne forces. The area primarily impacted by Operation *Paukenschlag* was designated the North Atlantic Naval Coastal Frontier by the United States Navy. Falling under the jurisdiction of Rear-Admiral Adolphus Andrews, this region, soon to be re-designated the Eastern Sea Frontier, encompassed the First, Third, Fourth and Fifth Naval Districts covering some 1,500 miles of coastline from the Canadian border to South Carolina. Against this vast expanse of territory, Admiral Andrews possessed a mere 20 assorted cutters, gunboats and patrol craft to provide protection for the multitude of vessels traversing these waters each day. Making matters worse, none of these vessels were ideally suited for anti-submarine operations due to their advanced age, marginal speeds and/or inadequate armament. In addition to these scanty naval assets, Andrews also had access to about 100 aircraft. Unfortunately, most of these were of limited capability and suffered from poor serviceability rates. Inadequate training and muddled command relationships further degraded the effectiveness of these aircraft as anti-submarine weapons.

Heightening these deficiencies was the intransigence and poor judgment displayed by key American leaders in response to this situation. From the onset of Operation *Paukenschlag*, British officials warned their American counterparts about the oncoming dispatch of German U-boats and lobbied for the institution of prudent countermeasures including a coastal convoy system. Sadly, most of these warnings and recommendations fell upon deaf ears. In particular, Admiral Ernest King, the US Chief of Naval Operations and Commander-in-Chief of the United States Fleet, refused to acquiesce on the matter of convoys claiming a lack of available escorts as his justification. In his opinion, a poorly defended convoy was worse off than no convoy at all. Unfortunately, this stance was at variance with British experience, and Admiral King's lack of escort vessels was partially a matter of his own making. Destroyers were available in the American Atlantic Fleet, but Admiral King stubbornly refused to release them for local defence. In many cases, American destroyers sat idly in port for days while U-boats ravaged shipping in the adjacent waters. So brazen did the U-boats become that they routinely operated in sight of major American cities with little fear of retaliation for their actions.

Not surprisingly, the British were greatly distressed by this growing calamity. It seemed particularly galling that in many cases the British and Canadians, with American participation, were able to safely convoy merchant ships across the Atlantic only to see them destroyed on America's doorstep. The British also lamented the fact that so many of these losses came in the form of tankers. During the first quarter of 1942 tankers made up 49 percent of the tonnage sunk by German and Italian submarines.[5] This was no accident since the Germans classified tankers as high priority targets and purposely sought them out from the myriad of vessels they encountered. In response to this dire situation, the British offered help to their beleaguered ally. Notwithstanding their own limited resources and worldwide commitments, in March the British assigned ten corvettes and 24 anti-submarine trawlers to perform defensive duties in American waters. Later, they transferred a Coastal Command squadron to the United States and assumed escort responsibility for convoys in the Caribbean and on the Aruba to New York tanker run. Finally, British technical missions provided advice and expertise regarding a number of issues including command and control, anti-submarine doctrine and weapons development.

While the carnage off America's Atlantic coast caused great concern, the British had reason for angst closer to home. For months the battlecruisers *Scharnhorst* and *Gneisenau* and the heavy cruiser *Prinz Eugen* had idly languished in the French Biscay port of Brest. In January 1942 Hitler directed these valuable warships to break out of Brest and return to Germany for subsequent reassignment to Norway. While the prospect of doing this was fraught with danger, the commander of the German Brest squadron, Vice-Admiral Otto Ciliax, determined that his best chance for success lay in a high-speed dash through the English Channel. Accordingly, the Germans immediately made plans and began assembling escort vessels to support this undertaking, which was designated Operation *Cerberus*. It was during this assembly process that the German destroyer *Bruno Heinemann* sank on a British-laid mine west of Ostend (as outlined in Chapter 5). For their part, the British observed this build-up and correctly surmised that a breakout attempt was its ultimate purpose. They further predicted that the breakout would proceed through the English Channel and made preparations accordingly to counter this attempt. This included the re-deployment of selected warships, placing Bomber Command at a heightened level of readiness and increasing Coastal Command surveillance of the southwestern approaches.

At 2245 hours on the evening of 11 February *Scharnhorst* (Flag), *Gneisenau*, *Prinz Eugen*, six destroyers and several minor vessels departed Brest to begin their dash up the Channel. Although the British had anticipated this move for weeks, the timing came as a surprise since they had expected the Germans to begin their sortie during the day to facilitate a nocturnal passage through the Straits of Dover. Sadly, British patrol aircraft failed to discover this movement due to inclement weather and technical problems with their ASV radar sets. As such, the German squadron proceeded undetected for 12 hours. Finally, at 1045 hours on the 12th British shore-based radar detected the force 27 miles southwest of Cap Gris Nez, and reconnaissance aircraft confirmed the presence of the German heavy ships 25 minutes later. By this time the German squadron had already progressed over 80 percent of its way through the English Channel and was now only an hour's steaming time from the Dover narrows. As such, the British found themselves at a great disadvantage as they scrambled to react to this surprising and unwelcome news.

Hampered by inclement weather as well as this tardy notification, various British elements began a series of disjointed attacks against the transiting German warships, which now included 14 torpedo boats from the 2nd, 3rd and 5th Flotillas. The first of these occurred at 1219 hours when the coastal batteries at Dover engaged the squadron at long range using radar fire control. For the next 17 minutes these guns fired 33 rounds but failed to score any hits. While this was underway five British motor torpedo boats from Dover and six Swordfish torpedo bombers attempted to attack the squadron. In both cases the attacks failed due to the heavy German defences, and in terms of the latter, all six torpedo bombers were shot down with the loss of 13 out of 18 crewmen involved. Despite this unsuccessful outcome, British authorities later recognised the great gallantry displayed by these aircrews in the face of overwhelming opposition, and the flight leader, Lieutenant-Commander E. Esmonde, was awarded a posthumous Victoria Cross. Meanwhile, a follow-up attack by three motor torpedo boats from Ramsgate also ended in failure, and in the early afternoon the German squadron emerged unscathed out of the English Channel.

Up until now, everything had gone exceedingly well for the Germans, but danger still loomed ahead. At 1431 hours *Scharnhorst* struck a mine while travelling at reduced speed through the Ruytingen Narrows. The blast left the battlecruiser temporarily immobilised and without power. Unfortunately, the British failed to take advantage of this vulnerability, and within 30 minutes *Scharnhorst* was underway again. A primary reason for this was the RAF's slow and uncoordinated response to the unexpected discovery of the German squadron in the eastern English Channel. It took until mid-afternoon before RAF bombers joined the battle, and then their efforts were severely hampered by harsh weather conditions including rain squalls, visibility down to less than a mile and cloud ceilings below 1,000 feet. From 1445 to 1700 hours Bomber Command dispatched 242 aircraft against the German ships, but only 39 of these actually succeeded in carrying out attacks. At roughly the same time Coastal Command sent out 35 Beaufort and Hudson aircraft while Fighter Command flew 398 related sorties. Together these aircraft sank the 292-ton patrol vessel *Vp1302* and damaged the torpedo boats *T13* and *Jaguar*, but failed to cause any appreciable damage to the main German ships. A similar result occurred when the British destroyers *Campbell*, *Mackay*, *Vivacious*, *Worcester* and *Whitshed* launched a long-range torpedo attack against the superior German force. Despite their valiant efforts, these destroyers failed to score any hits, and *Worcester* sustained heavy damage from the return fire.

By nightfall the German squadron, now substantially dispersed, had reached the Dutch coast and was steaming north-north-east on the final leg of its journey. Yet despite its substantial progress, danger still lurked ahead. At 1955 hours *Gneisenau* struck a British air-laid mine off Vlieland. Fortunately for the Germans, damage to the battlecruiser was minor, and *Gneisenau* was able to continue on at 25 knots with *Prinz Eugen* in company. One hour and 39 minutes later *Scharnhorst*, which was travelling well behind *Gneisenau*, struck a similar mine in the same area. In this case, damage was far more substantial as *Scharnhorst*'s engines once again failed and the great ship helplessly drifted for 49 minutes. Eventually damage control parties restored propulsion, and the wounded battlecruiser limped along at 12 knots arriving at Wilhelmshaven on the morning of the 13th with 1,000 tons of water in its hull. For their part, *Gneisenau* and *Prinz Eugen* arrived at the Elba estuary that same morning thus concluding Operation *Cerberus*.

With this outcome, both sides evaluated the results and implications of the German movement. In materiel terms, Operation *Cerberus* cost the Germans *Vp1302* and 17 aircraft destroyed while the destroyer *Bruno Heinemann* and the 425-ton auxiliary minesweeper *M1208* were sunk on mines during its run-up.[6] A number of German ships, including both battlecruisers, sustained damage to varying degrees. By comparison, the British lost 42 aircraft and the destroyer *Worcester* was heavily damaged.[7] These aircraft losses on both sides reflected the heavy aerial combat that took place over the German warships. In psychological terms, Operation *Cerberus* was clearly a tactical and moral victory for the Germans and a major disappointment and embarrassment for the British. In terms of the latter, British newspapers editorialised the channel dash as a great affront to British naval prestige. Yet, notwithstanding these tactical and psychological considerations, Operation *Cerberus* also represented a strategic reversal for the Kriegsmarine. By retreating to Germany for subsequent re-deployment to Norway, the German surface fleet was less-ideally positioned to menace Allied convoys in the Atlantic. Likewise, this move signalled a shift away from offensive thinking to a posture that was far more defensive in its application.

Nor was this action to go without prompt retribution. On 23 February the British submarine *Trident* torpedoed *Prinz Eugen* as the latter was proceeding to Norway with the pocket battleship *Admiral Scheer* and five destroyers. Losing its stern to a single torpedo, the badly damaged heavy cruiser returned to port to undergo extensive repairs. Thereafter, *Prinz Eugen* transferred to the Baltic Training Squadron and would never again venture out to oppose the Western Allies. Three nights later 49 RAF bombers attacked Kiel. At the time *Gneisenau* was in a floating dock undergoing repairs for the recent mine damage sustained during Operation *Cerberus*. Due to the anticipated short duration of these repairs, the Germans failed to unload *Gneisenau*'s ammunition, as was the normal practice. This omission was to cost them dearly. Hit by a single bomb that penetrated the ship's foredeck, the subsequent explosion and fire detonated ammunition stored in *Gneisenau*'s first (Anton) 11-inch gun turret. This caused a massive explosion that blew the turret off its bearings and devastated the whole forward section of the ship. With 112 dead and extensive internal damage, *Gneisenau*'s active career was over. Although moved to Gotenhafen to enact repairs, reconstruction progressed slowly and then was abandoned all together. In the end, *Gneisenau*'s gun turrets were removed for coastal defence duties, and the once proud battlecruiser was reduced to a derelict hulk that was ultimately sunk as a blockship. Thus, of the three major combatants that broke out of Brest, only *Scharnhorst* remained available to threaten the Western Allies.

While Operation *Cerberus* represented a great embarrassment for the British (as well as a strategic reversal for the Germans), events of a far greater consequence were also unfolding. On 1 February the Kriegsmarine added a fourth rotor to its Enigma code machines for radio communications with Atlantic and Mediterranean-deployed U-boats. This action increased by a factor of ten the possible number of combinations the Germans could use to encrypt and decrypt their messages. The result of this was an immediate breakdown in GC and CS' ability to decipher and read radio transmissions using this enhanced key, known as Triton by the Germans and Shark by the British. With the exception of a few short days, this cryptic blackout would stay in effect for most of the remaining year. By a cruel twist of fate, the loss of Triton coincided with a major German intelligence breakthrough when B-Dienst penetrated Britain's Naval Cypher No. 3, the primary code used by Allied naval forces in support of North Atlantic convoy operations. For most of the next year the Germans would have the ability to read large portions of this important signal traffic. Thus, with these two developments, the cryptic advantage the British had enjoyed during the latter half of 1941 was abruptly reversed. Since most U-boat activity was concentrated in American waters at the time, this reversal did not manifest immediate results, but this promised to change as soon as the battle switched back to the North Atlantic convoy routes.

As it was, it would be some time before this transition occurred since America's eastern and southern seaboards remained the centre of attention for U-boat opera-tions in April and May. During this period the Germans dispatched 48 U-boats to these contested waters. Once again, these boats found favourable conditions that they quickly exploited to deadly effect. Even intransigent American officials could not ignore the continuing level of destruction plaguing their coastline. Bolstered by British reinforcements and a growing assembly of American escort vessels, Admiral Andrews finally implemented a limited convoy system in April. Likened to a bucket brigade, this system consisted of informal groups of ships travelling together during the day and seeking shelter in protected anchorages at night. Supported by whatever escorts were available, these improvised convoys and daily hops were immediately effective in degrading German nocturnal operations off America's eastern coastline.

Further emphasising this point, on the night of 13/14 April the United States Navy scored its first Atlantic success when the destroyer *Roper* sank *U85* off Cape Hatteras. Three and a half weeks later the coast guard cutter *Icarus* sank *U352* in the same area.

As additional escorts became available, the Americans quickly formalised and expanded their rudimentary convoy system. This process was assisted by an Allied decision in mid-April to extend the time interval between convoys running from Halifax to the United Kingdom and back thus freeing two escort groups for North American service. Meanwhile, the Canadians were already running escorted convoys from Halifax to Boston. On 14 May the United States conducted its first uninter-rupted convoy from Hampton Roads to Key West. Over the next two weeks the Americans extended this coverage northward and created a continuous chain of convoys stretching from Halifax to Florida. By the beginning of June the vast bulk of Allied merchant shipping travelling along America's eastern seaboard did so in escorted convoys, and the era of abundant, easy targets in these waters came to an abrupt end.

The Germans responded to this changing situation by shifting the focal point of their operations further south to the Gulf of Mexico and the Caribbean where the American convoy system had yet to reach. A new innovation that helped them do this was the introduction of the U-tanker. Referred to as '*milch cows*' by the Germans, these U-tankers were U-boats designed to serve as refuelling and support vessels for their combatant counterparts. The first U-tanker was a 1,000-ton submarine, built on Turkish account, that was taken over by the Kriegsmarine and converted to carry 250 tons of diesel oil for refuelling purposes. Simply named *UA*, this boat first left Lorient on 14 March 1942 and successfully refuelled three Type VII U-boats in the Western Approaches. A fortnight later the first purpose-build Type XIV U-tanker, *U459*, made its operational debut. Displacing a surfaced weight of 1,688 tons and capable of carrying 432 tons of diesel oil as well as spare parts and other stores for re-supply purposes, *U459* proceeded to America's eastern seaboard where it refuelled 15 operational U-boats, including two Type IXs.

The introduction of these two U-tankers was only the beginning. Beyond the converted *UA*, the Kriegsmarine eventually commissioned 10 Type XIV U-tankers of which *U459* was the first. Likewise, a handful of Type XB minelaying U-boats were also converted to perform re-supply operations. Over the next four months the Germans dispatched four additional U-tankers on refuelling sorties to American waters, and at times two or three U-tankers were engaged in re-supply missions at the same time. The impact these logistical support boats had was immediate and profound. Ocean refuelling effectively doubled the endurance of the Type VII U-boats thus allowing them to extend their patrols as far south as Cape Hatteras while the longer-range Type IX U-boats were soon operating deep in the Gulf of Mexico as far west as the Mississippi River Delta and as far south as the northern coast of South America. With this, the Kriegsmarine expanded its offensive into areas previously beyond its reach and generally devoid of effective defence. As such, the 48 U-boats dispatched to American waters in April and May ultimately sank a combined 217 merchant ships worth 1,047,645 tons.[8]

The fighting continued in June and July as the Germans dispatched a further 40 U-boats to American waters. However, unlike the previous five months, these U-boats encountered increasingly difficult conditions as the Allies continued to improve and expand their defensive network. In particular, in June the Allies began implementing a convoy system within the Gulf of Mexico and Caribbean. Week by week the Allies incorporated more territory into this convoy system, and the Germans found it progressively more difficult to find unescorted targets. Eventually, the Allies established a fully interlocking convoy network that linked the western terminals of the transatlantic convoys with coastal routes proceeding along the entire eastern seaboard to the Gulf ports as well as Central and South America. In turn, these coastal routes ultimately supported the transfer of 7,546 convoys containing 49,680 ships through the duration of the war.[9] The immediate result of this was a 52 percent reduction in regional shipping losses as the U-boats dispatched to American waters in June and July only succeeded in sinking 103 vessels worth 497,892 tons.[10] Likewise, the Germans paid a significantly higher price for these results with six U-boats sunk in American waters during June and July. Of these, Allied warships sank *U157*, *U215* and *U153*; aircraft sank *U701* and *U754*; and aircraft and a warship combined to sink *U576*. Meanwhile, during the same period three U-boats were sunk en route to or from American waters (*U158* by American aircraft and *U502* and *U751* by British aircraft).

In July Admiral Dönitz realised that the advantages associated with Operation *Paukenschlag* had largely run their course. Therefore, in August he only earmarked a few U-boats to continue harassing shipping off Central and South America while the bulk of his force returned to the North Atlantic convoy routes. Due to the duration of these deployments, activities in American waters lasted into October, but Operation *Paukenschlag* was effectively over. During a nine-month period culminating in August the Germans dispatched 184 U-boats to American waters. Together, these U-boats sank a total of 609 vessels worth 3,122,456 tons.[11] Against this impressive total, the Germans lost 15 U-boats in American waters with a further seven U-boats sunk in transit. Included in these numbers were *U166*, *U654*, *U94*, *U162*, *U165*, *U512* and *U171*, which were all lost from August through October (three to American aircraft, two to British warships and two to mines). Thus, this 'second happy time' netted an exchange rate of 27.7 vessels and 141,930 tons of shipping sunk for each U-boat casualty.

While Operation *Paukenschlag* was the predominant component of the Kriegsmarine's offensive during this period, it was by no means the only component. During the first eight months of 1942 the Allies lost 1,240 merchant ships worth 5,426,652 tons in all theatres, including the Mediterranean and Pacific, due to enemy action.[12] Britain's portion of this toll amounted to 426 vessels worth 2,075,200 tons.[13] Of the total Allied loss, German and Italian submarines accounted for 780 vessels worth 3,964,211 tons of which over 78 percent were sunk in American waters.[14] Against this, the Germans lost the U-boats already mentioned plus *U93*, *U581*, *U252*, *U136*, *U90*, *U213* and *U588* that were all sunk by British warships in Atlantic operations not related to Operation *Paukenschlag*. The British sloop *Lulworth* and unknown causes also claimed the destruction of the Italian submarines *Pietro Calvi* and *Morosini* in the Central Atlantic and Bay of Biscay respectively. Japanese forces in the Pacific and Indian Oceans accounted for the bulk of the remaining Allied merchant losses. When broken down, this total loss equated to 678,331.5 tons of Allied or neutral shipping sunk per month. This was an almost threefold increase compared to the monthly average lost during the latter half of 1941 and came very close to the 700,000-ton threshold the Germans had originally calculated they would need to wear down the British merchant fleet.

Fortunately for the Allies, this tonnage calculation was grossly out of date based upon America's entry into the war. In 1939 the United States had possessed the world's second largest merchant fleet (behind Great Britain) consisting of 2,345 vessels worth 8,909,892 tons.[15] By the end of 1941 a further 1,937,090 tons of shipping had emerged from American shipyards.[16] During the same period about a million tons of shipping had been sold or transferred to Great Britain thus leaving the United States with about ten million tons of shipping within its merchant fleet at the beginning of 1942. In addition to this, when the United States entered the war, many Latin American countries followed suit thus further expanding the shipping pool available to the Allied cause. The entry of the United States and other American countries into the conflict also facilitated the seizure of some 111 German and Italian merchant ships worth almost 725,000 tons that had previously sought refuge in the then neutral American ports. Thus, by the beginning of 1942, the total amount of shipping available to the Allies stood at well over thirty million tons. While much of this tonnage was needed to support the conflict in the Pacific, the amount of shipping available for operations in the Atlantic had clearly improved.

A second major factor contributing to the growing irrelevance of Dönitz's original tonnage calculation was America's immense shipbuilding capacity. With the rapid mobilisation of America's vast economic and industrial power, the United States possessed unparalleled resources to produce new shipping at an unheard of pace. To this end, the Deputy Director of the United States Maritime Commission, Howard Vickery, publicly forecast that American shipyards would produce over 2,500 new merchant ships with a combined carrying capacity of 27.4 million deadweight tons (roughly 18 million gross registered tons) in 1942 and 1943.[17] When combined with expected output from British and Commonwealth shipyards, this meant that Axis forces would have to sink an average of nearly 900,000 tons of shipping each month just to compensate for the new Allied construction projected to be completed during this period. This requirement expanded to at least a million tons of shipping sunk each month if the Axis hoped to cause an even moderate reduction in the overall size of the combined Allied merchant fleet.

Of course, these developments only represented a portion of the advantages that America's entry into the war provided to Britain in its Atlantic struggle. In addition to merchant tonnage, the United States also provided a major influx of combat resources. In March 1942 Britain and the United States possessed a total of 383 and 122 assorted escort vessels respectively. This was against a projected requirement of 725 and 590 such vessels for each nation.[18] Fortunately, America's vast industrial power was also poised to help address these shortfalls. Among other things, American shipyards had orders for 300 escort vessels to be built on British account with 200 of these vessels expected to be completed by the end of 1943.[19] When added to production for the United States Navy as well as British and Commonwealth production, the Allied escort situation was poised for dramatic improvement. The same held true for nearly every category of weapon system as American industry expanded to become the arsenal of democracy. Increasingly, the United States Navy and United States Army Air Force (USAAF) were becoming full partners in the battle of the Atlantic while American-built ships, planes and other products augmented the resources of the various British and Allied services.

If the United States was a major maritime boon for the United Kingdom, the same could not be said for Britain's other principal ally, the Soviet Union. To the contrary, while the Soviets performed an essential task in tying down the bulk of the German army, this service came as a heavy burden to the Royal Navy and the Allied merchant marine. In particular, the British were compelled to continue their efforts to provide materiel aid to the hard-pressed Soviets through a series of increasingly larger Arctic convoys. This was no simple task given the many challenges confronting the Royal Navy at this time including the disaster unfolding in the Far East, the continuing struggle in the Mediterranean and the intensifying conflict in the Atlantic. Acquiring the necessary resources to carry out these convoys was a constant source of strain for British authorities. Likewise, these convoys represented extremely difficult and dangerous undertakings given the conditions arrayed against them including numerous hazards of both natural and manmade design.

The dangers associated with the Arctic convoys came in three major categories. To begin with, the convoys had to endure some of the world's harshest climatic conditions. In addition to the oppressive cold normally associated with these northern latitudes, the waters through which the convoys passed were prone to gales and blizzards of great intensity. Fog was often a problem due to the warmer waters of the Gulf Stream, which run in a northeastern direction along the Norwegian coast, mixing with the colder waters of the Arctic. This same factor created poor Asdic conditions that made submarine detection extremely difficult. Drift and pack ice were an ever-present danger that often caused delays and/or impacted convoy routing.

Finally, the high northern latitudes resulted in long periods of darkness during the winter and near-perpetual daylight in the summer. These two extremes facilitated differing challenges ranging from difficulty in maintaining convoy integrity during the long hours of darkness to an increased threat of detection and air attack during periods of perpetual light.

Geography and the routes the Arctic convoys were compelled to take constituted the second major challenge confronting the British. Departing from either Scotland or Iceland, these convoys faced a trek of about 2,000 miles before reaching their Russian destinations. Much of this journey was through a relatively narrow corridor formed by the polar ice fields in the west and north and the Norwegian coastline in the south and east. The size of this corridor fluctuated seasonally as the ice fields receded during the summer, allowing the convoys to make a more northerly passage, but expanded in the winter, forcing the convoys closer to German-held Norway. Anchorages and airfields dotted the length of the Norwegian coastline giving the Germans excellent bases from which to menace the passing convoys. As such, the Luftwaffe was capable of dominating 1,400 miles of the journey, while British shore-based air support was limited to bases no further north and east than Iceland and the Shetland Islands. For the bulk of the journey the convoys were compelled to pass through waters potentially dominated by the Luftwaffe with no protection other than their own inherent defences.

Relating to this, the third challenge facing the British was the opposition they would likely encounter from the Germans. While Hitler's decision to divert naval units to Norway was clearly a strategic error in the context of the overall maritime war, it had the benefit of providing Germany with ample means to attack the Arctic convoys. These means came in three forms. First, there was the U-boat arm, which constituted a threat for the entire length of each convoy's passage. Once the convoys came closer to Norway, they encountered the prospect of direct attacks from German warships ranging in size from destroyers to battleships. In these same waters, the convoys also faced the spectre of intervention from the Luftwaffe. By the beginning of 1942 the Luftwaffe had some 250 aircraft stationed in Norway. As time went on, this number was bolstered by additional reinforcements including air units specifically designated for anti-shipping operations. Thus, the British faced the prospect of attacks from a number of quarters including from the air and both above and below the waves.

To counter this substantial and comprehensive threat, the British were forced to commit extensive resources to the defence of each convoy. This included close escorts consisting of various combinations of minesweepers, trawlers, corvettes and destroyers to protect the convoys against U-boats, minor surface warships and air attacks. Covering forces consisting of heavier warships augmented these defensive arrangements to deal with the larger German surface threats. Often, these covering forces were split into close and distant contingents with the former including cruisers while the latter contained capital ships at their cores. In order to maintain superiority over any potential German foe, the British tried to send at least two battleships/ battlecruisers out with each distant covering force. When available, they also sent an aircraft carrier to provide fighter protection and strike capabilities. Thus, the dispatch of each Arctic convoy constituted a major fleet operation. To help mitigate this commitment, the British conducted their outward-bound PQ and homeward bound QP convoys simultaneously, but this added to the complexity of each undertaking. Finally, because of the limited facilities and resources available in Murmansk and Archangel, British ships were often compelled to carry the fuel, ammunition and supplies they would need for their return journeys. Likewise, extricating damaged vessels promised to be a difficult task.

Given the increased resources committed by both sides, it did not take long for the struggle in the Arctic to intensify. On 2 January 1942 the Allies suffered their first Arctic casualty when *U134* sank the 5,135-ton British merchant ship *Waziristan* from convoy PQ.7A. Fifteen days later *U454* sank the British destroyer *Matabele* from convoy PQ.8. After this, convoys PQ.9 through PQ.11 (along with concurrent QP convoys) progressed without incident. Unfortunately, this proved to be a lull before the storm as the Germans used this period to send substantial reinforcements to Norway including the battleship *Tirpitz*, the pocket battleship *Admiral Scheer* and a handful of destroyers. In early March the Germans dispatched *Tirpitz* and three destroyers to interdict convoys PQ.12/QP.8 (16 and 15 merchant ships respectively). Alerted to this movement by a submarine sighting, the British countered with a significantly stronger force including the battleships *King George V* and *Duke of York*, the battlecruiser *Renown* and the aircraft carrier *Victorious*. With these deployments, both sides braced for a potential surface action as the Germans sought to intercept one or both of the convoys while the British manoeuvred to bring *Tirpitz* into battle.

As it turned out, neither of these eventualities materialised. Hindered by poor weather and limited visibility, the German force, under the command of Admiral Ciliax, was unable to locate either of the British convoys, which passed each other off Bear Island on 7 March. The sole German success for the sortie was the destruction of a single straggler from QP.8, the 2,815-ton Soviet merchant ship *Ijora*. For their part, the British fleet, under the command of Admiral John Tovey, was equally unsuccessful in locating *Tirpitz* or its accompanying destroyers. Finally, with the assistance of radio intercepts, a reconnaissance aircraft from *Victorious* discovered *Tirpitz* off Vestfjord on the morning of the 9th as the latter was returning to base. A strike of 12 Albacore torpedo-bombers soon followed, but these aircraft failed to score any hits, and *Tirpitz* was able to divert to Narvik undamaged. Thus, both sides had reason for disappointment. Nevertheless, the British did gain a minor victory from the encounter as Hitler subsequently ordered *Tirpitz* not to put to sea when the possibility of interference from British carrier aircraft existed. As such, the Kriegsmarine's ability to utilise *Tirpitz* offensively was significantly restricted.

The next series of convoys, designated PQ.13 and QP.9 consisting of 19 merchant ships each, occurred at the end of March. Of the two, QP.9 fared the best with no losses sustained despite attempted interference from German U-boats. Further adding to this success, on 24 March the British minesweeper *Sharpshooter* sank *U655* off Bear Island as the latter was conducting operations against the convoy. The passage of PQ.13 was far more problematic as severe weather, U-boats, air attacks and German destroyers beset the hapless convoy. Four days after departing Reykjavik a fierce storm descended upon PQ.13 and scattered it over a 150-mile area. When the weather finally moderated on 27 March, not a single merchant ship was in contact with any of their escorts. On the same day German reconnaissance aircraft located some of these scattered vessels, and German forces proceeded into the area to pick off stragglers. In all, five merchant ships worth a combined 28,016 tons were sunk of which U-boats accounted for two, Luftwaffe aircraft accounted for two and the German destroyer *Z26* accounted for one. For their part, the Germans lost *U585*, which accidentally strayed into a German minefield north of Murmansk.

Meanwhile, on the morning of the 29th the British light cruiser *Trinidad* came upon the German destroyers *Z24*, *Z25* and *Z26* as the latter were searching for Allied merchant ships in the Barents Sea. Despite appalling weather conditions and limited visibility, *Trinidad* used radar to engage the German destroyers and scored disabling hits on *Z26* with its second salvo. As the battle progressed, *Trinidad* continued to pound *Z26* while the other two German destroyers hastily withdrew from the area. *Trinidad* then moved in to finish off the battered destroyer, but two of its torpedoes failed to leave their tubes while the third malfunctioned due to the intense cold and circled back to strike the British cruiser. Now heavily damaged itself, *Trinidad* was forced to leave the area, but the British destroyer *Eclipse* soon took its place to deliver the *coup de grâce* against *Z26*. After inflicting further damage, *Eclipse* also departed the area when *Z24* and *Z25* reappeared, but this intervention was too late to save the foundering destroyer, and *Z26* sank shortly thereafter. For its part, the heavily damaged *Trinidad* arrived in Murmansk the next day after a difficult passage.

By this time, the Admiralty was expressing increased apprehension regarding the continuation of Arctic convoys due to the lengthening hours of daylight and increased exposure to attack. The Germans had continued to send reinforcements to Norway including the heavy cruiser *Admiral Hipper* and additional destroyers. In the upcoming weeks the pocket battleship *Lützow* would also arrive in Norwegian waters. Despite these adversities, the political leadership in both London and Washington determined that the convoys must continue. Therefore, on 8 April PQ.14 departed Iceland with 24 merchant ships. Two days later the convoy encountered heavy ice further south than normal, and 16 merchant ships were forced to turn back to Iceland after becoming hopelessly scattered. Seven of the remaining ships continued their journey and arrived safely at Murmansk despite intermittent air attacks, but the eighth, the 6,985-ton *Empire Howard*, was sunk by *U403*. Meanwhile, the homeward-bound QP.10 had an equally difficult passage losing four of its 16 merchant ships to German attacks. Of these, Luftwaffe aircraft accounted for the 7,164-ton *Empire Cowper* and the 5,486-ton *Harpalion* while *U435* sank the 6,008-ton *El Occidente* and the 5,823-ton *Kiev*.

At the end of the month the next series of convoys occurred with equally deadly results. Of the 38 merchant ships making up PQ.15 and QP.11, only four worth a combined 18,655 tons were sunk in passage despite heavy attacks from German air, submarine and surface units. Unfortunately, this success came at a heavy cost for the escort and covering forces. First, on 1 May the destroyer *Punjabi* was sunk in an accidental collision with the battleship *King George V* in heavy fog off Iceland. As the destroyer sank, its ready-use depth charges exploded causing shock damage to the British battleship. The next day the British suffered a second accidental loss when the Polish-manned submarine *Jastrzab* (ex *P551*) strayed out of its designated patrol area and was sunk by escort vessels from PQ.15. Finally, on 30 April the British light cruiser *Edinburgh*, which was part of the close escort for QP.11, sustained torpedo damage from *U456*. Two days later German destroyers attacked the crippled British cruiser as it was being towed to Murmansk. Despite its heavily damaged state, *Edinburgh* savaged the lead German destroyer, *Hermann Schoemann*, with 6-inch gunfire. Sadly, this proved to be a last act of defiance as the remaining two German destroyers scored a single torpedo hit on *Edinburgh* as well as damage to two British destroyers. Thereafter, both sides disengaged to assist their distressed comrades, but *Edinburgh* and *Hermann Schoemann* both proved to be beyond salvation and had to be scuttled.

In the days and weeks that followed, the Allies continued to suffer a steady stream of losses in what the First Sea Lord, Admiral Dudley Pound, described as a 'regular millstone round our necks' and 'a most unsound operation with the dice loaded against us in every direction.'[20] On 14 May German aircraft attacked the cruiser *Trinidad*, which was homeward bound in the Barents Sea, and damaged it so severely that it had to be scuttled. A week later PQ.16 departed Hvalfjord with 35 merchant ships and proceeded into Luftwaffe-dominated waters during a period of near-perpetual daylight. Four days later (25 May) German reconnaissance aircraft located the convoy, and PQ.16 endured repeated air attacks for the next five days resulting in the destruction of six merchant ships (three British and three American) worth a combined 36,963 tons. Likewise, *U703* added a seventh victim when it sank the 6,191-ton American merchant ship *Syros*. The materiel losses associated with this tally amounted to 32,400 tons of cargo including 147 tanks, 77 aircraft and 770 vehicles.[21] On a positive note, the homeward-bound QP.12 made an uneventful passage with no losses sustained largely due to the German preoccupation with PQ.16.

It would be almost a month before the Allies attempted their next series of convoys. On 27 June PQ.17 departed Reykjavik with 36 merchant ships while at roughly the same time QP.13 departed Archangel and Murmansk with 35 merchant ships. The Allies assembled sizable assets to escort and cover these convoys including the battleships *Duke of York* and *Washington* (American), the aircraft carrier *Victorious*, six cruisers, 29 destroyers, eight corvettes, 15 submarines and various other vessels. In addition to *Washington*, a number of these cruisers and destroyers were also American, indicating the increased role the United States Navy was playing in Arctic operations. A reason for this extensive escort was intelligence indicating that the Germans intended to use *Tirpitz* and other heavy units to seek out and destroy PQ.17. In fact, this was exactly what the Germans hoped to do. Ignoring QP.13, the Germans focused all of their attention on PQ.17, and on 2 July they dispatched *Tirpitz, Admiral Hipper*, four destroyers and two torpedo boats from Trondheim to Altenfjord in Northern Norway. The next day a second German force consisting of the pocket battleships *Lützow* and *Admiral Scheer* and six destroyers departed Narvik to make a similar trek northward. As it turned out, these moves were marred when accidental groundings at Grimsöystraumen put *Lützow* and three of the destroyers out of action. Nevertheless, a powerful German force was poised to strike at PQ.17.

The Admiralty was generally aware of these movements through Ultra intelligence, but lacked specific information regarding the intentions and location of *Tirpitz*. They also knew that the Germans were tracking the progress of PQ.17, which had already had several encounters with U-boats and Luftwaffe aircraft. On the evening of the 4th the British learned that both *Tirpitz* and *Admiral Scheer* had arrived at Altenfjord as of 0900 hours that morning, but this information was several hours old and still left open the question of whether these vessels had re-sailed or were still in port. Additional Ultra intercepts failed to provide any conclusive information regarding this matter, and at about 2100 hours Admiral Pound assumed the worst-case scenario and proceeded on the assumption that *Tirpitz* was at sea and closing on the convoy. Accordingly, the Admiralty dispatched instructions for the covering cruiser force to withdraw westward and for the convoy to scatter. As it turned out, *Tirpitz* was not at sea and did not sail until the next day only to be hastily recalled.

Unfortunately, by the time this information became known to the British, it was too late to avert the disaster that was about to befall the convoy. The scattering of PQ.17 reduced the convoy to a collection of isolated and largely undefended ships that the Germans were quick to exploit. For the next five days swarms of U-boats and aircraft attacked the disorganised convoy, picking off victims one by one in what became a near slaughter. In the end, 24 of the 36 merchant ships that had set out from Reykjavik were sunk. Of these, all but three were sunk after the convoy had scattered. In materiel terms, this amounted to 142,695 tons of shipping sunk along with the loss of 430 tanks, 210 aircraft, 3,350 vehicles and 99,316 tons of related military stores and equipment.[22] Put into the context of a land battle, this constituted a major military defeat. Adding insult to injury, QP.13, which had largely avoided interference from the Germans, strayed into an Allied minefield in

Despite ongoing campaigns in the Atlantic, Mediterranean and Indian Ocean, the British embarked upon a series of difficult Arctic convoys to assist their Soviet allies in the spring and summer of 1942. Pictured here is an assembly of vessels in Hvalfjord, Iceland for convoy PQ.17. (Ware C. J. (Lt), Royal Navy official photographer, public domain)

the Denmark Straits on 5 July resulting in the destruction of five merchant ships worth 30,909 tons and the minesweeper *Niger*. Total German losses for the convoy battle amounted to just five aircraft.

Following the disaster of PQ.17, the Allies waited two months before attempting the next series of convoys. During the interim, the British destroyers *Martin*, *Marne* and *Onslaught*, which were en route back to the United Kingdom from Russia, intercepted and sank the German minelayer *Ulm* (3,071 tons) south of Bear Island on 25 August. This small victory largely eliminated the German mining threat from the region. Then on 2 September PQ.18 departed Lock Ewe in Scotland with 40 merchant ships. The convoy initially proceeded to Iceland where it rendezvoused with its escort before continuing on to Russia. The British provided PQ.18 with a particularly strong close escort that included the newly completed escort carrier *Avenger*, the anti-aircraft cruiser *Scylla* and 20 destroyers. Embarked upon *Avenger* were 12 Sea Hurricane fighters for convoy defence and three Swordfish torpedo-bombers for anti-submarine operations. Six additional Hurricanes were stowed disassembled within *Avenger* to be used as replacement aircraft. Thus, although limited in size, this air group gave

PQ.18 its own organic air cover, which was a first for an Arctic convoy.[23] Likewise, *Scylla* and the accompanying destroyers were capable of putting up heavy volumes of anti-aircraft fire if called upon to do so. This was a likely scenario since the Admiralty estimated that the Luftwaffe possessed 65 torpedo-bombers and 120 bombers for possible use against the convoy. In fact, this was an underestimate since the Germans actually possessed 92 torpedo-bombers within the area.[24]

The first few days of PQ.18 passed without undue incident, and the British were able to score a minor victory when the destroyer *Faulknor* sank *U88* near Bear Island on the 12th. However, this good fortune changed the next day when the convoy experienced a series of deadly mishaps. First, at 0855 hours a combined attack by three German U-boats sank two merchant ships from the convoy's starboard column.[25] Later in the day the convoy experienced a number of air attacks. Of these, the most serious occurred at 1530 hours when some 40 Luftwaffe torpedo-bombers carried out a low-level attack against the convoy. This attack was aided by two factors. First, *Avenger*'s fighters were out of position to interdict it due to their preoccupation with shadowing aircraft and high-altitude bombers. Second, when the convoy commander, Rear-Admiral E. K. Boddam-Whetham, ordered a 45-degree turn to starboard to render a reduced posture to the attack, the starboard columns failed to comply thus presenting themselves as ideal targets for the oncoming Luftwaffe aircraft. The Germans were quick to exploit these mistakes and carried out a devastating torpedo attack resulting in the destruction of eight merchant ships in a matter of minutes. Heavy German attacks continued over the next few days, but improved British tactics frustrated most of these efforts. In all, only three more merchant ships were sunk, while British destroyers sank *U589* and *U457* and British fighters and anti-aircraft fire took a heavy toll on attacking German aircraft.

When it was over, the Allies had reason to be satisfied with the results of PQ.18. Overall, the convoy lost 13 merchant ships worth a combined 75,657 tons. While this still represented a heavy toll, it was significantly less than the losses suffered during PQ.17. The British were also able to inflict a far heavier price upon their attackers than in the previous convoy battle. In addition to the three U-boats that were sunk, four more sustained serious damage. More importantly, the Luftwaffe lost 41 aircraft in operations against PQ.18. These losses, plus the transfer of aircraft to the Mediterranean, reduced the Luftwaffe's strength in Norway to the point where it would never again be able to repeat the same scale of attacks against subsequent Arctic convoys. Thus, despite its heavy losses, and the losses sustained during the concurrent QP.14 which consisted of four merchant ships worth 20,769 tons, the destroyer *Somali* and the minesweeper *Leda* (all sunk by U-boats), PQ.18 represented a turning point victory for the Allies. Nevertheless, it would be a few months before the Allies attempted their next Arctic convoy due to commitments in the Mediterranean.

With operations in the Arctic paused, the struggle in the Atlantic intensified as Dönitz progressively refocused his U-boat campaign against the Allied convoy routes. In this, Dönitz benefitted from having significantly greater resources than during earlier onslaughts into the North Atlantic. In July 1942 Germany had 331 U-boats in commission of which 140 were on operational status. Of the remaining 191 boats that were in training or working up, most would be operational by the end of the year.[26] Likewise, U-boat production was now averaging about 20 new boats per month thus proceeding at a pace that far exceeded the current rate of losses. Of those U-boats on operational status, 91 were stationed in the French Biscay ports and were thus fully available for operations in the Atlantic. Meanwhile, a further 23 U-boats were located in Norway and were available to participate in Atlantic operations on at least a limited basis.[27] Therefore, unlike the previous year when only a handful of U-boats were typically available to operate against the Allied convoys at any given time, Dönitz was now positioned to engage these same convoys with a few dozen U-boats on a fairly regular basis. As time went on, it seemed likely that this numerical advantage would increase assuming U-boat losses remained relatively constant.

Augmenting this growing U-boat force were two other factors that promised to benefit Dönitz's renewed offensive into the North Atlantic. The first of these was the advantage that Germany had recently attained in the area of naval intelligence. With Germany breaking Britain's Naval Cypher No. 3, which was used jointly by the British, Canadians and Americans to conduct convoy operations in the North Atlantic, B-Dienst was now able to provide Dönitz with a steady flow of actionable intelligence regarding the timing and routing of these Allied convoys. As well as this, Germany's introduction of the four-rotor Triton key had effectively blocked GC and CS' ability to decipher and read U-boat radio traffic, making it exceedingly more difficult to route convoys away from U-boat concentrations. As such, the Germans were in a far better position to find and engage the Allied convoys than they had been in 1941 while the British were in a far worse position to be able to avoid these attacks or shift resources to meet them.

The second factor complementing this advantage was the increasing number of *milch cow* U-tankers that were coming into service. By utilising these U-tankers to conduct refuelling at sea, the Germans were able to substantially extend the patrol times and reach of their U-boats. This gave the Type VIIs the ability to effectively operate throughout the North Atlantic while the Type IXs could reach into the South Atlantic and Indian Ocean. This provided a number of advantages to the Germans. First, with their increased endurance, the U-boats were able to stay on station longer thus improving their chances of locating and engaging the Allied convoys. This also gave the U-boats the ability to operate far from land thus reducing their exposure to detection and attack from shore-based aircraft. Finally, by dispatching a handful of Type IX U-boats to operate in distant waters, the Germans induced the Allies to maintain a broad defence that prevented them from solely concentrating their resources in the North Atlantic.

Fortunately for the Allies, they too enjoyed a number of quantitative and qualitative improvements that would help them meet this renewed offensive. First, by the end of July the Allies possessed a total of 97 destroyers, 26 sloops, 167 corvettes and 54 other vessels assigned to escort duty in the Atlantic.[28] While this combined number of 344 warships fell short of the requirements set forth earlier in the year, it still represented a sizable force to be reckoned with. If necessary, the Allies could draw reinforcements from the large numbers of destroyers and escort vessels assigned to the Mediterranean, Pacific and Indian Oceans. The bulk of these warships were divided into three commands: the Canadian Western Local Escort Force (WLEF), the Allied Mid-Ocean Escort Force (MOEF) and the British Eastern Local Escort Force (ELEF). The WLEF, which consisted of both British and Canadian warships, escorted convoys in Canadian waters to and from the Western Ocean Meeting Point (WESTOMP). From there, warships of the MOEF operating out of Newfoundland and Londonderry escorted convoys between the WESTOMP and the Eastern Meeting Point (EASTOMP). Finally, the ELEF escorted the convoys between the EASTOMP and the United Kingdom.

While the vast bulk of the warships in the WLEF, MOEF and ELEF were British or Canadian, the Allies were soon to open a second major transit route that would be predominantly an American affair. Created to support operations in the Mediterranean, this route was located in the more southerly latitudes of the Middle Atlantic. Fast and slow convoys outbound from the United States to Gibraltar were designated UGF and UGS convoys respectively while the reverse were designated GUF and GUS. Established in the late autumn of 1942 and lasting for the duration of the European war, this Middle Atlantic convoy route became the major link between the United States and Allied forces serving in the Mediterranean theatre and eventually supported the passage of 11,795 merchant ships to and from the region.[29] Thus, while the British and Canadians maintained primary responsibility for the North Atlantic, the Middle Atlantic became an American area of responsibility. Accordingly, within a few months increasing numbers of American destroyers, escort destroyers and other related warships would join their British and Canadian counterparts in confronting the U-boat threat.

The situation was much the same in the air. By the second half of 1942 the Allies possessed some 700 aircraft assigned to front-line anti-submarine squadrons in the area surrounding the North Atlantic. Of these, Coastal Command still provided the lion's share with 31 squadrons consisting of 489 aircraft available as of 1 July.[30] Nevertheless, the USAAF and United States Navy also provided increasing numbers of aircraft to perform this task. Operating from a variety of airfields in North America, Greenland, Iceland, the United Kingdom, Gibraltar and Bermuda, these aircraft were able to range far into the Atlantic to provide airborne coverage throughout most of the contested area. The British also flew regular patrols over the Bay of Biscay where the vast majority of U-boats transited into and out of the Atlantic. As such, other than an air gap that existed in the centre of the North Atlantic, Allied convoys could expect at least the potential for airborne coverage for most of their voyages while the German U-boats operated under a constant threat of Allied air attack.

Augmenting these quantitative gains were similar gains in technical quality. By this time in the war, the majority of British and American escorts were fitted with the improved rotating centimetric-wavelength Type 271 radar that greatly enhanced their ability to locate surfaced U-boats. Every convoy generally contained at least one and often two ships fitted with High Frequency Direction Finders (HF/DF) that could provide the bearing and general proximity of U-boats broadcasting radio transmissions near the convoy. While these innovations seriously restricted the U-boats' ability to avoid detection around the convoys, the Allies also possessed new and improved weapons to bring about their demise. In terms of the former, many escorts were armed with the new Hedgehog forward-firing mortar system that was capable of firing patterns of 24 contact bombs at submerged U-boats. The main benefit of this was that it allowed the escort vessel to maintain Asdic contact with the U-boat while carrying out the attack, which was not the case during conventional depth charge engagements. Of course, in those times when depth charges were used, all Allied escorts carried improved Torpex depth charges that delivered more powerful blasts and could be set to explode as deep as 600 feet.

The Allies also enjoyed similar innovations in the air. Long gone were the days when patrolling aircraft had to depend upon visual observation as their sole means to locate U-boats. By 1942 the vast majority of patrolling aircraft carried the Mark II or the improved Mark III ASV radar to assist this process. Certain aircraft also carried the Leigh Light airborne-mounted spotlight, which gave them the ability to attack surfaced U-boats at night. This device was commonly used in the Bay of Biscay where modified Wellington bombers used ASV radar to acquire and vector in on the U-boats before switching on their powerful Leigh Lights to carry out their attacks. This gave the bomb aimers clear views of their targets while the surprised U-boats had little time to react. The first success by a Leigh Light-equipped Wellington occurred on 6 July with the destruction of the previously mentioned *U502* off La Rochelle. Other nocturnal attacks soon followed thus expanding the airborne threat to both night and day. The standard ordnance carried by most of these aircraft was the Mark XIII aerial depth charge with a Torpex warhead and a shallow-set fuse that exploded at a depth of 25 feet thus giving the attacking aircraft an improved ability to sink crash-diving U-boats.

With the increased numbers and improved capabilities of the competing forces, it came as little surprise that the renewed German offensive in the North Atlantic brought about a heightened intensity in the U-boat conflict. The refocusing of Germany's U-boat effort manifested itself in August with the dispatch of 30 U-boats to operate in the North Atlantic compared to 28 to operate in American coastal waters and the South Atlantic. During the same month German and Italian

Shore-based patrol aircraft made key contributions to the Allied anti-submarine effort and eventually accounted for roughly a quarter of all U-boat kills during the war. Pictured here is a Coastal Command Sunderland about to take off from Oban Bay, Scotland. (Devon, S. A., Royal Air Force official photographer, public domain)

submarines sank a total of 117 merchant ships worth 587,245 tons of which 45 of 236,713 tons were sunk while proceeding under the protection of an Atlantic convoy.[31] Against this, nine U-boats were sunk of which eight were lost in the Atlantic. In terms of the latter: British escorts accounted for *U210* and *U379*; the British submarine *Saracen* claimed *U335*; British aircraft sank *U578;* American aircraft sank *U166* and *U654* and American aircraft and the Canadian corvette *Oakville* combined to sink *U94.* The eighth U-boat sunk in the Atlantic during August was the Type XIV U-tanker *U464*, which was dispatched by an American Catalina aircraft off Iceland. This was the first of Dönitz's valuable *milch cows* to be lost.

While August was a transitional month, September and October clearly brought the North Atlantic to the forefront of Germany's U-boat effort. During these two months the Germans dispatched a total of 73 attack boats and five U-tankers to operate in the North Atlantic compared to 36 attack boats and two U-tankers to operate off the Americas and Africa. Despite this heavy effort, Allied merchant losses actually declined during this period while German U-boat losses increased to the highest level yet experienced in the war. In terms of the former, 185 Allied and neutral merchant ships worth 1,045,484 tons were sunk by German and Italian submarines during September and October.[32] By comparison, no fewer than 27 German U-boats were lost during this two-month period of which 23 met their demise in the Atlantic or Baltic. Of the latter, British and Canadian aircraft accounted for the destruction of an unprecedented ten U-boats (*U705*, *U261*, *U619*, *U597*, *U216*, *U412*, *U599*, *U627*, *U520* and *U658*) while American aircraft added a further two U-boats (*U512* and *U582*) to this total. Of the remaining German losses, British and Canadian warships destroyed *U756*, *U162*, *U179*, *U661* and *U353* while mines accounted for *U253*, *U165*, *U446* and *U171*. Finally, accidental and unknown causes brought about the demise of *U222* and *U116*.

While these losses in the Atlantic and Baltic were significant, the most important U-boat casualty to occur during this time frame happened in the Mediterranean with the destruction of *U559*. Patrolling in the Eastern Mediterranean on the morning of 30 October, a RAF Sunderland reported a possible submarine contact some 70 miles north-northeast of Port Said. Initially the British destroyer *Hero* and then later the destroyers *Pakenham*, *Petard*, *Dulverton* and *Hurworth* arrived on the scene to carry out a search. With the help of a Wellesley aircraft, these destroyers located the submerged *U559* in the early afternoon and subjected it to a series of depth charge attacks lasting nearly ten hours. Finally, at 2240 hours the badly damaged *U559* broke the surface and was immediately engaged by gunfire from *Petard*. Realising that escape was impossible, the German crew blew scuttling charges and abandoned ship. However, *U559* did not immediately sink, and a boarding party from *Petard* was able to enter the submarine and secure numerous classified documents before the U-boat foundered.[33] Included in this haul were the current editions of the short-signal codebook and the weather cipher, which were immediately sent to Bletchley Park. With this invaluable information, the codebreakers at GC and CS were finally able to make significant progress against the four-rotor Triton key, although it was well into 1943 before the code was fully mastered.

While the capture of classified materials from *U559* signalled the beginning of a technological shift in favour of the Allies, the Germans were in the process of securing their own technological success in a different area. The loss of 12 U-boats to Allied aircraft during September and October came as a nasty shock to the Germans. For quite some time German authorities had known that the Allies possessed ASV radar, but it was not until the summer of 1942 that they finally recognised the threat this posed to their U-boat operations. The Germans immediately set out to acquire countermeasures to neutralise this threat. Included in this was the transfer of two dozen long-range Ju 88 fighters to Lorient and Bordeaux to engage Allied anti-submarine aircraft over the Bay of Biscay. The Germans also began increasing the anti-aircraft armament on their U-boats to give them more effective means to fight back against attacking aircraft. Soon U-boats possessed ever-increasing varieties of automatic weapons on their conning towers and specially built adjacent gun platforms.

But of all of these countermeasures, none was more important than the acquisition of an effective radar detector to give the U-boats warning of approaching aircraft. After looking at a number of different options, the Germans settled upon a French-built device called *Metox* that could detect signals over a bandwidth that included the frequency range of the Mark II ASV radar. Rushed into production in August, by November a growing number of U-boats possessed this crude, but effective, countermeasure. When on the surface, *Metox*-equipped boats erected an antenna on a simple wooden frame, which became known as the Biscay Cross, thus allowing them to search for the tell-tale pulses of Allied ASV radar. Upon receipt of such signals, the U-boats could submerge long before an aircraft could get within range to positively identify its presence or carry out an attack. With the increased introduction of *Metox*, U-boat sightings by aircraft fell off significantly. While the ability of aircraft to drive down U-boats was still potent and valuable, their ability to kill them had been greatly diminished.

The sudden loss of aircraft lethality was only one of many factors that boosted U-boat fortunes during the month of November. They also benefitted from increased numbers of U-boats on patrol, longer nights that favoured their ability to carry out attacks, deteriorating weather conditions that impeded Allied detection equipment and the temporary diversion of numerous Allied escort vessels to support operations off North Africa. Likewise, these operations off North Africa provided the U-boats with a plethora of targets in a relatively confined area, which was particularly beneficial to Mediterranean-based submarines, giving them the ability to make a meaningful contribution to the attrition of Allied merchant tonnage. The result of this was in November 1942 German and Italian submarines had their most successful month of the entire war in terms of Allied merchant tonnage sunk. To be specific, these submarines sank a total of 126 Allied and neutral merchant ships worth a combined 802,160 tons.[34] Nevertheless, this impressive success came at a heavy cost as 13 U-boats were sunk in November of which eight were lost in the Atlantic and Baltic. Of the latter, British warships sank *U98* and *U184*, American warships sank *U173*, Allied aircraft sank *U408*, *U411* and *U517* (one each by an American naval aircraft, a RAF Hudson and a FAA Albacore from the aircraft carrier *Victorious*) and accidental causes claimed *U132* and *U272*.

If November saw a flurry of activities and heavy losses on both sides, December was significantly different as severe winter weather markedly curtailed a repetition of similar results. Despite the fact that Dönitz dispatched a record 50 attack boats and two U-tankers into the North Atlantic, a mere 64 Allied and neutral merchant ships worth 337,618 tons were sunk by German and Italian submarines during December.[35] This represented a 58 percent decline in sinkings from the previous month and the lowest monthly total to be achieved since January of the same year.

On the other hand, if there was a bright spot for Dönitz, it was that his own losses in U-boats had also declined sharply during this period. In all, only five U-boats were sunk in December, which represented their lowest monthly loss rate since June. Of those U-boats sunk, British warships sank *U357* and *U356*, an American coast guard cutter sank *U626*, a British aircraft claimed *U611* and accidental causes accounted for *U254*. Dönitz could also take solace in knowing that severe weather, and not Allied countermeasures, was the main impetus behind the reduced results gained by his U-boats. To this point, when his U-boats were able to concentrate against convoy ONS.154 at the end of the month, they overwhelmed the accompanying escorts and sank 14 merchant ships worth 69,378 tons for the loss of just one of their number. Given good weather, Dönitz had every reason to believe that his U-boats would repeat this level of success on a regular basis.

With this, 1942 came to a close. During the last four months of the year total Allied and neutral merchant shipping losses due to enemy action amounted to 422 vessels worth 2,361,816 tons.[36] Britain's portion of this loss amounted to 231 merchant ships worth 1,386,300 tons.[37] The vast majority of these losses occurred in the Atlantic as a result of U-boat actions, but operations in other theatres and activities by aircraft, mines and surface ships also claimed a portion of this total. When looking at the year as a whole, total Allied and neutral merchant shipping losses for 1942 due to enemy action amounted to 1,664 vessels worth 7,790,697 tons including 657 British flagged ships worth 3,461,500 tons.[38] This represented a near doubling of the Allied and neutral merchant tonnage sunk the year before and constituted almost half the tonnage sunk since the beginning of the war. When broken down on a monthly basis, this constituted 649,225 tons of shipping sunk per month in 1942 compared to 360,713 and 332,637 tons sunk per month in 1941 and 1940 respectively.

While this result was a major improvement for Dönitz and his U-boats, it fell far short of a decisive victory when viewed in the larger context. During 1942 American shipyards produced 5.4 million tons of new merchant shipping while British yards added another 1.3 million tons to this total.[39] Thus, when taking new construction into account, the net loss of Allied merchant shipping for 1942 only amounted to approximately 1.1 million tons. Making matters worse from a German point of view, this net loss was taken against a far larger shipping pool then had been the case 13 months earlier. By 31 December 1942 the total amount of British-controlled merchant tonnage of vessels that were 1,600 gross tons or greater numbered 18,122,000 tons thus representing a decline of 2,571,000 tons since the beginning of the year.[40] Nevertheless, this shortfall was made up several times over by the addition of over 12 million tons of American shipping that was now active in the conflict. American merchant production in 1943 was projected to more than double, significantly exceeding the level of attrition suffered in 1942. Therefore, despite the sizable jump in Allied shipping losses, Dönitz had clearly failed to make meaningful progress in his overall tonnage strategy and was in fact continuing to fall behind.

Adding to Dönitz's concern was the increased number of U-boats lost during this period. In 1942 the Kriegsmarine lost a total of 86 U-boats, which more than doubled the number of U-boats sunk in 1941. Viewed another way, the casualties sustained in 1942 represented nearly 57 percent of the total U-boat losses suffered thus far in the entire war (from September 1939). Making matters worse for Dönitz, of the 86 U-boats sunk in 1942, 65 were lost in the last six months of the year thus representing a better than three-fold increase as compared to the previous six-month period. When viewed in terms of an exchange rate, during the first half of 1942 some 138,567 tons of Allied and neutral merchant shipping was lost for every U-boat sunk, but this rate dropped to 49,839 tons during the second half of the year.[41] While this increase in U-boat losses had yet to surpass the level of new construction, it still represented a worrisome trend that threatened to become pro-hibitive if left unchecked. Just as the U-boat arm was growing in size, so too were the Allied countermeasures arrayed against it. Therefore, Dönitz faced the daunting requirement to significantly increase attrition against the Allied merchant fleet while keeping his own losses to an acceptable level against an adversary that was growing in size and capability.

The Allies had challenges of their own to overcome. While the Allied shipping pool had grown with America's entry into the war, so too had the requirements placed against these assets. Unlike World War I where the conflict had overwhelmingly centred in Europe and the adjacent waters, the current conflict was truly a global struggle with powerful adversaries located in both Europe and the Pacific. As such, the Allies were forced to concurrently wage major maritime campaigns in the North Atlantic, Pacific and Mediterranean with lesser operations underway in the Indian Ocean, South Atlantic and Arctic. The Allies also had to maintain the economic and civilian needs of their home nations, colonial possessions and other territories under their control. Thus, despite America's entry into the war with its sizable mer-chant fleet and immense production capabilities, the Allies regularly faced shipping shortages that forced them to limit their efforts in a number of areas during 1942.

One area particularly hard hit was the level of imports arriving in Britain. Despite the fact that an ever-increasing percentage of merchant ships now travelled in con-voys, the total number of merchant ships dispatched in these convoys to the United Kingdom had actually dropped from 7,898 in 1940 to 6,588 in 1941 and 5,892 in 1942.[42] Likewise, the loss rate for convoyed merchant ships travelling to and from the United Kingdom increased from 0.7 percent in 1940 to 1.5 percent in 1942.[43] As a result of these combined factors, total imports to the United Kingdom in 1942 amounted to just 34,090,000 tons, which constituted a reduction of roughly 24 and 38 percent compared to the levels attained in 1941 and 1940 respectively. When broken down by category, 10,606,000 tons of these imports were foodstuffs,

11,505,000 tons were raw materials, 10,710,000 tons were tanker commodities (petroleum products, molasses, unrefined whale oil and industrial alcohol), 780,000 tons were munitions and manufactured goods and 489,000 tons were various items from Ireland.[44] While increased domestic production and rationing made up for part of this shortfall, this reduced level of imports came dangerously close to the minimum import requirement of 27 million tons per year that the British government determined was absolutely essential in meeting the nation's basic needs.[45] Therefore, if this trend continued, Britain's war effort and very survival would become increasingly threatened.

So as 1942 drew to a close, both sides had reasons for optimism and concern regarding the upcoming year. For the Germans, the substantial increase in Allied merchant losses and approaching threshold of 300 operational U-boats were positive developments, but this was countered by extensive Allied shipbuilding capacity, accelerated U-boat losses and growing Allied defensive capabilities. By comparison, the Allies faced an immediate continuation of their shipping availability crisis and a numerically more powerful enemy, but they countered this with anticipated record output from their shipyards and substantial improvements in the quantity and quality of their defences. One thing was certain; the battle was heading into an intense and climactic period. Gone were the days when U-boats were primarily able to operate against independently sailed vessels or when the Allies only had to contend with a relative handful of raiders. The battle was now poised to become a head-to-head contest of brute force against brute force along the North Atlantic convoy routes. The results of this titanic struggle would likely determine the outcome of the war.

CHAPTER 7

Turning Point

With the diversion of resources to support the landings in North Africa (Operation *Torch*), the Allies temporarily suspended convoy operations to the Soviet Union in the autumn of 1942. While this measure curtailed the dispatch of convoys, the Allies did attempt to run a handful of independently sailed merchant ships to Russia using severe weather and the increasingly long hours of darkness as cover for their movements. Of 13 vessels dispatched during this period, five made it through, three turned back and five worth 34,079 tons were lost. During the same time frame 23 ships sailed from the Soviet Union to Iceland with the 7,925-ton Soviet tanker *Donbass* as their only loss.[1] Then in mid-November the Allies attempted to retrieve the remaining ships left stranded in Russia from the earlier PQ convoys with the dispatch of QP.15. Aided by inclement weather and an almost complete lack of daylight, 26 merchant ships successfully completed this passage while two vessels worth 9,825 tons were lost to U-boats.[2]

In December the Allies were finally ready to reinitiate convoy service to the Soviet Union. By this time a number of conditions in the Arctic had changed to benefit this effort. First, the near-perpetual darkness and prevailing poor weather made aerial detection and attacks exceedingly difficult. These same factors also impacted the ability of German U-boats to effectively operate in the area. Finally, recent losses and transfers to the Mediterranean theatre had left the Luftwaffe in Norway markedly reduced compared to its status of just a few months earlier. With the two most successful components of Germany's offensive strength in Norway now hindered, the onus for causing serious damage to the Allied Arctic convoys passed to the local German surface forces. Unfortunately for them, surface warships could not respond as quickly as aircraft and were not kept in a perpetual state of patrolling like U-boats. Likewise, fuel shortages limited the operational readiness and training proficiency of the larger combatants. As such, good intelligence, early detection and precise coordination were required if the Germans hoped to intercept and engage a convoy with their major surface units. The same factors limiting the effectiveness of German aircraft and U-boats also degraded the likelihood of attaining these necessary prerequisites.

As it was, the Germans did not have long to wait before their forces were tested against these new conditions. Using revised convoy code designators, the British dispatched JW.51 to the Soviet Union during the latter half of December 1942. Split into two parts to provide better control under the difficult Arctic winter conditions, JW.51A departed Lock Ewe on 15 December and made an uneventful passage to successfully deliver 15 merchant ships to the Kola Inlet ten days later. JW.51B departed Lock Ewe on 22 December and proceeded on a similar trek with 14 merchant ships carrying 120 aircraft, 202 tanks, 2,046 vehicles, 11,500 tons of fuel oil, 12,650 tons of aviation spirits and 54,321 tons of general cargo.[3] The close escort for JW.51B consisted of the destroyers *Onslow* (flag), *Oribi*, *Orwell*, *Obedient*, *Obdurate* and *Achates*; two corvettes; a minesweeper and two trawlers and fell under the command of Captain Robert St. Vincent Sherbrooke. Further protection was provided by Force R, which was commanded by Rear-Admiral Robert Burnett and consisted of the light cruisers *Sheffield* and *Jamaica*. These latter cruisers departed Kola on the 27th and proceeded into the Barents Sea to provide close cover. Finally, the battleship *Anson*, the cruiser *Cumberland* and five destroyers provided distant cover for the small Russia-bound convoy.

For several days JW.51B proceeded unmolested with inclement weather as its only antagonist. Finally, on 30 December a sighting report from *U354* prompted the Germans into action. Informed of the presence of a weakly protected convoy south of Bear Island, the Germans dispatched the pocket battleship *Lützow*, the heavy cruiser *Admiral Hipper* and six destroyers into the Barents Sea to seek out and engage this convoy. Under the command of Vice-Admiral Oscar Kummetz, the German force split into two sections to trap the convoy in a pincer movement. By mid-morning on the 31st *Admiral Hipper* and three destroyers were northwest of the convoy while *Lützow* and its destroyers were 50 miles to the south and closing. Kummetz's plan called for *Admiral Hipper* to engage first from astern to draw off the escorts while *Lützow* subsequently destroyed the undefended convoy from the south. For their part, the British had four groups of ships scattered within the area with none knowing the exact positions of the others. The first was the convoy itself, which was steering east with 12 merchant ships and eight escort vessels. Forty-five miles to the north the trawler *Vizalma* was shepherding the detached merchant ship *Chester Valley* while to the northeast the minesweeper *Bramble* was searching for a second straggler. Finally, Rear-Admiral Burnett's Force R was located between the convoy and *Vizalma,* being some 30 miles from the former.[4]

At 0830 hours the destroyer *Obdurate* reported two unidentified ships to the stern of the convoy. These vessels were destroyers from the *Admiral Hipper* group, which made their identities known at 0930 hours when they opened fire on the investigating *Obdurate*. Alerted by *Obdurate*'s alarm, Captain Sherbrooke ordered the destroyers *Onslow*, *Obedient* and *Orwell* to assist their sister and engage the enemy while *Achates* and the three smaller escorts cloaked the convoy in smoke. At

0939 hours *Admiral Hipper* appeared on the port side of the convoy and opened fire on *Achates. Onslow* and *Orwell* immediately counterattacked, and for nearly two hours both sides engaged in a running battle around the convoy. Taking advantage of the smoke screen and feigning numerous torpedo attacks, the British destroyers stymied their vastly superior opponent for a while, but eventually *Admiral Hipper's* powerful gunfire began taking its toll. At about 1020 hours *Admiral Hipper* found the range on *Onslow* and scored a number of hits that forced the badly damaged British destroyer to withdraw. Shortly thereafter the German cruiser happened upon the minesweeper *Bramble* and reduced the lightly armed warship to a battered hulk that was subsequently sunk by the trailing German destroyers. Then at 1115 hours *Admiral Hipper* re-engaged *Achates* at the stern of the convoy and severely damaged the gallant British destroyer.

Up until this point, the battle had largely gone in favour of the Germans, but this was about to change. At 1130 hours *Admiral Hipper* suddenly found itself bracketed by a double salvo of 6-inch shells. *Sheffield* and *Jamaica* had finally arrived upon the scene. Caught completely by surprise and unsure where the fire was coming from, *Admiral Hipper* soon sustained three hits that disabled a boiler, caused flooding and started a fire. At 1137 hours Admiral Kummetz ordered his force to break off to

Arguably the best light cruiser class of the war, Britain's Town-class saw extensive action in a variety of theatres. Pictured here is HMS *Sheffield*, which played an important role in the successful defence of convoy JW.51B during the battle of the Barents Sea. (Royal Navy official photographer, public domain)

the west. The British cruisers pursued, but *Admiral Hipper* was able to escape into a snow squall. The same was not true for the German destroyer *Friedrich Echoldt*, which mistook *Sheffield* for *Admiral Hipper* and was quickly shot to pieces by the larger British warship. At about the same time *Lützow,* which had been loitering in the area for almost two hours, finally gained a clear view of the convoy and opened fire. Fortunately, this fire was largely ineffective, and the pocket battleship soon disengaged upon receipt of an order to withdraw. At 1215 hours the British cruisers and German warships briefly re-engaged, but neither side pressed the issue, and the battle soon ended, this time for good. Thereafter, the British suffered no further losses, and JW.51B arrived safely at the Kola inlet on 3 January.

The British hailed this action, which later became known as the battle of the Barents Sea, as a great victory. For the loss of the minesweeper *Bramble* and the destroyer *Achates*, which sank shortly after the battle concluded, the British repulsed a markedly superior enemy force and safely brought through their convoy without the loss of a single merchant ship. In the process of doing so, they sank the German destroyer *Friedrich Echoldt* thus roughly balancing the materiel scorecard for the action.[5] When combined with JW.51A and the subsequent returning RA.51, not a single merchant ship was lost in the Arctic during this period thus signalling a notable triumph for the Allies. In addition to these tangible results, the battle of the Barents Sea represented a clear moral victory for the Royal Navy as British tenacity and aggressiveness had once again prevailed over dire circumstances. Much of the credit for this success went to Captain Sherbrooke, who was severely wounded during the action and subsequently received the Victoria Cross for his role in the battle. By comparison, the Kriegsmarine's tepid and disappointing performance only served to lower morale and shake confidence in the competency and value of the surface fleet.

This latter point was no truer than in the case of Adolf Hitler. Keenly focused on the outcome of the battle while in his headquarters at Rastenburg in East Prussia, Hitler was initially bolstered by an ambiguous report received at 1145 hours on the 31st from *U354* that seemed to indicate a great victory was at hand. After this however, no further information was forthcoming, and Hitler grew increasingly impatient to learn the details of his presumed triumph. Plans were even made to broadcast a special New Year's Day announcement proclaiming the victory to the world. Still, no word arrived. The reason for this blackout was Admiral Kummetz's use of radio silence during his return to Altenfjord – a journey made longer by the need to nurse the wounded *Admiral Hipper*, which at times could only make 15 knots. Then, once safely in port, a communication breakdown between Norway and Berlin further delayed reporting. As a result, the first concrete news that an already agitated Hitler received regarding the battle came from a British broadcast on the afternoon of the 1st. It was then that Hitler learned the truth about his presumed victory, and he flew into a rage.

The consequence of Hitler's fury nearly signalled the end of the German battle fleet. Ranting that the major surface ships were just a waste of men and materiel, Hitler announced his decision to pay off and scrap the fleet's heavy units. Five days later Grand-Admiral Raeder appeared before Hitler to urge a reprieve for the fleet, but Hitler would hear none of it. Finally, Raeder did the only thing he could do under the circumstances and asked to be relieved. Admiral Raeder's departure from duty became effective on 30 January 1943, and Admiral Karl Dönitz assumed command of the Kriegsmarine. Being a U-boat man, Hitler expected Dönitz to agree with his decision to scrap the surface fleet, but this was not the case. Instead, Dönitz recognised the value the major surface ships brought in tying down comparable British forces and as weapons for both offensive and defensive applications. Therefore, soon after taking command of the Kriegsmarine, Dönitz began advocating for the fleet's retention and eventually convinced Hitler to alter his decision. With this, some of the major surface combatants remained on active service while others were shifted to training duties or paid off, but not scrapped thus preserving their potential availability for future operations. In this manner, the surface fleet survived to fight another day.

A factor that may have contributed to Hitler's overreaction to this event was the deteriorating situation facing Germany at the beginning of 1943. In many respects, the results of the battle of the Barents Sea were indicative of the waning fortunes confronting the Germans on a number of fronts. In the Soviet Union, a major Axis offensive in the Caucasus had been reversed by Russian counterattacks, and the German Sixth Army was trapped and fighting for its survival in the city of Stalingrad. When this embattled army finally surrendered at the end of January, some 91,000 German soldiers went into captivity while another 160,000 were left dead in the ruins of the devastated city. As bad as this was, this only represented a small portion of Germany's overall losses on the Eastern Front, which in 1942 totalled 1,080,950 casualties.[6] Meanwhile, in North Africa the British Eighth Army was pursuing the defeated German-Italian *Panzerarmee* across the sands of Libya while the Anglo-American First Army confronted an improvised Axis force in Tunisia. The resolution of these operations would take a little longer than at Stalingrad, but the ultimate outcome was equally pronounced – the destruction of all Axis forces in North Africa including 238,243 prisoners taken during the final capitulation.[7] Meanwhile, on the home front, German cities were coming under increased attack by British bombers. Many of these raids consisted of between 100 to 300 bombers, and in May 1942 the RAF conducted its first 1,000-bomber raid. Soon the USAAF would join this assault subjecting Germany to round-the-clock bombing.

The net result of these various calamities was a bleak strategic outlook for Germany as its prospect for outright victory had now diminished to a point of near impossibility. In fact, the best the Germans could realistically hope to accomplish in terms of conventional warfare was to fight the Allies to a standstill and seek a negotiated settlement that allowed them to retain a portion of their recently conquered empire.

In terms of achieving this, it was the Kriegsmarine that gave Germany its best chance for victory, limited though it was. If the Germans could sink adequate numbers of Allied merchant ships, they could blunt Britain's ability to wage war and neutralise America's immense human and materiel resources. This, in turn, would delay or even render impossible an Allied return to the continent. Finally, it was conceivable, if highly unlikely given America's immense shipbuilding capacity, that the Germans could so deprive Britain of imports that they would reduce the island nation to a level of impotency or even force it to capitulate.

By the beginning of 1943 the only weapon in the Kriegsmarine's arsenal remotely capable of inflicting the levels of destruction necessary to bring about these outcomes was the U-boat. While other weapons such as aircraft, mines and surface warships could play contributing roles, it was the U-boat that would either win or lose the tonnage campaign for Germany. This struggle would predominately occur in the Atlantic. To this end, in January 1943 the Kriegsmarine had 393 U-boats in commission of which 212 were considered operational and 181 were in trials or training.[8] Of the former, 168 U-boats were assigned to the critical Atlantic area.[9] This represented a 51 percent increase in operational U-boats and an 85 percent increase in U-boats assigned to the Atlantic when compared to the situation of six months prior. Meanwhile, production was proceeding at a rate of 23 new boats per month, and about 120 additional U-boats were expected to be operational by June.[10] Thus, assuming a loss rate similar to that in the latter half of 1942, the Germans could expect to have between 270 and 285 operational U-boats by mid-year, the vast majority of which would likely be assigned to Atlantic operations.

While the U-boat arm continued to enjoy meaningful numerical expansion, the situation regarding qualitative and technical improvements was far less satisfactory. By 1943 the performance characteristics of German U-boats had improved little since the beginning of the war. The Type VII and Type IX U-boats that dominated the Kriegsmarine's inventory were essentially improved versions of the submarines the Germans had used during World War I. The Germans did have radical new designs under development that promised to revolutionise submarine warfare, but it would be at least a year before these designs were ready for production. In the meantime, the Kriegsmarine would have to make do with its veteran Type VII and Type IX models. Complicating this situation, German electronic technology had fallen behind that of the Allies. For instance, whereas the vast majority of Allied escort vessels possessed some sort of surface search radar, the U-boats had no such equivalent. Likewise, despite extensive experimentation with acoustic absorbent coatings and decoys, the Germans had yet to develop an effective countermeasure to Allied Asdic. While *Metox* could detect certain Allied search radar, the increased introduction of centimetric-wavelength radar rendered this device useless. The Germans had limited awareness of ship-based HF/DF and had no means to counter this important Allied detection device other than to curtail their radio transmissions.

This is not to say there were no German technical advances. By the beginning of 1943 increasing numbers of U-boats were sailing with improved weapons and related devices. Paramount amongst these was improved passive array sonar that could detect the propeller noises of surface vessels up to 20 miles away depending upon weather conditions. Many of these U-boats also carried various new torpedoes including the pattern-running or looping G7a FAT torpedo and the T-3 *Falke* acoustic torpedo. The former was a programmable torpedo that could run set patterns while the latter was designed to go into a tight circling pattern once the noise of a nearby merchant ship was detected. It was believed that both would increase the chances of scoring hits at long range or in poor visibility. Finally, German U-boats were increasingly armed with growing arrays of anti-aircraft guns including single, twin or quadruple 20mm cannons; the new rapid firing 37mm cannon and twin Breda 13.2mm machine guns. To compensate for the increased topside weight and underwater resistance these weapons created, the Germans removed the 88mm deck guns from most of their Type VII U-boats.

In terms of quality, there was one other factor that had to be taken into consideration. By this time in the war, many U-boats sailed with new or inexperienced captains and crews. Part of this was due to the rapid expansion of the U-boat arm, and part of this was due to the heavy losses the U-boats had thus far sustained. To this latter point, by 1943 many of the most experienced U-boat captains and crewmen had either been killed or captured as a result of earlier operations. Making matters worse, unlike their earlier counterparts who had largely operated against weak Allied defences during the first and second 'happy times', these new U-boat captains and crews faced an ever-expanding gauntlet of Allied countermeasures ranging from increasingly potent surface escorts to equally deadly aircraft. The result of this was a growing tendency for U-boat captains to act cautiously or with timidity in the face of Allied opposition. Soon Dönitz would lament the lack of aggressiveness displayed by many of his captains as he relentlessly urged them to close with the enemy.

For their part, the Allies were equally aware of the criticality of the U-boat campaign. In January the senior leadership of the Western Allied nations conducted a conference in Casablanca to map out their future strategy for the conduct of the war. During this conference the Allies acknowledged the urgent and overriding need to secure their seaborne lines of communication and mount an all-out offensive against the U-boat threat. As part of this key strategic tenant, the Allies adopted a number of tangible measures regarding both airborne and seaborne assets. In terms of the former, they agreed to step-up bombing attacks against U-boat bases and production facilities. They likewise resolved to intensify the RAF's interdiction campaign in the Bay of Biscay and reinforce this effort with USAAF aircraft. They also undertook a number of measures to maximise airborne patrol coverage along the North Atlantic convoy routes including the conversion of certain B-24 Liberator bombers into very long-range aircraft with the installation of additional fuel tanks in their bomb bays. Finally, on the decision of the highest British authorities, the RAF took 40 new H2S centimetric-wavelength radar sets that were earmarked for Bomber Command and redirected them to Coastal Command.

In terms of seaborne initiatives, the Allies agreed to create a number of hunter-killer support groups consisting of a variety of escort vessels including destroyers, frigates and sloops. The purpose of these support groups was to patrol the convoy routes and reinforce threatened convoys as needed. Since a support group was not part of a convoy's dedicated defence, it had greater latitude to destroy U-boats and not merely suppress them. Quite often when convoy escorts located a U-boat, they were unable to press home their attacks or conduct sustained search operations due to their need to remain with the convoy. Support group vessels were less impacted by this requirement and could thus linger in an area to hunt suspected U-boats to their ultimate demise. In January the Allies decided to increase the interval of eastbound HX convoys from an eight-day cycle to a ten-day cycle. In doing so, they released enough escort vessels to create a minimum of five support groups. Later, as additional escort vessels became available due to new construction, the number of support groups would increase. Within a few months escort carriers would begin joining the ranks of the support groups thus giving them their own integrated air support. When coupled with good intelligence from Ultra, HF/DF or other sources, these support groups would be able to use their aircraft to proactively hunt for targeted U-boats and not merely respond to their incursions.

In a related decision, the United States assumed a greater direct role in the Atlantic struggle by expanding operations in the Middle Atlantic. In addition to the American-run UG and GU convoys operating between the United States and Gibraltar, the Allies created two new Middle Atlantic convoys to transport oil from North America to Africa and Europe. The first, designated OT, delivered oil from the Caribbean to Gibraltar and the Mediterranean while the second, designated CU, delivered oil from Curaçao to the United Kingdom. Returning convoys in ballast fell under the designation of TO and UC respectively. Once again, the United States assumed full responsibility for the operation and protection of these convoys, which typically ran at cruising speeds of 14.5 knots due to their use of specially built fast tankers. Other fast merchant ships regularly joined these convoys to take advantage of their unusual speed capabilities. Meanwhile, increasing numbers of American warships and aircraft were earmarked to support this expanding operation, which quickly became an integral part of the Allies' transatlantic logistical network. Eventually, 206 and 2,254 merchant ships participated in these OT and CU convoys respectively through the duration of the war.[11]

Beyond the Casablanca Conference, the beginning of 1943 saw the development of a number of Allied technical innovations that would soon make their operational debuts against the U-boats. Perhaps the most deadly of these was the FIDO air-dropped anti-submarine acoustic homing torpedo. Developed by the Americans and designated the Mark 24 mine for security purposes, the FIDO homed in on screw noises, making it highly effective against submerged U-boats. A second air-launched weapon to soon make its operational debut was the British-developed rocket projectile. Featuring a solid, 25-pound semi-armoured piercing head, these lightweight rockets were capable of piercing a surfaced submarine's pressure hull with little difficulty and could be delivered from a variety of aircraft. In terms of warship weaponry, the British had the Squid forward-firing mortar system under development as a follow-up to Hedgehog. Controlled automatically by Asdic, the Squid could fire three 390-pound depth charges in a triangular pattern up to 275 yards in front of a ship. Many Squid-armed ships possessed two sets of mortars so that six depth charges could be fired at once with three set to explode above the U-boat and three set to explode below it for maximum destructive power. Finally, the Allies continued to acquire improved versions of radar and Asdic that enhanced their ability to locate and target both surfaced and submerged U-boats.

Still, of all these technical innovations, none was more important than the progress made in the cryptic intelligence field. The main focus of this concerned the breaking of the four-rotor Triton key used by the Kriegsmarine to communicate with Atlantic and Mediterranean-based U-boats. Initially broken in December 1942 with the aid of captured materials from *U559*, GC and CS continued to enjoy growing success against Triton throughout 1943. In partnership with the cryptanalytic branch of the United States Navy, GC and CS was able to read a majority of daily Triton intercepts, although often with significant time delays. This ability was temporarily lost on 10 March when the Germans changed their weather cipher, but was quickly regained nine days later thus allowing GC and CS to successfully break Triton for 90 out of 112 days culminating on 30 June. By the end of this period, the British had begun using four-rotor bombes, which were electromechanical deciphering machines, to help break the code. This was a major aid, and by September the British were consistently breaking Triton intercepts in less than 24 hours. They would maintain this ability for the remainder of the war.

By comparison, Germany's ability to read Britain's Naval Cypher No. 3 had a reverse transition. On 15 December 1942 British authorities introduced changes to this code that temporarily interrupted B-Dienst's ability to read it. By placing most of their cryptanalytic efforts on it, B-Dienst restored their ability to read Naval Cypher No. 3 in February. Over the next few months the Germans were able to read the Admiralty's U-boat disposition signals on most days thus giving them valuable insights into convoy routing. By April, however, the British learned through Ultra intercepts that the Germans had compromised Naval Cypher No. 3 and took immediate actions to counter this intelligence breach. The final solution occurred on 10 June when the Allies replaced Naval Cypher No. 3 with Naval Cypher No. 5, abruptly ending B-Dienst's ability to read this valuable signal traffic. Thereafter, German codebreakers remained extensively deaf and blind to Allied convoy movements with only sporadic reprieves. Thus, by the latter half of the year and for the remainder of the war, the cryptic intelligence pendulum that had swung back and forth in terms of the naval struggle would finally swing irrevocably in favour of the Allies.

While the Allies had many reasons for optimism at the beginning of 1943, not all areas progressed as quickly as desired. Despite the promise of America's vast ship-building potential, the Allies lacked the merchant ships and escort vessels necessary to meet all of their many competing needs. Eventually time would correct this, but the situation as it stood in January 1943 was less than satisfactory. In the Atlantic, these shortages particularly manifested themselves in terms of the escort force. At the time the Allies possessed 383 assorted escort vessels earmarked for Atlantic service.[12] This constituted an increase of 39 vessels compared to the Allied escort strength of some five months prior. Nevertheless, in terms of percentages, this 11 percent growth rate was markedly less than the 85 percent expansion that German U-boats operating in the Atlantic had experienced during roughly the same period. Making matters worse, while the Allies were required to spread their escorts over a wide area and across multiple convoys, the Germans were able to mass their U-boats at times and places of their choosing. The result of this was that the U-boats often attained numerical superiority over the local convoy defences, which typically consisted of no more than five to ten escort vessels.

With all of these factors in play, 1943 promised to be a time of colossal struggle. Nevertheless, the year began with a whimper instead of a bang. To a large extent, January was just a continuation of the reduced activity experienced in December. Early in the month the Germans scored a meaningful success when U-boats sank seven out of nine tankers from the oil convoy TM.1, but this proved to be an isolated occurrence as the Germans generally had great difficulty in locating the Allied convoys. Part of this difficulty was due to the poor weather that continued to impede U-boat operations, and part of this was due to Ultra intelligence that allowed the British to successfully route convoys around U-boat concentrations. The result of this was despite the dispatch of 61 attack boats and two *milch cows* into the Atlantic and adjacent waters, Allied and neutral merchant losses due to European-based Axis submarines in January amounted to just 44 vessels worth 307,196 tons.[13] Against this, six U-boats were sunk of which four were lost in the Atlantic. Of the latter, American naval aircraft accounted for *U164* and *U507* while a Coastal Command aircraft was responsible for the destruction of *U337*. Finally, *U553* was lost due to unknown causes.

If January was a bad month for the Germans, February proved to be worse. During this month the Germans dispatched a record 71 attack boats, two *milch cows* and one minelaying U-boat into the Atlantic and adjacent waters. Combining with previously deployed U-boats and in conjunction with their comrades in the Mediterranean and Arctic, these boats sank a total of 67 merchant ships worth 362,081 tons in February.[14] While this toll represented a marginal improvement compared to the anaemic successes attained during the previous two months, it still fell far short of the required tonnage the Germans needed to sink in order to inflict meaningful attrition against the Allied merchant fleet. Making matters worse for the Germans, no fewer than 19 U-boats were lost during the month of which 15 were sunk in the Atlantic. Of these, British aircraft accounted for *U265*, *U624*, *U442*, *U620*, *U225*, *U268* and *U623* while American aircraft caused the demise of *U519*. British warships destroyed *U187*, *U609*, *U69*, *U201* and *U522*. Finally American and Polish warships combined to sink *U606* while unknown causes accounted for *U529*. In addition to these Atlantic losses, *U649* suffered a fatal accident in the Baltic while three further U-boats were destroyed in the Mediterranean. When combined together, this tally constituted the worst month for U-boat losses thus far in the war and came close to matching the U-boat replacement rate.

In many respects, these results reflected the growing influence of Allied strategy and technology on the campaign. Of the eight U-boats sunk by Allied aircraft, seven were lost to long-range or very long-range types. This demonstrated the increasing reach that Allied aircraft could now extend into the Atlantic. Likewise, aircraft flying in direct support of specific convoys sank five of these U-boats, indicating the integral and coordinated role that aircraft now played in convoy defence. With over 1,100 Allied aircraft now ringing the Atlantic from Brazil to South Africa, it was often possible to provide daytime air coverage for the entire length of a convoy's passage depending upon routing and weather conditions. As for the three U-boats that were sunk by routine air patrols, one was lost to a Leigh Light Wellington, demonstrating the continued threat menacing U-boats during nocturnal passages. HF/DF detection led to the destruction of three of the six U-boats sunk by surface escorts during the month, giving clear indication of how technology was also impacting surface operations. To this end, with each passing month, Allied surface escorts enjoyed an increased ability to locate and kill U-boats.

Under these conditions, the only realistic prospect the Germans had to inflict truly debilitating casualties depended upon their ability to attain numerical superiority. To bring this about, they required large numbers of U-boats to saturate the Atlantic in a continuous rotation that allowed them to locate and mass against transiting convoys. In March, a number of factors came together to facilitate this outcome. First, many of the record number of U-boats dispatched in February remained on patrol into March where they joined the 57 attack boats dispatched during that month to form a sizable presence in the North Atlantic and adjacent waters. Taking into account U-boats that were transiting to or from their patrol areas or undergoing re-supply, this allowed the Germans to maintain an average force of some 50 U-boats on station in the North Atlantic throughout the month. The Germans also benefitted from a favourable intelligence situation. For seven out of the first ten days in March, GC and CS had longer than average delays in reading Triton followed by a complete blackout from the 10th to the 19th. By comparison, B-Dienst had little difficulty in reading corresponding Allied radio traffic thus giving Dönitz an accurate picture of Allied naval and convoy dispositions. At various times throughout the month the Germans benefitted from changing weather conditions that grounded Allied aircraft, dispersed Allied defences and provided favourable gaps to mass and carry out their attacks.

Reflecting the culmination of these various advantages were two convoy battles fought in March. The first of these was SC.121, which consisted of 59 merchant ships and an escort of one coast guard cutter, one destroyer and three corvettes from the American Escort Group A-3. Forewarned of its passage by B-Dienst and located by *U405* on 6 March, the Germans deployed 27 U-boats to engage the lumbering convoy, which had become partially scattered due to relentless stormy weather. Although stoutly defended by its accompanying warships, the meagre escort was unable to cope with the series of attacks that followed. Taking advantage of gaps in the defence as well as the presence of associated stragglers, the Germans inflicted a steady toll upon the convoy over a three-day period. Eventually the arrival of reinforcements on the 9th and 10th prompted the Germans to break off their assault, but not before they had destroyed 12 merchant ships worth 55,661 tons for the loss of a single U-boat (*U633*).

One week later a second major convoy battle erupted in the North Atlantic. This battle actually involved two convoys, SC.122 and HX.229, which were in close proximity to each other due to evasive routing and speed variances. Once again, B-Dienst provided the Germans with timely intelligence that allowed them to concentrate 38 U-boats against the two converging convoys, which consisted of a combined 89 merchant ships. Against this onslaught, the British possessed an initial escort of two destroyers, one sloop and five corvettes with SC.122 and two destroyers and two corvettes with HX.229. This number increased as the battle progressed, and the Allies were also able to provide the convoys with air support from the 17th on. Nevertheless, the Germans were able to take advantage of the convoys' initial weakness and sank 13 vessels on the night of 16/17 March. Thereafter, the Germans continued to probe the convoys sinking a further nine merchant ships through the 19th. Finally, on 20 March the Germans called off their assault having sunk 22 merchant ships worth a combined 146,596 tons. Their own losses for the four-day battle amounted to one U-boat (*U384*) sunk and three others damaged.

When viewed as individual actions, these two convoy battles (SC.121 and SC.122/HX.229) were clear German victories. For the loss of two U-boats, the Germans destroyed a combined 34 merchant ships worth 202,257 tons. This was an exchange rate that hearkened back to the earlier days of great success for the U-boats. Even more importantly, unlike these earlier periods, which were largely waged against independently sailed and undefended merchant ships, the Germans attained these results against defended convoys. Fortunately for the Allies, these convoy battles proved to be anomalies as the U-boats were only able to score against three other eastbound convoys in the North Atlantic during March. Of these, HX.228 was the hardest hit losing four merchant ships and the British destroyer *Harvester* in exchange for two U-boats (*U444* and *U432*) sunk while HX.227 and HX.230 lost one ship each. Meanwhile, 11 other Allied convoys travelling to and from the United Kingdom during this period suffered no losses whatsoever.

Of course, these results only reflected a portion of the U-boat effort and the corresponding Allied supply operation. Throughout the entire Atlantic and in the adjacent waters of the Arctic, Mediterranean and Indian Ocean, Axis submarines sank a combined 110 Allied and neutral merchant ships worth 633,731 tons.[15] This roughly doubled the tonnage sunk in any of the three preceding months and proved to be the third most destructive month attained by the U-boats during the entire war. Despite this success, the Germans continued to pay a heavy price for their efforts. In all, 15 U-boats were sunk in March of which 12 were lost in the Atlantic. Of these latter boats, British escorts sank *U87*, *U444*, *U432* and *U163*; an American warship sank *U130* and the British merchant ship *Scorton* rammed and destroyed *U633*. RAF aircraft accounted for *U384*, *U665*, *U469* and *U169* while American aircraft dispatched *U156* and *U524*. In addition to these Atlantic losses, *U5* succumbed to a diving accident in the Baltic while *U83* and *U77* were lost in the Mediterranean. Thus, when viewed as a whole, the exchange rate attained by the German U-boats in March was far less advantageous than their celebrated successes against SC.121, SC.122 and HX.229 might have indicated.

Making matters worse for the Germans, they were unable to maintain this same level of destruction into the following month. A number of factors contributed to this reduction in results. Part of this dealt with the normal ebb and flow of U-boat operations as many of the U-boats that saw action in March were forced to return to base in April for replenishment and maintenance. This large number of returning U-boats put a strain upon the German infrastructure causing longer-than-expected delays in the Biscay ports. As such, the number of U-boats available for operations fell off substantially, and on 13 April a mere 33 U-boats were on station in the Atlantic. By the second half of the month the Germans were able to turn around many of their replenished U-boats and dispatched a sizable force back into the Atlantic. However, many of these boats arrived too late in their patrol areas to have a meaningful impact upon April operations. A second factor contributing to Germany's reduced success was the advent of better seasonal weather and longer days that improved the effectiveness of Allied detection equipment while concurrently robbing the U-boats of stealthy conditions. Finally, the Germans were hampered by continually improving Allied defences that challenged them both numerically and technically in all aspects of U-boat operations from departure to return to their Biscay bases.

Expanding upon this latter dynamic, by April many of the measures agreed to at the Casablanca Conference were finally bearing fruit. Paramount amongst these was the deployment of one American and five British support groups for operations in the North Atlantic. Three of these support groups possessed an escort carrier and all had between four and seven destroyers or other related escort vessels. With this and through the continuing expansion of their forces, the Allies were now capable of regularly having more than 100 anti-submarine escorts active in the North Atlantic at any given time as demonstrated by the 125 such vessels deployed on 1 April.[16] Also benefitting the Allies was the substantial increase in very long-range aircraft now available to them. In the winter of 1942 the Allies had possessed a mere six of these aircraft, but by May this number increased to 49, all of which were equipped with 10-centimetre ASV Mark III radar. These were split between the United Kingdom, Iceland and Newfoundland with 12 to 15 being operational at any given time.[17] Between the escort carriers and these very long-range aircraft, the air gap that existed in the centre of the North Atlantic was rapidly shrinking. Of course, this only represented a fraction of the anti-submarine aircraft available to the Allies, which in late April also included 72 10-centimetre radar-equipped Wellingtons, Liberators and Halifaxes that were earmarked for operations over the Bay of Biscay.[18]

The very-long range, American-built Consolidated B-24 Liberator was the most successful patrol aircraft in Coastal Command eventually accounting for or sharing in the destruction of some 70 U-boats during the war. Beyond this, the Liberator served as an effective minelayer and anti-shipping bomber in the Mediterranean and Far East. (Woodbine, G. (F/O), Royal Air Force official photographer, public domain)

The net result of these many factors was the loss of just 50 Allied and neutral merchant ships worth a combined 287,137 tons to German and Italian submarines in April.[19] This was less than half of March's total and represented the poorest output attained by the U-boats since December 1941. Making matters worse from a German point of view, their own losses remained high with at least 15 German U-boats and one Atlantic-based Italian submarine sunk during the month. As was now a regular pattern, the RAF sank the majority of these with *U635*, *U167*, *U632*, *U376*, *U189*, *U710*, *U332* and *U227* all succumbing to British aircraft.[20] Meanwhile, British warships accounted for *U124* and *U191* while a Swordfish from the escort carrier *Biter* combined with the destroyer *Pathfinder* to sink *U203*. This latter success represented the first kill attained by one of the new support groups. Of the remaining Axis losses, the British submarine *Tuna* sank *U644*, a British-laid mine destroyed *U526*, the American coast guard cutter *Spencer* accounted for *U175* and American aircraft sank *U174* and the Italian *Archimede*. Finally, sometime in late April or early May *U602* was lost due to unknown causes in the Mediterranean thus representing a probable sixteenth U-boat casualty for the month.[21]

As bad as this was from a German perspective, things became much worse when looking at the overall Allied shipping situation. During the first four months of 1943 Axis forces sank a combined 307 Allied and neutral merchant ships worth 1,702,490 tons in all theatres.[22] Of these, 194 merchant ships worth 1,173,143 tons were lost in the North Atlantic of which the overwhelming majority was sunk by German U-boats. U-boats also sank a sizable portion of the 85 merchant ships worth 427,886 tons that were sunk in the South Atlantic, Mediterranean and Indian Ocean.[23] When averaged out, this overall figure equated to roughly 77 merchant ships worth 425,623 tons sunk per month, which was nowhere near the tonnage necessary to cause meaningful attrition to the Allied merchant fleet. As emphasis for this point, during the same four-month period American shipyards alone produced 546 new merchant ships worth some 3,520,000 tons.[24] Thus, the resulting surplus of output over losses more than compensated for the shipping deficit that had occurred in 1942 and added almost an additional million tons to the Allied shipping pool. With production poised to continue increasing, the Germans now faced the implausible task of having to sink 1.3 million tons of shipping per month just to keep even.[25] Therefore, by the spring of 1943 Dönitz's tonnage campaign had clearly become a lost cause.

On the other hand, despite their improving shipping situation, the Allies had yet to decisively defeat the U-boat threat. Notwithstanding the loss of at least 49 U-boats from February through April, the U-boat arm had continued to grow. In April the number of U-boats in commission had reached 425 of which 240 were considered operational.[26] By the beginning of May 186 attack boats were earmarked for Atlantic service.[27] While these U-boats were incapable of achieving decisive victory, they still constituted a powerful force capable of inflicting heavy losses upon the Allies as indicated by March's results. In fact, a repetition of similar results on a consistent basis posed a serious impediment to the Allies' build-up in Britain and potentially even jeopardised the timetable for their return to mainland Europe. It was in this light that Dönitz and a now increasingly defensively minded Hitler saw the U-boat arm as Germany's first line of defence against the Western Allies.

The next opportunity for the Germans to exercise this defence was in May. With the return of large numbers of U-boats to the North Atlantic following their replenishment periods in the Biscay ports, the Germans were once again poised to launch major assaults against the transiting Allied convoys. The beginning of May found a staggering 113 U-boats present in the North Atlantic and the waters off the Americas (excluding those boats transiting to or from the South Atlantic). Some of these boats would soon arrive back in port, but the vast majority were available for operations. During the month a further 56 U-boats joined this sizable force thus maintaining a continuous rotation.[28] Unfortunately for them, these boats faced an ever-improving array of Allied countermeasures. With each passing month the Allies' technological and qualitative advantage became more pronounced as centimetric-wavelength radar, HF/DF and improved Asdic became increasingly prevalent and new weapons such as FIDO and aerial rockets made their operational debuts. Allied surface escorts and aircraft were now overwhelmingly manned by well-trained and motivated personnel that contrasted with their often inexperienced and timid counterparts in the U-boat fleet. Finally, Allied numbers in both warships and aircraft continued to grow. Given these competing factors, a clash of immense proportions was about to begin.

The two adversaries did not have long to wait. In the closing days of April, 16 U-boats formed a patrol line south of Iceland in search of Allied convoys. On 28 April one of these boats, *U650*, located westbound ONS.5 consisting of 42 merchant ships. Despite the intervention of a Catalina flying boat, the U-boat was able to report this contact thus putting in motion one of the greatest convoy battles of the war. Soon other U-boats arrived on the scene, but the convoy's defence, which consisted of two destroyers, a frigate, four corvettes and two trawlers of Escort Group B7, generally held them off. Finally, on 29 April *U258* sank the 6,198-ton American tanker *McKeespor*. Thereafter, the weather, which was already foul, deteriorated further, impeding U-boat operations. On 1 May the Germans lost contact with the convoy, which itself was having difficulty maintaining formation under the gale force conditions.

During the next three days the Germans carried out an extensive search for ONS.5 and two other convoys (SC.128 and HX.236) that were in the vicinity. In doing so, they eventually gathered 53 U-boats in the area directly south of Greenland and east of Newfoundland. On 4 May the Germans organised this force into a primary patrol line (Group *Fink*) and four smaller patrol lines (Group *Amsel*). That same day a Canadian patrol aircraft encountered and destroyed one of the *Fink* boats (most likely *U209*).[29] Despite this loss, the remaining 52 U-boats in Groups *Fink* and *Amsel* represented the largest concentration of U-boats ever assembled in the same patrol area. For their part, the British used this period to reinforce ONS.5 and collect stragglers. Unfortunately, the arrival of reinforcements was offset by the need to detach a number of escorts to St. John's for refuelling. Despite the large number of U-boats in the area, SC.128 and HX.236 avoided detection, but ONS.5 was not so fortunate, sailing directly into the centre of Group *Fink*.

On the afternoon of 4 May three U-boats reported contact with ONS.5. At the time the convoy had 30 ships in its main body with the destroyers *Vidette*, *Oribi* and *Offa*, the frigate *Tay* and the corvettes *Sunflower*, *Snowflake* and *Loosestrife* in escort. Astern of the convoy were two groups of stragglers under the escort of the corvette *Pink* and the trawler *Northern Spray*. This presented a nearly ideal tactical situation for the Germans as they were in position to menace the convoy from the north, west and south. Taking advantage of this opportunity, *Befehlshaber der Unterseeboote* (U-boat headquarters) ordered all of Group *Fink* and the two northernmost sections of Group *Amsel* to close in upon the convoy. In all, 40 U-boats were directed to attack ONS.5 thus constituting the largest wolf pack action of the war. With this, and the timely onset of moderate weather, conditions seemed ideal for the Germans to deliver a devastating assault against the convoy. Dönitz and his senior staff had high expectations for the outcome of the operation.

Over the next 36 hours the battle played itself out as the U-boats repeatedly probed the convoy's defences. In some cases the U-boats were able to penetrate the screen and inflict damage, but in most cases the skilled and determined British defenders frustrated their efforts. When the fighting finally subsided on 6 May due to the arrival of British reinforcements, the U-boats had sunk 12 merchant ships worth 55,760 tons. Unfortunately for them, this success came at a heavy price as the convoy's escorts sank no fewer than six U-boats (*U630*, *U192*, *U638*, *U125*, *U531* and *U438*) and damaged several other boats during the same time frame. When combined with the earlier destruction of the tanker *McKeespor* and *U209*, the final tally for the convoy action came to 13 merchant ships worth 61,958 tons sunk for the loss of seven U-boats. This equated to 1.86 merchant ships worth 8,851 tons sunk for each U-boat casualty thus representing an intolerable exchange rate for the Germans and a major turnaround from the March convoy battles of SC.121, SC.122 and HX.229. Even worse from a German point of view, given the many advantages the U-boats had going into their assault, it was now abundantly clear that the Allies had gained an operational ascendancy over the wolf packs.

It did not take long for this fact to be further proven. During the second week in May the Germans directed a combined 46 U-boats to operate against convoys HX.237 and SC.129. In the case of the former, the Germans succeeded in sinking three merchant ships worth 21,389 tons, but lost *U89*, *U456* and *U753* in return to British aircraft and escorts. The situation was much the same for convoy SC.129, which lost two merchant ships worth 7,627 tons, but extracted the destruction of

U186 and *U266* in return. A week later the British gained an even greater victory when aircraft and escorts defending convoy SC.130 destroyed *U273*, *U381*, *U258* and *U954* for no loss to themselves. Of the remaining 13 convoys proceeding east and west in the North Atlantic during May, the Germans only succeeded in sinking a single merchant ship worth 5,196 tons. Against this, the British frigate *Swale* from ONS.7 sank *U640* while aircraft from the escort carriers *Bogue* (American) and *Archer* (British) destroyed *U569* and *U752* respectively during operations in support of ON.184 and HX.239. Finally, British aircraft and warships covering southbound convoys OS.47, KX.10 and KMF.15 sank *U528*, *U436* and the Italian *Leonardo da Vinci* respectively.

As substantial as these results were, they only represented a portion of the U-boats lost during the month. RAF aircraft operating over the Bay of Biscay and other North Atlantic transit routes destroyed *U465*, *U109*, *U447*, *U663*, *U463*, *U646*, *U304*, *U440*, *U563* and the Italian *Enrico Tazzoli* while American aircraft in the same area added *U657* and *U467*. In southern waters American warships and aircraft sank *U176*, *U182* and *U128*. *U439* and *U659* were lost in an accidental collision while Allied forces in the Mediterranean accounted for *U303*, *U414* and *U755*. When it was all added up, a record 40 German U-boats and two Atlantic-based Italian submarines were lost during May. This unprecedented tally more than doubled the previous monthly record for U-boat losses set in February and significantly exceeded the concurrent U-boat production. Against this, German and Italian submarines only succeeded in sinking 45 Allied and neutral merchant ships worth 237,182 tons in May.[30] Not only was this a mere fraction of the tonnage necessary to inflict meaningful attrition against the Allies, but it constituted an exchange rate of 1.13 merchant ships worth 5,930 tons sunk for every U-boat lost. With such a rate, the prospect of any kind of real success for the U-boats was now gone, and the Kriegsmarine faced looming disaster.

This dire realisation was not lost to Dönitz or his senior staff. By the third week in May it was abundantly clear that operations under the current conditions substantially favoured the Allies and could only result in further intolerable losses for the Kriegsmarine. Therefore, on 24 May Dönitz suspended U-boat operations in the North Atlantic and ordered a phased withdrawal from the area. He redirected the bulk of his forces to concentrate on secondary areas that he speculated were less heavily defended, particularly by aircraft, such as the Caribbean Sea, the waters off Trinidad and Brazil and the west coast of Africa. Dönitz intended this to be a temporary measure until he could re-equip his U-boats with new weapons to counter the growing technical ascendancy the Allies had gained during recent months. In particular, he cited the acquisition of even more anti-aircraft guns, improved radar detectors and new anti-escort homing torpedoes as prerequisites before his U-boats could return to the North Atlantic. Nevertheless, despite the temporary nature of this move, Dönitz's withdrawal from the North Atlantic represented a strategic

The employment of support groups was just one of the many Allied innovations that turned the tide against the U-boat threat during the spring and summer of 1943. Pictured here is the sloop *Starling* from the British 2nd Support Group. (Beadell S. J. (Lt), public domain)

reversal of immense proportions and a clear admission of defeat that was beyond contention. After months of slowly gaining the initiative, the tide had abruptly and decisively turned in the Allies' favour.

Over the next few months the Allies consolidated and expanded this advantageous position as their anti-submarine forces continued to grow in size and capability. Included in the materiel side of this expansion was the recent procurement of new American-built destroyer escorts. Specifically designed for convoy defence applications, these destroyer escorts weighed in at between 1,100 and 1,400 tons, were capable of speeds of 21 knots or better and carried a variety of devices and weapons for the detection and killing of submarines. During the three-month period ending in June 1943 46 of these useful vessels were commissioned into Allied service including 19 that were sent to the Atlantic for escort duty. Production increased as the year progressed, and by war's end a total of 565 destroyer escorts were completed. Of these, 78 were transferred to the Royal Navy while many more saw service in the Atlantic as American naval vessels.[31]

This only represented a portion of the new warship construction that was underway at the time. A second major escort type to see widespread production during this period was the British River-class frigate. Weighing in at 1,310 to 1,460 tons and topping off at speeds of 21 knots, this design was well suited for conditions in the North Atlantic and carried the latest anti-submarine weapons and detection equipment. In all, British and Commonwealth shipyards produced 136 of these frigates during the duration of the war.[32] Meanwhile, the United States produced its own version of the River-class, called the *Tacoma*-class, of which 96 were built including 21 that were transferred to the Royal Navy.[33] While the Hedgehog forward-firing mortar system was standard issue on these various escorts, the British had two new warship designs under development/production to accommodate the forthcoming Squid system. The first of these was the Castle-class corvette, which was a follow-up to the widely successful Flower-class. Superior in both sea-keeping and anti-submarine capabilities, the British produced 39 'Castles' of which the first became available in the latter half of 1943. The second new warship design was the Loch-class frigate, which was an improved version of the River-class and arguably the best anti-submarine vessel of the war. The British produced 26 of these Loch-class frigates before war's end with the first entering service in 1944.[34]

Another major warship category that played an increasing role in Allied Atlantic operations was the escort carrier. Built using modified commercial designs and capable of operating up to 28 aircraft, although British carriers usually operated substantially less, these escort carriers were long in coming to the Atlantic. This was true for a number of reasons. First, escort carriers were highly versatile warships capable of performing a number of functions including many normally associated with fleet carriers. As such, they were highly prized assets and saw service in every maritime theatre of the war. For instance, during the summer of 1943 a number of British escort carriers were sent to the Mediterranean to support operations there. A second factor limiting Atlantic service was attrition. In November 1942 *Avenger* was sunk by *U155* while supporting Operation *Torch*. Four months later *Dasher* was lost in the Firth of Clyde when a faulty aircraft fuelling system

Table 7.1 Characteristics of Key Allied Escort Vessels during the period of 1943–1945

	Tonnage	Maximum speed (knots)	Standard main armament
Flower-class corvettes	925–1,110	16	1 × 4in gun, 1 Hedgehog, 70 DCs
Various destroyer escort classes	1,100–1,400	21+	3 × 3in guns, 1 Hedgehog, up to 200 DCs
River-class frigates	1,310–1,460	21	2 × 4in guns, 1 Hedgehog, up to 150 DCs
Castle-class corvettes	1,060	16.5	1 × 4in gun, 1 Squid, 1 rail for 15 DCs
Loch-class frigates	1,435	19.5	1 × 4in gun, 2 Squids, 1 rail and 2 throwers for 15 DCs
Various escort carrier classes	7,800–11,800	high teens	up to 28 aircraft

caused an accidental explosion. Finally, during the summer of 1943 *Archer* was withdrawn from service due to chronic engine problems. As a result of these mishaps and other functional concerns, the British had to extensively modify their American-built escort carriers to bring them up to an acceptable level of technical reliability, causing further delays. Yet, despite these various obstacles, a total of six American and two British escort carriers were available for duty in the Atlantic by summer's end.

Augmenting this growing number of purpose-built escort carriers was a supplemental development known as merchant aircraft carriers (MACs). These MACs were active merchant ships that retained their commercial purpose while concurrently fulfilling a limited military role. By constructing a simple flight deck over the superstructure of a grain carrier or tanker, the British were able to operate a small contingent of aircraft from these vessels while still retaining 80 percent of their cargo carrying capacity. In all, the British produced 19 MACs (six grain carriers and 13 tankers) with the first, *Empire MacAlpine*, entering service in April 1943. Since these vessels had minimal or non-existent hanger facilities, the typical complement on a MAC was only three or four Swordfish patrol aircraft for anti-submarine operations. While this contingent was certainly limited in size and capability, it still gave local escort commanders internal air assets to augment their organic defences. Thus, through the use of escort carriers and MACs, the Allies finally had the means to close the remaining air gaps that still existed within the Atlantic.

For operations closer to shore, Coastal Command and its comparable American and Canadian counterparts also enjoyed tangible improvements during this time. While the number of shore-based aircraft engaged in anti-submarine duties remained fairly constant, the percentage capable of very long-range operations continued to increase. With each passing month, more and more aircraft were equipped with 10-centimetre ASV Mark III radar and/or Leigh Lights. As such, Allied aircraft were increasingly able to saturate the Bay of Biscay and other targeted areas with both day- and night-time coverage. In doing so, they employed a deadly array of weapons that enhanced their ability to inflict fatal or severe damage upon the U-boats. In particular, following their successful debuts in May resulting in the destruction of three and two U-boats respectively, FIDO and aerial rockets became part of the standard weapon's mix carried on many aircraft.[35]

Beyond these materiel improvements, the Allies also enjoyed progress in a number of organisational and functional areas. Already discussed was the reversal of fortunes to occur in the area of cryptic intelligence during the summer of 1943. During the same period the United States established a new command to centralise and oversee American naval operations pertaining to the U-boat campaign in the Atlantic. Designated the Tenth Fleet, this command greatly improved America's ability to process applicable intelligence and orchestrate effective countermeasures to the U-boat threat. Part of this included assuming a more aggressive posture. On both sides of the Atlantic, Allied authorities increasingly moved away from a strategy of avoiding or deterring U-boats to a strategy of actively seeking them out and destroying them. For the Americans, this included a concerted effort to use HF/DF, Ultra intelligence and hunter-killer groups based around escort carriers to hunt down and destroy U-boats operating in the middle Atlantic. Particularly targeted during these operations were the limited number of U-tankers that facilitated long-range German patrols. Meanwhile, Britain's primary manifestation of this new policy revolved around their Bay of Biscay offensive, where support group warships soon augmented the ongoing aerial campaign.

Against this continually improving Allied position, the Germans were slow in making corresponding progress as their scientific and technical communities failed to provide the Kriegsmarine with relevant or effective countermeasures. The best example of this involved the development of a viable radar detector to counter 10-centimetre radar. It was understood that *Metox* emitted a small amount of radiation when in use. Unaware of Ultra and HF/DF, which in and of itself was a major intelligence and technical failure, the Germans erroneously surmised that the Allies had developed a means to home in on this radiation signature. Accordingly, the Germans expended a great deal of time and effort to develop an emissions-free substitute while severely restricting the use of *Metox*. Despite the recovery of a centimetric-wavelength radar set from a downed British aircraft in February, German scientists were slow to accept the feasibility of an airborne radar capable of operating at a 10-centimetre wavelength. As such, when the Germans deployed a supposedly non-emitting replacement for *Metox* in August, this device, called *Wanze*, searched in an 80-centimetre range and was thus ineffective against the Allies' 10-centimetre radar.

Compounding Germany's technical inadequacies were a number of tactical decisions that proved to be counterproductive. Throughout this period Dönitz issued a flurry of directives designed to blunt what he saw as the greatest threat to his U-boats – the proliferation and increased lethality of Allied aircraft engaged in anti-submarine operations. Already mentioned were his directives to first restrict, and then abandon the use of *Metox*. He also ordered his U-boats to remain submerged at night when crossing the Bay of Biscay to avoid Leigh Light-equipped aircraft. In doing so, U-boats were compelled to surface during the day to recharge their batteries. He further instructed his U-boats to remain on the surface and fight it out with attacking aircraft rather than crash dive, which was the common practice. Meanwhile, to multiply firepower, U-boats traversing the Bay of Biscay were to do so in groups of three to five whenever possible. Finally, when on the surface at night or in conditions of low visibility, U-boats were to run on a single motor to give lookouts a better chance of hearing approaching aircraft. Unfortunately for the Germans, these directives had little positive impact and actually made it easier for the Allies to locate and destroy transiting U-boats.

Given these conditions, the Allies continued to build upon the strategic success they had gained in May. In June the number of Allied and neutral merchant ships

The increased use of escort carriers in both convoy defence and hunter-killer groups represented a major weapon in the Allies' arsenal against the U-boats. Beyond that, escort carriers regularly participated in mining and antishipping operations off Norway. Pictured here is the escort carrier HMS *Pretoria Castle*. (Royal Navy official photographer, public domain)

sunk by German and Italian submarines dropped to the lowest level attained in a year and a half at 17 vessels worth 76,090 tons. Against this, Allied forces destroyed 17 German U-boats and one Atlantic-based Italian submarine for an exchange rate of roughly one-to-one. The fighting increased in July with losses on both sides jumping back up to May levels. In this case, the exchange rate was 46 merchant ships worth 237, 777 tons sunk for the loss of 37 U-boats. Thus, for the second time in three months, German U-boat losses far exceeded corresponding production levels. Finally, in August the Germans suffered a defeat yet unparalleled in the war. Not only did Allied losses drop back below 100,000 tons, but for the first time German U-boat losses exceeded the number of merchant ships they were able to sink. In this case, the Germans lost 25 U-boats for the destruction of 20 merchant ships worth 92,443 tons.[36]

Of the 79 U-boats sunk during this three-month period, almost half were lost due to the Allied offensive in the Bay of Biscay or the activities of American hunter-killer groups. In terms of the former, RAF Coastal Command deployed 20 squadrons of aircraft (including four American squadrons) in a massive assault against the Bay of Biscay transit routes. During this time RAF or RAF-affiliated aircraft destroyed *U418, U564, U126, U628, U535, U514, U607, U459, U614, U461, U383, U454, U106* and *U134* while American aircraft accounted for *U506* and *U706*. Meanwhile, British and American aircraft combined to sink *U558* and *U404*. Finally, warships of the soon to be famous British 2nd Support Group, under the command of Captain Johnny Walker, sank *U119, U449* and *U504* and shared in the destruction of *U462* with British aircraft while patrolling the outer portions of the bay. For their part, American hunter-killer groups built around the escort carriers *Bogue, Core, Santee* and *Card*, destroyed *U217, U118, U487, U160, U509, U67, U613, U527, U43, U117, U664, U525, U185, U84* and *U847*. Thus, from these two means, a total of 37 U-boats were destroyed including seven of the valuable U-tankers (four in the Bay and three by the hunter-killer groups).

The remaining 42 U-boats sunk during this time frame met their demises due to a number of causes. Since the Germans had largely pulled out of the North Atlantic, American forces operating predominately in more southerly waters accounted for the largest portion of these. Beyond the activities of the hunter-killer groups, American aircraft and ships accounted for *U521, U388, U194, U951, U232, U590, U159, U513, U662, U598, U622, U759, U359, U591, U199, U572, U615* and *U604* as well as the Italian *Barbarigo*. For their part, British naval and air units operating outside of the Bay of Biscay destroyed *U202, U308, U594, U417, U334, U200, U435, U135, U489* (U-tanker), *U468, U403, U523* and *U634*. These latter losses included residual U-boats left behind or passing through the North Atlantic, U-boats deploying out of Germany and U-boats operating off the west coast of Africa. Of the remaining 11 U-boat casualties, nine were sunk in areas outside of the Atlantic while a French aircraft accounted for *U105* and a probable mine strike claimed *U647*.

The three-month period following the climactic battles of May solidified the Allies' ascendancy over the U-boats. In practical terms, it was a sharp rebuke of German efforts to bypass the North Atlantic and find areas where they could attain meaningful results while mitigating their own losses. In fact, these operations in secondary areas yielded even worse results than had been the case in the highly contested North Atlantic. When compared to the previous three-month period culminating in May, everything had gone wrong for the Germans. Allied merchant losses had declined sharply, German U-boat losses had increased marginally and the corresponding exchange rate had reached an intolerable level. The recent loss of nine U-tankers, including *U463* sunk in May, severely restricted Germany's ability to continue operations in the Caribbean, South Atlantic and Indian Ocean. This latter point was important because the Indian Ocean was one of the only areas left where U-boats could still operate with reasonable impunity. Finally, heavy losses and the need to send reinforcements to the Arctic and Mediterranean had reduced the number of attack boats available for Atlantic operations to 115 by the end of August.[37]

When combining these factors together, it was clear that Germany had suffered a reversal of immense proportions. By turning the tide against the U-boats, the Allies had destroyed Germany's last, best hope for victory, slim though it was. Now nothing could stop the immense Allied build-up that was underway. This was not to say that the battle was over. Despite the disastrous turn of events that had befallen them, Dönitz and his U-boat arm would continue to fight on. In doing so, however, they abandoned all notions of a victorious tonnage campaign as Allied merchant losses fell to a point of being little more than a nuisance. Instead, they fought to maintain a degree of relevance within the overall war effort. The Kriegsmarine had invested considerable time and treasure in building its sizable U-boat force, and it simply could not allow this substantial asset to sit idly by while the rest of the nation waged war. If nothing else, the continuation of U-boat operations would tie down valuable Allied resources confronting this threat. Of course, this was an immensely dangerous task. Given the ever-increasing strength of the countermeasures arrayed against them, the U-boats, which for so long had been the hunters, were now largely the hunted, and a watery grave awaited most of Dönitz's crews. Only time would tell if their sacrifices netted consequential results in return.

CHAPTER 8

Retaining the Initiative

By the autumn of 1943 the tide of war had clearly turned against Germany. In the East, Soviet forces had blunted Germany's final attempt to regain the initiative, and the Germans were now irretrievably on the defensive. In the Mediterranean, the Allies had invaded Sicily and driven Italy out of the war. Soon, Allied armies would be advancing up the Italian peninsula, compelling the Germans to divert some two dozen divisions to defend the territory of their former Axis partner. Meanwhile, over Germany itself, the Allied bombing campaign was beginning to bear significant results, and the Germans were forced to devote ever-increasing resources to defend their homeland. In the maritime conflict, recent German U-boat losses had risen beyond their replacement rate while successes against Allied merchant shipping had fallen to inconsequential levels. This decline had prompted Grand-Admiral Dönitz to withdraw his U-boats from the North Atlantic to preserve their strength. In doing so, he abandoned the focal region of the entire maritime war and handed the Allies a substantial moral victory.

Yet, despite this momentous development, Dönitz had always intended this withdrawal to be temporary, and in September a handful of German U-boats re-entered the North Atlantic to re-establish operations against the transiting Allied convoys. Forming Group *Leuthen*, a total of 21 Type VII U-boats departed France and Norway for the North Atlantic. Each of these boats carried recent upgrades to redress the technical ascendancy the Allies had gained during the previous year. This included increased anti-aircraft armament, the new *Wanze* radar detector and the equally new T-5 *Zaunkönig* acoustic homing torpedo. This latter weapon was an improvement over the largely ineffective T-3 *Falke* acoustic torpedo and was specially earmarked for use against Allied escort vessels. Travelling predominately submerged and minimising radio transmissions to facilitate surprise, the Group *Leuthen* U-boats slowly made their way into the North Atlantic. By mid-September these U-boats congregated southeast of Greenland where they established a patrol line to catch westbound convoys entering the Greenland Air Gap. Because of this area's substantial distance from land, the Germans hoped to minimise interference from Allied shore-based aircraft as they assaulted westbound convoys passing through the gap. They would then repeat the same process in the opposite direction with eastbound convoys. Once engaged, they would use their T-5 acoustic homing torpedoes to dispose of the convoy escorts and then destroy the exposed merchant ships at will with conventional torpedoes.

Despite German efforts to maintain stealth and security, these movements quickly garnered Allied attention. British authorities had long anticipated a German return to the North Atlantic, and Ultra intelligence soon confirmed this development. By this time, the British had two converging convoys moving into the danger zone presented by Group *Leuthen*. These were ONS.18 and ON.202 with a combined 65 merchant ships and 15 escort vessels. To counter the presence of Group *Leuthen*, the British ordered the newly formed Canadian 9th Support Group, consisting of a further five escort vessels, into the area to assist the convoys. This brought the total number of escorts available for defence to five destroyers, three frigates, 11 corvettes and a trawler. Additionally, ONS.18 contained the merchant aircraft carrier *Empire MacAlpine*, which carried three Swordfish aircraft. Finally, the British ordered the convoys to alter course northward to bring them closer to shore-based air support and to potentially avoid the German patrol line.

Despite this latter move, a number of *Leuthen* U-boats encountered British escorts on the 19th, and early the next day *U270* reported the presence of ON.202. This began a three-day convoy battle resulting in the destruction of six Allied merchant ships worth 36,422 tons along with the Canadian destroyer *St. Croix*, the British frigate *Itchen* and the British corvette *Polyanthus*. Against this, the Germans lost *U341* to a Canadian aircraft while Canadian/British warships destroyed *U338* and *U229*. Compared to other recent convoy battles, this result was clearly an improvement for the Germans, but the three-to-one exchange rate still represented an unsustainable level of attrition for their forces. Making matters worse, the impact of Dönitz's new weapons was less than hoped for. Of these, the T-5 *Zaunkönig* torpedo was by far the most successful resulting in the destruction of all three Allied escorts. Still, the Allies had long anticipated the development of this weapon, and they immediately devised effective countermeasures in the form of Foxer and CAT acoustic decoys. Thereafter, the T-5's lethality was greatly diminished, although never entirely eliminated. *Wanze* proved to be a substantial failure due to its inability to detect 10-centimetre radar. While the increased anti-aircraft armament certainly improved U-boat defences against attacking aircraft, it was not a conclusive deterrent as demonstrated by the loss of *U341*.

Nor were the Germans able to maintain this level of relative success. In October the Germans established three new U-boat groups in the North Atlantic. Unfortunately for them, the Allies monitored each of these deployments and successfully routed the majority of threatened convoys around the danger. When contacts were made, these were largely intentional as Allied authorities sent heavily defended convoys into the heart of U-boat concentrations to draw the Germans out under favourable conditions. The result of this was catastrophic for the Kriegsmarine. On 6–9 October a battle around convoy SC.143 resulted in the destruction of the Polish destroyer *Orkan* and the 5,612-ton American merchant ship *Yorkmar* for the loss of three U-boats (*U419*, *U643* and *U610*) to British aircraft. One week later an even larger battle developed around the closely proceeding convoys ON.206 and ONS.20, during which the U-boats sank a single British merchant ship worth 6,625 tons, but lost six of their own number in return. British aircraft sank *U844*, *U964*, *U470* and *U540* while British escorts accounted for *U631* and *U841*. Finally, at the end of the month there were a series of engagements in the vicinity of convoys ON.207 and ON.208 during which British aircraft and warships sank *U274*, *U420* and *U282* for no losses to themselves.

As bad as this was, it only represented part of the calamity to befall the U-boats during this period. Supported by Ultra and HF/DF intelligence, the Allies were able to saturate the U-boat transit routes and assembly areas with shore and carrier-based aircraft. In this manner, British aircraft destroyed *U669* and *U221* in September and *U336* and *U389* in October. Meanwhile, American naval aircraft operating predominately from hunter/killer escort carriers sank *U161*, *U279*, *U460* (U-tanker), *U422*, *U402*, *U378*, *U220* and *U584* (the first in September and the rest in October). British warships and aircraft sank *U566*, *U306* and *U732* in the waters off Gibraltar while five other U-boats were sunk in the Baltic, Mediterranean and Indian Ocean. When combined with the earlier-listed losses, the toll for U-boat casualties in September and October came to nine and 26 respectively. Added to this was a tenth U-boat, *U760*, lost in September due to Spanish internment. By comparison, German U-boats sank an unimpressive 16 and 20 Allied and neutral merchant ships worth 98,852 and 91,295 tons during these months.[1] Thus, notwithstanding the relative success of Group *Leuthen*, the overall period was one of continued failure for Germany's U-boat arm.

This reality continued even as November brought a number of changes to U-boat operations. Recognising the Allies' ability to route around and/or defeat concentrated U-boat groups, Dönitz dispersed his U-boats into smaller formations that covered greater expanses of ocean. He also ordered his U-boats to remain fully submerged during the day to avoid detection and rescinded the policy of fighting back against attacking aircraft. Finally, he ordered his U-boats to carry out attacks only at night. The result of this, along with the onset of winter weather, was a sharp decline in contacts and losses on both sides. For the remainder of the year German U-boats only succeeded in sinking a further 17 merchant ships worth 86,520 tons in all theatres.[2] Against this, 19 and eight U-boats were lost in November and December respectively. Of the 21 U-boats sunk in the Atlantic during this time frame: British warships accounted for *U226*, *U842*, *U536*, *U538*, *U648* and *U600*; RAF aircraft sank *U707*, *U280*, *U211*, *U542* and *U391*; American warships and aircraft sank

U405, U848, U508, U849, U86, U172, U850 and *U645*; and American and British aircraft combined to destroy *U966* while marine causes accounted for *U284*.

With this, another year in the Atlantic struggle came to an end. In every major respect, this milestone found the Allies in a significantly better position than they had been the year before. In 1943 total Allied and neutral merchant shipping losses due to hostile action numbered 597 vessels worth 3,220,137 tons of which 452 merchant ships worth 2,510,304 tons were sunk by German and Italian submarines.[3] These former figures represented a 64 and 59 percent reduction in the total number of vessels and tonnage sunk compared to the previous year. More importantly, during the same 12-month period American shipyards produced an incredible 1,949 merchant ships worth some 13 million tons while British yards added a further 1.2 million tons to the Allied shipping pool.[4] This represented a better than fourfold increase in production over losses thus resulting in an additional 11 million tons of shipping becoming available to the Allied cause. As such, the shipping availability crisis that had warranted such concern at the beginning of 1943 was largely abated by year's end.

A second major area enjoying considerable improvement during this period was Britain's import situation. In 1943 the total number of convoyed merchant ships proceeding to the United Kingdom increased to 6,903 compared to the previous year's 5,892.[5] Augmenting this increased activity was a corresponding reduction in the related convoy loss rate (both to and from the United Kingdom), which dropped to 0.95 percent from 1.5 percent.[6] Together, these improvements helped foster a 22.7 percent increase in annual British imports, which amounted to 41,836,000 tons in 1943 compared to 34,090,000 tons in 1942.[7] While still far short of Britain's pre-war norms, this result reversed the downward trend of the previous three years and eased restrictions on Britain's industrial base and civilian population. No longer was the nation threatened by the prospect of economic starvation as stockpiles of many key resources rebounded. Britain also saw a substantial increase in military activity as several hundred thousand American (and to a far lesser extent Canadian) troops and millions of tons of supplies and equipment arrived in preparation for the upcoming invasion of Northwest Europe. When added to their own internal armed forces, this flow of men and materiel rapidly turned Britain into an armed camp that would soon unleash its fury on the beaches of France.

For their part, the Germans suffered a significantly different outcome. In 1943 the Kriegsmarine lost a total of 238 U-boats in all theatres. This came close to tripling the number of U-boats sunk in 1942 and was significantly greater than the total number of U-boats lost during the first 40 months of the war (up until the beginning of 1943). This level of attrition largely halted expansion within the German U-boat arm and facilitated a decline in the number of operational U-boats. In fairness, the Kriegsmarine was not in any danger of immediate impotency since it still possessed 436 commissioned U-boats at the beginning of 1944. However, only

Table 8.1 Key Performance Indices from the Battle of the Atlantic

	Total allied tonnage lost due to submarine attack	Total allied tonnage lost due to other military means	Total British tonnage lost due to submarine attack	Total British tonnage lost due to other military means	Additional merchant tonnage added to the British flag	Total import tons delivered to the United Kingdom	German U-boats sunk
Jan–Mar 42	1,341,788	591,915	527,400	185,400	347,000	8,845,000	11
Apr–Jun 42	1,739,146	474,557	537,000	247,800	563,000	8,808,000	10
Jul–Sep 42	1,505,888	340,685	687,300	165,000	536,000	9,333,000	31
Oct–Dec 42	1,679,393	117,325*	1,010,000	101,300	665,000	7,481,000	34
Jan–Mar 43	1,189,833	167,977	542,800	100,100	489,000	7,296,000	40
Apr–Jun 43	688,548	79,385	342,900	42,700	653,000	11,068,000	73
Jul–Sep 43	457,565	184,053	190,900	120,200	850,000	13,100,000	72
Oct–Dec 43	250,959	201,817	98,500	76,200	1,065,000	10,748,000	53

Source: The Central Statistical Office, *Statistical Digest of the War* (London: Her Majesty's Stationery Office, 1975), pp. 177–181, 184–185 and S. W. Roskill, *The War at Sea 1939–1945, Volume II: The Period of Balance* (London: Her Majesty's Stationery Office, 1956), p. 485 and *Volume III, Part I: The Offensive* (London: Her Majesty's Stationery Office, 1960), p. 388.
Note: See Note from Table 4.3.
* This includes two vessels worth 2,229 tons that were lost on unknown dates and are rolled into the fourth quarter to capture their presence.

168 of these were considered operational thus representing a 19 percent decline in this category from six months earlier.[8] Compounding this materiel situation was the loss of related crews. Due to the high fatality/capture rate associated with these events, only a minimal number of crewmen from the 238 U-boats sunk in 1943 ever returned to fight again. As such, inexperienced crewmen would predominately staff the new U-boats attaining operational status in 1944. Considering that these fledgling crews faced the same conditions that had bested their more experienced predecessors, their prospects for success and survival were limited.

No one was more aware of this reality than Dönitz. Given the current qualitative inferiority plaguing his forces, he could expect nothing more than a continuation of the recent failures that had befallen them. Fortunately for him, new weapons were in the works that promised to remedy the technical side of this imbalance. Of these, none was more important than a new generation of submarines known as electro-boats. Featuring streamlined hulls and substantially increased battery capacity, these electro-boats possessed significantly better underwater performance than their conventional counterparts and came in two variants. The first was the large ocean-going Type XXI. With a surface displacement of 1,621 tons and an outfit of 23 torpedoes, the Type XXI was capable of submerged speeds in excess of 17 knots and underwater endurance of 60 hours when travelling at five knots. This performance, which more than doubled that of conventional U-boats, gave the

Type XXI an enhanced ability to penetrate convoy defences and elude Allied surface escorts. The second was a much smaller version designated the Type XXIII. Weighing in at a paltry 234 tons (surfaced), the Type XXIII lacked some of the Type XXI's enhanced performance and only carried two torpedoes. Still, the Germans hoped that the Type XXIII would effectively function in shallow coastal areas, such as the waters around Britain, where the deployment of larger submarines was impractical.

In the waning months of 1943 the Germans drew-up elaborate plans to produce their new U-boat types. Realising that traditional production methods were too slow to meet the aggressive delivery schedule demanded by Dönitz, the Germans opted to use a prefabrication system to facilitate this process. Under this system, a variety of auxiliary facilities located throughout Germany produced the U-boats in prefabricated sections and then sent these sections to major shipyards in Bremen, Hamburg and Danzig for final assembly. By doing this, the Germans estimated they would reduce the number of man-hours necessary to produce a Type XXI U-boat from 460,000 using traditional methods to 260,000–300,000 using this new prefabrication method.[9] This also allowed them to diversify their production efforts thus making them less vulnerable to Allied bombing while concurrently easing pressure on the limited space available in the major shipyards. With this plan in place, the Germans hoped to complete their first Type XXI in April 1944 and achieve a production rate of 30 U-boats per month by September. Of course, it would take several months after this before these newly produced U-boats attained operational status. As such, it would likely be 1945 before this new generation of U-boats made its presence felt.

In the meantime, the Germans had a second major technical innovation that promised a much faster implementation. This came in the form of the snorkel, which was a retractable double-barrelled breathing tube that allowed U-boats to run their diesel engines while submerged. It accomplished this by sucking fresh air into the submarine through one barrel while expelling exhaust gases through the other. Incorporated into the new electro-boats as well as retrofitted onto the older Type VII and IX models, the snorkel gave the German U-boats the ability (depending upon weather conditions) to operate in a perpetual submerged state. This, in turn, theoretically increased the

Table 8.2 Characteristics of Selected German U-boats during the period of 1942–1945

	Displacement (tons) surf/subm	Speed (knots) surf/subm	Surface range miles/knots	Submerged endurance miles/knots	Main armament
Type VIIC	749/851	17.7/7.6	8,500/10	80/4	5 TT, 14 Torpedoes
Type IXC	1,102/1,213	18.25/7.3	13,450/10	64/4	6 TT, 22 Torpedoes
Type XIV	1,688/1,932	14.9/6.2	12,300/10	55/4	AA Only – U-tanker
Type XXI	1,621/1,819	15.6/17.2	15,500/10	340/5	6 TT, 23 Torpedoes
Type XXIII	234/258	9.7/12.5	2,600/8	194/4	2 TT, 2 Torpedoes

U-boats survivability since the snorkel presented a significantly smaller profile to detect on radar or by visual observation than a fully surfaced submarine. On the other hand, the snorkel also had its deficiencies. Snorkels could only be used in relatively calm weather and then only when the U-boat was travelling at speeds of six knots or less. Submerged diesel operations were noisy thus increasing the possibility of hydrophone/passive sonar detection while simultaneously deafening the U-boat's own audio detection devices. Travelling submerged on diesel engines also consumed twice as much fuel as similar operations on the surface. Still, despite these shortcomings, the Germans went forward with the snorkel, which made its operational debut in early 1944.

While the Germans waited for their new weapons to materialise, the fighting in the Atlantic continued. By the beginning of 1944 German authorities assumed that an Allied invasion of Northwest Europe and/or Norway was imminent, and they progressively scaled back offensive U-boat operations to preserve strength for this expected onslaught. This is not to say that offensive patrols were entirely abandoned. Citing a need to tie down Allied resources, free up space in the Biscay ports, maintain the combat efficiency of their crews, test new equipment and do weather reporting, the Germans sent a handful of U-boats into the Atlantic to carry out largely independent patrols or small pack operations. From January through May the number of U-boats dispatched for patrols in the Atlantic, Indian Ocean and waters off the Americas numbered 41, 37, 30, 15 and 10 respectively.[10] During the same time numerous other U-boats deployed to Norway and the Mediterranean as Hitler ordered reinforcements to these secondary areas.

The Allies confronted these limited deployments with a powerful array of warships and aircraft bolstered by some new technical and tactical innovations of their own. This included improved Asdic that allowed surface escorts to better determine the depth of submerged U-boats and new depth charges that descended deeper and carried a more powerful punch. Squid-armed escorts were now becoming available thus bringing the navy's anti-submarine capabilities to a higher level yet. In those cases where new technology was not available, the British used tactics to compensate for these deficiencies. Largely perfected by Captain Johnny Walker and his British 2nd Support Group, these tactics called for two or more escorts to work in unison when engaging submerged U-boats. In its primary form, known as a creeping attack, one escort maintained Asdic contact while the other carried out the engagement. In a variation of this, known as a barrage attack, two or more escorts engaged in succession thus saturating the target area with depth charges. Using these tactics, Walker's 2nd Support Group became the most prolific U-boat killing unit of the war.

Meanwhile, in the air the Allies employed two innovations that had been around for a while, but now gained meaningful usage for the detection and tracking of submerged U-boats. The first of these was Magnetic Anomaly Detection (MAD), which used a magnetometer to detect anomalies in the earth's magnetic field caused by a U-boat's ferrous hull. This device was hampered by an extremely limited range of only 400 to 600 feet, but when used in confined areas, such as the Straits of Gibraltar, proved to be capable of detecting transiting U-boats. The second detection device came in the form of expendable air-dropped sonobuoys that deployed passive hydrophones upon entering the water. Released over a suspected target area, sonobuoys listened for the sounds of submerged submarines and then transmitted those sounds by means of radio to the parent aircraft. With these two systems, aircraft now had a limited capability to detect and track submerged U-boats as well as their already proven effectiveness against those travelling on the surface.

Given the disparity in effort, technology and tactical proficiency that existed during this period, it came as little surprise that the Germans continued to suffer limited success and heavy losses against the Allied anti-submarine juggernaut. From January through May 1944 German U-boats only succeeded in sinking a paltry 54 Allied and neutral merchant ships worth 322,152 tons in all wartime theatres.[11] When broken down, this amounted to an insignificant 10.8 merchant ships worth 64,430 tons sunk per month. Added to this were a number of Allied warships sunk by German U-boats. In the Atlantic and Arctic this included: the American escort carrier *Block Island*; the British destroyers *Hardy* and *Mahratta*; the assorted escort vessels *Tweed*, *Woodpecker*, *Warwick*, *Gould*, *Asphodel*, *Leopold* (American), and *Valleyfield* (Canadian). Against this, the Germans lost a total of 106 U-boats from January through May including 76 that were lost in the Atlantic or Arctic. When averaged out, this equated to slightly better than 21 U-boats sunk per month, which generally matched their commissioning rate. Even worse, German efforts to preserve their strength moderately degraded as losses and transfers reduced the number of attack boats assigned to the Atlantic from 121 at the beginning of January to just 89 at the beginning of May.[12]

Of the 76 U-boats lost in the Atlantic or Arctic during this period, no fewer than 58 were sunk solely or partially as a result of British action.[13] Reversing the trend of the past year and a half where aircraft attained the highest success figures, British warships accounted for or participated in the destruction of more than half of these. By themselves, the relentless British 2nd Support Group accounted for the destruction of *U592*, *U762*, *U238*, *U734*, *U424*, *U264*, *U653*, *U961* and *U473*. Other British and Canadian warships sank or participated in the destruction of *U757*, *U305*, *U641*, *U314*, *U406*, *U386*, *U257*, *U713*, *U91*, *U358*, *U472*, *U744*, *U845*, *U575*, *U355*, *U360*, *U302*, *U962*, *U448*, *U311*, *U765* and *U289*. For their part, British shore-based aircraft sank *U426*, *U231*, *U571*, *U364*, *U545*, *U283*, *U601*, *U625*, *U976*, *U342*, *U193*, *U846*, *U240*, *U241*, *U476*, *U675*, *U990* and *U292*. Meanwhile, by this stage in the war the FAA was able to make a more meaningful contribution as aircraft from the British escort carriers *Fencer*, *Chaser*, *Vindex*, *Tracker* and *Activity* sank *U666*, *U366*, *U973*, *U288*, *U277*, *U674* and *U959* and shared in the destruction of five other U-boats (listed above) with British warships. The remaining two U-boats, *U263* and *U974*, were sunk by a British-laid mine and the Norwegian submarine *Ula*.

During the last two years of the war improved weapons, organisation and tactics increasingly turned the U-boat struggle in favor of the Allies. Pictured here is a British Loch-class frigate, which armed with the Squid forward-firing mortar system, was the premier anti-submarine vessel of the war. (Royal Navy/MOD, OGL v1.0)

Mastery over the U-boats decisively secured the all-important North Atlantic, but in the autumn of 1943 there was still one major convoy route susceptible to meaningful German interference – the Arctic route to the Soviet Union. Following the battle of the Barents Sea at the end of 1942, the Allies ran two more convoys to and from Russia with the loss of four merchant ships worth 25,705 tons to U-boats and a fifth merchant ship worth 6,800 tons sunk due to marine causes. Then at the end of March 1943 the British suspended convoys to Russia due to the coming unfavourable summer weather and the need to concentrate escort strength in the North Atlantic. As the year progressed, a primary impediment to restarting these convoys was the powerful German surface force present in Norway, which by the summer included the battleship *Tirpitz*, the battlecruiser *Scharnhorst* and the pocket battleship *Lützow*. Not only did these powerful units impede a resumption of Arctic convoys, but they also posed a persistent breakout threat to the North Atlantic.

In September 1943 the British launched an operation to neutralise this threat utilising the recently developed X-craft midget submarine. Weighing in at 27 tons and staffed by a four-man crew, the X-craft had a top underwater speed of 5.5 knots and an armament consisting of two 4,480-pound detachable saddle charges. On the night of 11/12 September six conventional British submarines departed Loch Cairnbawn in Northwest Scotland to begin an eight-day journey to Altenfjord in Northern Norway. Each of these submarines had a single X-craft in tow, which they intended to launch once they arrived at their destination. From there, the X-craft would penetrate into the fjord and attack the German warships located at Kaafjord anchorage. The British planned to utilise three X-craft against *Tirpitz* while two others targeted *Scharnhorst* and the last went after *Lützow*. Unfortunately, two of the X-craft, *X8* and *X9*, were lost en route due to accidents and technical problems thus reducing the proposed assault force by a third.

On 20 September the remaining submarines arrived at various locations around Altenfjord where they waited until evening and then launched their respective X-craft. Of these, *X5* was never heard from again while *X10* experienced a series of technical difficulties that eventually forced it to abort its mission and return to the rendezvous point. The two remaining X-craft, *X6* and *X7*, continued their journey and successfully circumvented extensive net defences and other hazards to eventually reach Kaafjord anchorage on the morning of the 22nd. Once there, both X-craft located *Tirpitz* and successfully released their saddle charges below the moored battleship. With this accomplished, *X6* scuttled itself while *X7* attempted to escape, but was also subsequently lost. Of the eight men aboard these two midget submarines, six survived to be captured by the Germans while the other two perished. The sole-surviving *X10* eventually rendezvoused with the submarine *Stubborn*, but was scuttled later on the return trip to Britain. Thus, of the assault force, all six X-craft and 16 men were lost.[14]

Fortunately, this expenditure in men and materiel was not in vain. At 0812 hours the charges laid by *X6* and *X7* detonated. By this time the alerted Germans had winched *Tirpitz* to starboard, negating the worst effects of the blast, but the massive explosions still caused extensive shock damage to the stationary battleship. Of particular consequence, all three of *Tirpitz*'s main turbines were disabled thus immobilising the massive giant. German authorities soon reported that it would take at least six months to repair the damage. This was no easy task given the limited facilities available in Norway. To compensate for this, the Germans were compelled to dispatch the repair ship *Neumark*, the accommodation ship *New York* and an army of valuable technicians and yard workers to Altenfjord to enact repairs. Even so, without the use of a dry dock, the Germans were unable to fully repair the hull, retarding *Tirpitz*'s ability to ever again operate at full speed.

Ultra intelligence conveyed these realities to the British, who were also bolstered by the news that *Lützow* had departed Norway to return to Germany. As a result of these developments and upon the urging of the Soviet government, the British agreed to restart convoy service to the Soviet Union. The first of these operations began in November with both outbound and inbound convoys undertaken, and by the third week in December the British had successfully passed 73 merchant ships either to or from Russia without loss.[15] This success was largely due to the advent of the Arctic winter, which made detection difficult, and the fact that the Luftwaffe in Norway was now a mere shell of its former self. In the latter part of

December the British conducted another series of convoys with JW.55B consisting of 19 merchant ships heading to Russia while RA.55A returned with 22 merchant ships. Each of these convoys possessed an escort that included ten destroyers while Vice-Admiral Robert Burnett provided close cover with Force 1 consisting of the heavy cruiser *Norfolk* and the light cruisers *Belfast* and *Sheffield*. Meanwhile, Admiral Bruce Fraser, the new Commander-in-Chief of the Home Fleet, provided distant cover with Force 2 consisting of the battleship *Duke of York*, the light cruiser *Jamaica* and four destroyers.

On 20 December JW.55B departed Loch Ewe to be followed two days later by the departure of homeward-bound RA.55A from Kola. On the morning of 22 December a German aircraft on a routine meteorological flight detected JW.55B and reported it as a troop convoy. Based upon this erroneous report, the Germans initially concluded that an assault against Norway might be underway and took a number of preparatory measures to meet this threat. This included increasing air reconnaissance, repositioning U-boats around Vestfjord and putting *Scharnhorst* and its destroyers on three-hour sailing notice. That afternoon further reconnaissance reclassified the sighting as a convoy, and German aircraft and U-boats were able to maintain periodic contact with JW.55B over the next three days. Realizing that the convoy had been spotted, Admiral Fraser surmised that intervention from *Scharnhorst* was likely and ordered a number of course and speed alterations to better consolidate his scattered forces. Since German attention was focused on JW.55B, he ordered four destroyers from RA.55A to reinforce the more threatened convoy.

On the evening of 25 December Fraser's actions were validated when *Scharnhorst* and five destroyers departed Altenfjord with orders from Dönitz to seek out and destroy the eastbound British convoy. At 0218 hours the next morning Fraser and Burnett received an emergency Ultra intelligence warning that *Scharnhorst* was probably at sea. An hour and 21 minutes later the Admiralty broadcast a general message stating: 'Admiralty appreciates *Scharnhorst* at sea.' At about this time JW.55B was some 50 miles south of Bear Island heading east-northeast while RA.55A was 220 miles west of Bear Island and considered out of danger. Meanwhile, Admiral Burnett's Force 1 and Admiral Fraser's Force 2 were 150 and 210 miles east and west of the endangered convoy and proceeding quickly to close the distance. Shortly after 0700 hours the German squadron, under the command of Rear-Admiral Erich Bey, arrived east of the convoy's expected position and began a westward sweep with the destroyers line abreast in the lead. At 0820 hours Bey turned *Scharnhorst* northward, possibly to investigate an old sighting report from *U716*, and in the process of doing so lost contact with his destroyers. He would never again regain contact, and they would play no further part in the upcoming action.

At 0840 hours the British cruiser *Belfast* from Force 1 picked up *Scharnhorst* on its radar at 35,000 yards. Within minutes the other two British cruisers also gained radar contact, and Admiral Burnett manoeuvred his force to place it between the

German battlecruiser and the convoy. At 0921 hours *Sheffield* gained visual contact with *Scharnhorst* at 13,000 yards and eight minutes later Burnett ordered his cruisers to engage. As it was, only *Norfolk* was able to do so since the formation they were travelling in blocked the line of fire of the other two British cruisers. Still, *Norfolk's* shooting was good, and it managed to score two hits on *Scharnhorst* in its first three salvos. This onslaught took *Scharnhorst* completely by surprise, but the battlecruiser quickly recovered and turned away at high speed. Soon *Scharnhorst* was able to put distance between itself and the pursuing British cruisers. Nevertheless, *Scharnhorst* had already sustained serious damage as one of *Norfolk's* shells had disabled its main radar and port high-angle fire control director, rendering the battlecruiser partially blind in the Arctic winter darkness.

Meanwhile, Burnett quickly realised that the prevailing heavy seas impeded his ability to catch the fleeing German raider, and at 1014 hours he broke off his pursuit to remain with the convoy. A major factor in this decision was his belief that *Scharnhorst* would circle around to the north to make another attempt at JW.55B. Events soon proved him correct when at 1205 hours *Belfast* regained radar contact with the approaching German battlecruiser, and at 1221 hours all three British cruisers opened fire. Once again, *Scharnhorst* was caught by surprise, but quickly recovered to return fire. After a twenty-minute exchange that caused damage to both sides, *Scharnhorst* again broke away on a south-easterly heading. This time, Burnett chose to follow his quarry since the wind and sea were on his beam. Joined by the four destroyers detached from RA.55A, Burnett's ships remained out of visual range and tracked the German battlecruiser by radar, sending a steady stream of position reports.

The beneficiary of these reports was Admiral Fraser's Force 2, which was rapidly approaching from the southwest. At 1617 hours *Duke of York* picked up *Scharnhorst* on radar at a range of 45,000 yards. Over the next several minutes the range closed, and at about 1651 hours *Duke of York* opened fire with its main armament. For the third time that day *Scharnhorst* was caught by surprise as a hit from *Duke of York's* first salvo disabled its forward (Anton) gun turret. After receiving further hits, *Scharnhorst* turned first to the north, where it encountered Force 1, and then to the east as a running battle developed. In this, *Scharnhorst* was gradually able to pull away from its British pursuers, but at 1820 hours a 14-inch shell from *Duke of York* hit and disabled one of *Scharnhorst's* boiler rooms, reducing the battlecruiser's speed to 22 knots. Shortly thereafter, the British destroyers *Savage*, *Saumarez*, *Scorpion* and *Stord* (Norwegian) rushed forward and conducted a well-coordinated torpedo attack that scored four hits and further reduced *Scharnhorst's* speed.

Scharnhorst's fate was now sealed. Within minutes *Duke of York*, *Jamaica*, *Belfast* and *Norfolk* (*Sheffield* was no longer present due to a gearing problem) closed in upon the wounded German battlecruiser and pummelled it with a deluge of heavy calibre shells. *Scharnhorst* was soon reduced to a floating wreck, and at 1919 hours

Admiral Fraser ordered his cruisers and destroyers forward to finish off the stricken warship with torpedoes. Several vessels complied, and *Scharnhorst* was hit by at least seven torpedoes. Finally at 1945 hours there was a large explosion, and *Scharnhorst*, which was shrouded in smoke and mist, disappeared from British radar screens as it began its final plunge to the ocean bottom. When the British came forward, all they found of the once proud battlecruiser were scores of men bobbing in the freezing Arctic water. Of *Scharnhorst*'s original crew of 1,968 officers and men, a mere 36 survived to be made prisoners by the British. None of these were officers. For their part, several British ships suffered varying degrees of damage during the engagement, but none were severely injured. Finally, regarding the focal point of the whole undertaking, JW.55B and RA.55A successfully arrived at their respective destinations without loss to any of their merchant ships on 29 December and 1 January respectively.

This action, which later became known as the battle of North Cape, significantly improved the strategic situation for the British. With *Scharnhorst* sunk and *Tirpitz* temporarily disabled, the surface threat from Norway effectively ceased to exist for the time being. As 1944 dawned, U-boats remained the only meaningful threat to menace the Arctic convoys, and as previously discussed, the British were more than capable of dealing with this peril. For the remainder of the war the British dispatched 13 eastbound convoys to Russia that successfully delivered 368 merchant ships for the loss of just five of their number. During the same period 14 westbound convoys departed Russia and returned 386 merchant ships with only six lost en route and two more sunk at Kola before joining RA.64.[16] When combined together, this constituted an insignificant 1.7 percent loss rate. In addition, the neutralisation of Germany's surface threat allowed the British to reduce the Home Fleet and send sorely needed reinforcements to conduct operations against the Japanese in the Indian Ocean and Pacific. Finally, what remained of the Home Fleet was now in a position to go over to the offensive and conduct significant operations against German-controlled shipping in and around Norway.

Of course, these latter-mentioned operations constituted a mere fraction of the effort put forth by the British to disrupt German seaborne commerce. It is important to remember that while most attention was focused on Britain's defensive struggle in the Atlantic, a concurrent offensive campaign was relentlessly underway to diminish the German merchant marine and undermine German maritime trade. In this campaign, it was the RAF, and not the Royal Navy, that was the primary player. Of the various weapons employed, the most effective remained the aerial mine, which was laid in large quantities by RAF aircraft. A recap of the advantages these mines provided was their ability to impact areas, such as the Baltic, that were inaccessible to other means, their capacity to sink meaningful numbers of ships for a minimal outlay of effort and their potential to cause disruption to seaborne commerce even when losses did not occur.

During a period lasting almost four years the British conducted 40 outbound Arctic convoys that delivered 720 merchant ships containing nearly 4 million tons of vital war materiel to the Soviet Union. This persistent effort under often harsh conditions bolstered a beleaguered ally and constituted another valuable contribution made by British sea power in attaining the overall Allied victory. (Hampton, J. A. (Lt), Royal Navy official photographer, public domain)

The British benefitted from several improvements that increased the volume, reach and accuracy of their mining campaign. By this time in the war Bomber Command was the primary facilitator in the RAF's mining effort being responsible for the vast majority of mines laid in hostile waters. With the large expansion that Bomber Command was undergoing at the time, increased numbers of aircraft were available to conduct mining operations. Likewise, newer and better aircraft such as the Short Stirling and the Handley Page Halifax (both four-engine heavy bombers) were progressively used thus increasing the range and number of mines that each aircraft could carry. The net result of this was a substantially larger number of mines that the British were able to lay compared to previous years. The British also benefitted from improved navigational aids that increased accuracy and enhanced their ability to hit targeted areas, multiplying the effectiveness of their effort. Together, these improvements helped keep the pressure on the Germans and counteracted the expanding and increasingly effective countermeasures they were employing to protect their coastal waters and transit routes.

In 1943 and the first five months of 1944 RAF aircraft carried out 8,555 sorties during which they laid a total of 23,440 mines in German-controlled waters off Norway, Northwest Europe, the Bay of Biscay and the Baltic. This compared to 4,907 sorties and 9,711 mines laid in 1942 and came at a cost of 202 aircraft.[17]

Added to this were significantly smaller quantities of mines laid by British warships and submarines including 2,867 mines that were laid between mid-April and early June of 1944 during the run-up to the Normandy invasion.[18] Together, these mines sank a total of 169 German and German-affiliated merchant ships and commercial vessels worth a combined 137,162 tons and damaged a further 38 vessels worth 83,783 tons from January 1943 through May 1944.[19] In turn, these losses or the threat of losses caused significant commerce disruptions including an estimated traffic shortfall of 1,000,000 metric tons of ocean cargo and 350,000 metric tons of coastal cargo along the Kiel Canal alone.[20] Meanwhile, these mines also claimed the destruction of 67 warships and auxiliary vessels worth 34,302 tons including the fleet minesweepers *M152*, *M553*, *M515* and *M13* and seven *sperrbrechers*.[21] In terms of anti-submarine successes, British mines sank *U526*, *U647*, *U263*, *U854* and *U803* during this period and caused transit and training delays that disrupted operations and increased the working up periods for many newly commissioned U-boats. Finally, a number of warships were damaged by mine strikes including the torpedo boats *Kondor* and *T24* and the minesweeper *M84*.

The RAF's next major contribution to the anti-shipping campaign was through direct attacks. In this, Coastal Command was the primary player, although Fighter Command and attached FAA squadrons also participated in this ongoing offensive. Once again, the British benefitted from a number of materiel, organisational and tactical improvements that progressively enhanced their effectiveness throughout 1943 and 1944. Together, these improvements helped the British contend with the growing defences employed by the Germans to safeguard their coastal traffic. By this time in the war nearly all German and German-affiliated merchant ships travelled in heavily defended convoys when proceeding in the waters off Northwest Europe. The typical ratio of escort vessels to merchant ships in these convoys was at least one-to-one and often two-to-one or greater thus presenting a formidable counter to attacking British aircraft. German convoys often travelled predominately at night thus limiting their exposure to daytime attack. In such cases, large-scale attacks were often only possible at dawn or dusk when the convoys were entering or leaving their protected anchorages.

The first improvement to benefit the RAF's anti-shipping offensive was the procurement of better aircraft. Of these, none was more important that the Bristol Beaufighter. Originally employed as a night fighter, the versatile twin-engine Beaufighter quickly found employment in a variety of roles. In 1942 this included a number of Beaufighter Mk.VICs that were assigned to Coastal Command as anti-shipping strike aircraft. By the end of the year a handful of these were converted to carry torpedoes. Then, in 1943 a new version of the Beaufighter, the Mk.X, arrived to become the premier ship-killer in the RAF's inventory. Compared to earlier Coastal Command strike aircraft, the rugged Beaufighter Mk.X was relatively fast and agile with a top speed of 330 miles per hour. Even more impressive was its extensive firepower that consisted of four 20mm cannons, seven 0.303 machine guns (six in the wings and one in a dorsal position) and an external load of one 18-inch torpedo, 2,000 pounds of bombs or eight wing-mounted rocket projectiles.

The British augmented the Beaufighter with other capable aircraft. In 1944 the De Havilland Mosquito fighter-bomber joined Coastal Command in a strike capacity. With a top speed of 380 miles per hour, the twin-engine Mosquito was capable of carrying a similar weapon's load as the Beaufighter (with the exception of the torpedo), and certain Mosquitoes possessed a single 57mm 'Tsetse' cannon as part of their armament. Although not employed in comparable numbers as the Beaufighter, the Mosquito constituted Coastal Command's most capable strike aircraft. In fact, it was only the Mosquito's limited numbers and shorter duration of service that prevented it from surpassing the Beaufighter as the RAF's foremost ship-killer. Meanwhile, a number of Fighter Command aircraft also participated in the anti-shipping campaign including various fighter-types converted to carry bombs or rockets such as the twin-engine Westland Whirlwind and the single-engine Hawker Typhoon.

The British enhanced the effectiveness of their various strike aircraft with the acquisition of improved weapons and electronic aids. The most important of these in terms of the former was the deployment of wing-mounted rocket projectiles. Already proven a success against the U-boats, these rockets demonstrated similar effectiveness against German merchant ships and small to medium-sized warships. The British employed two types of rockets. The first had a 60-pound high explosive warhead that was primarily useful for flak suppression. The second possessed a solid, 25-pound semi-armoured piercing head that was used to punch holes in ships' hulls. Of the two, the 25-pound solid head quickly proved to be the more effective, being capable of sinking a small- to medium-sized vessel with as little as two underwater hits. Eventually, this 25-pound solid head rocket became the predominant weapon in Coastal Command's anti-shipping arsenal. Assisting in the deployment of these weapons were various electronic aids including ASV radar, 'Gee' navigational positioning devices and radio altimeters that helped British aircraft locate and engage elusive German ships under all types of visibility conditions.

While these various materiel and technical acquisitions were clearly advantageous, the British also benefitted from organisational, tactical and intelligence improvements. The primary manifestation of this was the establishment of strike wings that were exclusively dedicated to anti-shipping operations. Consisting of two or more Beaufighter and/or Mosquito squadrons, these specialised strike wings used well-coordinated mass attacks to better engage the heavily defended German convoys. In a typical strike wing operation, a portion of the attacking aircraft performed flak suppression to neutralise the convoy's defences while other aircraft carried out the main attack with torpedoes, bombs or rockets. To take advantage of this, good intelligence and precise coordination were necessary to catch the fleeting convoys as they darted into and out of their protected anchorages. To this end, the British utilised a number of sources including Ultra, aerial reconnaissance and information gained from various resistance groups in occupied Europe to establish a solid picture of German convoy movements and dispositions.

When combined together, these various improvements allowed the British to attain a higher degree of success with direct attacks than had been the case earlier in the war despite the increase in German defences. From January 1943 through May 1944 RAF aircraft conducted 21,025 anti-shipping sorties in Northern and Western European waters for the cost of 264 of their number.[22] In return, these aircraft sank 44 German and German-affiliated merchant ships and 44 German warships and auxiliaries worth 119,351 and 15,738 tons respectively.[23] Included in these latter losses were the torpedo boat *Grief*, the 1,281-ton minelayer *Skagerrak* and the fleet minesweepers *M414*, *M345*, *M483*, *M156* and *M435*. Likewise, these attacks also damaged 17 merchant ships and two auxiliary warships worth a combined 80,207 tons.[24] Finally, these attacks, or the threat of these attacks, caused further disruption to the already overstretched German transportation system. An example of this was the dramatic falloff in activity at Rotterdam, which handled a significant portion of Germany's trade with Scandinavia due to its easy access to the Ruhr via the Rhine River. From the summer of 1942 to the summer of 1943 Rotterdam experienced a better than 60 percent reduction in shipping activity, forcing the Germans to divert the difference to their farther removed and less efficient Baltic ports.[25]

Nor was this the extent of the Allies' direct attack effort. Naval aircraft operating from British and American aircraft carriers also conducted a number of profitable strikes against Norwegian-based maritime assets during the latter part of this period. For the British, the return to offensive carrier operations in Norwegian waters coincided with a revitalised FAA. After years of making do with substandard or makeshift designs, the FAA finally possessed a growing number of top line aircraft. This included the American-built Chance Vought Corsair and Grumman Hellcat, which were both well-armed, powerful and rugged carrier-borne fighters. Another American design that would eventually attain widespread use was the Grumman Avenger strike aircraft. Although designed as a torpedo-bomber, the British did not use the Avenger in this capacity, but rather used it as a glide bomber. In terms of British designs, the most notable was the Supermarine Seafire, which was a carrier-borne version of the famous Spitfire fighter. Although hampered by marginal deck-landing performance, the nimble Seafire eventually proved itself to be a capable fighter and fighter-bomber. A second British design that attained similar service was the Fairey Firefly. Finally, in terms of strike aircraft, the British produced the Fairey Barracuda, which was effective in both the torpedo and dive-bombing roles.

While these new British aircraft would soon make their presence felt in the waters off Norway, it was the Americans who drew first blood under the auspices of a Home

Table 8.3 Characteristics of Selected Fleet Air Arm Aircraft

	Top speed (mph)	Range (miles)	Armament
Torpedo/strike aircraft			
Fairey Swordfish	139	546	2 × .303 MGs, 1 × 18in torpedo or 1 × 1,610lb mine or 1,500lbs of assorted ordnance
Fairey Albacore	161	710	2 × .303 MGs, 1 × 18in torpedo or 1 × 1,610lb mine or 2,000lbs of assorted ordnance
Fairey Barracuda II	228	686	2 × .303 MGs, 1 × 18in torpedo or 1 × 1,610lb mine or 1,620lbs of assorted ordnance
Grumman Avenger	271	1,215	5 × .50 MGs, 1 × 22in torpedo or 2,000lbs of assorted ordnance
Fighter/fighter-bomber			
Fairey Fulmar	280	800	8 × .303 MGs
Grum. Martlet/Wildcat	331	845	4 or 6 × .50 MGs, 2 × 200lb bombs
Supermarine Seafire LIII	358	725	4 × .303 MGs, 2 × 20mm CAN, 500lbs of bombs
Grumman Hellcat	376	1,090	6 × .50 MGs, 2,000lbs of bombs
Chance Vought Corsair	425	1,015	6 × .50 MGs, 2,000lbs of bombs
Fairey Firefly	316	1,300	4 × 20mm CAN, 8 × rockets or 2,000lbs of bombs

Fleet operation. Anxious to take the offensive following the crippling of *Tirpitz*, Admiral Fraser departed Scapa Flow on 2 October 1943 with the battleships *Duke of York* and *Anson*, the American aircraft carrier *Ranger* (which was on temporary assignment to the Home Fleet), four cruisers and 10 destroyers. Two days later this force arrived 140 miles off the Norwegian port of Bodo where *Ranger* launched 30 strike aircraft and 14 fighters to attack two German convoys and other shipping in the roads. Together, these aircraft carried out a devastating attack that sank or otherwise destroyed five merchant ships worth 20,753 tons and damaged five more worth 19,042 tons.[26] The total cost for this undertaking (designated Operation *Leader*) was a mere three aircraft, which were partially avenged in the afternoon when American fighters destroyed two out of three shadowing German aircraft.

The FAA's return to offensive operations was less auspicious. On 9 February 1944 elements of the Home Fleet, consisting of the British battleship *Anson*, the Free-French battleship *Richelieu*, the aircraft carrier *Furious*, two cruisers and seven destroyers, departed Scapa Flow to conduct an offensive strike against shipping off Stadlandet. As it was, no shipping was found underway, but the British did locate the 5,170-ton German merchant ship *Emsland* aground off Eervik. Previously, *Emsland* had grounded due to severe damage sustained during a strike wing attack on 20 January and then had suffered further damage due to a torpedo hit from the British submarine *Satyr* on 5 February. On 11 February *Furious* launched a strike of ten Barracuda dive-bombers and 12 Seafire fighters to finish off the grounded ship. Despite opposition from German fighters that cost each side a single aircraft in aerial combat, the Barracudas scored eight bomb hits that broke *Emsland* in half and rendered the stricken vessel beyond salvage.

The FAA's next operation was against a far more substantial target. Realising that repairs on *Tirpitz* were nearing completion, the British resolved to strike the German battleship again. Therefore, on 30 March two separate forces departed Scapa Flow and proceeded north. On 2 April these forces, consisting of the battleships *Duke of York* and *Anson*, the aircraft carriers *Victorious* and *Furious*, the escort carriers *Searcher*, *Emperor*, *Pursuer* and *Fencer*, four cruisers and 11 destroyers, assembled some 220 miles northwest of Altenfjord. From there, the carriers and their escorts proceeded to a flying off position 120 miles northwest of Kaafjord, and on the morning of the 3rd they launched a two-wave strike consisting of 41 Barracuda dive-bombers and 80 fighters. Attaining surprise, these aircraft scored 14 bomb hits on *Tirpitz* causing substantial damage to the battleship's superstructure and inflicting 438 casualties on the crew (122 dead and 316 wounded). In all, it would take two and a half months to repair the damage thus giving the British further relief from the threat

In 1944 the British launched a series of carrier air strikes against Norwegian shipping. In addition to Operation *Tungsten*, which damaged the battleship *Tirpitz*, these attacks accounted for some 20 German vessels destroyed. Pictured here are Corsair and Barracuda strike aircraft on the aircraft carrier *Formidable*. (Hudson F. A. (Lt), Royal Navy official photographer, public domain)

of *Tirpitz*. In addition, British aircraft also damaged the tanker *CA Larsen* and two smaller vessels worth a combined 14,300 tons. The cost for this successful venture, codenamed Operation *Tungsten*, came to four aircraft lost.

Over the next two months the Home Fleet conducted further operations involving the FAA of which three were particularly successful. On 26 April a British task force containing the aircraft carriers *Victorious* and *Furious* and the escort carriers *Searcher*, *Striker*, *Emperor* and *Pursuer* launched 27 Barracudas and 56 assorted fighters to search for shipping targets in the Bodo area. Most of these fell upon a southbound ore convoy, and for the loss of six aircraft, the British sank three merchant ships worth 15,083 tons and severely damaged a fourth vessel worth 795 tons. Ten days later 18 Barracudas and 34 fighters from *Furious* and *Searcher* attacked two German convoys in the Kristiansund North area. For the loss of two of their number, these aircraft sank the 2,522-ton ore carrier *Almora* and the 7,913-ton tanker *Saarburg* and damaged a third merchant ship and two minor vessels worth 1,548 tons. Finally, on 1 June *Victorious* and *Furious* launched 16 Barracudas, 12 Seafires and 22 Corsairs to attack a German convoy north of Stadlandet. Together, these aircraft sank the 4,174-ton merchant ship *Hans Leonhardt* and the 2,297-ton *Sperrbrecher 181* and damaged two other vessels worth 5,792 tons. British losses for this operation amounted to two aircraft.

Returning now to the RAF, there was one final area where the air service played a significant role in the anti-shipping campaign – that being strategic bombing. In this, the British once again enjoyed a number of advancements that increasingly facilitated their efforts. As previously touched upon, this included a vastly expanded Bomber Command, the acquisition of substantially more capable aircraft such as the Handley Page Halifax and the Avro Lancaster four-engine heavy bombers and the development of improved technology and tactics that enhanced bombing accuracy and destructive power. With this, the British were capable of reaching farther into German-controlled territory and delivering substantially larger bomb loads with far greater accuracy. Of even greater consequence, the British were no longer alone in this effort as the USAAF became increasingly involved in the bombing campaign until it matched and eventually surpassed Bomber Command's contribution.

As a result of these factors, the impact of Allied bombing upon the Germans progressed from being a minor nuisance in 1941 and 1942 to becoming a truly viable impediment to their war effort in 1943 and 1944. This outcome manifested itself in a number of ways. First, despite progressive efforts to mobilise the German economy, the bombing campaign prevented the Germans from fully realising their true manufacturing potential. An example of this was an estimated eight percent loss in Ruhr steel production in 1943 that was attributed to the bombing campaign. This equated to an output loss of 1.9 million tons of crude steel in Germany's Northwest District, which primarily consisted of the Ruhr. This deficit continued into 1944 with the loss of a further 1.3 million tons of crude steel production in this area during the first nine months of that year.[27] Meanwhile, in cases where German production actually increased due to mobilisation efforts, Allied bombing still impeded projected output. For example, in 1944 German tank, aircraft and truck production failed to attain output goals by 35, 31 and 42 percent respectively.[28] According to German authorities, these shortfalls were primarily attributable to the effects of Allied bombing.

Beyond this impact, the Allied bombing campaign had other significant benefits. Of these, the most important was the diversion of resources it forced upon the Germans. By September 1943 approximately one million service members manned the German air defence network. Materiel assets dedicated to this purpose included 8,876 88mm heavy anti-aircraft guns, 24,500 light anti-aircraft guns and 7,000 searchlights.[29] As time went on, this commitment increased eventually peaking at 14,400 heavy and 42,000 light anti-aircraft guns.[30] To support this defensive effort, 82 percent of Germany's aircraft production in 1944 was dedicated to fighters while one-third of its artillery production consisted of anti-aircraft guns. Meanwhile, 20 percent of ammunition, one-third of optics and over 50 percent of radar and signal equipment output went to air defence applications.[31] When combined with similar, although smaller, personnel and resource allocations the Germans adopted to counter Britain's anti-shipping campaign, this represented the equivalent of a second front in Europe long before the Allies landed in France. Likewise, as the war progressed, the bombing campaign increasingly debilitated Germany's transportation system and oil producing industries, progressively restricting and/or damaging all aspects of the German war effort. Finally, the bombing campaign served as the primary catalyst by which the Allies engaged and ultimately defeated the Luftwaffe in the skies over Europe.

Table 8.4 Characteristics of Selected RAF Aircraft in the Maritime War

	Roles	Top speed (mph)	Range (miles)	Maximum ordnance load (lbs)
Bristol Beaufort	Strike	265	1,600	1,650
Bristol Beaufighter	Strike	330	1,470	2,127
De Havilland Mosquito	Strike	380	2,040	2,000
Short Sunderland	Anti-submarine patrol	210	2,980	2,000
Vickers Wellington	Bomber, strike, minelaying, anti-submarine patrol	235	2,200	4,500
Consolidated Liberator	Heavy bomber, minelaying, anti-submarine patrol	303	2,850	8,000
Handly Page Halifax	Heavy bomber, minelaying, anti-submarine patrol	265	1,860	13,000
Avro Lancaster	Heavy bomber, minelaying	270	2,250	22,000

While only a small portion of the Allied bombing effort was directed against maritime assets, the Allies attained meaningful results in this area as well. From January 1943 through May 1944 Allied bombing against ports in Northern and Western Europe sank a total of 64 merchant ships and minor craft and 36 military vessels worth 154,711 tons and 14,566 tons respectively. Likewise, this bombing further damaged 36 merchant ships and at least three warships worth a combined 137,026 tons. Of this total, the large majority were sunk or damaged by USAAF aircraft, but the RAF contributed at least 35 vessels worth 56,564 tons to this tally.[32] Beyond surface vessels, Allied bombing during this period also destroyed two commissioned U-boats (*U622* and *U108*) and no fewer than 32 pre-commissioned U-boats that were destroyed while under construction.[33] These latter casualties were in addition to U-boat losses already recorded since monthly and annual loss totals listed in this book only include commissioned U-boats and do not cover production attrition. Thus, these pre-commissioned losses heightened the calamity befalling the Kriegsmarine and give an indication of the stifling impact that Allied bombing had on U-boat expansion. Meanwhile, of the surface warships sunk, British bombers sank the escort destroyer *G1* (1,374 tons, 2 × 4.1-inch guns) while under construction in Hamburg on the night of 27/28 July 1943 while American bombers sank the escort destroyer *SG2* (1,372 tons, 3 × 4.1-inch guns) at Nantes and the torpedo boat *T15* at Kiel on 23 September and 13 December respectively.

Turning now to the naval portion of this effort, during most of 1943 British and Allied submarines attained limited success in the waters off Northern and Western Europe. Part of this was due to the normal difficulties associated with operating in these waters including their proximity to land, prevailing shallowness, unfavourable weather and lighting conditions and a general scarcity of worthwhile targets. Beyond this, the British also suffered from limited resources since many of their submarines were deployed to the Mediterranean while those that remained were often employed in generally unproductive defensive patrols. The result of this was that British and British-affiliated submarines only succeeded in sinking two U-boats (*U644* and *U308*) and a few small fishing vessels during the first ten months of 1943. Joining this failure was an even worse performance by supporting American submarines. From December 1942 through June 1943 an American submarine squadron operated out of Britain with six boats. During this time these American submarines conducted a total of 24 patrols, but only managed to sink a single patrol boat, *V408*, and damage the 6,344-ton blockade-runner *Pietro Orseolo*.

Fortunately for the British, things improved dramatically thereafter. From November 1943 through May 1944 Home Fleet submarines enjoyed a notable operational renaissance as intensified efforts and the cover of arctic darkness improved British fortunes. As a result, during this period British and British-affiliated submarines sank a total of 18 German and German-affiliated merchant ships worth 62,539 tons in Norwegian waters. Included in this was the 7,569-ton *Bärenfels*, which was sunk by a British X-craft in Bergen on 14 April. Meanwhile, the Norwegian submarine *Ula* sank *U974* off Stavanger five days later while other British submarines damaged at least four more merchant ships worth 24,758 tons during this period.[34] The cost the British paid for these successes going back to the beginning of 1943 amounted to just two submarines, *Uredd* (Norwegian) and *Syrtis*, which were both presumably mined off Bodo.

The final facet of the Royal Navy's anti-shipping effort (beyond the FAA and submarines) came in the form of surface actions. As previously discussed in Chapter 5, coastal forces consisting of motor torpedo boats (MTBs) and motor gunboats (MGBs) constituted the primary players in this effort, but occasionally escort destroyers, destroyers and cruisers also participated in these operations. On nearly a nightly basis (weather permitting) groups of British MTBs, MGBs and/ or other coastal warships ventured into the English Channel and North Sea to do battle against the local German coastal forces and convoy traffic. Occasionally these forays also ventured as far as the waters off Norway or into the Bay of Biscay. When intelligence warranted, the British dispatched cruisers and other warships to search for Axis blockade-runners. Together, these various operations netted positive results that generally compensated for the meagre returns attained by Allied submarines in 1943. During the first ten months of that year British coastal/surface forces sank 27 merchant ships worth 62,803 tons and 21 warships and auxiliaries worth 6,257 tons.[35] Included in this were the fleet minesweepers *M8* and *M534* sunk by British MTBs on 14 May and 27 September and *M153* sunk by the Hunt-class escort destroyers *Melbreak*, *Wensleydale* and *Glaisdale* on 10 July.

Unfortunately, not all of these encounters were successful, and the British suffered their share of losses too. One engagement that was particularly costly for the British occurred on the night of 22/23 October. Earlier that evening a British squadron consisting of the anti-aircraft cruiser *Charybdis*, two fleet destroyers and four Hunt-class escort destroyers departed Plymouth in search of the German blockade-runner *Münsterland* which was en route from Brest to Cherbourg. Defending *Münsterland* was an escort of 13 German warships including five torpedo boats from the 4th Torpedo Boat Flotilla. After midnight the British force arrived off the north coast of Brittany and began a westward sweep. At 0130 hours *Charybdis* made radar contact with the enemy force at 14,000 yards and manoeuvred to enact an engagement. The Germans were also aware of the British presence through hydrophone and radio intercepts, and the two forces closed rapidly. At 0143 hours the torpedo boats *T23* and *T26* sighted *Charybdis* against the lighter northern horizon and launched a snap torpedo attack. Two minutes later *Charybdis* fired star shells and spotted the incoming torpedoes, but it was too late. One of the torpedoes struck *Charybdis* causing an immediate list to port. Meanwhile, *T27* and *T22* came up and fired a second salvo of torpedoes that scored hits on the immobilised *Charybdis* and the escort destroyer *Limbourne*. Both British ships

196 • THE LONGEST CAMPAIGN

sank with the loss of 506 men while the German ships disengaged having suffered no losses to themselves.

While this action was a clear German victory, the British soon enacted revenge. On 27 December a mixed force of 11 German destroyers and torpedo boats from the 8th and 4th Flotillas departed France to provide escort for the incoming blockade-runner *Alsterufer*. That same day a British Sunderland sighted *Alsterufer* 500 nautical miles northwest of Cape Finisterre. At the time there were several Allied warships located throughout the area searching for the blockade-runner, but before any of them could intervene, a RAF Liberator sank the 2,729-ton *Alsterufer* with bombs and rockets. News of this development did not reach German authorities until the next morning at which time they recalled their escort force. Unfortunately for them, an American Liberator had previously located these vessels, and the British light cruisers *Enterprise* and *Glasgow* were already racing forward to block their return route to France. An attack by German aircraft failed to damage the British cruisers, and by early afternoon *Enterprise* and *Glasgow* were in position to intercept the oncoming German force.

In this, they did not have long to wait. At 1332 hours *Glasgow* sighted the German squadron, and the British cruisers opened fire 14 minutes later. At the onset of the battle the Germans had the advantage in combined firepower with 24×5.9-inch and 24×4.1-inch guns compared to 19×6-inch and 11×4-inch guns for the British. The Germans also possessed a combined 76 torpedo tubes compared to 18 for the British. Still, heavy seas impeded the effectiveness of the smaller German warships, and a poor decision by the German commander, Captain Hans Erdmenger, soon negated this advantage. After a brief long-range duel, Erdmenger split his squadron to facilitate a withdrawal. *Enterprise* and *Glasgow* pursued the smaller of the two forces thus giving them the firepower advantage. In the running battle that followed, the British cruisers systematically ran down and sank the German flagship *Z27* and the torpedo boats *T25* and *T26*. Then low on ammunition, the two British cruisers broke off the engagement and safely returned to Britain despite further German air attacks. For their part, the remaining German destroyers/torpedo boats also made good their return to France, but the loss of three of their number signalled another bitter blow for the Kriegsmarine following the loss of *Scharnhorst* just two days before.

The onset of the new year brought little relief for the Germans. During the first five months of 1944 British surface forces sank a further 15 German vessels worth 8,550 tons in Northern European waters.[36] Included in this number were four more principal warships.[37] The first of these occurred on the night of 14/15 March when a British MTB sank the German fleet minesweeper *M10* off Dunkirk. Then on the night of 25/26 April a mixed British/Canadian squadron consisting of the light cruiser *Black Prince* and the destroyers *Ashanti*, *Athabaskan*, *Haida* and *Huron* engaged three torpedo boats from the German 4th Flotilla off Brittany and sank

T29. Three nights later *Haida* and *Athabaskan* fought a similar engagement with two German torpedo boats in the same area. In this case, the honours were even as *Haida* drove *T27* ashore in a severely damaged state, but *Athabaskan* was hit by a torpedo and subsequently sank. German efforts to salvage *T27* were unsuccessful, and in early May British aircraft and MTBs finished off the wreck. Finally, on the night of 23/24 May British MTBs sank the German fleet minesweeper *M39* off Dunkirk.

Beyond the efforts of the RAF and Royal Navy, there were other means that accounted for German shipping losses during this period. British long-range shore batteries located in the Dover area sank four German merchant ships worth 17,424 tons.[38] Likewise, accidents, Soviet action, sabotage and defections accounted for dozens of additional vessels. When added together, total German and German-affiliated merchant losses in Northern and Western European waters amounted to 493 ships worth 817,251 tons from January 1943 through May 1944.[39] These losses far exceeded additions due to new construction and other acquisitions thus causing great strain to the already overburdened German merchant fleet. Making matters worse, scores of additional vessels sustained damage during this period, and by July 1944 a full 25.39 percent of Germany's remaining commercial shipping in Northwest Europe was laid up under or awaiting repairs.[40] As a result of these losses and damage, the amount of German shipping available to carry out the all-important Scandinavian trade dropped from 1,032,000 tons at the beginning of 1943 to 812,000 tons in July 1944.[41]

The impact this had on German imports was profound. In 1943 German imports from Sweden and Norway amounted to 11,947,600 tons including 9,975,900 tons of iron ore. These results constituted an 8.5 and 16.2 percent increase compared to corresponding import figures from 1942, although both categories still lagged markedly behind 1939 levels. This increase was largely due to the various efforts put in place by the German commissioner of shipping, Karl Kaufmann, to expand German shipping capacity (see Chapter 5) and the unusually mild winter that extended the use of Sweden's northern Baltic ports. Unfortunately for the Germans, these improvements were only temporary, and in 1944 Scandinavian imports declined sharply. During the first seven months of that year the Germans received 4,310,000 tons of imports from Sweden and Norway including 3,478,000 tons of iron ore.[42] When calculated out on an annual basis, this rate represented an import level of 7,388,571 and 5,962,286 tons or a 38.16 and 40.23 percent drop respectively. Most of this decline was attributable to Germany's deteriorating shipping situation, and British authorities later determined that Allied attacks on German sea communications cost Germany approximately three million tons of iron ore imports from October 1943 through September 1944.[43]

As bad as this was, the situation was even worse for Germany's other significant seaborne importation initiative. In December 1943 the Germans attempted to revive their flagging blockade-runner programme after an eight-month hiatus. This started poorly for them when Coastal Command Beaufighters sank the 6,344-ton outbound *Pietro Orseolo* during the middle of the month. Meanwhile, the Germans had five inbound ships that were carrying 33,095 tons of valuable cargo from the Far East. Of these, only one arrived in France to deliver 6,890 tons.[44] The remaining four were all sunk. The first of these was the aforementioned 2,729-ton *Alsterufer*, which was sunk by a RAF Liberator on 27 December. Then in the first week in January American and Allied forces in the South Atlantic sank or forced the scuttling of the blockade-runners *Weserland*, *Rio Grande* and *Burgenland* worth a combined 19,910 tons. With these disasters, Admiral Dönitz cancelled further blockade-runner operations thus depriving German industry of certain key resources not readily available in Europe. Some importation did continue using submarines, but this could only satisfy a fraction of Germany's industrial needs.

Of course, there were other impacts that the anti-shipping campaign had on the German economy and war effort. In many respects, the anti-shipping campaign was an adjunct to the strategic bombing campaign and contributed to the same successes already discussed earlier in the chapter. Among its impacts, in 1944 Ruhr crude steel production dropped to 980,000 metric tons per month compared to 1,150,000 tons in 1942 and 1,370,000 tons in 1939 thus constituting a 14.78 and 28.47 percent decline respectively. Then, in January and February of 1945 this output collapsed by two-thirds to an average of just 331,500 metric tons per month.[45] According to German industrialists after the war, Allied bombing was the principal cause for this lost steel production in 1944 and 1945, but many of them also cited shortages of raw materials due to Allied attacks as a major factor. In fact, half of the firms surveyed stated that difficulties in attaining ore supplies would have halted production if bombing had not done so.[46]

Meanwhile, the anti-shipping campaign was equally successful in forcing the Germans to divert limited resources to defensive purposes. In 1944 an estimated 82,000 naval personnel were directly employed in staffing German minesweepers and escort vessels as well as serving as anti-aircraft personnel assigned to merchant ships.[47] When support personnel were added in, this number swelled to over 200,000.[48] Meanwhile, tens of thousands of additional men staffed the hundreds of German gun batteries defending ports and waterways or were engaged in ship-building and repair activities related to the campaign. In materiel terms, by April 1944 the Kriegsmarine had 2,343 assorted vessels assigned to defensive applications broken down into 177 fleet minesweepers, 129 motor minesweepers, 349 auxiliary minesweepers, 46 *sperrbrechers*, 342 Vp patrol boats, 1,248 harbour defence boats and 52 UJ submarine chasers.[49] From 1942 through 1944 some 12 percent of German weapon's production and five percent of ammunition production went to the Kriegsmarine.[50] Much of this was dedicated to defensive applications.

Nor did this effort come cheap to the Kriegsmarine. During the same 17-month period culminating in May 1944 the Kriegsmarine lost a total of 252 surface warships and auxiliary vessels worth 137,252 tons in the waters off Northern and Western Europe.[51] Included in these losses were the battlecruiser *Scharnhorst*, seven destroyers/ torpedo boats, two escort destroyers and 19 fleet minesweepers. In addition to this, many other vessels, including the battleship *Tirpitz*, were rendered non-operational. Meanwhile, the period also saw the decisive defeat of the German U-boat arm as a significant weapon in the maritime war. While the apex of this defeat occurred in the spring and summer of 1943, it was finalised in the autumn and winter of 1943–1944. The result of these various calamities was devastating for the Germans. Whereas the Royal Navy had been the primary deterrent against a German invasion of Britain in 1940, the Kriegsmarine was woefully incapable of performing a similar function in 1944. Despite the fact that it still possessed large numbers of U-boats and surface warships, the Kriegsmarine was powerless to prevent, delay or seriously impede the expected Allied invasion of France. With the final chapter of the European war about to begin, the initiative was firmly in the hands of the Allies, and all the Germans could do was wait and hope they could withstand the oncoming onslaught.

CHAPTER 9

Operation *Neptune* and the Battle for Northwest Europe

By the spring of 1944 the European war was fast approaching its final climactic event. For the Germans, the prospect of outright victory had long since passed, and the best they could realistically hope for was attaining some sort of settled peace that fell short of complete surrender. Still, when looking at a map of Europe, this looming reality was hardly evident. To the contrary, by this late date in the war, Germany still controlled a vast European empire that stretched from Norway in the north to Greece in the south and France in the west to Belarus in the east. For their part, even though the Western Allies had enjoyed more than a year and a half of near continuous success, they were still little more than outsiders looking in when it came to mainland Europe. This had to change if the Allies were to attain total victory. Four years before, the Germans had ejected the British army from France. Now a vastly more capable British army and an equally capable and significantly larger American army were poised to make a dramatic return to this contested region. If the Allies succeeded in this endeavour, they would join with the massive Soviet armies in the east and the smaller Allied armies in the south to overwhelm and destroy the German war machine. On the other hand, if the Germans defeated the fledgling invasion before the Allies could bring their overwhelming materiel might to bear, it would be months or even years before the Allies would be ready to make a second attempt, giving Germany valuable time to pursue a negotiated settlement.

Given these stakes, the Allies left nothing to chance in their invasion preparations. For them, the invasion of France culminated years of planning, procurement, innovation and training. The British had literally begun this process mere months following the evacuation of Dunkirk when the prospect for such an undertaking was little more than wishful thinking. This remained true until December 1941 when the United States entered the war. Now bolstered by America's vast human and industrial might, what had been grossly impractical suddenly became completely feasible and arguably inevitable. Even so, it would take almost two and a half years for the Allies to build up sufficient strength and attain the type of conditions necessary to mount their invasion and successfully challenge the vaunted German army in Northwest Europe. During this time, a staff of thousands meticulously planned every detail of the massive venture while Allied innovators conceived, designed and produced a myriad of new weapons and devices to carry it out. When all was said and done, this enterprise, designated Operation *Overlord* for the overall undertaking and Operation *Neptune* for the naval portion of the invasion, constituted the largest amphibious assault ever envisioned and the focal point for the entire Allied war effort.

The basic plan for this undertaking called for the landing of elements from two Allied armies (the American First and the British Second) along a 50-mile front between Quinéville on the eastern base of the Cotentin Peninsula and the Orne River in the region of Normandy on the French side of the English Channel. This area was chosen for a number of reasons including its beach and tidal conditions, proximity to British ports and airfields that afforded reasonable transit times and optimum air cover, reduced German defences compared to other target areas (notably the Pas-de-Calais) and its exploitation potential including nearby ports that could be seized and used to support Allied logistical needs. Once firmly ashore, the Allies would consolidate their positions and establish a firm lodgement that included the port of Cherbourg in the west and the city of Caen in the east. While this was underway, the navies would conduct a rapid and sustained logistical effort to build-up the invasion forces. Stretched over a period of several weeks, this effort would fill out the initial assault armies and ultimately allow for the activation of two additional armies (the American Third and the Canadian First).[1]

Meanwhile, once the build-up attained sufficient strength and conditions were right on the ground, the Allies would conduct operations to break out of the lodgement area. General Bernard Montgomery, the Allied ground forces commander, anticipated that geographical and infrastructure considerations would prompt the Germans to concentrate their opposition against the British and Canadian forces positioned on the eastern side of the Allied line. Therefore, Montgomery planned to use these forces to form a strong shoulder to tie down the Germans while the Americans broke out from the west. Once through the German defences, the Americans would seize the valuable Atlantic ports located in Brittany and then swing northward using the British forces located in the Caen-Falaise area as the pivot. Montgomery estimated that the lodgement phase of the battle might last up to 40 days and that the Allied armies would reach the Loire River in the south and the Seine River in the northeast within 90 days, signalling an end to the campaign. Thereafter, follow-up operations would continue as dictated by the situation.

To carry out this plan, the Allies amassed an immense force in the United Kingdom. On the eve of Operation *Overlord*, the Allied armies stationed in Britain numbered some 3.5 million men. Of these, the British army contained nearly 1.75 million soldiers while the Dominion and lesser Allied nations provided a further 219,000 combatants. Rounding out this force was the United States army and USAAF, which contained another 1.5 million men.[2] Given the substantial administrative and logistical requirements posed by modern warfare, only a fraction of this manpower was actually earmarked for combat operations. Still, in terms of major combat units, this constituted a force of 39 divisions and a third as many independent brigades that were ready for immediate service in Northwest Europe. This included 19 divisions and 13 independent brigades that were British or British affiliated that would staff the two British/Commonwealth armies previously mentioned. After that, Britain's contribution to the Allied ground forces would largely be exhausted, but not so with the Americans who would still have some 35 divisions awaiting transport from the United States as well as forces from the Mediterranean theatre.[3] Thus, there would be relative parity between the two Allied contingents during the first few months of the campaign, but thereafter the Americans would assume an increasingly predominant role.

The existence of these sizable American and Canadian forces in Britain testified to the indispensable role played by Allied maritime power in preparing for Operation *Overlord*. By the end of May 1944 the Allies had transported over a million and a half men across the Atlantic to Britain. Of these, nearly 60 percent arrived in escorted convoys, but over 30 percent were delivered in unescorted British or British-controlled fast troopships. These latter vessels were all pre-war passenger liners that had been converted to fulfil a wartime role. Utilising their great speeds as a means to avoid U-boats, these converted liners could accommodate up to 15,000 men per trip. Of particular success were the liners *Queen Mary* and *Queen Elizabeth*, which combined to deliver a total of 425,000 men without a single fatality. To support the American forces in Great Britain, the Allied navies and merchant marines further delivered some 5.25 million tons of weapons and materiel of which 40 percent arrived in the first five months of 1944.[4]

Turning now to the actual landings, which were scheduled for early June following a month-long delay to allow for greater preparation time, the Allies planned to utilise five reinforced infantry divisions in their initial assault supported by three airborne divisions. On the left, the British would land three divisions along a 30-mile front running from the Orne River in the east to the small harbour of Port-en-Bessin in the west. Within this area, there were three primary landing areas designated Sword, Juno and Gold that would receive the British 3rd, Canadian 3rd and British 50th Divisions respectively. To their west, the Americans would land the 1st and 4th Divisions along a 25-mile front in two primary landing areas designated Omaha and Utah. Protecting the flanks of these landings were three airborne divisions that would be flown in the night before. In the east the British 6th Airborne Division would secure the left flank of the British Second Army while the American 82nd and 101st Airborne Divisions did the same for the Americans on the right. Finally, the Allies would quickly follow-up their initial assault forces with additional formations including the British 51st, 7th Armoured and 49th and the American 29th, 2nd, 2nd Armoured, 90th, 9th, and 79th Divisions within the first five days of operations.

To carry this out, the Allies needed to employ a massive naval effort. Requirements for this endeavour (Operation *Neptune*) included the safe and timely delivery of assault forces, execution of the landings, delivery of gunfire support and the subsequent maintenance and build-up of the forces ashore. Whereas the ground campaign envisioned an initial parity between the two Allied contingents, Operation *Neptune* would predominately be a British affair. The man charged with commanding this enormous undertaking was Britain's Admiral Bertram Ramsay. To fulfil his mission, Ramsay possessed a force of roughly 7,000 vessels.[5] Included in this were 1,213 combatant warships and 4,126 assorted landing ships and craft.[6] In terms of the former, 79 percent of the assigned warships, ranging from battleships to coastal craft, came from British or Canadian sources while a further 4.5 percent came from affiliated Allied navies.[7] Likewise, the British provided at least 60 percent of the assigned landing ships and associated craft for the invasion.[8] Finally, this force was rounded out by 1,600 to 1,683 ancillary vessels and merchant ships (depending upon the source) to fulfil a variety of logistical and support needs.[9]

The Allies split these forces between a variety of subordinate commands. The largest of these was the predominately British Eastern Naval Task Force under the command of Rear-Admiral Philip Vian. With an initial strength of 2,426 assorted landing ships and assault craft and 348 supporting warships, this task force would conduct the landings in the British zone utilising three assault forces under the commands of Rear-Admiral A. G. Talbot (Sword), Commodore G. N. Oliver (Juno) and Commodore C. E. Douglas-Pennant (Gold) and a follow-up force under the command of Rear-Admiral W. E. Perry. To their right, the Western Naval Task Force under Rear-Admiral A. G. Kirk (USN) would perform an identical function in the American zone with 2,024 assorted vessels (including a sizable number that were British). To accomplish this, they would utilise two assault forces and a follow-up force under the commands of Rear-Admiral D. P. Moon (Utah), Rear-Admiral J. L. Hall Jr. (Omaha) and Commodore C. D. Edgar (follow-up) respectively. Finally, 541 warships (overwhelmingly British) and a number of support vessels were assigned to various home commands to provide flank security and reserves for the invasion and follow-up effort.[10]

The staging, movement and deployment of this vast array of shipping required intense planning and coordination. The landings themselves represented major undertakings requiring the synchronised movement of multiple sub-units. First, each assault force was split into three or four subordinate assault groups representing the sequential waves that would land on the beaches. Follow-up forces would arrive in a similar systematic manner. A separate bombardment group was assigned to each assault force to provide fire support. Finally, 22 flotillas of minesweepers would precede the assault forces to clear safe channels through the

Table 9.1 Allied Maritime Forces Assigned to Operation *Neptune*

	Western Task Force	Eastern Task Force	Home commands and reserve forces	Total
Combatant warships				
Battleships	3	3	1	7
Monitors	1	1	-	2
Cruisers	10	13	-	23
Gunboats	1	2	-	3
Escort carriers	-	-	3	3
Fleet destroyers	30	30	34	94
Escort destroyers, frigates and sloops	17	37	89	143
Corvettes	4	17	50	71
Fleet minesweepers	56	42	-	98
Other minesweepers and danlayers	62	87	40	189
Patrol craft and anti-submarine trawlers	27	21	30	78
Minelayers and seaplane carriers	-	3	2	5
Coastal craft	113	90	292	495
Midget submarines	-	2	-	2
Assault and landing vessels				
Headquarters ships	2	4	-	6
Infantry landing ships	18	37	-	55
Landing ship tanks (LSTs)	106	130	-	236
Other landing ships	3	3	-	6
Assorted landing craft	1,351	1,941	-	3,292
Assorted barges, ferries and refuelling trawlers	220	311	-	531
Ancillary ships and craft	-	-	-	736
Merchant ships	-	-	-	864

Source: L. F. Ellis, *Victory in the West, Volume I: The Battle of Normandy* (London: Her Majesty's Stationery Office, 1962), pp. 508–510. Condensed and organised for easier presentation.

extensive German minefields. To manage this mass of shipping, the Allies staged their invasion fleet in progressive order. The initial landing forces were assembled in the southern English ports between Plymouth and Newhaven. Follow-up forces were staged in more distant locations as far away as the Thames and Bristol Channel. Meanwhile, the smaller warships of the covering forces were concentrated at Plymouth, Dartmouth, Portsmouth and Dover while the battleships, cruisers and other heavy units were based at Belfast and the Clyde to avoid potential Luftwaffe attack.

In keeping with the complexity of its planning, *Neptune*'s implementation required meticulous timing and execution. Allied planners used the term D-day to delineate the day when the assault landings occurred. These landings would commence at dawn at low tide with the actual crossings taking place the night before. When given the execution order, the various naval contingents would depart their diverse locations and concentrate in an area south of Portsmouth and the Isle of Wight. From there, these various elements would proceed south through an elaborate series of swept channels (some only a few hundred yards wide) to arrive at their assigned landing areas. This would be no easy task given the requirement to arrive at precise locations along the coastline in correct order and within a very tight time schedule. To assist this process, the Allies planned to use motor launches and lighted buoys to mark the routes. The British would also position the midget submarines *X20* and *X23* off Juno and Sword beaches to serve as navigational markers.

Another obvious factor that would determine the success or failure of the landings was the Allies' ability to overcome the extensive German beach defences. Allied planners recognised that the Normandy coastline was substantially better fortified than anything previously encountered in North Africa, Sicily or Italy. German defences included tens of thousands of mines and assorted obstacles located on the beaches and offshore as well as dozens of hardened bunkers and gun emplacements in the targeted areas. The Allies planned to use firepower and innovation to counter these threats. As part of the former, Allied planners dedicated 137 warships (including some held in reserve) to bombardment duties including the British battleships *Warspite, Ramillies, Rodney* and *Nelson*, the American battleships *Nevada, Texas* and *Arkansas*, the British monitors *Erebus* and *Roberts* and 23 cruisers (18 of which were British or British affiliated).[11] Regarding innovation, the British army developed a number of specialised tanks and armoured vehicles that were designed to overcome the German defences and/or support the invading infantry. Included in this were amphibious tanks, bunker-busting tanks, mine-clearing tanks and various other engineering vehicles. Finally, demolition teams made up of both naval and army personnel would accompany the assault forces to clear and open the beaches once they were secured.

Of course, the initial landings were only the beginning of the navy's commitment to Operation *Overlord*. The consolidation and build-up phase would begin as early as the second high tide on D-day. Thereafter, a steady stream of coasters and support vessels would venture across the English Channel to deposit their vital cargoes of men and materiel on the liberated beachheads. Allied planners anticipated a requirement to dispatch eight convoys plus separate groups of landing craft to Normandy each day. There were two objectives to this. The first was to build-up the armies ashore. The second was to logistically support this ever-expanding force. Thus, as the build-up continued, the rate of expansion would diminish as the logistical requirements increased. As previously discussed, the Allies planned to have 17 divisions ashore by five days into the operation (D + 4). This build-up would increase to 21 divisions by D + 12, 26 divisions by D + 20, 31 divisions by D + 35 and 39 divisions by D + 90.[12]

To help facilitate this, the Allies devised a number of engineering innovations. First, realising that it would take time to capture and open the local ports, the Allies planned to construct artificial breakwaters and harbours. The first part of this was to use 55 elderly merchant ships and four obsolete warships to construct five blockship breakwaters called Gooseberries. There would be one Gooseberry in each landing zone. Once in position, the Allies would scuttle these ships in lines parallel to the shore thus creating shelters for the beaches. In the Gold and Omaha sectors the Allies would further transform their two Gooseberries into fully-fledged harbours known as Mulberries. To carry this out, the Allies produced prefabricated sections that would be towed across the English Channel and assembled in their assigned zones. This included 213 concrete caissons weighing up to 6,000 tons that would extend the breakwaters and largely enclose the harbours. It also included 93 floating steel cruciform sections, each 200 feet long and 25 feet high, to create sheltered deep-water anchorages. Finally, split between the two harbours would be 23 floating pierheads and ten miles of floating roadway.[13] When fully assembled, the British Mulberry would be roughly the size of Dover harbour and be capable of handling seven deep-laden ships, 20 coasters, 400 tugs and auxiliary vessels and 1,000 small craft. The American Mulberry would be slightly smaller, but both would have a projected unload capacity of 7,000 tons per day.[14]

Beyond solid cargo, the Allies also developed innovative methods to transport fuel to France. Throughout the campaign, the Allies would deliver most of their fuel in cased containers using conventional transport, but they would augment this with two major engineering projects. The first was the creation of two improvised fuel depots at Port-en-Bessin and Ste. Honorine near the junction of the British and American armies. Once established, these facilities would receive fuel directly from tankers anchored offshore using buoyed steel pipelines and store it for distribution to the armies. Called Operation *Tombola*, the Allies hoped to have four discharge points operational by D + 18 thus giving them the capacity to offload a combined 600 tons of fuel per hour. The second project, called Pluto, proposed the laying of pipelines under the English Channel from the Isle of Wight to the small port of Querqueville near Cherbourg. When fully implemented by D + 75, the Allies projected that Pluto would give them the capacity to pump 2,500 tons of fuel to France per day without the benefit of shipping assets.[15]

Turning now to defensive measures, the Allies earmarked a total of 279 warships, ranging from destroyers to anti-submarine trawlers, plus upwards of 400 coastal craft to protect the invasion fleet and follow-up convoys. Many of these vessels would serve as direct escorts while others patrolled the approaches to the invasion area. In terms of the latter, the British assigned four naval support groups to Plymouth Command to patrol the western entrance of the English Channel while a further six support groups, along with three escort carriers, patrolled beyond Land's End to counter U-boats coming from the Bay of Biscay. Within the western Channel itself, the Allies planned to establish three destroyer patrols (two British and one American) plus six groups of coastal craft to deal with German surface vessels operating out of the Biscay ports. Meanwhile, on the eastern side of the Channel, Dover Command would add a further four destroyers, two frigates and 46 coastal craft to provide similar coverage for the invasion's left flank. Finally, the Home Fleet, which was not part of *Neptune*'s force structure, would nevertheless be prepared to act in case German warships tried to intervene or break out into the Atlantic from Germany or Norway.

Joining this naval effort were thousands of aircraft from the Allied air forces. In all, the Allies possessed 11,590 aircraft and 3,500 gliders for inclusion in Operation *Overlord* of which 5,510 of the former were British or British-affiliated. Included in this total force were 4,190 assorted fighters and fighter-bombers and 1,070 Coastal Command aircraft.[16] To defend against German air attacks, the Allies planned to have five squadrons of fighters in constant patrol over the invasion routes while a further ten squadrons maintained vigilance over the beaches. Meanwhile, Coastal Command aircraft would conduct a continual series of patrols over the seaward approaches to the invasion area. Of particular importance was No. 19 Group, which would utilise 29 squadrons to saturate the western approaches and Bay of Biscay to counter the U-boat threat.[17] So intense would this presence be that the British planned to put every part of the approaches between Southern Ireland and the Brest Peninsula under aerial observation every half-hour both day and night. To the east, No. 16 Group would predominately concern itself with German surface traffic in the eastern Channel and North Sea while in the north No.18 Group would patrol the U-boat transit routes coming from Germany and Norway.

The Germans confronted this massive outlay of naval and aerial resources with markedly smaller counterparts. It was clear that the Kriegsmarine and Luftwaffe lacked sufficient strength to exclusively defeat the Allied invasion, but they could still play a role in its attempted demise. Starting with the former, on the eve of D-day the Germans possessed 517 surface warships stationed in the Channel area and the French Atlantic coast. Unfortunately for them, only a fraction of these vessels were suited for offensive action against the Allied invasion fleet. This included five destroyers, six torpedo boats and 39 E-boats. The remainder of this force consisted of various types of minesweepers and escort vessels of which the majority were commercial conversions. Beyond surface vessels, the Germans also possessed 49 Biscay-based U-boats that were earmarked for anti-invasion duties. Of these, 35 were operational at the time of the invasion, but only nine were equipped with snorkels.[18] Thus, when combined together, the Kriegsmarine had fewer than 100 U-boats and offensive surface warships readily available to confront an Allied invasion fleet that numbered in the thousands.

This disparity was much the same regarding the Luftwaffe. In the past the Luftwaffe had routinely compensated for Germany's lack of naval power, but this would not be the case under the current situation. Already, from January through May the Luftwaffe had carried out a series of nocturnal bombing raids against London, Portsmouth, Plymouth and other targets in southern England to retaliate for concurrent Allied strategic bombing and disrupt Allied invasion preparations. As it was, these raids caused minimal damage and utterly failed to impede the Allied build-up while costing the Germans 329 sorely needed bombers that would have been better utilised if saved to confront the invasion.[19] Now, at the end of May the German Third Air Fleet, which was stationed in France and Belgium, reported its strength at 891 aircraft of which only 497 were operational. Included in this number were 402 bombers, 336 fighters and 89 assorted reconnaissance aircraft.[20] Thus, at the onset of the battle, the Third Air Fleet would be outnumbered by a factor of at least 12 to one. While it was likely that the Luftwaffe would bring in additional aircraft from Germany and other theatres once the invasion occurred, it would still only possess a fraction of the strength available to the Allies. Under these conditions, it was clear that the Luftwaffe would only be able to conduct small hit and run raids and aerial minelaying that could cause some damage but would hardly be decisive against the massive Allied invasion fleet.

Given these disparities in resources, the Germans had to depend upon their army as the primary opponent to the Allied invasion. Fortunately for them, this was by far their strongest service. By the end of May the Germans possessed 58 divisions in France and the Low Countries, which were more divisions than the Allies had in Britain. Still, there were a number of factors that limited this force. First, the 58 divisions were spread over a wide area that precluded their ability to confront the Allies in mass. In keeping with this, 32 of these divisions were coastal or reserve formations that were largely immobile, under-strength and/or of marginal combat value. This left only ten panzer and panzer grenadier and 16 infantry and parachute divisions to make up the core of the army's combat power.[21] Of course, the Germans could again bring additional forces in from Germany or other theatres, but this would take time. Finally, air and naval firepower would provide the Allies with force multipliers that the Germans lacked due to the weakness of the Luftwaffe and Kriegsmarine. As such, the German ground forces would have to exercise increased operational prowess to compensate for this shortcoming.

Under these circumstances, leaders on both sides recognised the crucial role logistics would play in the upcoming battle. Simply put, the antagonist that could build up and sustain its forces in the quickest and most satisfactory manner would likely prevail. In this regard, established ground lines of communication offered the Germans some advantage. To counter this, the Allies employed two strategies. First, the Allies would utilise their substantial air power to interdict the movement of German units and supplies. Allied bombers had already begun this effort by targeting transportation hubs and infrastructure across France to cripple the German logistical network. In this assault, 21,949 British and American aircraft dropped 66,517 tons of bombs against 80 specified transportation targets destroying or severely damaging 76 of them.[22] This, in turn, helped foster a roughly 50 percent drop in rail traffic across France from January through the beginning of June including an 85–90 percent decline in the northern and western portions of the nation.[23] The Allies would continue these attacks once the invasion occurred with a greater emphasis put upon isolating the Normandy battlefield from outside support. This would include thousands of fighter and fighter-bomber sorties that would target the movement of German units trying to reach the contested area.

Second, the Allies would use deception to keep German units frozen away from Normandy. Under the codename Operation *Fortitude*, the Allies utilised a variety of means including double agents, dummy units and false radio traffic to convince the Germans that the Allied attack would take place at the Pas-de-Calais. Then after the invasion occurred, the Allies would continue these deception efforts to persuade the Germans that the Normandy landings were just a prelude to the primary attack, which was still targeted against the Pas-de-Calais. Finally, the Allies sought to convince the Germans that there would be an attack against Norway independent of the Normandy invasion. During the build-up to D-day Operation *Fortitude* proved highly successful in misdirecting the Germans and prompted them to station substantially more divisions in the Pas-de-Calais than at Normandy. It remained to be seen how successful the Allies would be at maintaining this ruse once the invasion occurred, but that answer would soon be known.

By the end of May everything was ready, and the Allies put their invasion plans into motion with an anticipated D-day of 5 June. All across southern England men and materiel congregated at ports to embark upon the ships and vessels that would transport them to France. Meanwhile, more distant naval and maritime assets began preliminary movements that would bring them into position to meet the meticulous timing of the *Neptune* plan. On 2 June the midget submarines *X20* and *X23* departed Portsmouth to begin their trek across the English Channel as the vanguard for the entire invasion. Unfortunately, despite all the planning and preparation, the Allies soon encountered the one thing they could not control – the weather. By the 4th weather conditions had deteriorated to such an extent that General Dwight Eisenhower, the Supreme Allied Commander, was compelled to postpone the invasion for 24 hours. Even then, it was questionable whether the invasion would go forth or have to be postponed further. If postponed beyond the 7th, the Allies would have to wait a fortnight before the moon and tidal conditions were right again. Fortunately, on the 5th Allied meteorologists forecasted a window of tolerable weather that would begin that night and carry on at least through the 8th, and General Eisenhower issued the final order to execute Operation *Overlord*.

With this, the great enterprise, which had been years in the making, finally got underway. As the day progressed, vessels of all kinds emerged from their respective ports of origination and proceeded to their assembly points off Portsmouth and the

Isle of Wight. Then as day turned into night, this vast armada turned south and began its fateful journey across the English Channel. Leading this procession were 255 minesweepers, motor launches and dan-layers that swept and marked ten approach channels through the German minefields. At the end of these approach channels, the minesweepers radiated out to sweep lanes to the assault beaches. Meanwhile, overhead thousands of Allied aircraft proceeded to France to fulfil their portion of the *Overlord* plan. This included 1,056 British bombers that dropped over 5,000 tons of bombs against ten selected German gun batteries in the assault area. It also included a vast fleet of transport aircraft and gliders that delivered the three Allied airborne divisions to secure the invasion's flanks.

As these airborne forces made first contact with the German defenders, the seaborne forces continued their plodding trek towards the Norman coastline. This journey did not go without incident as the American minesweeper *Osprey* was sunk on a mine while a handful of minor craft floundered in the heavy seas. Fortunately, beyond mines, the crossing encountered no opposition from the Luftwaffe or Kriegsmarine. Part of this was due to the recent bad weather, which had lulled the Germans into a false sense of security and even prompted them to cancel normal patrol activity in the English Channel. In addition, the Allies extensively jammed the handful of German coastal radar stations that were still operating following recent Allied bombing, blinding them to the approaching threat. The exception to this was in the eastern Channel where the British used chaff and various electronic devices to simulate a decoy naval force approaching the Pas-de-Calais. Finally, the Allies benefitted from German confusion and denials that caused them to hesitate and act indecisively once reports of airborne landings and other tell-tale incidents arrived at their headquarters.

Aided by these factors, the initial assault forces successfully completed their respective movements and were in position to begin landing operations at dawn's first light. Between 0525 and 0550 hours the various assault groups announced their presence with the roar of naval gunfire as the bombardment groups engaged assigned targets along the Normandy coastline. In this, Allied battleships, monitors and cruisers primarily focused their attention on silencing 23 German gun batteries that were spread throughout the region. Meanwhile, 1,630 American bombers and waves of Allied fighter-bombers attacked German coastal fortifications, command facilities and assembly points within the targeted areas. While this was underway, assault landing craft began their run-ins to the beaches while Allied destroyers and special rocket-firing craft provided fire support for these movements. At 0630 and 0730 hours the first waves of landing craft touched down in the American and British sectors respectively thus constituting H-hour for the invasion.

As these initial actions unfolded, the Kriegsmarine made its only effective appearance for the day. At 0442 hours the German torpedo boats *T28*, *Möwe* and *Jaguar* departed Le Havre with a flotilla of patrol boats to investigate reports of

Allied landings in the Seine Bay. Heading west, the torpedo boats soon encountered Bombardment Force D on the extreme left flank of the Eastern Task Force consisting of the battleships *Warspite* and *Ramillies*, the monitor *Roberts*, five cruisers and 13 destroyers. Fortunately for the Germans, an Allied smoke screen obscured their approach as they advanced to within 7,000 yards of the British warships. At 0535 hours the German torpedo boats turned and launched their torpedoes just as the British became aware of their presence. *Warspite* and *Ramillies* immediately engaged the German warships with their secondary armament while the cruisers *Mauritius* and *Arethusa* engaged them with their main guns. Despite this deluge of fire, the German torpedo boats were able to escape unharmed through the smoke screen, but a 6-inch shell from *Warspite* did hit and sink one of the attending patrol boats. As for the German torpedoes, one hit and sank the Norwegian-manned destroyer *Svenner*, but the remaining British warships escaped harm.

This brief, but deadly, engagement proved to be the only effective response the Germans were able to make against the Allied armada on D-day. In other skirmishes, German E-boats from both Cherbourg and Le Havre failed to inflict any damage against the mass of shipping present in the Seine Bay and/or were driven off by Allied countermeasures. The same held true that night when *Möwe* and *Jaguar* tried to repeat their earlier success, but accomplished nothing for their effort. Meanwhile, the Luftwaffe was practically a non-factor in the day's activities flying a paltry 319 sorties against 14,674 for the Allies.[24] This is not to say that the Allies escaped the remainder of the day unscathed. Mines continued to be a significant danger accounting for the loss of the American destroyer *Corry* and the British escort destroyer *Wrestler*. Likewise, large numbers of landing craft and other minor vessels were wrecked or damaged due to the inclement weather and shore obstacles encountered on the beaches. In the British areas alone 258 landing craft were lost or disabled in this manner.[25] Still, given the size of the Allied effort, these casualties were not prohibitive as wave after wave of men and materiel arrived in the assault areas. By 1000 hours over 31,000 men, 700 armoured vehicles and 300 guns had landed on the British beaches alone.[26]

With this inflow of resources and aided by the massive fire support previously mentioned, the Allied ground forces battled their way through the initial German defences. In the British sector this outcome was overwhelmingly positive. On the extreme left flank the British 6th Airborne Division was almost universally successful in achieving its objectives. Meanwhile, on the Second Army beaches the British and Canadians encountered heavy opposition, but were able to breach the strong German fortifications and advance inland with the help of their specialised armour. By nightfall the British firmly controlled all three beaches with perimeters extending five to six miles wide and four to six miles deep. During this advance the British blunted the only serious counterattack for the day when they repulsed the German 21th Panzer Division disabling as many as 50 tanks in the process. Against this comprehensive British success, results in the American sector were more sporadic, but still generally positive. Of particular concern was the situation at Omaha Beach where the Americans encountered heavy opposition and were only able to gain a shallow lodgement by day's end. Likewise, the American airborne forces were badly scattered and disorganised upon their landings in France and thus failed to achieve most of their assigned objectives. Still, by nightfall the American First Army had sizable forces ashore and held a firm, if uneven, toehold on the European continent.

When viewed together, these results constituted a decisive victory for the Allies. Barely 24 hours before the Allies had been foreigners to Northwest Europe, and now at the close of D-day they controlled some 130 square miles of French territory and had approximately 156,000 men ashore of which 75,215 British and Canadians and 57,500 Americans had landed on the beaches while a further 23,400 men had arrived with the airborne divisions.[27] In accomplishing this, the Allies eliminated Germany's best opportunity to defeat the invasion and brought themselves immensely closer to their own ultimate victory in Europe. The cost in achieving this great triumph came to some 4,300 British and 6,000 American ground casualties. In addition, 127 Allied aircraft were lost during the day of which the vast majority were shot

British troops passing a Royal Navy beach party during the early stages of Operation *Overlord*. Seventy-nine percent of the combatant warships and more than 60 percent of the landing vessels used in the Normandy invasion came from British or Commonwealth sources. (Norway (Lt Cdr), Royal Navy official photographer, public domain)

down by anti-aircraft fire.[28] Finally, naval casualties consisted of three destroyers and a minesweeper lost plus scores of minor craft sunk or damaged. Included in these latter numbers were an estimated 304 landing craft that were lost or disabled during the assault.[29] While not insignificant, these losses were less than Allied planners had anticipated thus further contributing to the day's success. German casualties for D-day are not precisely known, but the 716th Infantry Division, which was the primary German formation present in the British assault area, was effectively destroyed as a coherent fighting force. The Luftwaffe's Third Air Fleet lost 36 aircraft while the Kriegsmarine lost six auxiliary vessels sunk or scuttled in the assault area.[30]

Over the next several days the Allies moved quickly to maintain the initiative. On the ground Allied forces launched follow-up operations to expand and link their individual beachheads, forming a continuous lodgement by the 10th. While this was underway, the Allies began the all-important race to build up and sustain their deployed armies so as to disallow the Germans any opportunity to conduct a viable counterattack. On 7 June eight replenishment convoys arrived off Normandy to begin this process, but quickly encountered sea conditions that impeded their unloading efforts. Fortunately, on the same day the first Mulberry convoys arrived to begin construction of the artificial breakwaters and ports. This started with the sinking of blockships to form the Gooseberry breakwaters, but quickly included the placement of prefabricated caisson, cruciform and pierhead sections. Within a few days the Gooseberries were completed thus providing a degree of shelter for the unloading ships. Meanwhile, construction on the Mulberries continued at a rapid pace, and on the 16th the American Mulberry was put into limited operation. Finally, the minor ports of Coursuelles and Port-en-Bessin were captured largely intact, and on 12 June the British opened them for use with a combined capacity to handle 2,000 tons per day. Together, these factors combined to ease the burdens faced by Allied logisticians, and the pace of unloading increased.

For their part, the Germans did what they could to disrupt this logistical effort. On the morning of the Allied landings the Kriegsmarine ordered their U-boat forces stationed in France and Norway to come to immediate notice for sea while five snorkel-equipped U-boats that were en route to the Atlantic were diverted to Brest. A few hours later Admiral Dönitz exhorted his forces to exert a maximum effort regardless of cost. Despite this heroic proclamation, German authorities recognised that conventional U-boats stood little chance of success operating in the channel given the massive Allied defences arrayed against them. Therefore, the Germans only ordered their snorkel-equipped U-boats to proceed into the Channel with a patrol area centring 25 miles south of the Isle of Wight. As it was, they only had nine such U-boats ready to proceed on the 6th, so the Germans also ordered seven non-snorkel boats to accompany these transiting U-boats as far as the area between the Isles of Scilly and the Start Point in Devon. Finally, 19 additional non-snorkel U-boats were ordered to form a patrol line in the Bay of Biscay to prohibit a possible invasion of that coast.

By midnight on D-day, all 35 of these U-boats had departed their respective Biscay ports to proceed to their assigned patrol areas, but this was only the beginning of the Kriegsmarine's anti-invasion disposition. As further U-boats became available, they too would sortie out to join this effort. For the remainder of June this included seven additional snorkel-equipped U-boats that departed the Biscay ports to proceed into the English Channel. The Germans also dispatched supplementary U-boats from Norway and Germany to reinforce this undertaking. In addition to the five Atlantic-bound U-boats that were diverted to Brest on D-day, the Germans dispatched a further ten snorkel and four non-snorkel boats from Germany and Norway to proceed into these contested waters. While this was underway, the Germans retained 21 non-snorkel U-boats in Norwegian waters as a precaution against an invasion of that country. Given these various moves, some 80 German U-boats were present in the waters around Britain during June, but less than half of these were directly earmarked to contest the Allied invasion of Normandy.

Beyond this U-boat effort, the Germans also attempted to use surface ships to attack the Allied fleet. Of the limited assets available to them, the most formidable were the five destroyers of the 8th Destroyer Flotilla located in the Biscay ports. On the morning of D-day two of these vessels were undergoing refits and were thus unavailable for immediate service, but the remaining three flotilla members, *Z32*, *Z24* and *ZH1*, departed the Gironde and made for Brest. Of these vessels, the first two were large 1936A Narvik-class destroyers that were almost the equivalent of small light cruisers while the third was the captured Dutch destroyer *Gerard Callenburgh* (1,628 tons, 5 × 4.7-inch guns) that had been put into German service. While en route this small flotilla came under attack by Coastal Command Beaufighters, but managed to complete its journey with only minor damage. Two nights later the three destroyers departed Brest accompanied by the torpedo boat *T24* to conduct an offensive sweep northeast of Cherbourg.

Unbeknown to them, Allied authorities tracked this movement through Ultra intercepts and aerial reconnaissance and dispatched the British 10th Destroyer Flotilla to enact an intercept. Consisting of four British, two Canadian and two Polish destroyers and under the command of Captain Basil Jones, the 10th Flotilla positioned itself some 20 miles off the Breton coast and began a search for the oncoming German vessels. At 0116 hours on the morning of 9 June the British flagship, *Tartar*, detected the German warships on radar at a range of ten miles, and the Allied destroyers altered course to investigate. At the time the Allied force was split into two divisions of which the southernmost one was closest to the Germans. At 0125 hours this division, consisting of the British *Tartar* and *Ashanti* and the Canadian *Haida* and *Huron*, opened fire at a range of 5,000 yards. The German warships immediately responded by launching torpedoes while turning away to escape the Allied trap.

What followed was a prolonged and confused running battle that soon saw the German ships split into three separate elements. Of these, *Z24* and *T24* made good their escape to the southwest, but only after the former suffered heavy damage from at least six shell hits. Meanwhile, *ZH1* suffered even worse damage and soon found itself immobilised and adrift in a shroud of smoke and steam. The darkness and smoke gave *ZH1* a temporary reprieve from final destruction, but shortly after 0215 hours *Tartar* and *Ashanti* happened upon and sank the crippled destroyer. Finally, the German flagship, *Z32*, veered to the northwest and quickly found itself isolated from the rest of its flotilla. Over the next four and a half hours *Z32* fought a series of running engagements with various groupings of Allied destroyers during which it sustained considerable damage from multiple shell hits. Finally at 0500 hours a 4.7-inch shell struck *Z32*'s starboard engine room and reduced the destroyer's speed to 15 knots. Realising that escape was now impossible, *Z32*'s commander drove the severely wounded warship aground off Île de Batz. A few hours later British Beaufighters attacked the wreck and rendered it beyond salvage. With this and for no loss to themselves, the British decisively reduced the German destroyer threat from the west.

Still, this was only one of many surface actions that occurred during this period. On a nightly basis German E-boats and occasional torpedo boats sortied out of Cherbourg, Le Havre, and Boulogne to conduct minelaying and conventional attacks against the Allied invasion fleet and follow-up convoys. The Allies contested these movements with mines, aircraft and warships, and there were numerous clashes between the opposing forces. In most cases, these engagements produced limited casualties on either side, but these actions generally thwarted German intentions to attain more meaningful results. Baring this out, in the ten days following D-day German surface craft only succeeded in sinking three LSTs, one motor torpedo boat, three coasters, two landing craft and two tugs.[31] Against this, mines and British coastal craft sank three E-boats during the first few days of the campaign and then on the morning of 13 June RAF Beaufighters destroyed three more E-boats and a motor minesweeper. Likewise, in peripheral fighting British motor torpedo boats sank three German patrol boats off Den Helder on 10 June. Four days later the destroyers *Ashanti* (British) and *Piorun* (Polish) sank the German fleet minesweepers *M83* and *M343* off Cap de la Hague. Finally, on the night of 17/18 June British motor torpedo boats torpedoed the fleet minesweeper *M133* off Jersey and rendered it a total loss.

Meanwhile, in the middle of the month the heavy bombers of RAF Bomber Command also joined the struggle. For days British Intelligence had tracked the movements and whereabouts of the local German surface forces. On the 14th these authorities determined that the bulk of the available German torpedo boats and E-boats were congregated in Le Havre, and Admiral Ramsay petitioned Bomber Command to attack the port. That evening 234 Lancaster and Mosquito bombers attacked Le Havre in three waves. In this, the British were aided by the local German commander who had forbidden the use of anti-aircraft fire over the port since Luftwaffe aircraft were scheduled to conduct local minelaying operations at the same time. For the loss of a single bomber, the British dropped 1,230 tons of bombs on the German naval base. Together, these attacks devastated the local German forces costing them the torpedo boats *Falke, Jaguar, Möwe* and *Kondor*; the corvettes *PA1, PA2* and *PA3*;[32] 14 E-boats; 18 minor minesweepers and patrol vessels and 19 tugs sunk or damaged so severely they would subsequently be scuttled.

Over the next few days the RAF continued its onslaught against the Kriegsmarine. On the night following the Le Havre raid 297 Lancaster, Halifax and Mosquito bombers carried out a similar attack against Boulogne where they sank the fleet minesweepers *M402, M507, M546* and *M550* (the latter three were employed as tenders), seven motor minesweepers and 16 auxiliary vessels. Complementing these major raids were strikes by Coastal and Fighter Command aircraft against transiting and sheltering German vessels. Of particular consequence was a strike by RAF Beaufighters on 15 June that sank the fleet minesweeper *M103*, the 7,900-ton transport *Coburg* and the 3,500-ton depot ship *Gustav Nachtigal* off the Ems estuary. During other attacks in June British aircraft sank two minor merchant ships worth 1,201 tons and seven minor or auxiliary warships (excluding those already mentioned).[33] When combined together, these actions, and particularly the raid against Le Havre, all but eliminated the German surface threat within the English Channel for the remainder of June.

If the experiences of the German surface forces were less than satisfactory, those of the U-boat arm were equally adverse. By midnight on the 6th 35 U-boats had departed the Biscay ports for anti-invasion duties of which 16 were earmarked to proceed to the English Channel. Almost immediately these U-boats found themselves beset upon by Coastal Command aircraft in what proved to be the most intense aerial interdiction effort yet encountered. Harried both day and night, the Germans suffered a steady stream of attrition that quickly reduced their limited forces. Particularly hard hit were the non-snorkel boats which suffered the loss of six of their number (*U955, U970, U629, U373, U740* and *U821*) to British aircraft in just four days.[34] Beyond this, several additional U-boats suffered damage that forced them to return to port. By the 13th the Germans realised the folly in trying to sail non-snorkel U-boats under these conditions and recalled all such units. Meanwhile, the snorkel-equipped U-boats fared better in terms of their own survival, but could make little headway towards the English Channel in the face of the overwhelming Allied defences. One by one battle damage or exhaustion forced many of these U-boats to abort their missions while two, *U441* and *U269*, were lost to British aircraft and warships.

Despite these initial setbacks, the Germans continued their efforts to engage the invasion forces. Much of this focused on the snorkel-equipped U-boats attempting to circumvent Britain from the north. Unfortunately for them, these northern U-boats fared even worse than their Biscay counterparts. Of the 19 U-boats diverted or dispatched south to reinforce the anti-invasion effort, no fewer than ten were destroyed before month's end. Of these, British aircraft accounted for *U980*, *U715*, *U998*, *U423* and *U478* while British warships sank *U767*, *U971*, *U1191*, *U719* and *U988*. A further three aborted or were recalled leaving a net gain of just four snorkel-equipped U-boats present in the Bay of Biscay or western Channel by the beginning of July.[35] Meanwhile, in other actions not directly related to the invasion, British aircraft and submarines sank *U477*, *U987*, *U1225* and *U317* in Norwegian waters. Thus, when combined together, this brought the total number of U-boats sunk in Western European waters during June to 22. Against this loss, only a handful of U-boats were actually able to penetrate the British defences and engage elements of the invasion fleet. Of these, even fewer scored successes sinking a paltry three American liberty ships worth 21,550 tons, a LST and the British frigates *Mourne* and *Blackwood*.

While these results clearly represented a costly failure for the Kriegsmarine, the Germans were able to do marginally better with some of the other weapons available in their anti-shipping arsenal. In particular, mines proved to be a constant antagonist to the Allied effort. On nearly a nightly basis German aircraft and coastal vessels proceeded into the Seine Bay to conduct minelaying operations. In this, the Germans utilised a new pressure-operated mine that was impervious to traditional sweeping methods. Fortunately, the British were able to recover one of these mines and quickly devise countermeasures to mitigate its effectiveness. Still, these mines and their conventional counterparts remained constant threats accounting for 26 Allied ships sunk by the end of June including the American destroyers *Meredith*, *Glennon* and *Rich*, the British destroyers *Fury* and *Swift* and the American minesweeper *Tide*. During the same period, Luftwaffe aircraft supplemented their minelaying activities with bombing and torpedo attacks. Carried out mostly at night by individual or small groups of aircraft, these raids managed to sink five vessels during June including the British frigate *Lawford* and the British escort destroyer *Boadicea*. When combined together and including casualties from other or unspecified causes, the Allies lost a total of 59 vessels of appreciable size during June.[36] Given the scope of the Allied undertaking, this level of loss was regrettable but had no meaningful impact upon the Allied build-up.

In fact, weather was a far greater hindrance to Allied logistical operations than were the Germans. This was particularly true in the middle of the month when a major storm struck the channel area. Beginning on the 19th and lasting for four days, this storm severely restricted unloading operations and caused widespread damage to the Allied anchorages. Illustrating this former point, in the four days prior to the storm the Allies landed an average of 34,712 men, 5,894 vehicles and 24,974 tons of stores per day, but this dropped to a daily average of just 9,847 men, 2,426 vehicles and 7,350 tons of stores during the period of the storm.[37] In terms of damage, the storm pushed some 800 (mostly minor) vessels onto the beaches causing many to become a total loss. This would have been far worse if not for the shelter provided by the Gooseberry breakwaters. Tragically, while the Gooseberries generally survived and would continue to provide valuable service, the cruciform sections and harbour installations at the American Mulberry largely disintegrated thus rendering it unusable. As such, the Allies abandoned further work on the American Mulberry and reallocated its remaining prefabricated components to the British Mulberry, which although damaged, remained intact. When combined together, this disruption and damage caused a deficit to the Allied logistical schedule of 20,000 vehicles and 105,000 tons of stores that would take until 26 July to remedy.[38]

Fortunately, despite this shortfall, the Allied build-up still progressed at a sufficient pace to facilitate a viable ground operation thus ensuring the success of the entire campaign. By 30 June Allied supply convoys saw the arrival of 570 liberty ships, 788 coasters, 905 LSTs, 1,814 assorted landing craft and 180 troop transports to the Allied beaches.[39] On the same day the total number of Allied forces landed in France by sea since the beginning of the invasion numbered 861,838 men, 157,633 vehicles and 501,834 tons of supplies.[40] In terms of major units, the end of the month saw the Allies with 26 divisions plus numerous lesser formations ashore in Normandy of which roughly half were deployed with each army. Against this, the Germans, plagued by Allied interdiction efforts and their own limited mobility, only managed to deploy 16 divisions plus elements of seven others to Normandy during June.[41] Making matters worse from a German perspective, three of these divisions were largely destroyed by month's end, further exasperating the force imbalance. The Germans had additional units en route to Normandy that would arrive in July, but it was clear that the Allies were winning the build-up race.

Turning now to the ground campaign, despite the overarching strategic success that was unfolding, initial Allied progress following the link-up of the lodgement area was actually quite limited. This was particularly true in the British sector, where as Montgomery had predicted, the Germans directed their main defensive effort. As the month progressed, the British launched a series of attacks to challenge this defence, and while little ground was gained, the British succeeded in their primary mission of tying down German units including the vaunted German panzer formations. By 15 June the Germans had 520 tanks facing the Second Army compared to only 70 facing the Americans. Over the next six weeks this number fluctuated, but on average there were over 600 tanks confronting the British compared to 190 deployed against the Americans.[42] Likewise, the forces facing the British tended to be of better calibre and greater capability than those facing the Americans and included a higher percentage of elite formations. Given these realities, the Second Army found itself performing an essential, but unenviable task that quickly tested its mettle.

Of course, the payoff for this strategy was to occur on the western flank. The first major task confronting the American First Army was to capture the port of Cherbourg, which the Allies hoped to have in their possession by D + 8 (14 June). Unfortunately, the pace of the initial American advance was only marginally better than that of the British. Although predominately opposed by weaker infantry and static formations, the American First Army had to contend with closed and segmented terrain that severely restricted large-scale offensive operations. Referred to as *bocage*, this terrain was characterised by a series of small fields, sunken lanes and thick hedgerows that reduced the effectiveness of Allied firepower and mobility while concurrently providing the Germans with excellent defensive positions. As such, the Americans made slow progress in their lateral advance across the Cotentin Peninsula reaching the far side on the evening of the 17th. After that, it took a further week of heavy fighting for the Americans to battle their way into Cherbourg itself. By the time the last resistance ceased on 29 June, the Germans had so thoroughly blocked and wrecked the harbour that it would take another two and a half weeks before its capture rendered meaningful benefit.

Still, if the Allies were frustrated by this seemingly slow progress, things were far worse for the Germans. With their failure to defeat the Allied invasion on D-day, the Germans knew they must act quickly to destroy the Allied lodgement before it became too powerful. On the days immediately following the Allied landings, the Germans launched a series of limited and disjointed counterattacks against the British Second Army, but these were blunted with no appreciable gains. Then as the Germans brought additional panzer formations into the battle area, they were forced to deploy them in a piecemeal fashion to contain the burgeoning British presence. While these actions generally stymied British attempts to make significant territorial gains, they also denied the Germans the opportunity to accumulate a meaningful reserve to launch a decisive counterattack. With each passing day the prospect for a successful counterattack diminished. Finally, at the end of the month the Germans received two SS panzer divisions that had been transferred to Normandy from Eastern Europe, and they launched their attack. Utilising these units plus elements of two other panzer divisions, the Germans attacked a British salient west of Caen. Unfortunately for them, the British had anticipated this move, and the German attacks were decisively defeated with heavy losses. After this, the Germans went completely over to the defensive, and their last chance for victory was shattered.

Given this reality, the beginning of July saw the Allies in complete control of the initiative despite their seemingly slow progress on the ground. By applying continuous pressure over a wide area, Montgomery forced the Germans into a reactive posture that thwarted their ability to launch effective counterstrokes. As such, the ongoing struggle increasingly resembled an El Alamein-type contest in which Montgomery systematically crumbled the German defences in a battle of attrition they were ill prepared to wage. To this point, in June Allied ground casualties in Normandy numbered 24,698 for the British, 37,034 for the Americans and 80,783 for the Germans.[43] Included in these German losses were 46,913 prisoners of which the majority were taken in the Cherbourg area.[44] Given this scale of loss and the growing imbalance of men and resources coming into the fight, it would only be a matter of time before the Allied pressure became too great and the German defences cracked.

An essential factor in this calculation was the continued success of the Allied build-up and logistical effort. To ease this process, a number of Allied initiatives came to fruition in July and August. First, on 29 June the British Mulberry became operational, and by 8 July it was receiving some 6,000 tons of cargo per day. As the month progressed the British further expanded the harbour, increasing its capacity to over 7,000 tons per day culminating in a record 11,000 tons unloaded on 29 July.[45] The Allies accompanied this achievement with the activation of their *Tombola* fuel depots at Port-en-Bessin and Ste. Honorine. In July these depots attained the capability to unload and store up to 8,000 tons of fuel per day, and by the end of August the Allies had received over 175,000 tons of fuel through this system.[46] During the first two weeks of July the Allies also carried out extensive clearing and renovation efforts to put Cherbourg harbour back into service. For the cost of three minesweepers and seven other minor vessels, the Allies cleared 111 mines and had the port ready to receive deep-draught ships by the 16th. Thereafter, the Allies expanded the port's capacity until it could handle 12,000 tons per day in September.[47] Finally, by the beginning of the fourth week in July the Allies had recovered some 700 vessels driven ashore during the 19–22 June storm, substantially clearing the beaches and easing unloading efforts.[48]

Accompanying these technical feats, the Allies also continued to mitigate the effectiveness of the German interdiction efforts. During July and the first half of August, 20 snorkel-equipped U-boats attempted to penetrate into the English Channel and operate against the Allied invasion forces while nine non-snorkel boats made brief sorties into the Bay of Biscay as defensive precautions. During this two-month period the German U-boats enjoyed greater success than that gained in June by sinking eight merchant ships worth 28,237 tons, the 2,938-ton landing ship *Prince Leopold*, the Canadian corvettes *Regina* and *Alberni*, the British minesweeper *Loyalty* and three auxiliary vessels. Still, these losses had a negligible impact upon the Allied logistical effort. Meanwhile, the Allies continued to take a heavy toll upon the Germans including the destruction of 11 U-boats in the English Channel and Bay of Biscay during July and the first week of August. Of these, British warships sank *U390*, *U678*, *U672*, *U212*, *U214*, *U333*, *U671* and *U736* while British aircraft and mines accounted for *U243*, *U1222* and *U415*.

During this time the Allies also effectively dealt with the introduction of new German weapons into the local maritime struggle. Classified as small battle units, these weapons included *Linsen* explosive motor boats, *Neger* and *Marder* human torpedoes and *Biber* midget submarines. The first of these weapons arrived in the area at the end of June and consisted of a flotilla of 34 *Linsen* explosive motor boats. As it was, this initial deployment had no impact on the campaign since accidents and bad weather destroyed or damaged most of the *Linsens* before they could cause any damage to the Allies. Unfortunately, this respite was short-lived as a flotilla of 40 *Neger* human torpedoes soon appeared on the scene. On the nights of 5/6 and 7/8 July these *Negers* attacked shipping in the Seine Bay during which they sank the British minesweepers *Magic*, *Cato* and *Pylades* and damaged the Polish-manned cruiser *Dragon* so severely that it was declared a total loss. Still, during these same assaults British warships and aircraft along with marine hazards destroyed 36 of the attacking *Negers* thus impeding further small battle unit operations for the remainder of the month.

After a nearly four-week pause to bring in reinforcements, the Kriegsmarine renewed its offensive. On the night of 2/3 August the Germans launched a mass attack with 44 *Linsen* explosive motor boats and 58 *Marder* human torpedoes. Supported by Luftwaffe aircraft armed with *Dackel* long-range circling torpedoes, these units sank the British escort destroyer *Quorn*, the auxiliary minesweeper *Gairsay*, the 7,219-ton liberty ship *Samlong* and a landing craft. However, the Germans paid a heavy price for this success with at least 34 *Linsens* and 41 *Marders* destroyed in the operation. Six nights later 28 *Linsens* set out again to attack the Allied anchorage, but they failed to cause any damage and lost 20 of their number

Table 9.2 Characteristics of Selected German Small Battle Units and Special Weapons

Designation	Description
Linsen Explosive motor boat	Radio-controlled explosive motor boat. 1.2 tons. 660-pound explosive charge in stern. 31-knot maximum speed. 60-nautical mile standard range.
Neger Human torpedo	Non-submergible manned torpedo with second 21-inch explosive torpedo slung below carrier body. 2.75 tons. 4.2 knots. 48-nautical mile standard range.
Marder Human torpedo	Submergible manned torpedo with second 21-inch explosive torpedo slung below carrier body. 3 tons. 4.2 knots. 35-nautical mile standard range.
Biber Midget submarine	One-man midget submarine armed with two 21-inch torpedoes or two mines. 6.2 tons. 6.5 knots. 130-nautical mile standard range.
Molch Midget submarine	One-man midget submarine armed with two 21-inch torpedoes or two mines. 11 tons. 5 knots. 43-nautical mile standard range.
Seehund Midget submarine	Two-man midget submarine armed with two 21-inch torpedoes. 14.9 tons. 7.75 knots. 300-nautical mile standard range.
Dackel Long-Range torpedo	Long-range pattern running torpedo. 9 knots. Running range of 57,000 meters with initial straight run being 27,000 meters.

for the effort. Then in the middle of the month 42 *Marders* launched a renewed attack that sank two auxiliary vessels and damaged the 5,205-ton merchant ship *Iddesleigh* but cost them 26 craft in return. This proved to be the last *Marder* operation for the campaign, but the Germans made one last attempt to incorporate small battle units into their interdiction effort. On the night of 30/31 August 22 *Biber* midget submarines set out to attack Allied shipping but accomplished nothing due to bad weather.

In other interdiction operations during this period the Germans used E-boats, mines, aircraft and land-based artillery to confront the Allied logistical tide. In terms of the former, the Germans acquired additional E-boat reinforcements to compensate for the heavy losses sustained during the Le Havre bombing raid of 14/15 June. During July and August, these E-boats conducted regular nightly sorties to challenge the endless procession of Allied convoys transiting the English Channel. In most cases, these raids failed to breach the powerful Allied defences, and the E-boats only succeeded in sinking two liberty ships worth 14,395 tons as well as damaging a number of other vessels including seven merchant ships worth 48,124 tons, the British cruiser *Frobisher* and the frigate *Trollope*. Against this, British bombers sank *S144*, *S39* and *S114* while British surface craft destroyed *S182* and *S91* during this period. Meanwhile, German mines continued to be a persistent threat accounting for the destruction of a handful of vessels in July and August including the British destroyer *Isis* and the corvette *Orchis* and damage to the escort destroyer *Goathland* and the minesweeper *Chamois*. Still, as time progressed, the Allies became more adept at locating, contending with and destroying these mines thus rendering them less effective. Finally, Luftwaffe aircraft and shore artillery also continued to engage the Allied anchorages on a periodic basis, but these actions caused little damage to the vast Allied armada.

When combined together, these interdiction results were woefully inadequate in impeding the Allied build-up. From 24 June through 12 September the Germans only succeeded in destroying a paltry 8,260 tons of stores en route to France.[49] In early July, the Allies landed their millionth man in Normandy, and this process continued unabated for the next eight weeks. By 31 August the Allies had 2,052,299 men, 438,471 vehicles and 3,098,259 tons of stores ashore of which 829,640 men, 202,789 vehicles and 1,245,625 tons of supplies were British or British-affiliated.[50] In terms of major units, this constituted a force of 40 divisions plus numerous independent battalions and brigades.[51] Against this, a total of 37 German divisions saw service at one time or another against the Allied armies in Normandy. While this sounds roughly equivalent, most German divisions were smaller than their Allied counterparts, and the Germans lacked the elaborate support formations present in the Allied armies. As such, the total number of German soldiers that saw action in Normandy or supported operations there probably never exceeded much more than 640,000 men.[52]

As previously discussed, the Allies augmented their growing numerical advantage with the extensive use of aerial and naval firepower. In terms of the former, during the period of 6–30 June the Allied air forces in Northwest Europe flew 163,403 sorties of which 131,263 were directly or indirectly related to ground operations in Normandy. Included in this latter number were 37,266 bomber and 29,957 offensive fighter and fighter-bomber sorties. The German Third Air Fleet was only able to mount a scant 13,829 sorties during the same period.[53] Meanwhile, the navy's heavy warships maintained a constant presence off the Normandy coastline and provided extensive fire support against German defensive positions and troop concentrations. Through the duration of the campaign (into early September) British battleships, monitors and cruisers conducted over 750 support engagements during which they fired 34,621 shells ranging from 5.25-inch to 16-inch in calibre. Added to this were some 24,000 shells fired by British destroyers.[54] In one famous case, the battleship *Rodney* played a key role in defeating a major German counterattack when its 16-inch shells devastated a concentration of German armour located an astonishing 17 miles inland from Gold Beach.

Given this burgeoning imbalance in both forces and firepower, the German defences became increasingly strained, and the Allies began making appreciable gains on the ground. The first such success occurred on 9 July when British forces, bolstered by a massive aerial and naval bombardment, captured the strategically important city of Caen and attained a prize that had eluded them since D-day. Nine days later on the 18th the Americans culminated two weeks of heavy fighting by capturing the key town of St. Lô thus gaining them the necessary jumping off point for their forthcoming breakout offensive. That same day the British launched a massive attack (Operation *Goodwood*) that cleared Caen's southern suburbs and made advances towards the commanding terrain of the Bourguébus Ridge. Notwithstanding these territorial gains, *Goodwood*'s greatest contribution to the Allied effort was its continued lure of German reserves to the British sector. To this point, by 24 July the Germans had 13 divisions (seven panzer and six infantry) confronting the British while only nine divisions, of which only two were panzers, opposed the Americans.[55] Equally important, many of these German formations were severely depleted since the local German forces had suffered 116,863 casualties since D-day against the receipt of only 10,078 replacements.[56] German materiel losses were similarly high with upwards of 480 tanks and assault guns irretrievably lost during this period with hundreds more temporarily disabled.[57]

Together, these results served to ease the main American breakout attempt, which commenced on 25 July. Designated Operation *Cobra*, the American First Army launched this offensive using 15 divisions and extensive artillery and bomber support against the now thinly held German line. During two days of heavy fighting the Americans progressively crumbled the German defences until on the 27th large portions of the German line collapsed allowing the Americans to surge forward.

With their forward defences now compromised, the Germans lacked the immediate reserves to seal off these breaches or form a new comprehensive line, and the American advance continued against sporadic resistance. By 31 July the westernmost American spearheads had broken free of the *bocage* and were advancing into the open terrain south of the Cotentin. Progress on the eastern portion of the American line was more deliberate as the advancing formations encountered greater German resistance including newly arrived reinforcements from the Caen sector, but the Americans still made meaningful gains. Adding to this success, during the last six days of July the American First Army took some 20,000 German prisoners.[58] This brought the total German prisoner count taken since D-day to 82,520.[59] Included in this number were 12,301 prisoners taken by the British Second Army through 29 July.[60]

With their long-awaited breakout now at hand, the Allies moved quickly to maintain and exploit the situation. On 1 August the newly activated American Third Army passed through Avranches and began its conquest of Brittany. In this, the Americans made great strides as they advanced through largely undefended territory. Meanwhile, just prior to this event, six divisions of the British Second Army launched Operation *Bluecoat* in the Caumont area to expand the base of the American breakout and protect its flank from German interference. Against heavy resistance, the British made a strong advance in the area northeast of Vire, although less so at Mont Pincon, and fought to a standstill four German panzer divisions that would have otherwise been available to engage the Americans. In turn, this action delayed and weakened the proposed German counterattack that Hitler had ordered to seal off the Cotentin Peninsula. When the Germans finally launched this attack on 7 August, they did so with just four depleted panzer divisions that mustered fewer than 190 tanks between them. Not surprisingly, this attack, which occurred in the vicinity of Mortain, failed to make appreciable progress, and the flood of American forces advancing through Western France continued unabated.

This rapidly deteriorating situation had major implications for the German naval forces stationed in Western Europe. Already in July British warships and Coastal Command aircraft had destroyed (or in some cases captured) 40 German and German-controlled vessels in the English Channel, North Sea and adjacent areas including the fleet minesweepers *M469*, *M264* and *M307* and five sizable merchant ships worth 12,535 tons. During the same period, British bombing raids against ports destroyed *U239* and *U1164* along with a further five merchant ships and seven minor vessels worth 22,090 tons. Likewise, American bombers sank the incomplete destroyer *Z44*, the torpedo boats *T2* and *T7* and the submarines *U872*, *U890*, *U891* and *U892* in a raid against Bremen.[61] Now, with the ongoing collapse of their armies in Normandy and the appearance of American forces in Brittany, the Germans realised that their retention of the French Atlantic ports was clearly jeopardised. As such, they began a series of evacuation operations to save as many assets as possible before the Americans arrived.

Starting first with their U-boat forces, in early August German authorities ordered the transfer of all seaworthy U-boats from the immediately threatened ports of Brest, Lorient and St. Nazaire to the less endangered ports of La Pallice and Bordeaux on France's southern Atlantic coast. While this was underway, the Germans also ordered five additional U-boats into the English Channel to engage Allied shipping. Forewarned of these pending actions through Ultra intercepts, the British dispatched six groups of destroyers along with three cruisers into the Bay of Biscay and intensified Coastal Command activity within the area. During a nine-day period beginning on 10 August these warships and aircraft destroyed no fewer than seven relocating U-boats and two of the U-boats en route to the English Channel. The vessels in question were *U608*, *U385*, *U981*, *U270*, *U618*, *U741*, *U107*, *U621* and *U766* of which the former eight were sunk outright while the ninth was damaged so severely it was declared a total loss and subsequently scuttled.

Unfortunately for the Germans, this was only the beginning of their ordeal as a new threat burst upon their southern flank. On 15 August Allied forces in the Mediterranean launched a large-scale invasion of Southern France. Unlike Operation *Neptune* or earlier amphibious landings in North Africa, Sicily and Italy, the British were not the predominant maritime players in this undertaking. The distinction for this went to the United States Navy. Still, the British did provide 35.6 percent of the 1,034 primary vessels used in the invasion and its follow up. This contribution included the battleship *Ramillies*; the escort carriers *Emperor*, *Pursuer*, *Searcher*, *Attacker*, *Khedive*, *Hunter* and *Stalker*; 11 cruisers; 29 destroyers and escorts; 18 minesweepers; two gunboats and 300 assorted support and landing vessels.[62] Against this onslaught, the local Kriegsmarine and Luftwaffe were virtually non-existent, and the invasion proceeded without significant mishap. By the evening of the 17th the Allies had 86,575 men, 12,250 vehicles and 46,140 tons of supplies ashore, and by 2 September this number increased to 190,565 men, 41,534 vehicles and 219,205 tons of supplies.[63]

Given this result and the ongoing calamity unfolding in Normandy, the Germans realised that the entire region was now irretrievably compromised. Accordingly, on the 18th Hitler ordered the evacuation of Southern and Southwestern France with the exception of Brest, Lorient, St. Nazaire, La Pallice, La Rochelle and parts of the Gironde, which would be turned into fortresses to deny their use to the Allies. In accordance with this, all serviceable U-boats were ordered to leave these ports and proceed to Norway while U-boats that could not be made seaworthy were scuttled. Over the next couple of weeks a total of 27 Type VII and seven Type IX U-boats departed the area. Most of these boats proceeded directly to Norway, but a handful conducted war patrols en route. U-boats that were already deployed continued their patrols until also diverting to Norway. Finally, three U-cruisers departed Bordeaux with cargo for the Far East. Against this great mass of transiting U-boats, British warships sank *U413*, *U984*, *U445* and *U247* while mines claimed *U180* and *U667* from 20 August through 1 September. Meanwhile, of the U-boats that were unable to proceed, the Germans scuttled *U178*, *U188*, *UIT21*, *U123*, *U129* and the aforementioned *U766*. When combined together, this brought the total number of U-boats lost in the Biscay area from 1 August through 1 September to 22.

Still, as bad as this was, it was nothing compared to the carnage unleashed against the local German surface forces. In addition to hunting U-boats, the British warships and aircraft dispatched into the Bay of Biscay also destroyed large numbers of German surface vessels. Starting first with the British warships, on the night of 5/6 August the light cruiser *Bellona* and a mixed force of four British/Canadian destroyers engaged a German convoy off Île d'Yeu and destroyed the fleet minesweepers *M263* and *M486*, the patrol boat *V414* and two coasters. During the same engagement the Allies severely damaged the German escort destroyer *SG3* (ex-French *Sans Pareil*, 1,372 tons, 3 × 4.1-inch guns) which was finished off by Beaufighter strike aircraft the next day. Then on 12 August the light cruiser *Diadem* and two destroyers teamed up with Beaufighters to sink the 7,087-ton *Sperrbrecher 7* off La Rochelle while Canadian and British destroyers sank three patrol craft south of Brest. Two nights later the light cruiser *Mauritius* and the destroyers *Ursa* and *Iroquois* (Canadian) intercepted a German convoy off Les Sables d'Olonne and destroyed the fleet minesweeper *M385*, the 1,495-ton *Sperrbrecher 157* and a coaster. Finally, on 23 August these same three Allied warships attacked a group of German patrol boats off Audierne and sank *VP702*, *VP717*, *VP720*, *VP729* and *VP730*.[64] All of these actions occurred for no Allied losses in return.

For its part, the RAF contributed to the local interdiction campaign in three ways. First, strike aircraft from Fighter Command and Coastal Command's No. 19 Group flew extensive sweeps over the contested waters in search of German vessels. Some highlights of these operations included strikes by British aircraft that wrecked the fleet minesweepers *M422*, *M424* and *M206* at St. Malo on 4 and 6 August. Two days later two squadrons of Beaufighters sank the fleet minesweepers *M366*, *M367*, *M428* and *M438* off St. Nazaire while other Coastal Command aircraft sank the 997-ton *Sperrbrecher 134* off Lorient. Then from 10 to 21 August these aircraft launched a series of attacks throughout the area that helped sink the aforementioned *Sperrbrecher 7* and sank *Sperrbrechers 5* and *6* (5,339 and 6,128 tons respectively), the fleet minesweepers *M370* and *M292*, five auxiliary escort vessels and a tug. Likewise, on the 12th British aircraft attacked the destroyer *Z23* at La Pallice and damaged it so severely that the Germans were compelled to scuttle it nine days later. Finally, on 24 August British Beaufighters sank the destroyer *Z24* and the torpedo boat *T24* at Le Verdon.[65]

The second major component in this aerial offensive was Bomber Command, which contributed to the campaign in two ways. First, in August Bomber Command

Whether armed with bombs, torpedoes or rockets, the Bristol Beaufighter was the RAF's most prolific ship-killer in a direct attack role and saw service as such in every major theatre of the war including Northwest Europe where it excelled in strike wing operations. (Daventry, B. J. (Flt Lt), Royal Air Force official photographer, public domain)

carried out a series of raids against the Brittany and Biscay ports with Brest being particularly hard hit. During these raids Bomber Command aircraft sank 23 assorted vessels worth a combined 44,864 tons including the fleet minesweepers *M271*, *M325* and *M444* and five *sperrbrechers*. During the same period USAAF bombers added a further six vessels worth 12,368 tons to this total. Beyond these direct attacks, Bomber Command aircraft also flew multiple minelaying sorties in August against the Biscay area. In addition to the already mentioned *U180* and *U667*, these mines sank the fleet minesweeper *M27* and nine minor vessels. These mines also severely damaged the minesweepers *M304* and *M363* thus leading to their scuttling at Bordeaux on 25 August.[66]

While most attention was focused on the Biscay area, the Allies also scored a number of successes against German naval and maritime assets located in Northern European waters. In August British strike aircraft, predominately from Coastal Command's No. 16 Group, flew extensive sorties in the North Sea and off Norway where they sank 13 German vessels including two sizable merchant ships and two *sperrbrechers* worth a combined 10,710 tons along with the fleet minesweepers

M383 and *M347*. During the same period Bomber Command carried out major raids against Le Havre, Stettin, Ymuiden and Kiel where they sank 26 ships worth 21,256 tons including the minesweeper *M266* and damaged 13 more worth 28,862 tons. Likewise, Allied mines accounted for 22 assorted vessels in these waters and the Baltic including two merchant ships worth 4,141 tons, the submarine *U1000* and the minesweeper *M468*. Finally, British coastal craft destroyed 11 minor warships in the Channel area.[67]

Unfortunately for the Germans, the grievous losses sustained by the Kriegsmarine only exacerbated the calamity befalling their ground forces. By the second week in August Allied advances threatened to encircle much of the German army in Normandy with the British and Canadians pressing in from the north and west while the Americans proceeded around the southern flank. Over the next several days the Allies applied continuous pressure along the entire perimeter causing it to progressively collapse. Of particular consequence, on 13 August American forces arrived in the vicinity of Argentan while three days later elements of the recently activated Canadian First Army captured Falaise thus reducing the distance between the two converging armies to about 15 miles. With the German defensive pocket now rapidly shrinking and Allied artillery and aircraft turning the area into a vast killing ground, Hitler finally authorised a withdrawal. Unfortunately for many of his impacted units, it was already too late. On 19 August Canadian and American forces made contact with each other at Chambois thus closing the pincer, although it would take two more days of heavy fighting to fully seal the gap.

With this, a sizable portion of the German army was cut off and destroyed. During the final phase of the encirclement, 16–21 August, the British and Canadians took some 20,000 German prisoners while the Americans took a similar number on their side of the pocket.[68] When expanding the period to encompass the totality of the victory, the total number of prisoners taken by British and Canadian forces increased to 34,524 from 30 July (the beginning of Operation *Bluecoat*) through 23 August.[69] An estimated 10,000 Germans died in the pocket while many thousands more were wounded.[70] Beyond this human toll, the Germans also suffered extensive materiel losses including 344 tanks and armoured vehicles, 2,447 trucks and cars and 252 towed guns found destroyed or abandoned in the British/Canadian portion of the pocket alone.[71] Of the German units that did escape, most were mere shadows of their former selves with the all-important panzer divisions being particularly depleted. This was demonstrated by the fact that when the seven impacted panzer divisions crossed the Seine a few days later, they did so with a combined strength of just 24 tanks and 60 artillery pieces.[72]

Nor was this the extent of the German disaster. Even as the bulk of the Allied armies conducted operations in the Falaise-Argentan area, other Allied formations advanced through large swaths of Northern France against minimal opposition. With the destruction of German forces in the pocket, the remaining Allied units joined this advance and quickly made impressive territorial gains against the shattered German army. On 25 August Paris was liberated, and by the end of the month all of the Allied armies were over the Seine River thus completing the Normandy portion of the campaign. During this time large numbers of prisoners continued to flow into the Allied cages. An example of this occurred on 31 August when British XXX Corps took some 5,000 prisoners in the Amiens area alone.[73] Together, this brought the total number of German prisoners taken in France from D-day through the end of August to a staggering 233,023.[74] Added to this were at least 23,019 German soldiers killed and 67,060 wounded in France from June through August.[75] When combined with Luftwaffe and Kriegsmarine losses, total German casualties during this period easily exceeded 330,000 men. Meanwhile, German materiel losses were equally high including an estimated 1,300 tanks, 20,000 vehicles, 500 assault guns and 1,500 field guns and larger artillery pieces destroyed or abandoned.[76] The regional Luftwaffe commands (the Third Air Fleet and Reich Defence Force) lost 3,656 aircraft during roughly the same period.[77]

For its part, the Kriegsmarine was a full participant in this disaster. Already discussed were the many ships destroyed as a result of Allied action, but in addition to this the Germans also scuttled scores of vessels that were unable to attempt an escape from the threatened Biscay or Channel ports. As these ports fell, the Allies captured many ships intact. The result, in August German losses from scuttling or capture amounted to 56 military and 116 commercial vessels worth a combined 332,975 tons. Included in this number were the destroyer *Z37* and the fleet minesweepers *M384*, *M262*, *M344* and *M463* as well as the previously mentioned *Z23*, *M133*, *M206*, *M84*, *M304* and *M363* that were all scuttled after being disabled by British aircraft, warships or mines. When viewing the entire period of June through August, total German maritime losses from all causes (including accidents and Russian action) in the waters off Northwest Europe and the Baltic consisted of 346 military and 287 commercial vessels worth 179,906 and 506,980 tons respectively.[78] In terms of principal warships, this toll included six destroyers, eleven torpedo boats, one escort destroyer, three corvettes and 41 fleet minesweepers. During the same period the Germans also lost 68 U-boats in these waters of which 48 were destroyed in actions related directly or indirectly to Operation *Overlord*. Beyond vessels already mentioned, this included *U319*, *U361*, *U347*, *U742*, *U354* and *U344* that were sunk by British aircraft or warships in the Arctic and Norwegian Sea and *U2323* and *U1000* that were sunk by British mines in the Baltic.

Against these staggering totals, Allied losses were also high, but nowhere near the carnage suffered by the Germans. Through the end of August Allied ground casualties in Normandy numbered 209,672 of which Britain's portion (including British-affiliated units) came to 16,138 dead, 58,594 wounded and 9,093 missing.[79] Allied materiel losses were equally high and in some cases worse than those suffered by the Germans. This latter point was certainly true when it came to the Allied air forces, which lost 4,101 aircraft in Northwest Europe from 6 June through 31 August.[80] Still, given the Allies' industrial might and vast materiel superiority, they were far better positioned to replace their losses than were the Germans. Also, since the Allies retained the battlefield, they were able to recover and repair much of their disabled equipment whereas the vast bulk of disabled German equipment was irretrievably spent.

Regarding the maritime portion of the campaign, the Allies lost 60 military vessels, 45 supply ships/transports and 419 landing craft worth a combined 242,196 tons due to hostile and operational causes.[81] Included in the former were 27 principal warships. Added to this were three additional warships that were sunk in the theatre during the period but not in operations related to the campaign. The majority of these warship losses were British or British-affiliated consisting of one cruiser, four destroyers, three escort destroyers, one sloop, four frigates, three corvettes and six minesweepers. This number includes the British minesweepers *Britomart* and *Hussar* that were misidentified and accidently sunk by RAF strike aircraft on 27 August off Cap d' Antifer in what proved to be one of the worst cases of maritime fratricide during the war. A third minesweeper, *Salamander*, was heavily damaged during this strike but made it back to port. Meanwhile, during the same month U-boats sank the escort destroyer *Fiske* (American) 470 miles north-north-west of the Azores and the sloop *Kite* and frigate *Bickerton* in Norwegian waters thus constituting the three Allied naval losses that were unrelated to the Normandy fighting.

Of course, the true significance of the Allied victory went far beyond a simple accounting of the casualties suffered by both sides. By the end of August the Allies had six field armies present in France including two armies that had recently landed in the Toulon area through the Mediterranean. This force would soon increase to seven field armies with the activation of the American Ninth Army in Northern France on 5 September. There would be no reversing this presence. By successfully carrying out the invasion of France, the Allies had overcome the last strategic barrier to their ultimate victory. Germany was now caught in a powerful vice of converging forces from both east and west, and there was absolutely nothing the Germans could do to stave off defeat. While additional resistance was likely, it was only a matter of time

Table 9.3 Principal Allied and Axis Warship Losses in Northern European Waters (and Related Areas) during the Period of June 1944 through August 1944

	Cruisers	Destroyers	Torpedo boats/escort destroyers/frigates/sloops	Corvettes/fleet minesweepers	Submarines
British/Allied	1	8	10	11	-
German	-	6	12	44	68

before Germany collapsed. How long this would take still depended upon events, but prevailing thought indicated it would only be a matter of months. Therefore, after nearly five years of blood, sweat, toil and tears, Britain's epic struggle against Nazi Germany was almost over.

CHAPTER 10

Victory in Europe

In the early days of September 1944, a growing sense of euphoria rapidly spread throughout the Allied camp in Northwest Europe. From commanding generals to lower enlisted men and political leaders to common civilians, a collective belief prevailed that the war was almost over. For the advancing Allied armies, the spectacular progress being made clearly bolstered this belief. This was no truer than with the British Second Army, which advanced 250 miles in six days and liberated much of Northern France and Belgium including the major cities of Ghent, Brussels and Antwerp. In the process of this advance, which became known as the Great Swan, the British took large numbers of German prisoners for minimal cost to themselves. During the week ending on 10 September the British Second Army took 28,557 prisoners, which excluded thousands more taken during the first three days of the month.[1] While this was underway, the Canadian First Army invested the port of Le Havre and advanced up the channel coastline. When combined together with earlier operations, these actions brought the total number of prisoners taken by the British and Canadian forces in Northwest Europe from D-day through 8 September to 97,163.[2]

Meanwhile, on the right, the American 12th Army Group, consisting of the American First and Third Armies, advanced on a broad front that brought it to the vicinity of the German border in the north to the Moselle River in the south. With this advance, the Americans took even greater numbers of prisoners for minimal losses to themselves, and by 10 September their total prisoner count for the campaign reached 239,679.[3] Similar events unfolded in the south where elements of the 6th Army Group (American Seventh and French First Armies) advanced up the Rhône valley from Southern France. In five weeks of fighting (15 August through 20 September) these forces reached the outskirts of Southern Germany and added a further 87,705 prisoners to the growing Allied bag.[4] Thus, in a matter of only a few weeks the Allies attained success on an immense scale and established a continuous front ranging from the Dutch frontier in the north to the Swiss border in the south.

Yet, despite these dramatic developments and the euphoria they induced, a number of significant adversities still existed that threatened to delay the Allies' final victory.

Chief amongst these were various logistical constraints that portended to stall the Allied advance. In this regard, the Allies were largely victims of their own success. Before the Normandy invasion Allied planners had forecast that their forces would reach the Seine River by D + 90 and then pause there for 30 days to build-up logistical stockpiles before advancing further. Even then, they did not anticipate an advance beyond the Aisne River in Northern France until D + 150. As it was, by D + 90 (4 September) Allied forces were 150 to 180 miles beyond the Seine River and were there in greater strength than Allied planners had ever anticipated. As such, the Allies were quickly outrunning their supply lines. Making matters worse, the initial Allied plan had called for the Americans to quickly seize the Brittany ports after breaking out from Normandy. Instead, the bulk of the American forces had turned eastward to pursue the retreating German army, and the Brittany ports remained in German hands with the exception of St. Malo. By early September this decision resulted in a discharge shortfall of some 14,000 tons per day compared to earlier Allied projections.[5]

Given these circumstances, it was only a matter of time before logistical constraints compelled the Allies to pause their offensive and give their overextended lines of communication a chance to catch up. As if on cue, the Allied advance began to sputter and stall as various formations ran out of fuel and other essential materiel. This problem was particularly acute in the American area of operations, but soon the British 21st Army Group (British Second and Canadian First Armies) experienced similar disruptions. Unfortunately, this brought about another problem. While the German army had suffered a severe mauling, it was far from a vanquished force. What the Germans needed most was a pause in the action to give them time to regroup and re-establish a comprehensive defensive line. On numerous occasions in the past the Germans had demonstrated an uncanny ability to recover from earlier defeats, and the Allies feared that a respite of even a few days might give them the opportunity to do so again. Thus, the Allies sought a way to maintain the initiative while still addressing the logistical constraints that confronted them. In this, they faced a fast-closing window of opportunity to deliver a decisive blow that might still prematurely end the war or at least hasten this outcome.

To achieve this, the Allies considered a number of options. Most of these deliberations broke down along nationalistic lines. The British position, advocated by newly promoted Field Marshal Bernard Montgomery, called for the husbanding of all available resources to support a single thrust by British and American forces in the north to seize Germany's industrial heartland of the Ruhr. This proposal was largely in line with pre-invasion strategy that saw the seizure of the Ruhr as a key strategic objective. Against this, American Lieutenant-General Omar Bradley proposed a similar thrust to be delivered by his 12th Army Group against the Saar region. This proposal was not in keeping with earlier Allied planning, but reflected an opportunity to exploit the great successes attain by his armies in Eastern France. Weighing these competing options was the Supreme Allied Commander, General Dwight Eisenhower, who had also recently assumed the role as ground forces commander from Montgomery (thus relegating the latter to command the British 21st Army Group). Considering a variety of factors, both military and political, Eisenhower decided upon a compromise strategy that split the available resources and authorised both army groups to continue their respective advances.

Unfortunately, this decision failed to attain the hoped-for results. In the north the British Second Army launched a bold and elaborate enterprise, designated Operation *Market-Garden*, to seize a crossing over the Rhine River and circumvent the main German defences along the West Wall.[6] The key to this was the planned seizure of a road bridge at Arnhem, which spanned the Lower Rhine. Launched on 17 September and lasting the duration of a week, *Market-Garden* made some territorial gains that would provide future benefits, but failed to capture the Arnhem bridge thus rendering the operation a strategic failure. Sadly, this setback came at a heavy cost as the British and supporting American forces suffered a total of 16,482 ground casualties during the operation.[7] Estimates of the corresponding German casualties ranged between 6,300 and 10,000.[8] Meanwhile, in the south the American First and Third Armies launched a series of attacks in the areas around Aachen and Metz to advance to and breach the German West Wall defences. Unfortunately, in each case the Americans encountered growing German resistance that capitalised upon the region's formidable natural and manmade defences. Both American armies also continued to suffer persistent supply shortages due to the conditions previously mentioned. The result, in three weeks of costly fighting the Americans failed to attain a decisive breakthrough anywhere, and the front stabilised, ending the prospect for an early victory.

With this window now closed, the Allies refocused their attention on the mundane task of shoring up their overextended supply lines. A critical factor in this was attaining additional port capacity that was closer to the deployed armies thus alleviating pressure on the local road and rail networks. At the time the Allies were still landing the bulk of their supplies in Normandy, which was located several hundred road-miles from their forward-deployed units. In the third week in September American forces, with fire support from the battleship *Warspite* and other British warships, finally captured the port of Brest after a 40-day siege costing 9,831 American casualties.[9] Unfortunately, this was little more than a pyrrhic victory. Not only was Brest located even farther away from the forward-deployed Allied troops than Normandy, but its port was so thoroughly devastated by German demolition efforts and the recent heavy fighting that it was practically useless to the Allied cause. Based upon this result, the Americans decided to forgo further attempts to capture the remaining Atlantic ports and instead chose to let the isolated German garrisons wither on the vine.

With the Americans now stymied in this effort, all attention turned to the British and Canadians in the north to alleviate the growing Allied logistical shortfall. In this, the Allies recognised that the key to resolving their logistical problems rested in opening the port of Antwerp, which was the second largest port in Europe with a discharge capacity of over 40,000 tons per day. The British had captured Antwerp largely intact on 4 September, but this was of no use by itself. Antwerp is located more than 60 miles inland from the Atlantic Ocean with its access to the sea coming from the Scheldt Estuary. In early September the Germans still controlled the entire length of this estuary including Zeelandic Flanders in the south and Walcheren Island and the South Beveland peninsula in the north. In order to open Antwerp, the Allies first had to gain control over this vital waterway. This was no easy task since the Germans also recognised the area's strategic value and thus resolved to mount a resolute defence. Much of this territory was sodden polder land, which restricted mobility and offered limited cover for attacking forces. The island of Walcheren, which controlled access to the Scheldt, possessed a number of built-up fortifications and heavy artillery batteries that made it an extremely formidable obstacle that had to be overcome.

The responsibility for clearing the area around the Scheldt fell upon the Canadian First Army. This was one of two major tasks given to the Canadians in the autumn of 1944. The other was to liberate the coastal areas of Northern France and Belgium and to seize the various local ports including St. Valéry-en-Caux, Dieppe, Le Havre, Boulogne, Calais, Dunkirk and Ostend. While Antwerp was clearly the biggest prize, the capture and use of these lesser ports would also provide some logistical relief for the Allies. St. Valéry-en-Caux, Dieppe and Ostend were largely undefended and fell easily enough, but the remaining ports promised to be more difficult since Hitler had designated them fortresses. Defending this area was the German Fifteenth Army, which was largely intact having escaped most of the fighting around Normandy. For its part, the Canadian First Army was the smallest active Allied army operating in Northwest Europe at the time consisting of only two corps (I British and II Canadian) with a total of six divisions (British 49th and 51st, Canadian 2nd, 3rd and 4th [Armoured] and Polish 1st [Armoured]). Now that the euphoric days of early September were clearly waning, it appeared that these British and Canadian forces had their work cut out for them.

Yet despite this reality, the task of clearing the coastal areas and seizing the channel ports went surprisingly well. Supported by numerous British and Canadian artillery units, the specialised armour of the British 79th Armoured Division, the heavy bombers of RAF Bomber Command and gunfire from various British warships including the battleship *Warspite* and the monitor *Erebus*, First Army launched a series of highly successful assaults that systematically reduced the German fortresses. First to go was Le Havre, which fell to the British 49th and 51st Divisions on 12 September along with 11,302 prisoners. Ten days later the Canadian 2nd and 3rd Divisions captured Boulogne and took another 9,517 prisoners. Then at the end of the month the Canadian 3rd Division captured Calais and cleared the coastal batteries at Cap Gris Nez collecting a further 9,128 prisoners in the process. Together these combined operations, which netted almost 30,000 prisoners, cost the British and Canadians fewer than 1,500 casualties in return.[10] Meanwhile, the Allies immediately went to work putting these ports back into operation, and by the middle of November the channel ports were receiving nearly 30,000 tons of supplies per day.[11] The exception to this was Dunkirk, which the Allies decided to leave in German hands as an isolated garrison.

Against these successes, clearing the Scheldt proved to be a far more difficult undertaking. After preliminary operations in September that expanded Allied control around Antwerp and cleared portions of East Zeelandic Flanders, First Army began its main effort to open the Scheldt Estuary on 2 October. Over the next month the Canadian 2nd and 3rd Divisions and the newly arrived British 52nd Division conducted a series of operations to seal off and capture the South Beveland peninsula, North Beveland and the Breskens pocket (West Zeelandic Flanders). While this was underway, eight divisions from I and XII British Corps (the latter from Second Army) launched a series of attacks to clear the territory south of the Maas River from Nijmegen to St. Philipsland and Tholen on the North Sea. In doing so, they formed a more linear front between the First and Second Armies that added depth to the defence of Antwerp and secured the Scheldt's eastern flank.

By the beginning of November all of these operations were complete or nearing completion and the only major task that remained was the capture of Walcheren Island. The Germans defended Walcheren with a force of over 8,000 men, although most of these were garrison troops of dubious combat value. Nevertheless, these troops manned strong defensive positions with considerable firepower to compensate for their limited tactical prowess. On the seaward side of the island the Germans had ten coastal batteries with some 40 guns, mostly in fixed concrete casements, ranging in calibre from 3-inch to 8.7-inch. They had additional batteries positioned around the town of Flushing on the southern tip of the island that could engage targets approaching from the south or east via the Scheldt. Meanwhile, the beaches around Walcheren were fortified with bunkers, mines and a variety of obstacles similar to those used in Normandy while the sea approaches were also heavily mined.

To overcome these considerable defences, the British proposed to launch a major amphibious operation to capture Walcheren. Serious planning for this operation began in September and eventually developed into a two-pronged assault with the British 4th Special Service Brigade (Commandos) landing at Weskapelle on the west end of the island while a reinforced brigade from the British 52nd Division landed at Flushing in the south. In terms of these two landings, the former represented a full-blown seaborne assault reminiscent of the Normandy operation while the latter essentially constituted an oversized river crossing of about three miles distance.

Under the overall command of Captain A. F. Pugsley, the British assembled two naval forces to carry out these landings. The Weskapelle force, which assembled at Ostend, consisted of 181 assorted landing craft, barges and motor launches for the assault while an additional 27 specialised gun- and rocket-fitted landing craft were earmarked for fire support.[12] Utilising the frigate *Kingsmill* as a headquarters ship, the British further assigned the battleship *Warspite* and the monitors *Erebus* and *Roberts* for heavy bombardment duties. Meanwhile, the Flushing force, which consisted of about 90 landing craft and amphibious vehicles, assembled at Breskens directly across the Scheldt from the landing area.[13]

While these preparations were underway, RAF Bomber Command carried out a series of raids against Walcheren to weaken its defences and reduce the garrison's morale. Of particular consequence, the RAF launched an effort to flood the island. Topographically, Walcheren resembled a giant saucer plate with most of the island's interior located below sea level. By breaching the surrounding dikes, the British planned to flood the island's interior, compromising many of the German defences and forcing the Germans to concentrate their forces on the remaining dry ground. These floodwaters would impede German efforts to reinforce and support their isolated forces once the British attacked. Of course, these same waters would also impede British mobility, but this would be less problematic for them given their abundance in specialised amphibious vehicles. Based upon these considerations, the RAF carried out a series of raids in October that breached the dikes in four places and caused flooding to 80 percent of the island.

With these preparations complete, the British launched their invasion of Walcheren on 1 November. The first phase of this operation commenced at 0545 hours when British assault forces, supported by a 284-gun artillery barrage, crossed the Scheldt and began their conquest of Flushing. Although some heavy fighting ensued, the crossing went reasonably well, and the British were able to progressively seize their objectives. The assault against Weskapelle, which occurred four hours later, proved to be a more difficult undertaking as the British encountered heavy fire from the German shore batteries. Return fire from the British warships, including 353 shells from *Warspite*, only partially succeeded in subduing this opposition.[14] Fortunately, the Germans concentrated most of their fire against the British support squadron thus allowing the assault craft to proceed against lighter resistance. Once ashore, the commandos, supported by specialised armour, began the process of clearing the German defences, and the situation steadily improved. By day's end the British were firmly ashore, but this success cost them 26 assorted landing craft thus attesting to the difficulty of the landings.[15]

It took another week of fighting for the British to complete their conquest of Walcheren, which signalled the end of the Scheldt campaign. Even before this occurred, ten flotillas of minesweepers began the process of clearing the vital waterway leading to Antwerp. After sweeping 267 mines, the British declared the channel

On hundreds of occasions during the Northwest Europe campaign British warships provided valuable gunfire support for their army brethren. Of the various warships involved, none was more notable than the veteran battleship *Warspite,* which conducted engagements against Normandy (pictured here), Brest, Le Havre and Walcheren Island. (McNeill M. H. A. (Lt), Royal Navy official photographer, public domain)

clear on 26 November, and two days later the first convoy of 19 deep-laden vessels arrived in Antwerp.[16] This was the first of what would quickly become a flood of ships, and in December the Allies discharged 427,592 tons of supplies (excluding bulk fuel and vehicles) in the great port.[17] When combined with tonnage from the channel ports and other infrastructure improvements, the Allies' logistical dilemma was largely resolved. Sadly, this success came at a high cost. During the heaviest period of fighting to clear the Scheldt (1 October to 8 November) First Army suffered 12,873 casualties split almost equally between its British and Canadian contingents. Against this, the army took 41,043 prisoners with thousands of additional Germans killed or wounded during this same period.[18] When combined with concurrent results from Second Army, this helped bring the overall haul of prisoners taken by the British 21st Army Group through the end of November to 222,987.[19]

Unfortunately, the restoration of the logistical situation had little immediate impact in helping the Allies regain the strategic initiative. Already, throughout this period the various Allied armies had carried out a series of operations to gain territory and consolidate their positions. Unfortunately, many of these ended in costly frustration for the participating commands. This was particularly true in the 12 Army Group's sector where the Americans conducted unproductive campaigns in the areas around Aachen, the Hürtgen forest and the Lorraine region that made minimal territorial gains and cost the three participating American armies a total of 112,277 combat and 113,742 non-battle casualties.[20] As frustrating as this was, things got worse in the second half of December when the Germans launched a major counterattack in the Ardennes region of Belgium with three reconstituted armies consisting of seven panzer and 13 infantry divisions. Although the Allies eventually repulsed this attack and inflicted some 80,000 to 90,000 casualties on the Germans, this came at a terrible cost in terms of lost time and casualties. Regarding the former, the fighting and its aftermath cost the Allies two months of valuable time during which they were unable to pursue their own strategic ambitions. It would now be the middle of February before the Allies were ready to resume the offensive in a meaningful way. In terms of the latter, the six-week long battle cost the participating American forces 75,482 casualties including 29,402 killed, missing or taken prisoner. Added to this were a further 1,408 casualties suffered by the participating British units.[21]

For the Western Allies, the conclusion of the Ardennes offensive signalled the end of a disappointing period. Looking back at the heady days of late August and early September, it had appeared that victory was just around the corner and that the war would be over by Christmas. Instead, by the beginning of February, five months had passed since these euphoric days, and the war still raged on. Making matters worse, during the intervening time the Allies had suffered some 300,000 combat casualties, but made little appreciable headway in their advance towards Germany. This had been a time of great frustration for the Allies, and yet the period was not a complete waste. To the contrary, the Allies had used this period to substantially build-up their forces and put their logistical situation in order. As such, by the beginning of 1945 the Allies had 3,724,927 men in Northwest Europe thus giving them a force of 73 divisions. The Allies also possessed over 17,500 assorted combat aircraft in Britain, France and the Low Countries.[22] Finally and perhaps equally important, the Allies now possessed the logistical means to utilise this force to its full potential. Against this was a German army that was still sizable in numbers, due to the call-up of civilian reserves, but increasingly hollow in terms of its combat effectiveness and resolve. The situation was much the same for the Luftwaffe. Given these realities, after five months of frustrating delay, the Allies were finally poised to fulfil the promise of the previous autumn.

Before proceeding on, however, we will first go back to review the maritime conflict that was ongoing during this same period. Given the events on the ground at this late stage in the war, observers might reasonably conclude that the concurrent maritime struggle was of little consequence. By any measure, maritime power had been absolutely essential in propelling the Allies to this point, but with their armies now positioned on the outskirts of Germany itself, was this maritime contribution still relevant? In at least one vital respect, the answer to this was a resounding yes. In November 1944 the Allies required the intake of two million tons of supplies per month to support their forces in Northwest Europe. By April 1945 this monthly requirement was expected to increase to over three million tons. Other than a negligible amount that was flown in by air or pumped in via Pluto pipelines, the vast majority of these supplies had to arrive by sea. A significant portion of this came directly from Britain while the remainder came from across the Atlantic or through the Mediterranean. In practical terms, this translated into a continuous flow of ships and vessels that had to arrive daily in France and Belgium to unload their valuable cargoes. Thus, while the means of victory in Europe now clearly rested with the ground forces, this was only possible through the continued support of the Allied navies and merchant marines.

Putting this task into perspective, during the first half of the war the Axis had struggled, and usually failed, to deliver a mere 100,000 tons of supplies to their forces in North Africa on a monthly basis. Now the Allies were compelled to execute an effort some twenty to thirty times larger. Perhaps even more revealing, if extended out for a year, this immense supply effort was roughly equivalent to the total tonnage of imports that had arrived in Britain in 1942. Thus, to support their armies in Northwest Europe, the Allies had to conduct the type of effort that had sustained an entire nation just two years before. Of course, this latter requirement had not disappeared. In addition to supporting their armies, the Allies still had to fulfil Britain's import needs, which in 1944 amounted to the receipt of some 46 million tons. When combined together, this constituted a requirement to transport upwards of 80 million tons of cargo and materiel into or through the still contested waters around Britain and Western Europe on an annual basis. As such, this represented a scale of prolonged seaborne transport exceeding anything previously undertaken in the European conflict. Fortunately from their point of view, the Allies possessed adequate resources to fulfil this task, but they still had to execute the mission on a consistent basis despite German opposition.

For their part, the corresponding German task in this ongoing maritime struggle was to cause as much disruption to the Allied logistical effort as possible. By this stage in the war Germany clearly lacked the means to fully sever or even substantially disrupt this flow of maritime traffic, but as ongoing events in France and Belgium had demonstrated, even a partial disruption to the Allied logistical network could have meaningful ramifications on the battlefield. Likewise, any successes attained at sea reduced the burden shouldered by the German army. Grand Admiral Dönitz articulated this latter point by stating, 'On the other hand every ship, laden with war materiel and bound for France or for the Scheldt estuary, which we could sink under the English coast, lightened the burden of our struggle ashore.'[23] Over the previous year and a half the Kriegsmarine had suffered a series of significant reversals, but it was far from a spent force. Now with the German homeland directly threatened by the encroaching Allied armies, the Kriegsmarine moved to fulfil its part in the German defence.

The key component in this effort was the launching of a renewed U-boat offensive directed primarily against Allied shipping in the waters around Britain. Despite reoccurring heavy losses, the U-boat arm had maintained its strength at about 400 boats through new construction, although only about a third of these were operational. Of the latter, only a portion were available for sea duty at any given time. A major factor in this was the loss of the Biscay ports, which left Bergen and Trondheim in Norway as the only front-line bases now available to support U-boat operations. As it was, these Norwegian bases only possessed sufficient repair and refit facilities to handle about 30 boats. The Germans immediately began efforts to boost this capacity, but despite increases in dockyard personnel and equipment, these bases could only accommodate about a third of the boats that the Biscay ports had handled. As such, the overflow had to divert to Germany to fulfil their support needs. The results of this were threefold. First, the reduced dockyard capacity significantly increased the average turnaround time to enact repairs and refits. Second, these Norwegian/German bases were located further away from the U-boat patrol areas thus increasing transit times. Finally, the diversion of front-line U-boats to Germany took resources away from the production and working up of new U-boats thus further stifling the expansion of the operational fleet.

Given these circumstances, from the middle of August through the end of December the Germans were only able to dispatch 59 U-boats on offensive patrols around Britain. Areas particularly targeted during these sorties included the English Channel, the Bristol Channel, the Irish Sea, the North Channel and the waters between the Orkneys and Iceland. By patrolling these areas, the Germans sought to impede both shipping movements to France as well as transatlantic convoys culminating in Britain. During roughly the same period a further 15 U-boats, which were unsuitable for in-shore operations, deployed farther into the Atlantic to patrol the waters off North America, Gibraltar and West Africa thus forcing the Allies to maintain a wide defensive posture. Finally, at least 30 more U-boats deployed to perform various support functions, such as weather reporting, or to operate against Allied Arctic convoys still running to and from the Soviet Union.

At the time none of the new Type XXI or Type XXIII electro-boats were operationally ready, so the Germans had to depend upon their veteran Type VIIs and Type IXs to carry out this offensive. Yet, despite their aging designs, these Type VII and Type IX U-boats still possessed formidable capabilities. First, the Germans had equipped all of these boats with snorkels, which allowed them to operate almost entirely submerged thus substantially enhancing their stealth and survivability. Adding to this was the fact that German crews were now more adept at using these snorkels. The Germans also finally possessed an effective radar detector called *Tunis* that could detect 10-centimetre radar. By attaching the *Tunis* receiver aerials to their snorkel masts, the Germans were generally able to detect radar signals from incoming aircraft or warships before they themselves were acquired thus allowing them to dive and avoid detection or effective attack. Finally, the U-boats carried a full complement of improved acoustic and pattern-steering torpedoes that made them deadly adversaries for both Allied merchant ships and escorts alike.

Beyond these technical improvements, there were operational and geographical factors that further enhanced the survivability of the German U-boats. In terms of the former, by operating almost exclusively submerged, the Germans significantly undermined the effectiveness of Allied anti-submarine aircraft, which had been the primary U-boat killers during the previous two years. With this, these aircraft became little more than sentinels that forced the U-boats to stay submerged. In the same light, since the Germans had abandoned wolf pack tactics, their radio transmissions dropped off significantly thus reducing the effectiveness of shore and ship-based HF/DF. This also curtailed the amount of intelligence gained through Ultra intercepts. By predominately operating in shallow in-shore waters, the U-boats were able to take advantage of natural conditions that restricted Asdic and hydrophone usage. This was true for two reasons. First, the rip currents and varying thermal layers that were prevalent in these waters often deflected Asdic beams and impaired hydrophone performance. Second, much of the seabed was covered with shipwrecks and rock formations that regularly caused Allied warships to respond to false Asdic echoes. Given these factors, the Allies soon found that many of the detection means that had served them so well in the past were now rendered far less effective.

On the other hand, not all of these variables benefitted the Germans. To the contrary, some of the same factors that enhanced U-boat survivability also impaired their ability to effectively engage Allied shipping. Of particular consequence, by operating almost exclusively submerged, U-boat mobility was greatly reduced. In a typical cruising day, the U-boats only snorkelled about four hours with the rest of the time spent fully submerged using battery power. Operating in this manner, the U-boats could only travel about 50 to 60 miles per day, significantly increasing the transit times to and from their patrol areas. This, in turn, reduced the amount of time these U-boats were actually on station to hunt Allied shipping. Even with the close proximity of the British Isles, the typical German U-boat was only able to spend about 10 days in its designated patrol area with at least four times that duration spent in transit. Added to this, German hydrophones were impacted by the same tidal and thermal conditions that plagued the Allies. As such, many U-boats found it difficult to locate targets or put themselves in position to carry out effective attacks. Finally and perhaps most importantly, limited numbers hampered the German offensive. The 74 U-boats that deployed on offensive patrols during this four and a half-month period compared quite feebly to the 269 attack U-boats that were dispatched into the Atlantic during a similar four-month period (February to May) in the spring of 1943.

Given these factors, the initial results from the renewed German U-boat offensive were largely anticlimactic. From September through December the U-boats were only able to sink 24 merchant ships worth 138,654 tons.[24] Of these, 14 were sunk in British coastal waters or the immediate area. These losses compared to 12,168 merchant ships that safely passed through the battle zone during the same period.[25] On top of this, these U-boats also sank the British frigates *Bullen* and *Capel*, the corvettes *Hurst Castle* and *Shawinigan* (Canadian) and the Canadian minesweeper *Clayoquot* and seriously damaged the frigates *Chebogue*, *Magog*, *Whittaker* and *Affleck*. Against this, the Germans lost a total of 61 U-boats in all theatres including at least 29 that were sunk by British means in the Atlantic, Baltic and Arctic. British warships sank *U247*, *U394*, *U484*, *U743*, *U1006*, *U1200*, *U322*, *U297*, *U387*, *U400* and *U877* while RAF aircraft accounted for *U867*, *U871*, *U1060* and *U772*.[26] FAA aircraft from the escort carrier *Campania* sank *U921* and *U365* while the submarine *Venturer* sank *U771*. Mines and Bomber Command air raids accounted for the remainder, which will be discussed later.

Making matters worse from the German point of view, these meagre results were replicated in their other interdiction efforts. Throughout this period the Germans conducted repeated sorties by aircraft, E-boats and small battle units to lay mines and/or attack Allied shipping in the English Channel and North Sea. This was particularly true in the Scheldt area where the Germans increasingly concentrated their efforts. The British responded to this with intense aerial and surface patrolling as well as periodic attacks against the German bases that staged these operations. During the four-month period culminating at the end of December, German mines sank 12 merchant ships worth 37,334 tons as well as the British escort destroyer *Rockingham* while E-boats and small battle units added two further merchant ships and an auxiliary vessel worth 6,395 tons.[27] Against this, British warships, shore batteries and aircraft sank seven E-boats in the Channel area and North Sea while the Germans scuttled an eighth E-boat at Brest. The Germans also lost 52 *Biber* midget submarines and 115 *Linsen* explosive motor boats to Allied defences and natural hazards during this period.[28]

Looking at the bigger picture, the conclusion of these actions brought about the end of another calendar year in the Atlantic war. For the Allies, this had been a period of great success that solidified their momentum from the previous year. First, with the loss of just 205 merchant ships worth 1,045,629 tons due to hostile action in 1944, the Allies experienced their lowest level of annual attrition suffered thus far in the conflict.[29] Put in perspective, this casualty rate was only about a third of that suffered in 1943 and an eighth of that suffered in 1942. In regards to the all-important Atlantic convoy routes, this contributed to an inconsequential loss rate of only 0.1 percent.[30] American shipyards produced 1,786 new merchant

VICTORY IN EUROPE • 245

ships worth 12.26 million tons in 1944 while British shipyards added another 1.014 million tons during the same period.[31] As such, new construction outpaced losses by a factor of almost thirteen to one in terms of tonnage. Meanwhile, imports to the United Kingdom increased to 46,093,000 tons in 1944 thus constituting the best import year since 1940.[32] The Allied merchant fleets successfully supported military campaigns in the Mediterranean, Northwest Europe, Indian Ocean and Pacific while also providing critical logistical assistance to the Soviet Union. German U-boat losses during the year numbered 254 boats, which represented their highest annual casualty rate of the war.

Despite these dismal results, the Germans continued their anti-shipping offensive into the new year. This was almost entirely a naval affair since the Luftwaffe ceased aerial mining in January. For the Kriegsmarine, the Germans were able to take some solace in the belief that their U-boats could now operate in Britain's well-defended coastal waters without undue loss. This conclusion was bolstered by the fact that only 11 of the 61 U-boats lost in the previous four months were sunk in these coastal waters. Likewise, the first of the new Type XXI and Type XXXIII electro-boats were almost ready for operational use. For their part, the British were well aware of the pending arrival of the new electro-boats as well as the improved survivability of the older models. To counter this, the Admiralty persuaded the Chiefs of Staff to increase bombing raids against the U-boat production facilities. They also intensified mine-laying activities in both the Baltic and the approaches to the U-boat patrol areas. By delaying the departure of resources to the Pacific as well as other measures, the British substantially increased their home defences, which at the beginning of January included 426 assorted destroyers, frigates, sloops and corvettes as well as 420 anti-submarine aircraft.[33] Finally, the Allies accelerated the operational deployment of 3-centimetre radar, which improved their ability to locate snorkel masts.

As it turned out, events proved this German optimism and British concern to be substantially overblown. In the first three months of 1945 the Germans dispatched 78 U-boats (including the first of the new Type XXIII electro-boats) on offensive patrols around Britain while at least 41 more deployed to various other locations such as the Arctic, the Americas and the mid and South Atlantic. During this period these U-boats and those present from earlier deployments sank 39 merchant ships worth 187,298 tons of which 28 worth 104,074 tons were sunk in British home waters.[34] Added to this, these U-boats also sank the Soviet destroyer *Deiatelnyi*, the British sloop *Lapwing*, the British corvettes *Denbigh Castle*, *Bluebell*, *Vervain* and *Trentonian* (Canadian) and the Canadian minesweeper *Guysborough*. Against this, German U-boat losses for the period numbered 73 boats of which 38 were destroyed in the British home waters or the greater Atlantic and Arctic areas. In terms of the latter, British warships sank *U482*, *U1199*, *U1051*, *U1172*, *U1279*, *U1014*, *U989*, *U309*, *U425*, *U1278*, *U300*, *U480*, *U1018*, *U327*, *U1208*, *U1302*, *U683*, *U714*, *U1003*, *U399*, *U722*, *U965*, *U246* and *U1021* while British aircraft accounted for

U927, *U905* and *U1106*. Meanwhile, the British submarine *Venturer* sank *U864* (its second such success in three months)[35] while the remaining were sunk by various other means, much of which will be discussed later.

The Germans also failed to score meaningful results with their E-boats and small battle units. This was true despite the operational debut of the new *Seehund* midget submarine, which represented the most capable small battle unit yet employed by the Germans. Weighing in at 14.9 tons and with a standard range of 300 nautical miles, the two-man *Seehund* was armed with two 21-inch torpedoes that gave it the same offensive sting as the Type XXIII electro-boat. From January through March the Germans launched 106 *Seehund* sorties, but these only succeeded in sinking six Allied ships worth 9,282 tons for the cost of 23 *Seehunds* in return. The E-boats fared better during this period destroying 29 Allied ships worth 80,598 tons (mostly by mines) against the loss of six E-boats. Finally, the Germans failed to score any appreciable results with their *Biber*, *Molch* and *Linsen* small battle units, but still lost 95 of their number to Allied defences and maritime hazards.[36]

Compounding these offensive failures for the Kriegsmarine, the Germans also reeled from a rapid deterioration in their own shipping and import situation. This was due to a combination of unrelenting Allied pressure and various political changes that diminished Germany's available shipping pool and access to natural resources. In September 1944 Finland signed an armistice with the Soviet Union thus abandoning the Axis cause and depriving Germany of 263,000 tons of Finish shipping.[37] During the same period Sweden (bowing to Allied pressure) enacted a series of policies that initially restricted and then ceased all trade with Germany. First, in August the Swedish government effectively banned its vessels from proceeding to German ports by discontinuing the insurance underwriting for these voyages thus eliminating a further 450,000 tons of shipping available for German use.[38] A month later the Swedes closed their own ports to this trade thus making Narvik the only access point Germany had to acquire Swedish exports. These actions contributed to a precipitous drop in the amount of Swedish iron ore that arrived in Germany amounting to just 1,235,000 tons in the last five months of 1944.[39] Finally in January 1945 the Swedish government ceased all trade with Germany, leaving Norway as Germany's only source for phosphorous-rich iron ore and other key minerals.

Unfortunately for the Germans, imports from Norway could only satisfy a small portion of their industrial needs, and the Kriegsmarine and German merchant fleet struggled to deliver even this reduced flow of commerce. Part of this was due to Allied countermeasures and part was due to diminished German resources. By this stage in the war, heavy losses had taken a debilitating toll on the German merchant fleet while new construction had slowed to a trickle amounting to just 80,000 tons built in the first seven months of 1944.[40] Germany still possessed a fair number of merchant ships, but this force was a dwindling asset and many of the vessels that did exist were non-operational due to battle damage or maritime wear. To this latter point, in November nearly one-third of the German merchant fleet (332,000 tons) was laid-up awaiting repairs or refit leaving only 694,000 tons available for service in the Baltic, North Sea and adjacent areas.[41] This available tonnage was further reduced as the Germans diverted increasing numbers of ships to support military requirements such as the maintenance of the growing U-boat force in Norway and the evacuation of German military and civilian personnel from Finland and the Eastern Baltic region. When coupled with fuel shortages, extended turnaround times and other organisational problems, the force that remained was inadequate to maintain a steady flow of imports.

This problem was further exacerbated by the resurgence of an old foe within the region. Since its invasion in the summer of 1941, the Soviet Union had played a minor role in the maritime war. This participation had been limited to the coastal waters of the Eastern Baltic, Arctic and Black Sea with Soviet forces exacting a small, but steady toll against the Kriegsmarine throughout the succeeding three years. Now, from the summer of 1944 onwards, the Soviets expanded their operations into the Baltic (and to a lesser extent the Arctic) as their land forces advanced westward towards Germany. In 1945, this compelled the Germans to launch a series of major seaborne evacuations to rescue as many troops and civilians as possible from the oncoming Soviet forces in Lithuania, East Prussia and Pomerania. This was a massive undertaking that dwarfed the Dunkirk evacuation and eventually resulted in the transport of 448,500 military personnel and 1,668,000 civilians over a four-month period.[42] Prior to and throughout this period the heavy units of the Kriegsmarine, including the pocket battleships *Lützow* and *Admiral Scheer*, the old battleship *Schlesien* and the heavy cruisers *Prinz Eugen* and *Admiral Hipper*, carried out numerous fire support missions that temporarily blunted or at least slowed some of the Soviet advances along the Baltic coastline.

While immensely successful in tactical and humanitarian terms, these operations were conducted within the framework of a losing cause and exacted a heavy toll upon the Germans in both allocated resources and shipping losses. Many of these stricken vessels were sunk by British means (which will be discussed later), but an increasing number fell to Soviet forces using aircraft, submarines, surface vessels, shore artillery and mines. From the beginning of September 1944 through the end of the war the Soviets sank a total of 147 German military and civilian vessels worth a combined 275,050 tons.[43] In terms of principal warships, this included the torpedo boat *T18* and the minesweepers *M303*, *M31* and *M376*. In addition, the Soviets played an active role in the destruction of the torpedo boat *T36* along with British means. Finally, during this period Soviet forces sank the U-boats *U362*, *U679*, *U763*, *U923*, *U676* and *U78*.

Of course, notwithstanding these Soviet successes, the British remained the primary antagonist to the Kriegsmarine and German merchant fleet. Of the hundreds of German ships attacked during the war's waning months, none was larger or more significant than the battleship *Tirpitz*, which still sheltered in the Norwegian fjords. During the summer FAA aircraft from the aircraft carriers *Furious*, *Indefatigable*, *Formidable*, *Nabob* and *Trumpeter* carried out a series of strikes against *Tirpitz* as a follow-up to April's highly successful Operation *Tungsten*. Unfortunately, these latter strikes were far less effective in the face of improved German defences. In particular, radar detection gave the Germans adequate time to shroud *Tirpitz* in thick smoke screens that rendered it practically invisible to the attacking British aircraft. As a result, the British had to drop their bombs blind through the smoke and only managed to score two hits that caused minimal damage to the German battleship.

Next, the RAF took its turn in attacking *Tirpitz*. On 15 September a force of 28 Lancaster bombers, operating from a forward base in Russia, attacked *Tirpitz* at Altenfjord in Northern Norway. Armed with special 12,000-pound bombs, known as Tallboys, the British bombers encountered the German smoke screen, but still managed to score a single hit on *Tirpitz*'s bow that caused extensive damage and ended the great battleship's seagoing capability for good. With this, the Germans decided to move *Tirpitz* to Tromsö, some 200 miles to the south, where it would be used as a floating coastal defence battery. After making temporary repairs, *Tirpitz* proceeded to Tromsö in the middle of October to assume this new role. To facilitate the battleship's survivability upon its arrival, the Germans began the process of constructing a large sand bank under and around the ship's hull to raise the seabed and eliminate the danger of the ship sinking or capsizing due to bomb-induced flooding.

However, before the Germans could complete this task, the British struck again. After an unsuccessful effort at the end of October, 29 Lancasters attacked *Tirpitz* on the morning of 12 November. In this case, the British bombers found *Tirpitz* only partially covered in its protective smoke screen, and they were able to mount an effective attack with their 12,000-pound Tallboy bombs that scored three hits and two near misses against the stationary giant. This caused catastrophic damage to *Tirpitz*, which immediately experienced heavy flooding and a progressive list to port. A few minutes later an internal fire caused one of *Tirpitz*'s magazines to explode thus hurling its massive Caesar gun turret into the sea. Thereafter, the great ship rapidly capsized to port and settled on the shallow seabed at an angle of 130°. In doing so, 1,204 members of *Tirpitz*'s crew, including its captain, perished along with the ship, and a threat that had plagued the British for over three years was finally and irretrievably eliminated.

With this loss, *Tirpitz* joined hundreds of other German vessels that were sunk or otherwise destroyed by Allied aircraft during this period. As usual, the RAF was at the forefront of this effort conducting 871 minelaying and 5,667 maritime strike sorties in Northern European waters during the last four months of 1944.[44] During this time RAF-laid mines sank a total of 15 German warships and 39 commercial vessels worth a combined 55,533 tons while RAF aircraft in direct attacks at sea added a further 42 military and 38 civilian vessels worth 65,821 tons sunk in the North

Beyond destroying the German battleships *Tirpitz* and *Lützow* in direct attacks, the Avro Lancaster served as the premier bomber in Bomber Command, which accounted for the loss of almost 1,100 German military and commercial vessels through minelaying and bombing raids during the war. (Devon, S. A., Royal Air Force Official photographer, public domain)

Sea and surrounding area.[45] In terms of principal warships, these losses included the torpedo boat *T34* and the minesweeper *M584*, which were sunk by mines, and the newly constructed torpedo boat *T61* (1,931 tons, 4 × 5-inch guns), the escort destroyer *K2* (1,200 tons, 4 × 4.7-inch guns) and the minesweepers *M426*, *M462* and *M471*, which were sunk by British strike aircraft. Finally, beyond these surface vessels, RAF-laid mines sank the U-boats *U855*, *U703*, *U547*, *U479* and *U2342*.

Added to this was the destruction that Allied bombers inflicted during raids against German-held ports. In addition to the previously mentioned *Tirpitz*, RAF bombers sank 39 assorted ships worth 63,421 tons during the last four months of the year while American bombers accounted for a further 16 vessels worth 21,763 tons during the same period. Beyond these surface losses, ten U-boats were also sunk during these attacks. Some notable raids that occurred during this period include a RAF attack against Bergen on 4 October that destroyed the U-boats *U92*, *U228*, *U437* and *U993* and three merchant ships worth 3,935 tons. Twelve days later British bombers attacked Wilhelmshaven and sank *U777* and a minor vessel. Then in the first week of November the USAAF launched two raids against Hamburg that sank four merchant ships and three minor craft worth a combined 10,372 tons. Six weeks later on the night of 18/19 December the RAF carried out a devastating attack against Gdynia that sank the old battleship *Schleswig-Holstein*, the torpedo boat *T10* and nine assorted merchant ships and auxiliaries worth 30,731 tons. Finally, at the end of the month British bombers sank *U735* and two merchant ships worth 4,902 tons at Horten while USAAF bombers sank *U906*, *U908*, *U2532* and *U2537*, the minesweeper *M445* and four merchant ships worth 8,761 tons at Hamburg.

This aerial onslaught continued into the new year with even greater results. By this stage in the war, the Germans found it increasingly difficult to cope with the relentless Allied assault assailing their maritime efforts. This was particularly true regarding their minesweeping programme, which progressively broke down thus exposing their shipping to increased dangers from Allied mines. These reduced defences along with the recent acquisition of Allied airfields on the European continent allowed Allied aircraft to reach farther into the Baltic than ever before. As part of this, two squadrons of radar-equipped Halifax bombers from RAF Coastal Command began nightly sweeps into the Skagerrak and Northern Kattegat to seek out and attack German shipping. Given these factors, during the first three months of 1945 a total of 20 German warships and 47 commercial vessels worth an unprecedented 145,859 tons were sunk by RAF-laid mines in Northern European waters. Included in this were the torpedo boats *T3* and *T5* and the escort destroyer *F5*. These mines also sank *U3520*, *U1273*, *U3519*, *U275*, *U260*, and *U367*. Meanwhile, RAF aircraft in direct attacks destroyed a further 13 warships and 33 civilian vessels worth 55,083 tons in the same area.

Similar results were enjoyed by the Allied heavy bombers, which continued to batter the various German-controlled ports from January through March. This was particularly true regarding the USAAF, which launched a series of devastating attacks against Hamburg, Kiel, Swinemünde, Wilhelmshaven and Bremen that targeted German U-boat production and support facilities as part of the effort to minimise the electro-boat threat. In this, the Americans were highly successful causing severe damage to these facilities and destroying no fewer than 20 U-boats (*U2523*, *U2515*, *U2530*, *U3007*, *U3036*, *U3508*, *U72*, *U96*, *U329*, *U348*, *U350*, *U429*, *U430*, *U870*, *U884*, *U886*, *U1167*, *U2340*, *U3042* and *U3043*) in their attacks. During these raids the Americans also destroyed 16 warships and 36 commercial vessels worth 106,287 tons. Included in this were the light cruiser *Köln*, the escort destroyer *F6* and the fleet minesweepers *M15*, *M16*, *M18*, *M19*, *M266*, *M329*, *M522*, *M804* and *M805*.[46]

For its part, RAF Bomber Command also carried out a number of raids during this period that resulted in the destruction of 16 assorted vessels worth 48,534 tons as well as a single U-boat. Included in this was an attack against Bergen on 12 January that sank the minesweeper *M1*. Then on the night of 23/24 February British bombers attacked Horten and sank the torpedo boat *TA8* (ex-Norwegian, 1,278 tons, 4 × 4.7-inch guns), the 2,112-ton merchant ship *Huldra* and five minor vessels. Ten days later a British raid against Sassnitz sank the destroyer *Z28*, the

3,344-ton evacuation transport *Robert Möhring* and three more minor vessels. This was followed by a RAF attack against Hamburg on the night of 8/9 March that sank *U682* and damaged the 27,288-ton liner *Robert Ley* so severely that it was rendered a total loss. Twelve days later a British attack against Bremen sank the destroyer *Z51*, which was in the process of fitting out. Finally, on 31 March British bombers attacked Hamburg and sank the 7,134-ton merchant ship *Ammon*.

Augmenting these air force efforts, the FAA was also active during this period. From September through March the British launched a series of minelaying and strike operations utilising carrier-borne aircraft in the waters off Norway. In terms of the former, FAA-laid mines accounted for two merchant ships and two minor vessels worth 8,675 tons that were sunk during this period. In terms of the latter, on 12 September aircraft from the carriers *Furious* and *Trumpeter* destroyed two small escorts worth 280 tons and damaged a 5,374-ton merchant ship from a German convoy off Stadlandet. Then from the middle of October through the first part of December the new fleet carrier *Implacable* launched a series of strikes with its Seafire, Barracuda and Firefly aircraft that sank or otherwise wrecked the minesweeper *M433* and seven merchant ships/auxiliaries worth 12,927 tons and damaged a further 11 vessels worth 13,800 tons. Also during this time *Implacable*'s Fireflies severely damaged and forced the grounding of *U1060*, which was later destroyed by RAF aircraft (as previously mentioned). Meanwhile, in November fighter-bombers from the escort carriers *Pursuer* and *Premier* sank a German escort vessel worth 742 tons off Trondheim and damaged two other vessels worth 701 tons. Finally, at the end of January Swordfish from the escort carriers *Campania* and *Nairana* destroy three small auxiliaries worth 398 tons during a nocturnal strike near Stadlandet. This final action was noteworthy in that it represented the last confirmed combat success of the venerable Swordfish, which had proven to be the FAA's most accomplished strike aircraft during the war despite its seemingly obsolescent status.[47]

Of course, these FAA activities were only part of the navy's interdiction effort as the British also used submarines and surface warships to attack German shipping. From September through March, British and British-affiliated submarines sank 23 assorted vessels worth 26,743 tons through minelaying and direct attacks in the waters off Norway including the fleet minesweepers *M132* and *M381*.[48] Also sunk by British submarines during this time were the aforementioned *U771* and *U864* and an 8,000-ton floating dock. Meanwhile, local British and British-affiliated warships sank 25 military and 22 commercial vessels worth a combined 60,269 tons during this period. This included the fleet minesweepers *M489* and *M382*, which were sunk by British motor torpedo boats. This also included the results of two major surface actions fought by heavier British warships. First, on the night of 12/13 November a British squadron consisting of the heavy cruiser *Kent*, the light cruiser *Bellona* and four destroyers attacked a German convoy off Listerfjord and sank the minesweepers *M416* and *M427*, the submarine chasers *KUJ14*, *KUJ15* and *KUJ25* and two merchant ships worth 4,320 tons for no loss to themselves. Then on the night of 11/12 January a second British force consisting of the heavy cruiser *Norfolk*, the light cruiser *Bellona* and three destroyers carried out a similar attack against a German convoy off Egersund and sank the minesweeper *M273* and two merchant ships worth 12,955 tons for again no loss to themselves.

When these various agents were combined together, the Western Allies sank a total of 180 military and 280 civilian ships and craft worth 176,449 and 544,888 tons respectively from September 1944 through March 1945. Added to this were 128 assorted vessels worth 227,205 tons that were scuttled or surrendered as the Germans gave ground to the various Allied advances. A further 243 vessels worth 271,357 tons were sunk by other means including Soviet actions as well as accidents, marine and unknown causes. Included in these latter categories were the destroyers *Z35* and *Z36*, which accidentally sank on German mines, the minesweepers *M25*, *M274* and *M276*, which were scuttled, and the minesweepers *M305*, *M421*, *M575* and *M412*, which were lost due to marine or accidental causes. Also scuttled during this period, although not counted in the numbers above or below, was the derelict hulk of the battlecruiser *Gneisenau*, which had been previously disabled by RAF bombers in 1942 (see Chapter 6). This brought Germany's total maritime loss during the seven-month period in question to 287 warships and 544 assorted merchant ships and civilian craft worth 215,052 and 1,004,847 tons respectively in the waters off Northern Europe.

These staggering losses were only one of the ongoing calamities befalling Germany at the time. By the beginning of 1945 German maritime imports had largely collapsed as manifested by the arrival of only 99,000 tons of iron ore during the first four months of the year.[49] When projected out on an annual basis, this paltry number reflected a staggering 97.3 percent loss to Germany's iron ore trade compared to what it had been in 1939. For all intents and purposes, the British had achieved the blockade objective they had been pursuing since the beginning of the war. Still, this accomplishment had little practical impact given the advanced stage of the conflict. Already, powerful formations of Allied bombers ranged over Germany attacking military, industrial and transportation targets at will. In 1943 and 1944 this bombing campaign had prevented German war production from meeting its full potential, but now in 1945 the relentless Allied bombing rapidly curtailed Germany's ability to materially support its armed forces. Of even greater consequence, with the massive Soviet and Allied armies pressing in on it from both east and west, it would only be a matter of weeks before Germany itself was overrun.

From the second week in February through the middle of March the various Allied armies, now largely recuperated and adequately supplied, launched a series of offensive operations designed to advance to and clear all of the territory west of the Rhine River. The British/Commonwealth portion of this was Operation *Veritable*, which sought to clear the area between the Maas and Rhine Rivers north of Venlo and Xanten using the Canadian First Army reinforced by eight British divisions. Launched on 8 February, Operation *Veritable* encountered heavy opposition that eventually involved 11 German divisions including some of the best formations still remaining in the German army.[50] Part of this was due to an earlier American failure to capture the Roer Dams, which allowed the Germans to flood much of the targeted terrain and forced the postponement of an adjacent American offensive that was supposed to begin two days after the launching of *Veritable*. As such, the Germans were able to concentrate most of their opposition against the First Army's advance. Yet, despite this adversity, the British and Canadians made slow but steady progress that eventually gained them all of their objectives and netted 22,239 prisoners by 10 March. Beyond that, a further 22,000 Germans were estimated killed or wounded during the month-long battle. For its part, First Army losses consisted of 15,634 casualties of which roughly two-thirds were British.[51]

While this was underway, the other Allied armies enjoyed similar success, and by the third week in March the Allies were firmly established on the western bank of the Rhine River with one of their armies, the American First, actually across due to the opportune seizure of an intact railway bridge at Remagen. In doing so, the Allies took more than 230,000 prisoners (from 8 February) including those captured by the Canadian First Army.[52] This, in turn, brought the total number of prisoners seized since the beginning of the campaign to well over a million including 248,533 that were taken by the British 21st Army Group (as of the morning of 23 March).[53] Now the next task at hand was to get the rest of the Allied armies across the great river. Over the next few weeks each of the Allied armies, excluding the Canadian First, conducted operations to do so. In the north, this consisted of a massive joint undertaking, known as Operation *Plunder*, which was carried out by the British Second and American Ninth Armies. Augmented by the British 6th and American 17th Airborne Divisions which carried out concurrent airborne landings, the two Allied armies launched Operation *Plunder* on 23 March with river crossings in the vicinity of Rees and Wesel north of the Ruhr. Utilising massive air and artillery support as well as a multitude of amphibious vehicles including 36 Royal Navy landing craft, these crossings were entirely successful, and by 27 March the Allies had a bridgehead 35 miles wide and 20 miles deep. They captured 16,259 prisoners including 11,161 taken by the British Second Army for the cost of 3,968 and 2,813 casualties for the British and American contingents respectively.[54]

With this and the other related crossings, the Allies had overcome the last great barrier protecting Germany's western frontier. Now with the German empire rapidly crumbling, the Allies began their final drive to end the war. Per General Eisenhower's instructions, the centrally located American 12th Army Group became the main effort in this process. Of particular consequence, in the closing days of March the American First and Ninth Armies launched converging offensives that rapidly enveloped the key industrial region of the Ruhr. On 1 April these two American armies met at Lippstadt thus completing this encirclement and entrapping two and a half German armies (the Fifth Panzer, the Fifteenth and part of First Parachute) in a pocket that was 75 miles long and 50 miles wide. Over the next two and a half weeks the Americans systematically collapsed this pocket and eliminated the forces inside. In doing so, they only encountered moderate resistance as many of the trapped German units were of poor quality and/or had lost their willingness to continue fighting. As such, on 18 April the last organised resistance ceased, and the Americans completed their task having taken over 317,000 prisoners. American casualties for the undertaking numbered fewer than 10,000 in return.[55]

While this was underway, the other Allied armies were also active enjoying considerable success. On the right flank the American Third and Seventh and French First Armies made deep penetrations into Central and Southern Germany taking large numbers of prisoners in the process. On the left the British Second Army, now 11 divisions strong, made similar advances into Northern Germany. In doing so, the British encountered surprisingly strong resistance from a number of German units including naval formations serving in a ground defence role. What these naval forces lacked in training and experience, they made up for in spirit and discipline and proved to be tough adversaries. Yet, despite this resistance, the British made steady progress and reached the Elbe River by mid-April having advanced some 200 miles and taken 78,108 prisoners since leaving the Rhine bridgehead for the cost of 7,665 casualties.[56] Finally, to their rear the Canadian First Army, now seven divisions strong including reinforcements from the Mediterranean, protected the Second Army's northern flank and cleared much of Western and Northern Holland.[57] In the process of this latter mission, First Army formations (including the British 49th Division) took some 18,460 prisoners while entrapping a further 117,000 Germans in the patches of Dutch territory remaining under their control.[58]

Meanwhile, from the east massive Soviet forces also encroached upon the beleaguered German homeland. In January the Soviets had launched a large winter offensive that gained them much of East Prussia, Lower Silesia, East Pomerania and Upper Silesia and brought their forces to the banks of the Oder River some 40 miles from Berlin. Now in April the Soviets launched a renewed offensive with the overriding goal of capturing the German capital. Utilising three army groups with over two and a half million men, the Soviets opened this offensive on the 16th against a severely depleted German force only about a third as strong. Despite initial stout resistance, the Soviets were able to break through the German defences and rapidly enveloped the German capital pushing aside all attempts to stop their advance. By 24 April this encirclement was complete, and the Soviets spend the next several days progressively reducing Berlin from all sides as their forces advanced block by block towards the city's centre. Among the two million souls trapped within this ever-tightening noose was Adolf Hitler, the German dictator, who had resigned himself to meet his fate within the crumbling capital.

Amazingly, even as the Nazi regime rapidly disintegrated, the Kriegsmarine continued to resist the Allies with whatever means were still at its disposal. In April and early May the Germans dispatched a total of 48 U-boats into the Atlantic to wage war against the Allied shipping lanes for a cause that was clearly doomed. Joining the U-boats in this defiant gesture were numerous E-boats and small battle units that continued to feebly confront the massive Allied supply effort. Tragically for the Germans, these operations had no hope of meaningful success and proved to be quite costly. During a five-week period beginning on 1 April the Germans succeeded in sinking 22 Allied merchant ships worth 91,712 tons along with the Canadian minesweeper *Esquimalt* and the British frigate *Goodall*.[59] Against this, the Germans lost a staggering 61 U-boats in April (their highest monthly casualty total of the war) of which 36 were sunk while underway in the Atlantic, North Sea,

U-boats remained an ongoing threat throughout the war. Of the nearly 1,200 U-boats on hand or acquired during the conflict, a staggering 1,015 were lost through combat action, maritime causes, accidents or scuttling. Roughly three-quarters of these losses were solely or partially attributable to British action. Pictured here is *U534*, which was sunk by Coastal Command Liberators on 5 May 1945. (Australian Armed Forces, public domain)

Arctic or Western Baltic. Of the latter, British warships, aircraft and mines sank *U321, U1276, U242, U1169, U1195, U774, U1001, U804, U1065, U843, U878, U486, U1024, U285, U1063, U1274, U251, U636, U396, U1223, U307, U286* and *U1017* while American naval forces, accidents and unknown causes claimed the rest. Meanwhile, during the same period the Germans lost six E-boats and 38 assorted small battle units to Allied defences and operational causes.[60]

For their part, the Allies enjoyed considerably greater success in their own interdiction efforts including the destruction of four major warships and numerous lesser vessels. RAF Bomber Command and the USAAF caused much of this outcome by sinking 22 and 12 assorted vessels worth 76,249 and 42,306 tons respectively during bombing raids in April. Added to this were 21 U-boats that were sunk or otherwise wrecked during these same raids. In terms of principal warships, these included the minesweeper *M802*, the minelayer *Brummer II* and the U-boats *U237, U749, U1221, U2542, U3003* and *U3505* that were sunk during USAAF raids against Kiel on 3–4 April. Then on the 8th American bombers attacked Hamburg followed by a large British raid that night and a second British raid the next day that combined to sink *U677, U747, U982, U2509, U2514, U2547, U2550* and *U3512*. The next night, 9/10 April, the RAF carried out a devastating raid against Kiel that sank or irretrievably damaged the pocket battleship *Admiral Scheer*, the heavy cruiser *Admiral Hipper*, the light cruiser *Emden*, the torpedo boat *T1*, the minesweeper *M504* and the U-boats *U1131, U1227, U2516, U3525* and *U4708*. Then on the 16th RAF Lancaster bombers attacked the pocket battleship *Lützow* at Swinemünde and sank it in shallow water with Tallboy bombs that ripped out the ship's bottom. Finally, in other attacks during the month RAF bombers sank *U103* and *U56* at Kiel and *M455* at Cuxhaven.

Of course, these raids were only part of the Allies' interdiction effort during this period. In April RAF aircraft in direct attacks at sea sank six military and 26 commercial ships worth a combined 53,503 tons while RAF-laid mines added a further 18 assorted vessels worth 12,706 tons in the waters off Northern Europe. Included in these losses were the torpedo boats *T13* and *T16* and the minesweepers *M2* and *M403* that were sunk by British aircraft and the destroyer *Z43* and minesweeper *M368* that were sunk by mines.[61] Meanwhile, the Royal Navy sank through all means (surface warships, submarines, mines) a total of five military and three commercial craft worth 3,763 tons. Soviet forces sank a further 32 vessels worth 50,306 tons. During the month the Germans scuttled 21 ships worth 42,375 tons while the Allies captured a further seven vessels worth 4,322 tons. This former number included the incomplete aircraft carrier *Graf Zeppelin*, which was scuttled as a blockship at Stettin on 25 April.

Meanwhile, in the waning days of April the Allies continued their conquest of Germany. By this time General Eisenhower had halted the American Ninth and First Armies along the Elbe River to await the arrival of the oncoming Soviets. The first link-up between these converging forces occurred at Torgau on the 25th thus essentially cutting Germany in half. Thereafter, the Allies shifted their main efforts to the northern and southern flanks. While American and French forces cleared Southern Germany and advanced towards the Czech and Austrian boarders, the British Second Army focused on capturing the port city of Bremen. This latter task absorbed four British infantry divisions in a week-long battle that culminated on the 26th with the surrender of the port and the seizure of 5,000 prisoners. This event along with other concurrent operations brought the total number of prisoners taken by the British 21st Army Group to 158,690 from the beginning of Operation *Plunder* (the evening of 23 March) through 27 April.[62] Meanwhile, in the city's shipyards the British took possession of 20 U-boats that were at various levels of construction as well as an incomplete Narvik-class destroyer.

The British next turned their attention northward towards the Baltic. The purpose of this was twofold. First, they sought to deprive Germany of any opportunity to move forces into Denmark and Norway for a last-ditch defensive stand. Second, they wanted to seal off Schleswig-Holstein and the Danish peninsula from the oncoming Soviets thus shielding this strategically important region from potential Soviet influence after the war. On 29 April British forces crossed the Elbe River and began their northward trek to the Baltic. Three days later on 2 May the British 6th Airborne Division reached Wismar on the Baltic coast thus beating the Soviet arrival by a matter of hours. At roughly the same time the British 11th Armoured Division captured Lübeck while the British 7th Armoured Division took the surrender of Hamburg. In terms of the latter, the British discovered almost 140 incomplete U-boats scuttled or abandoned in the city's ship yards and 59 large and medium ships, 19 floating docks and about 600 minor craft sunk or scuttled within the harbour.[63] Meanwhile, further to the west Canadian forces captured Delfzijl on Holland's northeast coast. Through these events and the related mopping up operations the British Second Army took 105,998 prisoners from 28 April through 4 May while the Canadian First Army added a further 8,122 prisoners through the morning of the 5th.[64]

Beyond its impact on the ground, the British advance also spurred an exodus of ships and craft attempting to escape from Northern Germany to Norway. Included in this were numerous U-boats, many of which were not fully worked up or capable of submerged travel. To prevent this transfer, the RAF conducted a massive interdiction effort utilising both Coastal Command and Second Tactical Air Force aircraft against these vessels. The result was a slaughter of massive proportions. During a period of just five days, 2–6 May, these British aircraft sank or destroyed 11 military and 26 commercial ships worth 13,358 and 118,546 tons respectively as well as 24 U-boats in the waters of the Western Baltic, Kattegat, Skagerrak and North Sea. In terms of the former, this included the escort destroyers *F3* and *K1*, the gunnery training ship *Nordland* (ex-Danish coastal defence ship *Niels Juel*, 3,800 tons, 10 × 5.9-inch guns) and the fleet minesweepers *M293*, *M301* and *M36*. Meanwhile, the U-boats involved consisted of *U1007*, *U2359*, *U2503*, *U1210*, *U2540*, *U3030*, *U3032*, *U2524*, *U3028*, *U236*, *U393*, *U2338*, *U534*, *U579*, *U2365*, *U2521*, *U3523*, *U1008*, *U2534*, *U3503*, *U904*, *U746*, *U876* and *U733*.

Added to this carnage were a number of warships sunk by other means. This included the battleship *Schlesien*, which struck a RAF-laid mine while conducting evacuation operations off Swinemünde on 2 May. Severely damaged, the battleship was towed back to Swinemünde where it was beached in shallow water and blown up two days later to avoid capture by the Soviets. Also blown up at the same time was the immobilised pocket battleship *Lützow*, which had been disabled by British Lancaster bombers two and a half weeks before. Other German ships sunk by RAF-laid mines in early May included the torpedo boat *T36* and the minesweeper *M14*. Meanwhile, the Germans scuttled numerous vessels during this period including most of their remaining U-boat fleet, which will be discussed momentarily, the cruisers *Admiral Hipper* and *Emden*, which were both in a wrecked state due to

Table 10.1 Principal German Surface Warships sunk in Northern European Waters from September 1944 through May 1945

	British aircraft, mines and naval units	USAAF aircraft	Soviet action	Scuttled	Accidents or marine causes	Total
Battleships	1	-	-	-	-	1
Old battleships/pocket battleships	4	-	-	-	-	4
Aircraft carriers	-	-	-	1	-	1
Cruisers	2	1	-	-	-	3
Destroyers/large torpedo boats	7	-	-	-	2	9
Small torpedo boats/ escort destroyers	10	1	1	2	-	14
Fleet minesweepers	22	11	3	5	4	45
Minelayers	-	1	-	-	-	1
Total	46	14	4	8	6	78

Note: These losses do not include the battlecruiser *Gneisenau*, which was effectively destroyed as an operational unit in 1942 and subsequently scuttled in 1945. Given these factors, *Gneisenau*'s loss is attributed to RAF bombing in 1942.

earlier RAF bombing, the torpedo boats *T8* and *T9* and the minesweepers *M387* and *M22*. Finally, on 4 May the FAA launched its final operation of the European war when aircraft from the escort carriers *Searcher*, *Queen* and *Trumpeter* attacked the anchorage at Harstad in Northern Norway and sank the 5,035-ton depot ship *Black Watch*, the nearby U-boat *U711* and a small merchant ship worth 858 tons.

This period also saw the departure of the final Allied Arctic convoy to the Soviet Union, which arrived there safely on 20 May. Summarising the results of the overall Allied effort, from August 1941 to May 1945, the Allies dispatched a total of 40 convoys containing 811 merchant ships to the Soviet Union of which 720 ships successfully arrived while 33 more turned back. During the same period, 35 westbound convoys containing 715 merchant ships departed the Soviet Union of which 680 successfully completed their journeys. Finally, 41 merchant ships sailed independently both to and from the Soviet Union of which 32 reached their destinations.[65] In the process of these operations, the Western Allies shipped a total of 3,964,000 tons of weapons and materiel to the Soviet Union of which 93 percent arrived.[66] In the last year of the war this included enough weapons, materiel and vehicles to equip 60 motorised Russian divisions, which according to German Vice-Admiral Friedrich Ruge, 'exerted a decisive influence on the land operations in eastern Europe.'[67] This success came at a heavy price as the Allies lost 100 merchant ships worth 604,837 tons during the duration of the campaign while British naval losses consisted of two cruisers, six destroyers, ten assorted escort vessels and one submarine.[68] Meanwhile, German losses included the battlecruiser *Scharnhorst*, three destroyers and 38 U-boats sunk in operations directly related to the Allied supply effort.[69]

While these events were underway, the European war rapidly moved to its final conclusion. On 30 April Adolf Hitler committed suicide in his Berlin bunker, and Grand-Admiral Dönitz, who had just been appointed Hitler's successor the day before, became the German head of state. Dönitz now faced an impossible task as most of Germany had already been overrun and the German armed forces, although still millions strong, were largely of limited combat value and lacking in any real possibility for long-term support. Given this situation, Dönitz fully realised that the war was lost, but he wished to delay this outcome for as long as possible to allow more of his countrymen to escape from the advancing Soviets. Unfortunately for him, the rapid deterioration of events over the next few days convinced Dönitz that time had run out. As such, on 3 May he dispatched a delegation to Field Marshal Montgomery's headquarters at Lüneburg Heath to negotiate the surrender of Army Group Vistula, which was streaming westward in front of the oncoming Soviets. Montgomery refused this offer and instead demanded the surrender of all German forces on his northern and western flanks. After consulting with Dönitz, the German delegation returned to Montgomery's headquarters on 4 May and agreed to these terms. The instrument of surrender was signed at 1830 hours that evening and came into effect the next day at 0800 hours covering all German forces and naval ships in Holland, Northwest Germany, Schleswig-Holstein, Denmark and their associated islands.

With this, major combat operations on the British front ended, and the British and Canadian forces spent the next several days implementing the provisions of the surrender document including the administration of the vast number of German prisoners resulting from it. This was no minor task given that the German forces within the impacted areas numbered more than 1.4 million men, which were more men than the British themselves had in Northwest Europe.[70] At the same time the British began efforts to gain control over what remained of the German fleet. On the 4th the German command ordered all U-boats at sea to cease hostilities and return to base while details of the surrender were transmitted to all Kriegsmarine units. As part of this, the various subordinate commands were forbidden to scuttle their ships. Many of the deployed U-boats failed to receive this message or chose to ignore it. The same held true in port where most of the U-boat commanders ignored the surrender directive and scuttled their boats in accordance with previously set plans. The Germans had already destroyed numerous U-boats during the first few days in May, and this subsequent demolition brought the total number of U-boats scuttled during this period to 208, which constituted approximately 55 percent of the total remaining force.

While the surrender of German forces in Northern Europe clearly constituted a tremendous British success, it was soon overshadowed by an even greater event. On 6 May a delegation led by General Alfred Jodl, the Chief-of-Staff of the German High Command, arrived at General Eisenhower's headquarters at Reims and offered the surrender of all German forces confronting the Western Allies. General Eisenhower, through his Chief-of-Staff, Lieutenant-General Walter Smith, refused this offer and instead threatened to break off all negotiations unless the Germans agreed to a complete unconditional surrender. In doing so, he also threatened to close off the Allied lines thus forcing the Germans to surrender to the Soviets. Given this ultimatum, the Germans felt compelled to accept, and at 0241 hours on 7 May Jodl signed the document of unconditional surrender. The next day the Germans conducted a similar signing ceremony for the Russians in Berlin. With this, German forces all across Europe, including Norway, laid down their arms, and the war in Europe came to an end effective at 2301 hours on 8 May.

For the Western Allies, this culminated an 11-month campaign that had started on the beaches of Normandy and ended with the complete destruction of the Nazi regime. During the intervening period the Allies had liberated the vast majority of France, Belgium, Holland and Luxembourg and conquered most of Germany. In doing so, they took 2,057,138 German prisoners during combat operations and at least a further four million prisoners at the end of hostilities (of which roughly one-quarter and one-third respectively were taken by British/Canadian forces).[71] Hundreds of thousands of additional German service members died or were wounded during this period. Allied ground casualties in gaining this great victory numbered 782,374 of which 164,954 were killed. Allied air and naval forces suffered a further 61,624 and 10,308 casualties respectively in support of the campaign. Finally, Britain's portion of this combined tally came to 223,644 casualties of which 63,362 were killed (including casualties suffered by Canadian and other British-affiliated units).[72]

The German surrender also signalled an end to the European naval war. Prior to this, combat operations claimed their last U-boat victims when American naval forces sank *U853* and *U881* in the Western Atlantic while a RAF aircraft wrecked *U320* in the Norwegian Sea on 6 and 7 May respectively. After this, the majority of German U-boats that were still at sea began the process of surrendering to the Allies or returning to their home ports. Many more were captured intact when the Allies occupied the various German naval bases. From 4 through 7 May British ground forces took possession of Kiel, Emden, Wilhelmshaven and Cuxhaven. Two

Table 10.2 Allied Forces Committed to the Northwest Europe Campaign (as of 30 April 1945) and Casualties Sustained during the Course of the Campaign

Contingents	Participating Allied forces	Allied personnel killed	Allied personnel wounded	Allied personnel missing or captured	Total Allied casualties
Army					
British	835,208	30,276	96,672	14,698	141,646
Canadian	183,421	10,739	30,906	2,247	43,892
Other British-affiliated allies	34,518	1,528	5,011	354	6,893
Americans	2,618,023	109,824	356,661	56,632	523,117
French	413,144	12,587	49,513	4,726	66,826
Air Force					
British/British-affiliated	522,000	16,589	1,746	5,314	23,649
Americans	447,482	14,034	5,545	18,067	37,646
French	24,000	222	49	58	329
Navy					
British	16,221	4,230	3,334	-	7,564
American	7,035	1,102	1,642	-	2,744

Source: L. F. Ellis, *Victory in the West, Volume II: The Defeat of Germany* (London: Her Majesty's Stationery Office, 1968), pp. 406–407.

Note: The strength figures above indicate the forces committed to the Northwest Europe campaign on 30 April 1945 and are not a cumulative tally for the campaign's duration. Casualty figures for army and naval personnel are from 6 June 1944 through 7 May 1945 while casualty figures for air force personnel are from 1 April 1944 through 7 May 1945.

days later a British squadron consisting of the cruisers *Birmingham* and *Dido* and the destroyers *Zealous*, *Zephyr*, *Zest* and *Zodiac* arrived in Copenhagen to accept the surrender of the local German surface fleet. At about the same time British airborne forces began landing in Norway to take control of that country and secure the 350,000 German military personnel stationed there. In the days that followed a number of British warships, including the cruiser *Devonshire* and 14 destroyers, arrived at key Norwegian ports to disembark additional troops and take possession of German naval assets. Through these efforts and those previously described, the allies eventually secured the surrender of what remained of the German navy including the heavy cruiser *Prinz Eugen*, the light cruisers *Nürnberg* and *Leipzig*, 15 destroyers, 17 torpedo boats, 10 escort destroyers, 123 fleet minesweepers and 163 assorted U-boats.

With this, Britain's epic struggle in the Atlantic and surrounding waters came to an end. This had been a hard fought and gruelling undertaking having stretched over 68 months thus making it the longest continuous campaign of the war. At its core was the battle against Germany's vaunted U-boat arm. In the end, Britain and its allies prevailed, but only after suffering very heavy losses. During the course of

Table 10.3 Key Performance Indices from the Battle of the Atlantic

	Total Allied tonnage lost due to submarine attack	Total Allied tonnage lost due to other military means	Total British tonnage lost due to submarine attack	Total British tonnage lost due to other military means	Additional merchant tonnage added to the British flag	Total import tons delivered to the United Kingdom	U-boats sunk
Jan–Mar 44	328,145	77,305	147,300	32,300	803,000	10,053,000	61
Apr–Jun 44	144,448	69,305	62,800	40,500	795,000	12,734,000	70
Jul–Sep 44	205,448	36,417	119,700	27,700	405,000	12,739,000	86
Oct–Dec 44	95,286	89,275	35,600	23,600	445,000	11,395,000	37
Jan–Mar 45	187,298	102,119	84,400	50,800	214,000	9,907,000	73
Apr–May 45*	82,979	40,537**	46,800	8,400	358,000	12,688,000	90***

Source: The Central Statistical Office, *Statistical Digest of the War* (London: Her Majesty's Stationery Office, 1975), pp. 177–181, 184–185 and S. W. Roskill, *The War at Sea 1939–1945, Volume III, Part I: The Offensive* (London: Her Majesty's Stationery Office, 1960), p. 388 and *Volume III, Part II* (London: Her Majesty's Stationery Office, 1961), p. 477.

Note: See Note from Table 4.3.

* Figures for the final period in most columns are from April to May 1945 with the exception of the additional merchant tonnage added to the British flag and total import tons delivered to the United Kingdom which are from April to June 1945.

**This includes two vessels worth 1,806 tons that were lost on unknown dates and are rolled into this period to capture their presence.

*** U-boat losses for the final period only include those sunk through combat or operational causes and do not include the 371 U-boats scuttled or captured during this time.

the war a total of 5,150 Allied and neutral merchant ships worth 21,570,720 tons were lost due to hostile action including 2,828 ships worth 14,687,231 tons that were sunk by Axis submarines.[73] Of the latter, German U-boats accounted for about 90 percent of these losses. German U-boats also sank 175 Allied warships of which the vast majority were British or British-affiliated. In the Atlantic (both North and South) and Arctic these British losses included the battleship *Royal Oak*, the aircraft carrier *Courageous*, the escort carriers *Audacity* and *Avenger*, one cruiser, 22 destroyers, three submarines, 16 sloops and frigates, 20 corvettes and five fleet minesweepers. Yet as bad as these losses were, they failed to keep pace with the massive Allied building programme or sever Allied lines of communication. As such, the campaign proved to be a strategic failure for the Germans, which led to their eventual defeat. The cost for this defeat was high as the Kriegsmarine lost a total of 1,015 U-boats during the war including those scuttled at the end of hostilities.[74] When combined with the boats that surrendered and six U-boats that were seized by the Japanese, this accounted for the entire German U-boat force.

The German surface fleet and merchant marine suffered similar heavy losses. During the war a total of 1,258 German surface warships and auxiliaries worth a combined 941,728 tons were sunk or otherwise lost in the waters around Europe (excluding the Mediterranean and Black Sea).[75] Included in this tally were two battleships, two battlecruisers, two pocket battleships, two pre-dreadnought battleships, one aircraft carrier, two heavy cruisers, four light cruisers, 65 destroyers/torpedo boats, eight assorted escort destroyers/sloops, three corvettes, 118 fleet minesweepers and three minelayers. During the same period a total of 2,495 German and German-affiliated merchant ships and commercial vessels worth 4,417,664 tons were sunk, wrecked or captured in the same area.[76] The tally was

Table 10.4 Axis Military and Commercial Surface Ships sunk, captured or destroyed in European Waters outside of the Mediterranean and Black Sea (Number of Ships/Tonnage)

	Mines laid by Allied aircraft and naval vessels	Allied air attacks against ships and ports	Allied naval/ submarine actions and seizures	Soviet actions, scuttlings, accidents and other causes	Total
Military					
1943	37/17,836	47/18,431	26/43,742	44/12,729	154/92,738
1944	94/40,755	273/219,856	84/37,763	177/69,941	628/368,315
1945	34/48,579	75/113,901	12/2,905	70/40,118	191/205,503
Commercial					
1943	117/87,229	91/241,548	32/72,402	103/133,363	343/534,542
1944	138/135,992	184/307,126	45/82,780	384/762,469	751/1,288,367
1945	61/133,885	147/406,256	12/32,375	141/308,746	361/881,262

Note: See Note from Table 5.2.

even higher in the Mediterranean where the Axis lost 1,817 military vessels and 3,179 merchant ships worth 1,044,722 and 4,147,523 tons respectively from 10 June 1940 through 2 May 1945.[77] Most of these losses were Italian, but the former included an aircraft carrier, three cruisers, nine destroyers, 31 torpedo boats, six escort destroyers and 18 corvettes that were all sunk while under German control.[78] The pocket battleship *Graf Spee* and 330 German and German-affiliated merchant ships worth 2,048,891 tons were sunk, scuttled or seized in the waters outside of Europe and the Mediterranean.[79] Given these atrocious losses, it was abundantly clear that the Kriegsmarine and German merchant marine had paid an exceedingly heavy price for Hitler's evil folly.

CHAPTER 11

The Reckoning

In reviewing the maritime conflict during World War II, many researchers will inherently focus upon the Pacific theatre where the United Sates Navy fought an epic struggle against the naval forces of Imperial Japan. Waged over vast expanses of ocean and featuring immense fleet actions that often involved dozens or even hundreds of principal warships, the Pacific conflict clearly exemplified the traditional view of naval warfare. This was highlighted by many notable battles including Midway, the Marianas and Leyte Gulf that rank in similar status to Salamis, Actium, Lepanto, Trafalgar and Jutland in the hierarchy of maritime history. Augmenting this exalted position was the execution of dozens of amphibious landings as American forces, supported by Commonwealth contingents, island-hopped their way across the Western Pacific to arrive on the doorsteps of Japan itself. Other distinctions include the conduct of a successful submarine interdiction campaign, the unprecedented ordeal of the Kamikaze onslaught and the death ride of the Japanese super-battleship *Yamato*. In all respects, the Pacific campaign constituted a naval-centric struggle that warrants justifiable interest from both casual and serious students of maritime history.

Moving the enquiry closer to Europe, some naval enthusiasts might be inclined to focus their attention on the struggle that occurred in the Mediterranean. Although lacking in the same scope as the Pacific campaign, the Mediterranean conflict also had its share of maritime combat. Fought predominately between the forces of Great Britain and Italy, the Mediterranean campaign featured such events as the bombardment of the Vichy Fleet at Mers-el-Kebir, the Fleet Air Arm raid against Taranto, the battle of Cape Matapan, the multi-service effort to interdict Axis maritime traffic to Africa, the epic struggle to maintain the island fortress of Malta and the execution of numerous amphibious landings in both North Africa and Southern Europe. In turn, these actions were essential in facilitating Allied victories that secured the region's vast oil supplies, provided an important logistical route to the Soviet Union, eliminated the Axis presence in Africa, brought France back into the Allied fold, drove Italy out of the war, forced Germany into a multi-front conflict, gained useful bases for the strategic bombing campaign, liberated nearly all of Southern Europe and turned the Mediterranean into a British-dominated sea.

As momentous as each of these campaigns were in both the Pacific and Mediterranean, neither constituted the premier maritime contest of the war. Instead, the distinction for this goes to the Atlantic and coastal waters of Northern Europe – the prolonged conflict fought predominately between Britain and Germany that is recounted in the preceding ten chapters. Unlike the Pacific campaign, this was not an ostentatious contest. There were no major fleet actions comparable to Midway, Leyte Gulf or even Cape Matapan. In many respects, the naval struggle between Britain and Germany resembled a long and gruelling slog in which the competing forces fought a multitude of minor and medium actions under often difficult conditions over a six-year period. For every time the two sides engaged each other, there were many additional instances where combat was avoided, but the actions undertaken still contributed to the overall war effort. Examples of this would include the safe arrival of a convoy or independently sailed merchant ship and the completion of an unproductive patrol, which nevertheless contributed to an offensive or defensive posture that helped shape the course of the campaign. In many respects, the conflict in the Atlantic and the surrounding area would seem an unlikely candidate to be the war's premier maritime contest, but in terms of impact and scope, that is precisely what it was.

To understand its relevance, it is necessary to place the naval conflict in the context of the greater war. Despite its seemingly global involvement, World War II was essentially a contest between six major powers divided evenly into two competing camps. For the Allies, these were the British Commonwealth of Nations, the Soviet Union and the United States. For the Axis, the belligerents were Germany, Italy and Japan. Beyond this breakdown of primary combatants, World War II was further divided into two portions: the war in Europe and the war in the Far East. Participants at the time and subsequent historians have all agreed that the war in Europe was the more critical of the two contests with Germany posing the greatest threat to the Allied cause. As such, all three of the major Allied powers devoted the bulk of their war efforts into defeating Germany and winning the war in Europe. As part of this, the Allies also vigorously engaged Italy, which was rightly seen as Germany's greatest supporter and an adjunct to German power. The war against Japan did not garner the same level of involvement. Of the three main Allied powers, the Soviet Union did not even confront Japan until the last few days of the war while the Americans and British considered the Asian/Pacific conflict to be a matter of secondary importance that could be dealt with once the war in Europe was over. The Western Allies only employed a minority of their resources against the Japanese, but this still proved to be enough to bring the island nation to its knees.

Compared to this, Germany was a much tougher adversary to subdue requiring the combined efforts of all three Allied powers. No one nation was solely responsible for the defeat of Germany, but instead this was a collective effort in which each of the major Allied belligerents played an essential role in securing this outcome. In viewing these contributions, it is fitting to start with the Soviet Union since it provided the bulk of the manpower and brute force to the Allied cause. The Soviets were also the main antagonists to the German army and the single greatest instrument in that army's destruction. Unlike the Western Allies, who waged war across multiple fronts and theatres, the Soviets almost exclusively limited their efforts to a single, colossal contest pitted against the bulk of the German army over a period of nearly four years. In doing so, they confronted between 60 and 80 percent of the German army's combat strength (depending upon the time frame) and inflicted up to 80 percent of Germany's total ground casualties for the duration of the war.[1] Looking at this another way, for nearly three years until the Western Allies landed in Normandy, the Soviet Union bore the overwhelming brunt of the fighting against the German army. During this period (22 June 1941 through 31 May 1944) German ground losses in the East numbered 4,120,232 total casualties.[2] By comparison, German casualties in North Africa, Sicily and Italy during this same period numbered fewer than half a million men.

Counterbalancing this Soviet contribution was the Western Alliance made up of the British Commonwealth and United States. Unlike the Soviets, who waged a largely one-dimensional war focused almost entirely on the destruction of the German army in the field, the Western Allies conducted the war on a multidimensional basis. Yet, even within the domain of the overarching Soviet goal, the Western Allies played a significant role in bringing about the destruction of German ground forces. By the spring of 1944, the German army was still largely intact despite the mauling it had received on both its eastern and (to a far lesser extent) southern flanks. Likewise, the Germans still controlled an empire that spanned across most of Europe. In less than one year, this army and empire were totally destroyed. During this period of climactic decision, the Soviets still confronted roughly 60 percent of the German army, but the Western Allies engaged the other 40 percent. This was no minor undertaking. In 11 months the Western Allies liberated four European countries, captured the northern half of Italy, conquered two-thirds of Germany and took roughly three times more German prisoners than did the Soviets. In fact, given this vast number of prisoners taken, the results of the last year of the war allowed the Western Allies to largely catch up to the number of casualties inflicted by the Soviets upon the Germans during the war's duration and therefore brought general parity between both sides in this regard. Thus, instead of merely being in on the kill, the Western Allies were major perpetrators of it.

Nor was this their only contribution. Throughout the war, the Western Allies provided considerable materiel support to the Soviet Union, which by the end of the war included 11 percent of its armour, 13 percent of its aircraft and 35 percent of its automotive transport.[3] The Western Allies were also the primary agents responsible for knocking Italy out of the war. From a Soviet perspective, this garnered little notice since the Italians were only minor players on their front, but Italy's departure from the war compelled the Germans to divert sizable forces into Southern Europe that could have otherwise been utilised in the East. It was also the Western Allies who conducted the strategic bombing campaign and related maritime blockade that severely degraded Germany's industrial output and forced the Germans to divert significant manpower and materiel resources into defensive applications. It was the

Western Allies who largely destroyed the Luftwaffe as an effective fighting force accounting for roughly 80 percent of all Axis aircraft losses sustained in Europe and the Middle East.[4] Finally, it was the Western Allies who compelled the Germans to wage a maritime war that obliged them to expend sizable resources in the construction and maintenance of a massive U-boat fleet that was otherwise useless in the land campaign against the Soviet Union. When reviewing these contributions, it is clear that the Western Allies ultimately forced the Germans into a five-front war (eastern, western, southern, aerial and maritime) as opposed to the single-front war they would have faced fighting the Soviets alone.

So what does this have to do with the maritime conflict in the Atlantic? The succinct answer is everything. Without success in the maritime conflict, none of the contributions made by the Western Allies would have been remotely possible. In fact, it was only through the successful application of maritime power that the Western Alliance was even able to exist. Most of this centred upon Britain's ability to stave off invasion and maintain access to seaborne commerce. In terms of the former, it was the strength of the Royal Navy and the corresponding weakness of the Kriegsmarine that provided the greatest deterrent to a German invasion of Britain in 1940. Even before this, the successful seaborne evacuation of the British Expeditionary Force from France was a major impetus to Britain's decision to fight on. In terms of the latter, once Britain's immediate survival was secured, it was only through the preservation of maritime lines of communication that the nation's long-term viability was maintained. Without this, Britain would have fallen or at least been rendered impotent. Likewise, these same maritime lines of communication were the primary means by which the United States brought its immense power to bear in the European conflict. As such, success in the maritime war was a vital component in the formation of the Western Alliance and set the conditions by which the Western Allies were able to execute their entire war effort against the Axis powers.

In terms of this greater effort, maritime power made many essential contributions to each and every campaign waged by the Western Allies. On a strategic level, this included the blockade against Germany, which when combined with the strategic bombing campaign, severely weakened that nation and forced it to divert substantial resources away from offensive and/or ground applications. Likewise, once the conditions were right, maritime power provided the means by which the Allies were able to launch Operation *Overlord* and conduct largescale combat operations in Northwest Europe. This was a massive undertaking that eventually required the monthly delivery of 3.5 million tons of supplies and cargo to support a force of over four million men by the end of the campaign.[5] Moving beyond this region, the successful execution of British maritime power played an indispensable role in supporting the army and helping it attain victory in theatres across the globe. Already described were the many benefits attained by British and Allied forces in the Mediterranean. Beyond this, maritime power also allowed British and Commonwealth forces to conduct successful campaigns in Southeast Asia against the Japanese.

None of this would have been remotely feasible without success in the maritime realm. This was particularly true regarding the maintenance of logistical support. From Africa to Southeast Asia and Italy to the plains of Northern Germany, nearly every man and item of equipment utilised by the Allied armies had to come in by sea. This was an enormous undertaking that compelled the British navy and merchant marine to simultaneously support various disparate operations throughout the world. In some cases, this effort included the maintenance of supply lines that stretched for more than 11,000 miles or literally to the other side of the globe. Beyond this, British maritime power provided many other strategic and tactical advantages including the successful execution of numerous amphibious landings, the conduct of innumerable fire support missions, the interdiction of Axis logistical efforts and the timely execution of seaborne evacuations to rescue situations when fortunes faltered on the battlefield. In the end, the eventual victory over Germany was gained on the plains of Northwest Europe with the defeat of the German army and the conquest of their homeland. In much the same light, the defeat of Italy was largely fashioned in the sands and mountains of North Africa. Still, without taking anything away from the ground forces involved, British sea power provided the essential foundation for each of these victories.

It is fitting to recognise that Britain was the predominant player in this maritime contest. In an overall sense, this was a collective effort shared jointly between the forces of the British Commonwealth and the United States with both combatants playing essential roles. Still, in both the Atlantic and Mediterranean, Britain was the predominant partner. It was the British who provided the majority of resources dedicated to this endeavour, conducted the majority of related operations, suffered the majority of related losses and scored the majority of successes against the Kriegsmarine and German merchant fleet. Britain's share of German maritime losses (both sole and partial) included 100 percent of their capital ships, 75 percent of their cruisers, 86 percent of their destroyers, 75 percent of their torpedo boats and escort destroyers, 86 percent of their fleet minesweepers, 77 percent of their U-boats and 73 percent of their merchant and commercial vessels. The British enjoyed similar success against the Italians accounting for 86 percent of Italy's principal warship losses during their time as an Axis partner. By comparison, the United States made several substantial inputs to the operational effort, but it was the output from American shipyards that proved to be America's greatest contribution to the maritime campaign. Indeed, it was this output that doomed Dönitz's tonnage strategy and ensured an Allied victory even before the U-boat threat was decisively defeated.

It is through this perspective that the predominance of the Atlantic theatre and the success and effectiveness of the British maritime effort are primarily evaluated, but there are other ways to assess these matters. As suggested above, we can also look at the materiel results. In this regard, the maritime conflict in the Atlantic and Northern Europe reigned supreme with more ships lost in this region during the war than any other theatre. Just one example highlighting this point is the fact that the Kriegsmarine alone suffered more principal warship losses in the Atlantic and Northern European

While its service history generally consisted of uneventful escort missions and sweeps, the battleship *Duke of York* enjoyed one spectacular success when it prevailed over the German battlecruiser *Scharnhorst* during the battle of North Cape in December 1943. (Royal Navy official photographer, public domain)

theatre than did all of the combatants involved in the Pacific conflict combined. When results from the Mediterranean are added into this calculation, these Kriegsmarine losses are still roughly equivalent to the total principal warship losses suffered by all of the combatants involved in both the Mediterranean and Pacific. This statistical fact reveals three major points. First, as already alluded to, it demonstrates the immense scale of the conflict in the Atlantic and waters off Northwest Europe. Second, it testifies to the vast resources that Germany invested into its naval forces. Finally, it validates the effectiveness of the British maritime effort, since as already mentioned, the British were solely or partially responsible for the vast majority of these losses.

Expanding this materiel enquiry further, there are many valuable insights to be learned in reviewing the maritime losses sustained by the competing sides. While war is not a sporting contest in which one simply tallies up the corresponding losses to determine winners and losers, a key element in any military conflict is the destruction of the enemy's will and ability to carry on while preserving your own to do the same. In order to provide context, we will look at the entire global struggle as a means to gauge the scale of the fighting and to evaluate Britain's effectiveness within the overall contest. This is also fitting because throughout the conflict Britain waged war on a global basis with major concurrent operations underway in disparate theatres around the world. This was something well beyond the capability of Italy, Japan, Germany or even the Soviet Union to emulate and thus served as a testimony to Britain's substantial power and impact. Only the United States waged war in a similar fashion. The primary component in Britain's ability to do this was maritime power. With the world's oceans as the battlefield, we will now compare the competing losses.

Starting first with principal warships, the hierarchy of these combatant vessels broke down into several classes based upon their size, configuration and role within the fleet organisation. The designation of some of these classes, such as battleships, aircraft carriers and submarines, were universally acknowledged and used within the various navies. Others were not. A prime example of the latter was the torpedo boat, which was a classification used extensively by the Kriegsmarine and Regia Marina (Italian navy), but not by the British or American navies. By comparison, the western navies categorised some of their warships as frigates, which was a designation not used by the Germans or Italians. When viewed globally, there were a number of warship types that were of similar size and configuration, but came under different classifications within their respective navies. Given this reality, it is prudent to group these similar warship variants into like categories to better evaluate the comparative warship losses suffered by the competing nations. While this is open to interpretation, my attempt in doing this resulted in the 12 categories listed below.

1. Battleships and battlecruisers. At the beginning of the war battleships and battlecruisers constituted the principal capital ships within the fleet hierarchy and the premier measure of maritime power. As such, all the major navies possessed varying numbers of battleships (and in some cases battlecruisers) within their ranks. The typical battleship/battlecruiser of the era weighed in at between 22,000 and 42,000 tons and possessed a primary armament ranging from 11- to 16-inch guns.

2. Pocket battleships, pre-dreadnought battleships, armoured cruisers and monitors. This grouping consists of a handful of disparate, large-gunned warships that existed outside the parameters of the standard battleship/battlecruiser classes and saw service within certain belligerent navies. Weighing in at 7,200 tons (the monitor) to 13,200 tons (the pre-dreadnought battleships) and armed with 10- to 15-inch guns, these warships fulfilled various tasks including surface raiding, coastal defence and naval gunfire support.

3. Fleet aircraft carriers. Although only actively used by three of the belligerent navies (British, American and Japanese), the aircraft carrier ended the war as the predominant warship within the fleet organisation usurping the battleship in this role. This was particularly true in the Pacific where the scope of carrier operations reached a level far exceeding that attain in European waters. The typical fleet carrier weighed in at between 11,000 and 36,000 tons and carried between 20 and 80 aircraft.

4. Escort carriers. The same three nations that actively used fleet carriers also used escort carriers to augment the defensive and offensive capabilities of their

respective naval aviation arms. Either converted from existing merchant ships or built based upon mercantile lines, these escort carriers generally weighed in at between 7,800 and 18,000 tons and carried between 10 and 30 aircraft.

5. Heavy cruisers. After the presence of capital ships, heavy cruisers constituted the most powerful surface combatants within the fleet organisation. Weighing in at between 8,000 and 14,000 tons and typically armed with 8-inch guns, these powerful warships served in all the major navies.

6. Light cruisers and anti-aircraft cruisers. Far more numerous than their heavy counterparts, these versatile warships saw substantial service in all the major navies where they performed a number of functions including fleet reconnaissance, offensive surface action, fleet and convoy defence, fast transport and naval gunfire support. The assorted variants weighed in at between 3,000 and 11,000 tons and usually possessed a main armament consisting of 5- to 6-inch guns.

7. Destroyers and large-class torpedo boats. Perhaps the most versatile warships in the fleet arsenal, these multipurpose vessels were equally capable of engaging in anti-surface, anti-aircraft or anti-submarine warfare. Whether utilised as part of a larger fleet or in more independent operations, these vessels performed a number of tasks both offensive and defensive and saw service in all the major navies as well as many minor navies of the era. These warships typically weighed in at between 900 and 2,600 tons and possessed a main armament of 4.1- to 5.9-inch guns. Likewise, most variants also carried torpedo tubes.

8. Escort destroyers, small-class torpedo boats, sloops, frigates and general purpose escorts. While this grouping of warships performed a variety of tasks, their overall orientation tended to be more defensive in nature compared to the destroyers listed above. Likewise, these vessels were generally ill-suited for fleet operations, but tended to serve as convoy escorts or shorter-range coastal combatants. Typically weighing in at between 600 and 2,000 tons and possessing a main armament consisting of 3.9- to 5-inch guns, this category of warships served in different variants (and in some cases under different designations including gunboats, patrol boats and fast transports) in all the combatant navies. Finally, this category only includes purpose-built warships and not converted auxiliary vessels.

9. Corvettes, cutters and large-class sub-chasers. Unlike the general-purpose escorts listed above, these specialised warships were primarily designed for anti-submarine warfare and were predominately used as such. This category only includes purpose-built warships that generally weighed in at between 600 and 1,000 tons and were armed with 3.9- to 4-inch guns. It does not include smaller sub-chaser classes in the 150- to 450-ton range or converted auxiliary vessels.

10. Submarines. With their ability to operate submerged, submarines were unique amongst the various warship categories and heavily used by all the major wartime combatants. While certain small-class coastal submarines are included in this category, mini-submarines and human torpedoes (typically less than 50 tons) are not. The standard size of most World War II-era submarines was between

600 and 1,600 tons, but there were classes that were smaller or larger thus producing an overall range of between 150 and 2,600 tons.

11. <u>Minelayers</u>. As the name suggests, these specialised warships were primarily designed to fulfil a mine-laying function, but they also served in various other roles including that of general-purpose escorts and fast transports. This category only includes purpose-built warships and not converted civilian vessels that also performed this task. Weighing in at between 450 and 2,600 tons, these vessels were primarily armed with 3- to 5.5-inch guns.

12. <u>Fleet minesweepers</u>. Like their counterparts above, these warships were primarily designed to fulfil a minesweeping function, but they also performed other activities including extensive use as convoy escorts. This category only includes purpose-built warships that weighed in at between 500 and 900 tons and were armed with 3- to 4.7-inch guns. It does not include smaller-sized motor minesweepers or converted auxiliary vessels.

Beyond understanding the make-up of the various warships involved, it is also important to specify what constituted a warship loss. My definition only consists of vessels that were a total loss split between two categories. First, it includes all vessels that were sunk, destroyed or irretrievably damaged as a result of military action, scuttling or non-combat related causes. Warships that were sunk in shallow waters, but subsequently raised, repaired and put back into service are not included in this category. Likewise, certain Allied warships that were damaged near the end of the war and not repaired due to economic or other elective considerations are also not included. This latter exclusion is warranted because the warships in question were repairable, but not repaired primarily due to a lack of need. With the war almost over and the massive resources available to the Allies, these vessels had become surplus and were thus little different than the significant numbers of warships that were idled once the conflict ended. The second category deals with warships that were captured during the course of the war or surrendered at the conclusion of hostilities. In the case of the surrendered vessels, this only covers Axis warships and is valid because the vessels in question were lost to their originating countries as completely as if they had been destroyed. For the nations involved, this was not an elective decision, but one imposed upon them by the Allies. Utilising these parameters, the breakdown of the war's principal warship losses by major naval power is presented in Table 11.1.

In viewing this data, one observation readily apparent is that Axis losses were substantially higher than those of the Allies. Being the losing side, one might reasonably expect this result, but with an exchange rate of almost four to one when comparing the three primary Axis powers to the three primary Allied powers, this disparity was pronounced. Of course, part of this was due to the seizure of surrendered Axis warships at the conclusion of hostilities, but even taking these capitulated vessels out of the equation, the exchange rate was still roughly three to one. In terms of unit numbers, Germany was far and away the greatest contributor to this disparity with

Table 11.1 Principal Warship Losses during World War II

	British Comm	USA	USSR	Germany	Italy	Japan	France
Battleships/battlecruisers	5	2	1	4	7	12	6
Pocket battleships/pre-dreadnought battleships/armored cruisers/monitors	1	-	-	5	1	-	-
Fleet aircraft carriers	5	5	-	2	1	17	-
Escort carriers	3	6	-	-	-	7	-
Heavy cruisers	5	7	-	5	7	18	4
Light cruisers/anti-aircraft cruisers	27	3	2	7	18	25	6
Destroyers/large-class torpedo boats	107	70	31	74	76	143	57
Escort destroyers/small-class torpedo boats/sloops/frigates/escorts	65	21	9	87	98	305	47
Corvettes/cutters/large-class sub-chasers	41	1	-	21	43	-	4
Submarines	76	52	103	1,184	151	232	64
Minelayers	3	1	-	4	10	5	2
Fleet minesweepers	39	21	23	241	6	9	-
Total	377	189	169	1,634	418	773	190

a total warship loss higher than the next three highest losers combined. Roughly 72 percent of these German losses consisted of U-boats, but they also included a mammoth 450 surface warships of which slightly more than half were minesweepers while destroyers and torpedo boats made up 36 percent. About 94 percent of Germany's total casualty figure consisted of German-built vessels while captured Italian, French and other foreign vessels made up the rest.

Moving beyond this unprecedented German number, the remaining Axis partners also suffered significant losses in their respective navies. This was particularly true regarding Japan, which suffered the loss of 773 principal warships. Adding to Japan's misfortune, these losses tended to be from warships of far greater tonnage than those sustained by the other participating powers. This is demonstrated by the fact that Japan decisively topped the loss results for battleships, aircraft carriers, heavy cruisers and destroyers while coming in a very close second for light cruisers. For their part, the Italians suffered 418 principal warship losses. In breaking down these Italian numbers, 46.4 percent were lost during the period of Italy's Axis partnership (10 June 1940 to 8 September 1943) while 25.8 percent surrendered to the Allies and 27.8 percent were sunk or seized by the Germans following Italy's capitulation.[6] Of this latter category, all of the seized vessels were subsequently sunk or scuttled while operating under German control. As such, these losses are counted twice being first tallied against the Italians and then later against the Germans. This practice is repeated for all vessels (both Allied and Axis) that were seized and subsequently lost in the service of the seizing power.

Continuing on, with a loss of 377 warships, the British Commonwealth suffered the highest butcher's bill for the Allied powers. Some 87 percent of these losses came from the Royal Navy while the remainder came from the various Commonwealth contingents or consisted of British-built ships manned by personnel from the lesser Allied nations. A number of factors contributed to this costly result. First, of the six principal combatant powers, the British Commonwealth was the only one to be actively engaged through the entire duration of the war from 3 September 1939 through 2 September 1945. All the other powers either joined the conflict late or ceased participation before the hostilities ended. As an example, the British were already 27 months into the war by the time the United States became an active participant. A second factor contributing to this was the extensive role played by the British navies in supporting the Allied war effort. As already established, this was a global undertaking in which the British navies were often at the forefront of the action. It was the British who confronted and defeated the bulk of German and Italian naval power while being the primary antagonist against the Vichy French. It was only in the case of Japan that the British were not the dominant partners in the maritime war. Thus, given this substantial role and extended involvement, it only makes sense that the British suffered higher losses than their Allied counterparts.

Turning now to the latter, the United States, Soviet Union and France all suffered comparable losses to each other. The loss of 189 warships represented a profoundly low cost paid by the United States given the overwhelming predominance the Americans played in defeating Japan as well as their sizable contribution to the European war.

As such, this result gives testimony to the effectiveness of American naval operations. By comparison, a similar level of loss by the Soviet Union represents poor performance given the negligible role the Soviets played in the maritime war. In a similar vein, the French also suffered heavy losses given their limited role in the conflict. Conquered early on, the French spent most of the war as uninvolved observers to the greater events going on around them. Yet, this lack of relevance did not shield them from suffering heavy naval losses. Making matters more interesting, nearly 36 percent of these losses came from warships that were sunk or seized by the Allies. This put France in a unique position of being an unintentional, quasi-Axis nation for part of the war. In either case as Ally or Axis, the French had little to show for the heavy losses they sustained.

So what of the British? How did the losses suffered by the British compare to the successes they achieved against the Axis navies? In evaluating this, we must again define some parameters. First, British forces are defined as all military forces (naval, air and ground) affiliated with the United Kingdom, the British Empire and the British Commonwealth. This includes Allied forces operating British vessels and equipment within the British force structure, but does not include American, Free-French or other Allied forces operating their own equipment in affiliation with the British. Axis warships are combatant vessels from Germany, Italy and Japan as well as the affiliated powers of Vichy France and Persia. They are broken down into the 12 classifications previously outlined, although abbreviated in the following tables to provide easier presentation. Exclusive British successes consist of all Axis warships that were lost solely or overwhelmingly as a result of British action. This includes Axis warships that were crippled or put out of action by British forces and subsequently scuttled. It also includes Axis warships that were scuttled to avoid action with British forces and those that were seized by force of arms. Shared British successes consist of all Axis warships that were lost due to the activities of British forces in conjunction with other Allied forces. This includes warships that were lost as a result of direct, collaborative action as well as those lost through more indirect means. Examples of the latter include vessels scuttled to avoid capture by Allied forces. Given the essential role played by Britain in the European war, this also includes Italian and German warships that surrendered at the end of their respective conflicts. On the other hand, given the secondary role played by British forces in the Pacific war, it does not include Japanese warships surrendered at the end of that conflict.

Utilising these parameters, the next three tables explore the materiel results attained by the British against the warship assets of the Axis nations. The first table compares British losses to British successes thus establishing an overall exchange rate between the competing sides. The second table breaks down the applicable Axis losses into major categories depicting the means by which the British caused or contributed to these losses. The final table breaks down these British successes (both exclusive and shared) by each Axis nation. In all cases, the data presented is the result of my calculation compiled from a variety of sources.

Table 11.2 Principal British Warship Losses Compared to Concurrent British Successes

	Total British warship losses	British ships lost due to hostile action	Axis ships lost solely or overwhelmingly as a result of British action	Axis ships lost partially as a result of British action	Total Axis ships lost solely or partially as a result of British action
Battleships	5	5	8	6	14
Pocket battleships	1	1	6	-	6
Aircraft carriers	5	5	-	2	2
Escort carriers	3	2	1	-	1
Heavy cruisers	5	5	9	2	11
Light cruisers	27	24	10	13	23
Destroyers	107	97	77	53	130
Escort destroyers	65	64	100	52	152
Corvettes	41	36	9	29	38
Submarines	76	66	617	435	1,052
Minelayers	3	3	7	3	10
Minesweepers	39	33	79	133	212
Total	377	341	923	728	1,651

Table 11.3 Breakdown of British Principal Warship Successes by Cause

	Exclusive British successes			Shared British successes		
	Lost in combat with British forces	Scuttled to avoid combat with British forces	Vichy warships seized by British forces	Lost in combat with British and other Allied forces	Scuttled to avoid capture by Allied forces	Surrendered Italian and German warships in Sep 43 and May 45
Battleships	6	-	2	1	-	5
Pocket battleships	4	2	-	-	-	-
Aircraft carriers	-	-	-	1	1	-
Escort carriers	1	-	-	-	-	-
Heavy cruisers	9	-	-	1	-	1
Light cruisers	10	-	-	2	-	11
Destroyers	72	1	4	10	5	38
Escort destroyers	82	-	18	6	4	42
Corvettes	9	-	-	1	9	19
Submarines	603	7	7	20	218	197
Minelayers	5	1	1	-	-	3
Minesweepers	79	-	-	1	9	123
Total	880	11	32	43	246	439

Table 11.4 Breakdown of British Principal Warship Successes by Axis Nation

	Germany		Italy		Japan		Vichy France & Persia		Total	
	Excl British success	Shared British success	Excl British success	Shared British success	Excl British success	Shared British success	Excl British success	Shared British success	Excl British success	Shared British success
Battleships	4	-	1	5	-	1	3	-	8	6
Pocket battleships	5	-	1	-	-	-	-	-	6	-
Aircraft carriers	-	2	-	-	-	-	-	-	1	2
Escort carriers	-	-	-	-	1	-	-	-	1	-
Heavy cruisers	2	2	4	-	3	-	-	-	9	2
Light cruisers	3	2	6	9	1	2	-	-	10	13
Destroyers	34	30	34	14	-	9	9	-	77	53
Escort destroyers	42	23	27	25	8	4	23	-	100	52
Corvettes	6	10	3	19	-	-	-	-	9	29
Submarines	518	398	69	35	9	2	21	-	617	435
Minelayers	3	-	2	3	1	-	1	-	7	3
Minesweepers	76	132	2	1	1	-	-	-	79	133
Total	693	599	149	111	24	18	57	-	923	728

In viewing these tables, the effectiveness of Britain's military effort is clearly demonstrated by the positive exchange rate it achieved. During the course of the war the British perpetuated or participated in the loss of 4.4 Axis warships for every corresponding British loss due to all causes. As good as this overall exchange rate is, it does not represent a fair comparison since the British figures include non-combat related losses whereas the Axis numbers do not (377 to 1,651). Examples of non-combat related losses include warships that were sunk through accidents, fratricide, storm damage or unknown causes. A total of 36 principal British warships were sunk by these non-combat related means. When excluding these non-combat related losses from the equation (341 to 1,651), this exchange rate improves to 4.8 to 1 in favour of the British. Thus, in comparing the competing combat losses of both sides, this latter exchange rate is more applicable to our purposes and is thus used for the remainder of our analysis. Breaking down this calculation further, the British achieved 2.7 exclusive and 2.1 shared successes for every warship loss they suffered through hostile action. Meanwhile, beyond this combined exchange rate, the British also enjoyed considerable success in the component warship categories comprising it. In nine out of the 12 warship categories, the British were able to inflict higher losses than they themselves suffered. This was particularly true in the area of submarines where the British attained a staggering 15.9 to 1 exchange rate.

Beyond this impressive box score, a second factor worth noting is the substantial contribution the British made in diminishing Axis naval power. With a total of 1,651 Axis warships lost solely or partially due to British action, the British played a role in 57 percent of the total Axis warship losses sustained during the war.[7] When broken down by the individual Axis nations, this contribution becomes even more pronounced. This is particularly true regarding Germany where the British were fully or partially responsible for 79.1 percent of total German losses. The British also contributed to 62.2 percent of the overall Italian losses, but this portion increases to 86.1 percent when just considering Italian losses incurred while facing the Allies. The situation is much the same with the Vichy French and Persians who lost 70 principal warships to the Allies of which 81.4 percent were attributable to British means. It was only in the case of the Japanese that the British were not the primary contributors to the Axis naval losses, but this number was so low (5.4 percent) that it limited Britain's overall contribution to the previously mentioned 57 percent despite the dominant role it played against the other Axis nations.

By comparison to these decisive results, the breakdown of merchant shipping losses (as displayed in Table 11.5) presents a mixed bag. This dichotomy is highlighted by the fact that in absolute terms the Axis suffered a higher number of merchant/commercial shipping casualties while the Allies suffered a higher tonnage loss. In fairness, these figures are compiled from incomplete data. In particular, some national casualty figures consist of all merchant/commercial ships that were lost while others are limited to the demise of merchant ships of 500 tons or greater. In the former

Table 11.5 Comparative Merchant/Commercial Shipping Losses

	Number of ships	Tonnage
British Empire and Commonwealth	2,627	11,396,900
Remaining Allied and Allied-Affiliated Nations	2,523	10,173,820
Total Allied losses	5,150	21,570,720
European Axis and Axis-affiliated nations	6,004	10,614,078
Japanese Empire	2,346	8,618,234
Total Axis losses	8,350	19,232,312

Source: The Central Statistical Office, *Statistical Digest of the War* (London: Her Majesty's Stationery Office, 1975), p. 180; S. W. Roskill, *The War at Sea 1939–1945, Volume III, Part II* (London: Her Majesty's Stationery Office, 1961), pp. 367, 479; *AIR 41/79, RAF in the Maritime War, Volume VIII: Statistics*; ADM 199/2447, German Ships: Losses and Damage in NW European Waters, 1939–1945; Roger Jordan, *The World's Merchant Fleets 1939, The Particulars and Wartime Fates of 6,000 ships* (Annapolis: Naval Institute Press, 1999); The Joint Army-Navy Assessment Committee, *Japanese Naval and Merchant Losses During World War II By all Causes* (Washington: US Government Printing Office, 1947), p. vi and minor inputs from other sources.

cases, there are also no tonnage figures available for many of these smaller vessels. Still, rectifying these data shortfalls, even if it were possible to do so, would unlikely change the overall dynamic stated above. If anything, the most likely outcome would be a substantial increase in the number of Axis merchant/commercial vessels sunk with a far smaller increase in their corresponding tonnage loss. This, in turn, would widen the gap between the competing numbers of ships lost while diminishing, but not entirely eliminating, the corresponding tonnage gap.

When viewed from a national perspective, the British Commonwealth suffered the highest merchant tonnage loss of any of the competing powers. Altogether, this represented about 28 percent of the worldwide merchant tonnage that was lost during the war. There were a number of factors that contributed to this high casualty rate. First, given the size of the British merchant fleet, which was more than twice the size of the next largest power at the beginning of the war, they had the ships available to lose. Beyond this size, the British merchant fleet was essential to the survival of the nation and the entire Allied effort. As such, it was extensively utilised throughout the duration of the war without any breaks in action, exposing it to constant usage and danger. Given its essential role, the British merchant fleet was highly targeted by the Axis, and in particular the Kriegsmarine, which made its destruction the overarching objective of the U-boat campaign. Thus, when considering the duration and scope of the British war effort and the central role played by the British merchant fleet in enabling it, these losses are put into a proper perspective. Through new construction and other acquisition means, the British were largely able to replace their losses and maintain the relative size of their merchant fleet throughout the war. Thus, while these losses were grievous, they never approached a point where they became truly debilitating or fatal to the overall British war effort.

By comparison, each of the Axis nations suffered less tonnage loss in numerical terms, but a far higher percentage of attrition against the size of their competing national merchant fleets. Unlike the British, these Axis nations ultimately lost or suffered great deprivation in their ability to use seaborne commerce as a means to advance their national objectives. The preservation of merchant shipping was not essential in and of itself, but rather only important to the extent in which these vessels were able to advance the strategic and tactical goals of the nations involved. When losses or the threat of losses precluded this, the nation's overall war standing suffered accordingly. In the case of the British, despite their heavy losses and the constant threats arrayed against them, they were always able to maintain sufficient merchant strength to fulfil the essential tasks needed to advance their war effort. This was not the case with the various Axis nations, which all suffered a far greater percentage of loss that ultimately degraded their ability to exploit sea power to a point of practical impotency.

The most obvious example of this was Japan, which, like Britain, depended upon seaborne commerce to support the viability of its homeland as well as the maintenance of its newly acquired regional empire. Given this reality, the Japanese merchant fleet was targeted by the Americans (and other Allied powers) in a similar way that the British merchant fleet was targeted by the Germans. However, unlike the British, the Japanese were unable to withstand this onslaught, and their merchant fleet became a dwindling asset that was reduced to the point of near extinction in less than four years. By the end of the war the Japanese only had 1,495,150 tons of merchant shipping remaining against a total loss of 8,618,234 tons.[8] This surviving tally constituted less than 14.8 percent of their total accumulated merchant strength since the beginning of the war. Of the tonnage still available to the Japanese, only about 557,000 tons were operational thus reducing this effective rate to a mere 5.5 percent.[9] Given these losses and the corresponding fuel shortages they helped facilitate, Japan's overseas commerce ground to a halt, leaving its home islands prostrate and vulnerable to invasion while its empire was isolated and powerless to assist or intervene.

The European Axis suffered similar high losses. Of greatest percentage magnitude, the Italian merchant fleet was almost entirely destroyed or seized by the Allies during the course of the war. The same was true for German-controlled shipping operating in the Mediterranean. In fact, by the end of the conflict there were virtually no merchant ships left under German control within the theatre, with an overall Axis loss of more than 4.1 million tons. The situation was somewhat better for the Germans in Northern Europe where they still had roughly 1.3 million tons of shipping available for their use at war's end against a regional loss of more than 4.4 million tons.[10] Still, even in this case, the majority of these surviving vessels were non-operational due to damage or logistical constraints. When combined together and including

German and Italian ships lost outside of European waters, this represented a rough survival rate of only 11 percent of their accumulated merchant tonnage. Of course, this percentage declines further if only considering operational vessels.

Given the lack of complete data, or in some cases contradictory information, a full accounting of Britain's role in bringing about these Axis merchant losses is extremely difficult to ascertain. To the contrary, an accurate estimate is the best we can reasonably hope to produce. In this regard, approximately 2,700 commercial vessels worth 5.5 million tons were lost solely or predominantly as a result of British action in the European conflict while a further 1,300 such vessels worth 2.6 million tons were lost partially attributable to this cause.[11] The latter primarily consists of Axis commercial vessels that were seized, surrendered or scuttled during the course of the conflict including merchant ships that were caught overseas and sought shelter in neutral ports to avoid the British blockade only to be seized by those nations or scuttled to avoid this outcome. On the other hand, this does not include Axis vessels that survived the war since the Allies generally let the conquered Axis nations retain these vessels for their own use.

Through the duration of the war the British used a combination of aircraft, mines, warships and submarines to wage a relentless interdiction campaign that eventually eliminated some 80 percent of Germany's accumulated merchant fleet and reduced its seaborne trade to a trickle. Pictured here is a Coastal Command strike against the German ship *Sauerland* off France. (HQ Coastal Command, Royal Air Force official photographer, public domain)

Compared to these European figures, an accurate accounting of British-inflicted Japanese losses is more difficult to determine. This is primarily due to the lack of records regarding Japanese merchant losses of less than 500 tons as well as other data shortfalls and contradictions. At a minimum, British and Commonwealth forces were responsible for the loss of at least 56 Japanese merchant ships (of 500 tons or greater) worth 138,529 tons and contributed to the destruction of a further 11 merchant ships worth 56,931 tons.[12] Added to this were several hundred minor craft worth at least 100,000 tons that were destroyed by British or Commonwealth means. Finally, it is almost certain that the British were solely or partially responsible for further Japanese losses ranging from at least 25,000 tons to perhaps as high as an additional 100,000 tons, but it is difficult to determine an exact number given the lack of Japanese confirmation and conflicting claims in the Allied records. Thus, when combined together, total Japanese commercial losses that were solely or partially attributable to British/Commonwealth means numbered upwards of 1,000 vessels worth somewhere between 300,000 and 400,000 tons. In turn, when combined with their European results, Britain's total commercial success rate stood at roughly 5,000 vessels worth upwards of 8.5 million tons. This almost doubled their own merchant losses in terms of numbers of vessels, but only represents about 75 percent of their tonnage loss, thus remaining consistent with the overall loss dynamic prevalent between the greater Allied/Axis sides.

Completing our analysis of maritime losses, the final area to review involves minor and auxiliary warships. Although often overlooked in the traditional fleet hierarchy, all of the naval powers utilised these unassuming vessels in a variety of roles, and they made innumerable contributions to the overall war effort. Yet, despite their prevalence, a complete accounting of these losses is extremely difficult to ascertain given gaps and/or contradictions in the various national records and the vast variety of vessel types involved. As such, we will only review the casualties sustained by the two primary competing powers, Great Britain and Germany. In terms of the former, this only includes British-controlled vessels or those loaned by them to Commonwealth and other Allied navies, but not vessels owned by those latter services. For their part, the German tally consists of units of German origin as well as captured Allied craft pressed into Kriegsmarine service. Finally, the casualties involved consist of all minor warships and auxiliary vessels that were lost, scuttled or captured during the course of the war. These losses are grouped in similar categories representing more than 60 different vessel types and functions and are presented in Table 11.6.

While clearly an incomplete accounting, this data gives an ample sampling of the scale of losses these lesser vessels sustained during the war. Of the two nations presented, this tally consists of almost 4,800 vessels that were sunk, scuttled or seized during the course of hostilities. Added to this were hundreds of additional German vessels that were seized by the Allies at the end of the war. Included in this latter number were all of the E-boats, R-boats and small battle units that survived the conflict. Of these combined German losses, the vast majority were solely or partially

Table 11.6 Comparative Losses of British and German Minor Warships and Auxiliary Vessels

British	Number lost	German	Number lost
Armed merchant cruisers/boarding vessels	25	Armed merchant cruisers	8
Auxiliary minelayers	5	Auxiliary minelayers	35
Auxiliary anti-aircraft ships	6	Sperrbrechers/old warships converted to anti-aircraft vessels	93
Auxiliary fighter catapult ships	2	Catapult ships	2
Navy depot ships	2	Navy depot ships/tenders	11
Motor torpedo boats/motor gunboats/motor launches	226	Motor torpedo boats (E-boats)	146
Motor minesweepers	24	Motor minesweepers (R-boats)	163
Midget submarines/human torpedoes	40	Small battle units	550+
Auxiliary minesweepers/anti-submarine craft/patrol vessels/trawlers/drifters	465	Auxiliary minesweepers/sub-chasers/patrol vessels/escorts	800+
Assorted landing ships	20	Kriegstransporters (KT Ships)	42
Assorted landing craft/landing barges	1,306	Assorted naval ferries/barges	500+
Other assorted support/military vessels	270	Other assorted support/military vessels	39+
Total	2,391	Total	2,389+

Source: S. W. Roskill, *The War at Sea 1939–1945, Volume III, Part II* (London: Her Majesty's Stationery Office, 1961), pp. 449–450, 461–462; H. T. Lenton, *German Warships of the Second World War* (New York: Areo Publishing Company Inc., 1976) and ADM 199/2447, German Ships: Losses and Damage in NW European Waters, 1939–1945.

the result of British action, although I have made no attempt to do a detailed analysis regarding this point. Meanwhile, going beyond Britain and Germany, it is likely that the overall casualty number for these types of vessels exceeded 10,000 when adding in the contributions of the other naval powers. In fairness, the vast majority of these losses consisted of small tonnage craft, but the sheer volume of destruction provides another example of the all-consuming nature of the war and its extraordinary cost.

Indeed, the war was unprecedented in many ways. In just reviewing the maritime struggle, the total number of vessels of all categories (principal warships, merchant/commercial ships and minor warships/auxiliaries) that were lost probably exceeded

27,000. Divided out equally, this equates to more than 12 vessels lost for every day of the war. Throughout history, there has never been anything approaching this scale of maritime carnage, and we will probably never again experience anything like this in the future. While more destructive wars are certainly conceivable given the advent of nuclear weapons and other instruments of mass destruction, it is hard to envision a prolonged maritime conflict ever again approaching the scale of World War II. In fact, the idea of major naval battles fought between competing fleets almost seems obsolete. After more than 2,500 years of related warfare, battles such as Salamis, Actium, Lepanto, Trafalgar, Jutland and Midway will only reign in the province of history.

World War II also represented the swansong of Britain's maritime legacy. In this, it provided a fitting close to a glorious period of history that had begun some 400 years before with the defeat of the Spanish Armada. When reviewing its many contributions during World War II, it is abundantly clear that Britain (including the Empire and Commonwealth) played a substantial role in bringing about the ultimate Allied victory. Without Britain, there would have been no effective Western Alliance, and the Soviet Union would have faced the full force of the European Axis alone. Beyond this, the British were active participants in every major campaign waged by the Western Allies during the course of the European war. In most cases, British leadership, manpower and resources played predominant or equal roles in the execution of these campaigns, and in the one instance where this was not the case (Northwest Europe), the British still made an essential, if subordinate, contribution to the overall Allied success. Britain's ability to make these contributions was attributable to a number of factors, but none was more important than the effective application of British maritime power. It was through this power that the British were able to sustain their own national survival, preserve the alliance and prosecute each of the campaigns mentioned above. In turn, the origins of this victory centred firmly upon the struggle in the Atlantic and adjacent waters and radiated outward from there. Thus, by playing this indispensable role, in the matter of Britain's maritime heritage, World War II truly was its finest hour.

Selected Bibliography

Unpublished Sources

ADM 186/798, Battle Summaries, No. 17: Naval Operations of the Campaign in Norway, April–June 1940.

ADM 186/802, The U-boat War in the Atlantic 1939–1945.

ADM 199/2447, German Ships: Losses and Damage in NW European Waters, 1939–1945.

ADM 234/218 British Minelaying Campaign, September 1939–May 1945.

ADM 234/322, Battle Summaries, No. 5, Chase and Sinking of the German Battleship *Bismarck*, May 23–27, 1941.

ADM 234/324, Battle Summaries, No. 13: Actions with Enemy Disguised Raiders 1940–1941.

ADM 234/342, Battle Summaries, No. 24: Sinking of *Scharnhorst*, 26 December 1943.

ADM 234/345, Battle Summaries, No. 27, Naval Aircraft Attack on *Tirpitz* (Operation *Tungsten*) 3 April 1944.

ADM 234/347, Battle Summaries, No. 29: Attack on *Tirpitz* by Midget submarines (Operation *Source*) 22 September 1943.

ADM 234/352, Battle Summaries, No. 31: Cruiser and Destroyer Action in English Channel 1943–1944.

ADM 234/355, Battle Summaries, No. 33: Raid on Dieppe: Naval Operations, 19 August 1942.

ADM 234/360, Battle Summaries, No. 41: Evacuation from Dunkirk (Operation *Dynamo*) 26 May–4 June 1940.

ADM 234/362 Battle Summaries, No. 12: Attack on St. Nazaire.

ADM 234/363, Battle Summaries, No. 49: Campaign in North-West Europe June 1944–May 1945.

ADM 234/366, Battle Summaries, No. 39, Volume I: Landings in Normandy (Operation *Neptune*) June 1944.

ADM 234/367, Battle Summaries, No. 39, Volume II: Landings in Normandy (Operation *Neptune*) June 1944: Appendices.

ADM 234/369, Battle Summaries, No. 22: Arctic Convoys 1941–1945.

ADM 234/370, Battle Summaries, No. 51: Convoy and Anti-submarine Warfare Reports.

ADM 234/578, Naval Staff History: Defeat of the Enemy Attack on Shipping, 1939–1945: A Study of Policy and Operations, Volume IA (Text and Appendices).

ADM 234/579, Naval Staff History: Defeat of the Enemy Attack on Shipping, 1939–1945: A Study of Policy and Operations, Volume IB (Plans and Tables).

ADM 234/67, The U-boat War in the Atlantic: Volume II, January 1942–May 1943.

ADM 234/68, The U-boat War in the Atlantic: Volume III, June 1943–May 1945.

AIR 40/2588, British Bombing Survey Unit: Sea Communications Panel; Report on Air Action against German Merchant Shipping.

AIR 41/47, The RAF in the Maritime War, Volume III: The Atlantic and Home Waters; The Preparative Phase July 1941–Feb 1943.

AIR 41/48, The RAF in the Maritime War, Volume IV: The Atlantic and Home Waters; The Offensive Phase, February 1943–May 1944.

AIR 41/74 The RAF in the Maritime War, Volume V: Atlantic and Home Waters; The Victory Phase, June 1944–May 1945.

AIR 41/79, RAF in the Maritime War, Volume VIII: Statistics.

CAB 106/992, Administrative History of Operations of 21st Army Group, 1944 June 6–1945 May 8.

WO 205/972A, Notes on the Operations of 21st Army Group 6 June 1944–5 May 1945.

Published Sources

Barnett, Correlli. *Engage the Enemy More Closely, the Royal Navy in the Second World War* (London: Hodder & Stoughton, 1991)

Behrens, C. B. A. *Merchant Shipping and the Demands of War* (London: Her Majesty's Stationery Office and Longmans, Green and Co., 1955)

Blair, Clay. *Hitler's U-boat War, the Hunters, 1939–1942* (New York: Random House, 1996)

———. *Hitler's U-boat War, the Hunted, 1942–1945* (New York: Random House, 1998)

Brown, David. *Warship Losses of World War Two* (London: Arms and Armour Press, 1990)

Campbell, Ian and Macintyre, Donald. *The Kola Run, A Record of Arctic Convoys, 1941–1945* (London: Frederick Muller, 1958)

Central Statistical Office. *Statistical Digest of the War* (London: Her Majesty's Stationery Office, 1975)

Delaforce, Patrick. *Smashing the Atlantic Wall, The Destruction of Hitler's Coastal Fortress* (London: Cassell & Co., 2001)

Dönitz, Karl. *Memoirs: Ten Years and Twenty Days* (London: Weidenfeld and Nicolson, 1959)

Ellis, John. *World War II, A Statistical Survey, the Essential Facts and Figures for all the Combatants* (New York: Facts on File, 1993)

Ellis, L. F. *Victory in the West, Volume I: The Battle of Normandy* (London: Her Majesty's Stationery Office, 1962)

———. *Victory in the West, Volume II: The Defeat of Germany* (London: Her Majesty's Stationery Office, 1968)

Fleming, Peter. *Operation Sea Lion* (New York: Ace Books, Inc., 1956)

Gannon, Michael. *Black May, The Epic Story of the Allies' Defeat of the German U-boats in May 1943* (New York: Dell Publishing, 1998)

Goulter, Christina J. M. *A Forgotten Offensive, Royal Air Force Coastal Command's Anti-Shipping Campaign, 1940–1945* (London: Frank Cass, 1995)

Hickman, Homer H. Jr. *Torpedo Junction, U-boat War off America's East Coast, 1942* (New York: Dell Publishing, 1991)

Jordan, Roger. *The World's Merchant Fleets 1939, The Particulars and Wartime Fates of 6,000 Ships* (Annapolis: Naval Institute Press, 1999)

Kemp, P. K, *Key to Victory, The Triumph of British Sea Power in World War II* (Boston: Little, Brown and Company, 1957)

Kemp, Paul. *Convoy, Drama in Arctic Waters*, (London: Brockhampton Press, 1999)

———. *U-boats Destroyed, German Submarine Losses in the World Wars* (London: Arms and Armour, 1997)

Milner, Marc. *Battle of the Atlantic* (Gloucestershire: Tempus, 2005)

O'Hara, Vincent P. *The German Fleet at War, 1939–1945* (Annapolis: Naval Institute Press, 2004)

Rohwer, J. and Hummelchen, G. *Chronology of the War at Sea 1939–1945* (Annapolis: Naval Institute Press, 1992)

Rohwer, Jürgen. *Allied Submarine Attacks of World War Two, European Theatre of Operations 1939–1945* (Annapolis: Naval Institute Press, 1997)

——. *Axis Submarine Successes 1939–1945* (Annapolis: Naval Institute Press, 1983)

Roskill, S. W. *The War at Sea 1939–1945, Volume I: The Defensive* (London: Her Majesty's Stationery Office, 1954)

——. *The War at Sea 1939–1945, Volume II: The Period of Balance* (London: Her Majesty's Stationery Office, 1956)

——. *The War at Sea 1939–1945, Volume III, Part I: The Offensive, 1st June 1943–31st May 1944* (London: Her Majesty's Stationery Office, 1960)

——. *The War at Sea 1939–1945, Volume III, Part II: The Offensive, 1st June 1944–14th August 1945* (London: Her Majesty's Stationery Office, 1961)

Ruge, Friedrich. *Der Seekrieg, The German Navy's Story, 1939–1945* (Annapolis, Naval Institute Press, 1957)

Stacey, C. P. *Official History of the Canadian Army in the Second World War, Volume III: The Victory Campaign, The Operations in North-West Europe 1944–1945* (Ottawa: Queen's Printer and Controller of Stationery, 1966)

Tarrant, V. E. *The Last Year of the Kriegsmarine, May 1944–May 1945* (Annapolis: Naval Institute Press, 1994)

——. *The U-boat Offensive, 1914–1945* (Annapolis, Naval Institute Press, 1989)

Terraine, John. *The Right of the Line, The Royal Air Force in the European War 1939–1945*, (Hodder and Stoughton, Sceptre edition, 1988)

Westwood, David. *The U-boat War, The German Submarine Service and the Battle of the Atlantic, 1935–1945* (London: Conway Maritime Press, 2005)

Endnotes

Chapter 1: A Not So Phoney War

1 I. C. B. Dear and M. R. D. Foot, *The Oxford Companion to World War II* (Oxford: Oxford University Press, 1995), p. 906.

2 This includes some ships held in reserve or under refit, but does not include ships held in the Commonwealth navies. Cruisers with 8-inch guns are classified as heavy cruisers. See S. W. Roskill, *The War at Sea 1939–1945, Volume I: The Defensive* (London: Her Majesty's Stationery Office, 1954), pp. 577–582, 586 and David Brown, *Warship Losses of World War Two* (London: Arms and Armour Press, 1990), pp. 161, 170–176.

3 Roskill, *The War at Sea 1939–1945, Volume I*, p. 586.

4 Ibid., pp. 588–589.

5 Ibid., pp. 49–50.

6 John Keegan, *The Rand McNally Encyclopedia of World War II* (Chicago: Rand McNally & Company, 1977), p. 95 and John Ellis, *World War II, A Statistical Survey, the Essential Facts and Figures for all the Combatants* (New York: Facts on File, 1993), p. 245.

7 Cajus Bekker, *Hitler's Naval War* (New York: Kensington Publishing Corp., 1977), pp. 369–371.

8 Roskill, *The War at Sea 1939–1945, Volume I*, p.32.

9 Due to manufacturing delays in the 5.25-inch guns, the British substituted eight 4.5-inch guns on the *Dido*-class cruisers *Scylla* and *Charybdis*.

10 In addition to Germany, many other nations including Italy, France and Japan used torpedo boats as a classification for small destroyer–type vessels. This is not to be confused with British-designated motor torpedo boats that were small, fast coastal craft weighing in at less than 100 tons and generally armed with two or four torpedoes and small arms.

11 Friedrich Ruge, *Der Seekrieg, The German Navy's Story, 1939–1945* (Annapolis, Naval Institute Press, 1957), p. 43.

12 Ibid., p. 42.

13 Roskill, *The War at Sea 1939–1945, Volume I*, p. 42.

14 Michael Gannon, *Black May, The Epic Story of the Allies' Defeat of the German U-boats in May 1943* (New York: Dell Publishing, 1998), p. 61 and ADM 234/579, Naval Staff History: Defeat of the Enemy Attack on Shipping, 1939–1945: A Study of Policy and Operations, Volume IB (Plans and Tables), Tables 12(ii) and 12(iii).

15 ADM 234/578, Naval Staff History: Defeat of the Enemy Attack on Shipping, 1939–1945: A Study of Policy and Operations, Volume IA (Text and Appendices), p. 30.

16 These were merchant ships, usually large passenger liners that were drafted into naval service to perform convoy escort and blockade enforcement duties. These were armed combatants that normally carried a main armament of eight 6-inch guns. The Germans employed similar merchant conversions to serve as surface raiders.

17 Roskill, *The War at Sea 1939–1945, Volume I*, p. 615.

18 These losses do not include ships sunk on submarine-laid mines. See Roskill, *The War at Sea 1939–1945, Volume I*, p. 615.

19 Jürgen Rohwer, *Axis Submarine Successes 1939–1945* (Annapolis: Naval Institute Press, 1983), pp. 1–16 and the Central Statistical Office, *Statistical Digest of the War* (London: Her Majesty's Stationery Office, 1975), p. 180.

20 Roskill, *The War at Sea 1939–1945, Volume I*, p. 614.

21 Ibid., p. 615.

22 The Central Statistical Office, *Statistical Digest of the War*, p. 180.

23 This latter figure came from the Germans themselves as reported to Uruguayan officials. This may have been an exaggeration and/or included splinter damage from near misses.

24 Roskill, *The War at Sea 1939–1945, Volume I*, p.151.

25 ADM 199/2447, German Ships: Losses and Damage in NW European Waters, 1939–1945; J. Rohwer and G. Hummelchen, *Chronology of the War at Sea 1939–1945* (Annapolis: Naval Institute Press, 1992), pp. 1–14; Roger Jordan, *The World's Merchant Fleets 1939, The Particulars and Wartime Fates of 6,000 ships* (Annapolis: Naval Institute Press, 1999), pp. 465–480 and Peter C. Smith and John R. Dominy, *Cruisers in Action 1939–1945* (London: William Kimber & Co., 1981), pp. 130–133.

26 ADM 199/2447, German Ships: Losses and Damage in NW European Waters, 1939–1945; Rohwer and Hummelchen, *Chronology of the War at Sea 1939–1945*, pp. 1–14 and Jordan, *The World's Merchant Fleets 1939, The Particulars and Wartime Fates of 6,000 ships*, pp. 465–480.

27 Rohwer and Hummelchen, *Chronology of the War at Sea 1939–1945*, pp. 1–14 and Jordan, *The World's Merchant Fleets 1939, The Particulars and Wartime Fates of 6,000 ships*, pp. 465–480.

28 ADM 199/2447, German Ships: Losses and Damage in NW European Waters, 1939–1945; Rohwer and Hummelchen, *Chronology of the War at Sea 1939–1945*, pp. 1–14 and Jordan, *The World's Merchant Fleets 1939, The Particulars and Wartime Fates of 6,000 ships*, pp. 465–480.

29 German and Russian mines accounted for 13 of the accidental sinkings while an erroneous attack by a Soviet submarine accounted for the loss of a fourteenth vessel. See ADM 199/2447, German Ships: Losses and Damage in NW European Waters, 1939–1945 and Jordan, *The World's Merchant Fleets 1939, The Particulars and Wartime Fates of 6,000 ships*, pp. 464–481.

30 S. W. Roskill, *The War at Sea 1939–1945, Volume I*, pp. 67, 149.

31 Ibid., p. 44.

32 P. K. Kemp, *Key to Victory, The Triumph of British Sea Power in World War II* (Boston: Little, Brown and Company, 1957), p. 37.

33 For these British submarine successes see Jürgen Rohwer, *Allied Submarine Attacks of World War Two, European Theatre of Operations 1939–1945* (Annapolis: Naval Institute Press, 1997), pp. 46–48.

34 Roskill, *The War at Sea 1939–1945, Volume I*, p. 96.

35 Ibid., p. 615.

36 Ibid., p. 63.

37 Ibid., p. 64.

Chapter 2: Blitzkrieg

1 AIR 40/2588, British Bombing Survey Unit: Sea Communications Panel; Report on Air Action against German Merchant Shipping, Appendix B.

2 Christina J. M. Goulter, *A Forgotten Offensive, Royal Air Force Coastal Command's Anti-Shipping Campaign, 1940–1945* (London: Frank Cass, 1995), p. 303 and AIR 40/2588, British Bombing

Survey Unit: Sea Communications Panel; Report on Air Action against German Merchant Shipping, Appendix B

3   Goulter, *A Forgotten Offensive, Royal Air Force Coastal Command's Anti-Shipping Campaign, 1940–1945*, p. 118.

4   Correlli Barnett, *Engage the Enemy More Closely, the Royal Navy in the Second World War* (London: Hodder & Stoughton, 1991), p. 103.

5   Donald Macintyre, *Narvik* (London: Pan Books LTD, 1959), p. 24.

6   The first three were total losses, but the Germans were able to raise and put *Kattegat* back into service. See Jordan, *The Worlds Merchant Fleets 1939, The Particulars and Wartime Fates of 6,000 Ships*, pp. 472–473, 477–478 and ADM 186/798, Battle Summaries, No. 17: Naval Operations of the Campaign in Norway, April–June 1940, pp. 31, 44, 48.

7   Interestingly enough, this first ship sunk under the new rules of engagement was not connected to the invasion, but was rather a blockade-runner returning to Germany.

8   Rohwer, *Allied Submarine Attacks of World War Two, European Theatre of Operations 1939–1945*, pp. 48–49.

9   ADM 186/798, Battle Summaries, No. 17: Naval Operations of the Campaign in Norway, April–June 1940, p. 28 and Jordan, *The Worlds Merchant Fleets 1939, The Particulars and Wartime Fates of 6,000 Ships*, pp. 465, 470, 474, 475, 481, 571.

10   Being sunk in shallow water, the Germans were able to raise and put *Bärenfels* back into service.

11   Jordan, *The Worlds Merchant Fleets 1939, The Particulars and Wartime Fates of 6,000 Ships*, pp. 465, 477–478.

12   Rohwer, *Allied Submarine Attacks of World War Two, European Theatre of Operations 1939–1945*, pp. 49–50.

13   ADM 186/798, Battle Summaries, No. 17: Naval Operations of the Campaign in Norway, April–June 1940, p. 61.

14   This ship was eventually raised and put back into service.

15   Rohwer, *Allied Submarine Attacks of World War Two, European Theatre of Operations 1939–1945*, pp. 48–53.

16   Rohwer, *Axis Submarine Successes 1939–1945*, pp. 17–18.

17   The count of British divisions only includes those deployed to France and designated for combat operations. It does not include three Territorial Army divisions that were deployed in France to provide logistical and service support.

18   Sources differ on the exact number of forces available to the competing sides during Germany's assault against France and the Low Countries. However, it is generally acknowledged that the combined Allied nations maintained at least parity and in many cases a numerical superiority in most force categories. The strength figures presented here come from Basil Liddell Hart (Editor In Chief), *World War II, An Illustrated History* (London: Purnell Reference Books, 1977), p. 96.

19   Roskill, *The War at Sea 1939–1945, Volume 1*, p. 210.

20   Ibid., p. 216.

21   Daily Dunkirk evacuation totals come from Admiralty figures listing the number of personnel landed in England between midnight and midnight each day. See ADM 234/360, Battle Summaries, No. 41: Evacuation from Dunkirk (Operation *Dynamo*) 26 May–4 June 1940, Table 3(c).

22   Rohwer and Hummelchen, *Chronology of the War at Sea 1939–1945*, p. 21.

23   Rohwer and Hummelchen, *Chronology of the War at Sea 1939–1045*, p. 21 and Robert Jackson, *Dunkirk* (New York: Playboy Press Paperbacks, 1980), p. 213.

24   ADM 234/360, Battle Summaries, No. 41: Evacuation from Dunkirk (Operation *Dynamo*) 26 May–4 June 1940, Table 3(b).

25   Ibid., p. 209.

26   Roskill, *The War at Sea 1939–1945, Volume 1*, p. 603.

27   John Terraine, *The Right of the Line, The Royal Air Force in the European War 1939–1945* (Hodder and Stoughton, Sceptre edition, 1988), p. 157.

28   Roskill, *The War at Sea 1939–1945, Volume 1*, pp. 231–232.

29   Ibid., p. 239.

30   Hart, *World War II, An Illustrated History*, p. 164.

31   Roskill, *The War at Sea 1939–1945, Volume 1*, p. 239.

32   Rohwer and Hummelchen, *Chronology of the War at Sea 1939–1045*, p. 21.

33   Alistair Horne, *To Lose a Battle, France 1940* (Boston: Little Brown and Company, 1969), p. 584.

34   J. L. Moulton, *The Norway Campaign of 1940, A Study in Three Dimensions* (London: Eyre & Spottiswoode, 1966), p. 259.

35   Denis Richards, *Royal Air Force 1939–1945, Volume I: The Fight at Odds* (London: Her Majesty's Stationery Office, 1953), p. 149 and T. K. Derry, *The Campaign in Norway* (London: Her Majesty's Stationery Office, 1952), p. 231.

36   Winston S. Churchill, *Never Give In, the Best of Winston Churchill's Speeches* (as selected by his grandson, Winston S. Churchill) (New York: Hyperion, 2003), p. 218.

37   Ibid., p. 229.

Chapter 3: Standing Alone

1   Peter Fleming, *Operation Sea Lion* (New York: Ace Books, Inc., 1956), p. 191 and David French, *Raising Churchill's Army, The British Army and the War against Germany, 1919–1945* (Oxford: Oxford University Press, 2000), p. 186.

2   Hart, *World War II, An Illustrated History*, p. 164.

3   Basil Collier, *The Defence of the United Kingdom* (London: Her Majesty's Stationery Office, 1957), p. 124.

4   Fleming, *Operation Sea Lion*, pp. 191–192.

5   Ibid., p. 191.

6   Ibid., p. 190.

7   Barnett, *Engage the Enemy More Closely, the Royal Navy in the Second World War*, p. 183.

8   Roskill, *The War at Sea 1939–1945, Volume 1*, p. 249.

9   Ibid., pp. 593–597.

10   Ibid., p. 250.

11   Fleming, *Operation Sea Lion*, p. 243.

12   Ibid., p. 248.

13   Bekker, *Hitler's Naval War*, p. 175.

14   Various sources have minor disagreements as to the exact number of Luftwaffe aircraft available at the beginning of the battle. Most sources give figures in a range of 2,400 to 2,600 aircraft. The figures stated in this text come from the Air Historical Branch Narrative. See Terraine, *The Right of the Line, The Royal Air Force in the European War 1939–1945*, p. 181.

15   Terraine, *The Right of the Line, The Royal Air Force in the European War 1939–1945*, p. 174.

16   In fact, the Spitfire was marginally superior in overall performance to the Messerschmitt Bf 109E while the Hurricane was marginally inferior. However, these performance variations were generally not pronounced enough to be decisive. Success in combat often depended upon other factors such as pilot skill, height and position advantage and tactics.

17   Various sources disagree on the actual number of aerial combat losses sustained by both sides during the Battle of Britain. A number of factors including incomplete and/or contradictory records, varying methods used to categorise destroyed and damage aircraft (at what point is a

damaged aircraft considered a total loss) and distinctions made between combat and non-combat related wastage all contribute to these variances. Unless stated otherwise, the loss figures cited in this book regarding the battle of Britain come from Collier, *The Defence of the United Kingdom*, pp. 450–451, 456–460.

18 Terraine, *The Right of the Line, The Royal Air Force in the European War 1939–1945*, p. 191.
19 Fleming, *Operation Sea Lion*, p. 207.
20 Rohwer and Hummelchen, *Chronology of the War At Sea 1939–1945*, p. 28.
21 The actual figure for German air strength as of 10 August 1940 was 3,021 aircraft broken down into 1,370 bombers, 406 dive-bombers, 813 single-engine fighters, 319 twin-engine fighters and fighter-bombers and 113 long-range reconnaissance. See Collier, *The Defence of the United Kingdom*, p. 452.
22 Richard Hough and Denis Richards, *The Battle of Britain, The Greatest Air Battle of World War II* (London: W. W. Norton & Company, 1989), p. 248.
23 Ibid., pp. 249–250.
24 Fleming, *Operation Sea Lion*, p. 283.
25 Terraine, *The Right of the Line, The Royal Air Force in the European War 1939–1945*, pp. 219–220.
26 *T3* was later recovered and put back into service.
27 ADM 199/2447, German Ships: Losses and Damage in NW European Waters, 1939–1945.
28 The Central Statistical Office, *Statistical Digest of the War*, p. 184.
29 Roskill, *The War at Sea 1939–1945, Volume 1*, pp. 617–618.
30 This number includes a handful of British ships lost in the Mediterranean. See The Central Statistical Office, *Statistical Digest of the War*, p. 180.
31 According to Admiralty sources, the total number of British, Allied and neutral merchant ships sunk by submarines during the period in question amounted to 403 worth 2,078,066 tons. Italian submarines operating in the Atlantic, Mediterranean and Indian Ocean reportedly accounted for 33 of these worth 138,202 tons. Subtracting these Italian numbers from the total arrives at the figures attributable to German U-boats. While statistically insignificant, it is entirely possible that these figures possess minor inaccuracies given discrepancies in claims and various methods used to classify ships, means of attack and victory results. See Roskill, *The War at Sea 1939–1945, Volume I*, pp. 615–616 and Rohwer, *Axis Submarine Successes 1939–1945*.
32 Barnett, *Engage the Enemy More Closely, the Royal Navy in the Second World War*, p. 194.
33 ADM 234/579, Naval Staff History: Defeat of the Enemy Attack on Shipping, 1939–1945: A Study of Policy and Operations, Volume IB (Plans and Tables), Table 11.
34 ADM 234/578, Naval Staff History: Defeat of the Enemy Attack on Shipping, 1939–1945: A Study of Policy and Operations, Volume IA (Text and Appendices), pp. 31, 58, 59.
35 Roskill, *The War at Sea 1939–1945, Volume 1*, p. 349.
36 ADM 234/578, Naval Staff History: Defeat of the Enemy Attack on Shipping, 1939–1945: A Study of Policy and Operations, Volume IA (Text and Appendices), Appendix 6.
37 This does not include Italian submarine successes in the Mediterranean. See Rohwer, *Axis Submarine Successes 1939–1945*, pp. 25–44.
38 The covered period for these merchant raider successes is from April 1940 through February 1941. See Roskill, *The War at Sea 1939–1945, Volume 1*, pp. 615–616.
39 Roskill, *The War at Sea 1939–1945, Volume 1*, p. 616.
40 Ibid., pp. 615–616.
41 Ibid.
42 ADM 234/579, Naval Staff History: Defeat of the Enemy Attack on Shipping, 1939–1945: A Study of Policy and Operations, Volume IB (Plans and Tables), Tables 12(ii) and 12(iii).
43 Clay Blair, *Hitler's U-boat War, the Hunters, 1939–1942* (New York: Random House, 1996), pp. 743–744.

Chapter 4: Respite in the Atlantic

1   Winston Churchill, *The Second World War, Volume II: Their Finest Hour* (Boston: Houghton Mifflin Company, 1949), p. 598.
2   In addition to the previously mentioned accomplishments of Otto Kretschmer, Günther Prien was responsible for the destruction of 28 merchant ships worth 160,939 tons and the battleship *Royal Oak* while Joachim Schepke accounted for the destruction of 39 merchant ships worth 159,130 tons. These two officers ranked tenth and eleventh on the list of top scoring U-boat aces during World War II. See Bekker, *Hitler's Naval War*, p. 380.
3   Roskill, *The War at Sea 1939–1945, Volume 1*, p. 616.
4   ADM 234/579, Naval Staff History: Defeat of the Enemy Attack on Shipping, 1939–1945: A Study of Policy and Operations, Volume IB (Plans and Tables), Table 11.
5   Gannon, *Black May, The Epic Story of the Allies' Defeat of the German U-boats in May 1943*, p. xxi.
6   Roskill, *The War at Sea 1939–1945, Volume 1*, pp. 615–616 and The Central Statistical Office, *Statistical Digest of the War*, p. 180.
7   The Central Statistical Office, *Statistical Digest of the War*, pp. 177–179.
8   Roskill, *The War at Sea 1939–1945, Volume 1*, pp. 616, 618.
9   Ibid., p. 618.
10   Barnett, *Engage the Enemy More Closely, the Royal Navy in the Second World War*, p. 266.
11   The agent of *Gneisenau's* damage was a Beaufort torpedo–bomber from No. 22 Squadron RAF Coastal Command. This aircraft, commanded by Flying Officer Kenneth Campbell, attacked *Gneisenau* at masthead height within Brest's inner harbor on 6 April 1941. The resulting torpedo hit wrecked the battlecruiser's stern thus forcing it into dry dock for repairs. During the attack the Beaufort aircraft was shot down killing Campbell and his crew. The British government later awarded Campbell a posthumous Victoria Cross for this action.
12   The Fulmar was the Fleet Air Arm's newest carrier-borne fighter. It possessed a top speed of 280 miles per hour, a range of 800 miles and an armament of eight .303 machine guns.
13   The British cruiser *Dorsetshire* rescued 85 men from *Bismarck's* crew while the destroyer *Maori* accounted for another 25. After the British departed the area *U74* and a German weather ship picked up an additional five survivors. Included in the dead were Admiral Lütjens and Captain Ernst Lindemann, *Bismarck's* commanding officer.
14   Rohwer and Hummelchen, *Chronology of the War at Sea 1939–1945*, pp. 66, 73, 75.
15   Rohwer and Hummelchen, *Chronology of the War at Sea 1939–1945*, pp. 68, 72, 75 and Jordan, *The World's Merchant Fleets 1939, The Particulars and Wartime Fates of 6,000 ships*, pp. 33, 458.
16   Roskill, *The War at Sea 1939–1945, Volume 1*, p. 464.
17   ADM 234/579, Naval Staff History: Defeat of the Enemy Attack on Shipping, 1939–1945: A Study of Policy and Operations, Volume IB (Plans and Tables), Table 11.
18   ADM 234/578, Naval Staff History: Defeat of the Enemy Attack on Shipping, 1939–1945: A Study of Policy and Operations, Volume IA (Text and Appendices), p. 31.
19   Barnett, *Engage the Enemy More Closely, the Royal Navy in the Second World War*, p. 265.
20   Roskill, *The War at Sea 1939–1945, Volume 1*, p. 456.
21   Ibid., pp. 453–454.
22   David Westwood, *The U-boat War, The German Submarine Service and the Battle of the Atlantic, 1935–1945* (London: Conway Maritime Press, 2005), p. 97.
23   Terraine, *The Right of the Line, The Royal Air Force in the European War 1939–1945*, p. 245.
24   Roskill, *The War at Sea 1939–1945, Volume 1*, p. 459.
25   The Martlet was the British designation for the American-build Grumman F3F Wildcat single-seat fighter. Specifically designed for carrier-borne operations, the Martlet was armed with four or six .50 caliber machine guns and had a top speed of 331 miles per hour.

26 ADM 234/579, Naval Staff History: Defeat of the Enemy Attack on Shipping, 1939–1945: A Study of Policy and Operations, Volume IB (Plans and Tables), Tables 12(ii) and 12(iii).

27 Roskill, *The War at Sea 1939–1945, Volume 1*, p. 616.

28 Calculated from loss data found in Appendix R of the official British history. See Roskill, *The War at Sea 1939–1945, Volume 1*, p. 616.

29 Ibid., p. 471.

30 ADM 234/369, Battle Summaries, No. 22: Arctic Convoys 1941–1945, Appendix A, Section I and II.

31 Blair, *Hitler's U-boat War, the Hunters, 1939–1942*, p. 356.

32 ADM 199/2447, German Ships: Losses and Damage in NW European Waters, 1939–1945.

33 Roskill, *The War at Sea 1939–1945, Volume 1*, p. 475.

34 This figure does not include merchant losses sustained in the Pacific during December. See Roskill, *The War at Sea 1939–1945, Volume 1*, p. 618.

35 Roskill, *The War at Sea 1939–1945, Volume 1*, p. 618 and The Central Statistical Office, *Statistical Digest of the War*, p. 180.

36 The Central Statistical Office, *Statistical Digest of the War*, p. 177.

37 Ibid., p. 184.

38 The Tripartite Pact was a defensive agreement signed on 27 September 1940 between Germany, Italy and Japan that obligated its signatories to provide political, economic and military support to each other in the event of an attack by a power not already involved in the European war or Sino-Japanese conflict.

39 Winston S. Churchill, *The Second World War, Volume III: The Grand Alliance* (Boston: Houghton Mifflin Company, 1950), p. 607.

Chapter 5: Offensive Operations

1 ADM 199/2447, German Ships: Losses and Damage in NW European Waters, 1939–1945.

2 Hart, *World War II, An Illustrated History*, p. 763.

3 Goulter, *A Forgotten Offensive, Royal Air Force Coastal Command's Anti-Shipping Campaign, 1940–1945*, p. 277.

4 C. B. A. Behrens, *Merchant Shipping and the Demands of War* (London: Her Majesty's Stationery Office and Longmans, Green and Co., 1955), p. 112.

5 This includes foreign merchant shipping seized by the Germans and allocated for trade, but does not include neutral tonnage on charter. See AIR 40/2588, British Bombing Survey Unit: Sea Communications Panel; Report on Air Action against German Merchant Shipping, Appendix E.

6 ADM 199/2447, German Ships: Losses and Damage in NW European Waters, 1939–1945.

7 Dispatch on Raid on Military and Economic Objectives in the Vicinity of Vaagso Island, submitted to the Lords Commissioners of the Admiralty on 7 January 1942 by Admiral Sir John C. Tovey, K.C.B., D.S.O., Commander-in-Chief, Home fleet as appearing in the *London Gazette* of Friday 2 July 1948.

8 Hart, *World War II, An Illustrated History*, p. 767.

9 ADM 234/362, Battle Summaries, No. 12: Attack on St. Nazaire, 28 March 1942, p. 22 and C. E. Lucas Phillips, *The Greatest Raid of All* (London: William Heinemann Ltd., 1958), p. 266.

10 ADM 234/362, Battle Summaries, No. 12: Attack on St. Nazaire, 28 March 1942, p. 27, Appendix D and Phillips, *The Greatest Raid of All*, pp. 256, 266.

11 The recipients of the Victoria Cross were Captain Robert Ryder, RN; Lieutenant-Commander Stephen Beattie, RN; Able Seaman William Savage, RN; Sergeant Thomas Durrant, Royal Engineers; and Lieutenant Colonel Augustus Newman, No 2 Commando.

12 ADM 199/2447, German Ships: Losses and Damage in NW European Waters, 1939–1945 and Jordan, *The World's Merchant Fleets 1939, The Particulars and Wartime Fates of 6,000 ships*, pp. 453–480, 526, 530–539, 551–566, 570.

13 ADM 234/218, British Minelaying Campaign, September 1939–May 1945, p. 19.

14 Roskill, *The War at Sea 1939–1945, Volume 1*, pp. 125, 336, 511.

15 This number includes seven barges and two fishing vessels of unknown, but presumably limited tonnage. See ADM 199/2447, German Ships: Losses and Damage in NW European Waters, 1939–1945 and AIR 41/79, RAF in the Maritime War, Volume VIII: Statistics.

16 ADM 199/2447, German Ships: Losses and Damage in NW European Waters, 1939–1945 and AIR 41/79, RAF in the Maritime War, Volume VIII: Statistics. Included in this number is *Sperrbrecher XII*, which the British initially recorded as being sunk by a submarine, but was in fact sunk by a mine. Likewise, a number of tonnage differences are taken from other sources.

17 Ibid.

18 Roskill, *The War at Sea 1939–1945, Volume 1*, p. 512. This includes a number of tonnage differences taken from other sources.

19 Ibid., pp. 334, 512.

20 Ibid., pp. 339, 507.

21 ADM 199/2447, German Ships: Losses and Damage in NW European Waters, 1939–1945 and AIR 41/79, RAF in the Maritime War, Volume VIII: Statistics. This includes some tonnage differences that are taken from other sources.

22 Roskill, *The War at Sea 1939–1945, Volume 1*, p. 512.

23 ADM 199/2447, German Ships: Losses and Damage in NW European Waters, 1939–1945 and Rohwer, *Allied Submarine Attacks of World War Two, European Theatre of Operations 1939–1945*, pp. 16–20, 53–60.

24 Initial British assessments attributed the vessels as being destroyed by British submarines, but other sources indicate different outcomes. The vessels in question are the 8,205-ton Norwegian *Drafn* which was attributed to *Sturgeon*, but may have survived; the 682-ton Norwegian *Vesteraalen* which was either sunk by *Tigris* or the Soviet submarine *SC-402*; the 1,930-ton German *Flottbek* which was either sunk by *Trident* or a Soviet mine; and the 1,774-ton Norwegian *Bessheim* which was either sunk by *Seawolf* or a Soviet mine.

25 Included in this number was the 6,322-ton merchant ship *Birkenfels*, which the British originally recorded as being sunk by a submarine, but was actually sunk by British motor torpedo boats. Also included are five minor vessels of unknown, but presumably, limited tonnage sunk during naval bombardments in September 1940. See ADM 199/2447, German Ships: Losses and Damage in NW European Waters, 1939–1945 and Rohwer, *Allied Submarine Attacks of World War Two, European Theatre of Operations 1939–1945*, p. 57.

26 ADM 199/2447, German Ships: Losses and Damage in NW European Waters, 1939–1945; AIR 41/79, RAF in the Maritime War, Volume VIII: Statistics and Jordan, *The World's Merchant Fleets 1939, The Particulars and Wartime Fates of 6,000 ships*, pp. 453–480, 526, 530–539, 551–566, 570.

27 AIR 40/2588, British Bombing Survey Unit: Sea Communications Panel; Report on Air Action against German Merchant Shipping, Appendix E.

28 Goulter, *A Forgotten Offensive, Royal Air Force Coastal Command's Anti-Shipping Campaign*, 1940–1945, p. 284.

29 All mine successes during this period are taken from ADM 199/2447, German Ships: Losses and Damage in NW European Waters, 1939–1945 and AIR 41/79, RAF in the Maritime War, Volume VIII: Statistics. However, there are a few tonnage differences that are taken from other sources.

30 S. W. Roskill, *The War at Sea 1939–1945, Volume II: The Period of Balance* (London: Her Majesty's Stationery Office, 1956), p. 395.

31 RAF aircraft sank or damaged the vast majority of these vessels while American aircraft accounted for the remainder. See ADM 199/2447, German Ships: Losses and Damage in NW European Waters, 1939–1945. Once again, a few tonnage differences are taken from other sources.

32 Included in this total are two outbound blockade-runners worth 15,143 tons covered later in the chapter and selected German warships sunk in the Arctic and covered in Chapters 6 and 7. Likewise, this includes three fishing vessels of unknown, but presumably limited tonnage. See ADM 199/2447, German Ships: Losses and Damage in NW European Waters, 1939–1945 and Rohwer, *Allied Submarine Attacks of World War Two, European Theatre of Operations 1939–1945*, pp. 61–63. Once again, a few tonnage differences are taken from other sources.

33 Roskill, *The War at Sea 1939–1945, Volume II*, p. 395 and S. W. Roskill, *The War at Sea 1939–1945, Volume III, Part II: The Offensive, 1st June 1944–14th August 1945* (London: Her Majesty's Stationery Office, 1961), p. 443.

34 AIR 41/79, RAF in the Maritime War, Volume VIII: Statistics.

35 Goulter, *A Forgotten Offensive, Royal Air Force Coastal Command's Anti–Shipping Campaign, 1940–1945*, p. 286.

36 AIR 40/2588, British Bombing Survey Unit: Sea Communications Panel; Report on Air Action against German Merchant Shipping, Appendix E.

37 Ibid., Appendix B.

38 Imperial War Museum, Speer Collection, Interrogation Reports, 3063/49. File 4, Report 35, Supplement II, 21 November 1945, p. 3.

39 AIR 41/48, The RAF in the Maritime War, Volume IV: The Atlantic and Home Waters; The Offensive Phase, February 1943–May 1944, Appendix XVI. Tonnage data for lost ships taken from Jordan, *The World's Merchant Fleets 1939, The Particulars and Wartime Fates of 6,000 ships*, and Rohwer and Hummelchen, *Chronology of the War at Sea 1939–1945*.

40 Ibid.

41 Compiled from multiple sources including Jordan, *The World's Merchant Fleets 1939, The Particulars and Wartime Fates of 6,000 ships*, pp. 453–480, 526, 530–539, 551–566, 570; Rohwer and Hummelchen, *Chronology of the War at Sea 1939–1945*, pp. 51, 57, 81; and ADM 199/1277, Madagascar.

42 ADM 234/355, Battle Summaries, No. 33: Raid on Dieppe: Naval Operations, 19 August 1942, Appendix C.

43 Roskill, *The War at Sea 1939–1945, Volume II*, p. 243 and Rohwer and Hummelchen, *Chronology of the War at Sea 1939–1945*, p. 158.

44 ADM 234/355, Battle Summaries, No. 33: Raid on Dieppe: Naval Operations, 19 August 1942, Appendix C.

Chapter 6: The Battle Intensifies

1 Karl Dönitz, *Memoirs: Ten Years and Twenty Days*, (London: Weidenfeld and Nicolson, 1959), p. 197 and Homer H. Hickam, Jr., *Torpedo Junction, U-boat War off America's East Coast, 1942* (New York: Dell Publishing, 1991), pp. 3–4.

2 Blair, *Hitler's U-boat War, the Hunters, 1939–1942*, p. 695.

3 Ibid.

4 *U82* and *U587* were both sunk during their return journeys to Europe after completing operations off North America while *U656* and *U503* were sunk in American waters.

5 Calculated from various tables in Blair, *Hitler's U-boat War, the Hunters, 1939–1942*, pp. 764–768, 771.

6 John Dean Potter, *Breakout* (London: Bantam Books, 1982), p. 200 and ADM 199/2447, German Ships: Losses and Damage in NW European Waters, 1939–1945.

7   Vincent P. O'Hara, *The German Fleet at War, 1939–1945* (Annapolis: Naval Institute Press, 2004), pp. 115–118.

8   Blair, *Hitler's U-boat War, the Hunters, 1939–1942*, p. 695.

9   ADM 234/579, Naval Staff History: Defeat of the Enemy Attack on Shipping, 1939–1945: A Study of Policy and Operations, Volume IB (Plans and Tables), Table 12(iv).

10 Blair, *Hitler's U-boat War, the Hunters, 1939–1942*, p. 695.

11 Ibid.

12 Roskill, *The War at Sea 1939–1945, Volume II*, p. 486.

13 The Central Statistical Office, *Statistical Digest of the War*, p. 180.

14 V. E. Tarrant, *The U-boat Offensive, 1914–1945* (Annapolis, Naval Institute Press, 1989), pp. 149–150. Please note that comparable Admiralty figures for each month as listed by S. W. Roskill are moderately different. This is true for a number of reasons including the fact that the Admiralty figures include all Axis submarine successes (including Japanese) whereas the Tarrant figures only include German and Italian submarine successes, the Admiralty figures do not include victims of submarine-laid mines whereas the Tarrant figures do, and the normal variations invariably found when compiling such comprehensive tallies due to claim and tonnage inconsistencies and gaps in the available information. While there are likely errors in both lists, those errors are probably minor.

15 Ellis, *World War II, A Statistical Survey, the Essential Facts and Figures for all the Combatants*, p. 249.

16 Ibid., p. 280.

17 Clay Blair, *Hitler's U-boat War, the Hunted, 1942–1945* (New York: Random House, 1998), p. 9. Please note that deadweight tonnage refers to the amount of cargo, stores and bunker fuel that a vessel can transport. It should not be confused with gross registered tonnage, which expresses the internal volume of the vessel itself. Unless indicated otherwise, all merchant tonnage figures listed in this book reflect gross registered tons.

18 Roskill, *The War at Sea 1939–1945, Volume II*, p. 92.

19 Ibid.

20 Taken from a letter sent to Admiral Ernest J. King describing the difficulties confronting the Royal Navy in the Arctic. See ADM 205/19, First Sea Lords Papers.

21 Rohwer and Hummelchen, *Chronology of the War at Sea 1939–1945*, p. 141.

22 Ibid., p. 148.

23 Some of the prior Arctic convoys did utilise CAM ships, but these vessels only offered token coverage given the single use limitation of their embarked fighters.

24 F. H. Hinsley, *British Intelligence in the Second World War, Its Influence on Strategy and Operations, Volume Two* (New York: Cambridge University Press, 1981), p. 225.

25 *U405, U408* and *U589* all engaged this side of the convoy at roughly the same time thus making it impossible to definitively determine which U-boats were responsible for the destruction of these merchant ships.

26 Roskill, *The War at Sea 1939–1945, Volume II*, p. 475.

27 Westwood, *The U-boat War, The German Submarine Service and the Battle of the Atlantic, 1935–1945*, p. 165.

28 Ibid., p. 166.

29 ADM 234/579, Naval Staff History: Defeat of the Enemy Attack on Shipping, 1939–1945: A Study of Policy and Operations, Volume IB (Plans and Tables), Tables 12(vi) and 12(vii).

30 Westwood, *The U-boat War, The German Submarine Service and the Battle of the Atlantic, 1935–1945*, p. 166

31 Tarrant, *The U-boat Offensive, 1914–1945*, p. 150 and Westwood, *The U-boat War, The German Submarine Service and the Battle of the Atlantic, 1935–1945*, p. 177.

32 Tarrant, *The U-boat Offensive, 1914–1945*, p. 150.

33 In their efforts to secure classified materials from *U559*, Lieutenant Anthony Fusson and Able Seaman Colin Grazier both lost their lives when the U-boat abruptly sank with them still inside. Both men posthumously received the George Cross for their sacrifice and contribution to the war effort.

34 Tarrant, *The U-boat Offensive, 1914–1945*, p. 150. As already pointed out in Endnote 14, there are variations between the Tarrant and Admiralty figures. While most of these variations are reasonably explainable, the deviation for November is more problematic. In particular, the Admiralty lists the total British, Allied and neutral merchant shipping losses for November at 134 ships worth 807,754 tons of which 119 ships worth 729,160 tons were lost to submarine attacks. It is possible that one or both lists have errors contributing to this seeming discrepancy.

35 Ibid.

36 Roskill, *The War at Sea 1939–1945, Volume II*, p. 485.

37 The Central Statistical Office, *Statistical Digest of the War*, p. 180.

38 Roskill, *The War at Sea 1939–1945, Volume II*, p. 485 and The Central Statistical Office, *Statistical Digest of the War*, p. 180.

39 The American total is taken from Blair, *Hitler's U-boat War, the Hunted, 1942–1945*, p. 161 and the British total is taken from The Central Statistical Office, *Statistical Digest of the War*, p. 135.

40 The Central Statistical Office, *Statistical Digest of the War*, p. 174.

41 This exchange rate is based upon U-boat losses verses merchant tonnage sunk by European-based Axis submarines. It does not take into account Italian submarine losses.

42 ADM 234/579, Naval Staff History: Defeat of the Enemy Attack on Shipping, 1939–1945: A Study of Policy and Operations, Volume IB (Plans and Tables), Table 10.

43 Ibid., Table 12(ii).

44 The Central Statistical Office, *Statistical Digest of the War*, p. 184.

45 Behrens, *Merchant Shipping and the Demands of War*, p. 363.

Chapter 7: Turning Point

1 ADM 234/369, Battle Summaries, No. 22: Arctic Convoys 1941–1945, Appendix A, Section III and IV.

2 Ibid., Appendix A, Sections II and IV.

3 Bernard Edwards, *Salvo! Classic Naval Gun Actions* (London: Arms & Armour Press, 1995), p. 165.

4 By this time *Oribi* had become separated from the convoy and was unable to regain contact due to a gyro compass failure. The British destroyer proceeded independently arriving in the Kola inlet on the 31st.

5 *Achates* weighed in at 1,350 tons and had a main armament of four 4.7-inch guns while *Bramble* weighed in at 815 tons and was armed with two 4-inch guns. By comparison, *Friedrich Echoldt* weighed in at 2,270 tons and had a main armament of five 5-inch guns. Thus, in terms of total tonnage and firepower, both sides suffered comparable losses.

6 Niklas Zetterling, *Normandy 1944, German Military Organization, Combat Power and Organizational Effectiveness* (Winnipeg: J.J. Fedorowicz Publishing, Inc., 2000), p. 91.

7 Total Axis casualties for the duration of the African campaign numbered some 950,000 men. See Thomas Parrish (Editor), *The Simon and Schuster Encyclopedia of World War II* (New York: Simon and Schuster, 1978), p. 446 and I.S.O. Playfair, *The Mediterranean and Middle East, Volume IV: The Destruction of Axis Forces in Africa* (London: Her Majesty's Stationery Office, 1966), p. 460.

8 Roskill, *The War at Sea 1939–1945, Volume II*, p. 475.

9   Westwood, *The U-boat War, The German Submarine Service and the Battle of the Atlantic, 1935–1945*, p. 187.

10 Roskill, *The War at Sea 1939–1945, Volume II*, p. 475.

11 ADM 234/579, Naval Staff History: Defeat of the Enemy Attack on Shipping, 1939–1945: A Study of Policy and Operations, Volume IB (Plans and Tables), Tables 10 and 12(v).

12 Westwood, *The U-boat War, The German Submarine Service and the Battle of the Atlantic, 1935–1945*, p. 187.

13 Tarrant, *The U-boat Offensive, 1914–1945*, pp. 150–151.

14 Ibid.

15 Ibid.

16 ADM 234/579, Naval Staff History: Defeat of the Enemy Attack on Shipping, 1939–1945: A Study of Policy and Operations, Volume IB (Plans and Tables), Table 11.

17 ADM 234/578, Naval Staff History: Defeat of the Enemy Attack on Shipping, 1939–1945: A Study of Policy and Operations, Volume IA (Text and Appendices), pp. 74, 95.

18 Marc Milner, *Battle of the Atlantic* (Gloucestershire: Tempus, 2005), p. 157.

19 Tarrant, *The U-boat Offensive, 1914–1945*, pp. 150–151.

20 The British originally assessed *U635* as having been sunk by the British frigate *Tay*, but this was later revised to credit a Liberator from No.120 Squadron with this success. Likewise, the British originally ascribed *U332*'s loss to a RAAF Sunderland on 2 May, but subsequent investigation amended the cause of this loss to a Liberator from No.224 Squadron on 29 April. Because of this latter reassessment, many early tallies of U-boat losses in April and May 1943 are in error.

21 Some sources indicate that a Hudson from No.500 Squadron sank *U602* on 23 April, but this attack was actually carried out on *U453*. Therefore, the cause and date of *U602*'s demise remains a mystery.

22 Roskill, *The War at Sea 1939–1945, Volume II*, p. 485.

23 Ibid., p. 486.

24 Blair, *Hitler's U-boat War, the Hunted, 1942–1945*, p. 168.

25 Gannon, *Black May, The Epic Story of the Allies' Defeat of the German U-boats in May 1943*, p. xxii.

26 Roskill, *The War at Sea 1939–1945, Volume II*, p. 475.

27 Blair, *Hitler's U-boat War, the Hunted, 1942–1945*, p. 166.

28 Ibid., pp. 740–744, 778–779.

29 Initially the Admiralty identified *U630* as the U-boat in question, but succeeding investigation indicates that the likely victim of this attack was *U209*. It now appears that *U209* survived the attack, although in a severely damaged state, and was subsequently lost on or about 7 May while trying to rendezvous with *U119*. Although the precise reason for this loss is unknown, it is generally believed that the damage sustained on 4 May was a primary factor in the submarine's demise.

30 Tarrant, *The U-boat Offensive, 1914–1945*, pp. 150–151.

31 Blair, *Hitler's U-boat War, the Hunted, 1942–1945*, pp. 809–810.

32 Richard Worth, *Fleets of World War II* (Cambridge: Da Capo Press, 2001), p. 126.

33 Ibid., p. 323.

34 Ibid., pp. 126–127.

35 Of the U-boats sunk in May, FIDO homing torpedoes sank or participated in the destruction of *U456*, *U657* and *U467* while aerial rockets accounted for *U752* and *U755*.

36 All merchant losses due to European-based Axis submarines in June, July and August come from Tarrant, *The U-boat Offensive, 1914–1945*, pp. 150–151.

37 This number includes non–operational attack boats, but does not include converted Type VII flak boats, XB minelayers, XIV U–tankers or IXD1 and IXD2 U–cruisers. See Blair, *Hitler's U-boat War, the Hunted, 1942–1945*, p. 418.

Chapter 8: Retaining the Initiative

1   Tarrant, *The U-boat Offensive, 1914–1945*, pp. 150–151.

2   Ibid.

3   For total Allied and neutral merchant losses see Roskill, *The War at Sea 1939–1945, Volume II: The Period of Balance* (London: Her Majesty's Stationery Office, 1956), p. 485 and S. W. Roskill, *The War at Sea 1939–1945, Volume III, Part I: The Offensive, 1st June 1943–31st May 1944* (London: Her Majesty's Stationery Office, 1960), p. 388. For losses due strictly to German and Italian submarine actions see Tarrant, *The U-boat Offensive, 1914–1945*, pp. 150–151.

4   The American total is taken from Blair, *Hitler's U-boat War, the Hunted, 1942–1945*, p. 708 and the British total is taken from The Central Statistical Office, *Statistical Digest of the War*, p. 135.

5   ADM 234/579, Naval Staff History: Defeat of the Enemy Attack on Shipping, 1939–1945: A Study of Policy and Operations, Volume IB (Plans and Tables), Table 10.

6   Ibid., Table 12(ii).

7   The Central Statistical Office, *Statistical Digest of the War*, p. 184.

8   Roskill, *The War at Sea 1939–1945, Volume III, Part I*, p. 364.

9   V. E. Tarrant, *The Last Year of the Kriegsmarine, May 1944–May 1945*, (Annapolis: Naval Institute Press, 1994), p. 27.

10   Blair, *Hitler's U-boat War, the Hunted, 1942–1945*, p. 482.

11   Tarrant, *The U-boat Offensive, 1914–1945*, pp. 150–151.

12   Blair, *Hitler's U-boat War, the Hunted, 1942–1945*, p. 481.

13   Of the remaining U-boats sunk in the Atlantic during this period, American forces sank *U544*, *U271*, *U177*, *U709*, *U603*, *U801*, *U1059*, *U856*, *U515*, *U68*, *U550*, *U986*, *U488*, *U66* and *U549* and shared in the destruction of *U575* while unknown causes accounted for *U377*, *U972* and *U851*. In addition to this, 18 U-boats were sunk in the Mediterranean, nine were sunk in the Baltic and three were sunk in the Indian Ocean.

14   Many of the men involved in the operation subsequently received awards including Lieutenant D. Cameron and Lieutenant B. G. Place (the commanders of *X6* and *X7*) who both received the Victoria Cross.

15   ADM 234/369, Battle Summaries, No. 22: Arctic Convoys 1941–1945, Appendix A, Sections I and II.

16   Ibid.

17   Roskill, *The War at Sea 1939–1945, Volume II*, p. 395 and Roskill, *The War at Sea 1939–1945, Volume III, Part I*, pp. 96, 289.

18   Roskill, *The War at Sea 1939–1945, Volume III, Part I*, p. 289.

19   This number includes four fishing vessels of unknown, but presumably limited tonnage. See ADM 199/2447, German Ships: Losses and Damage in NW European Waters, 1939–1945 and AIR 41/79, RAF in the Maritime War, Volume VIII: Statistics.

20   ADM 234/218, British Minelaying Campaign, September 1939–May 1945, p. 19.

21   ADM 199/2447, German Ships: Losses and Damage in NW European Waters, 1939–1945 and AIR 41/79, RAF in the Maritime War, Volume VIII: Statistics. Subtracted from these sources is *M372*, which the British initially recorded as being sunk by a mine, but was later determined to have been sunk by Soviet aircraft. Likewise, a number of tonnage differences are taken from other sources.

22   Roskill, *The War at Sea 1939–1945, Volume II*, p. 395 and Roskill, *The War at Sea 1939–1945, Volume III, Part I*, pp. 94, 288.

23   ADM 199/2447, German Ships: Losses and Damage in NW European Waters, 1939–1945. This includes a handful of tonnage differences taken from other sources relating specifically to the warship losses.

24 Ibid.

25 AIR 41/48, The RAF in the Maritime War, Volume IV: The Atlantic and Home Waters; The Offensive Phase, February 1943–May 1944, pp. 265–266.

26 ADM 199/2447, German Ships: Losses and Damage in NW European Waters, 1939–1945.

27 United States Strategic Bombing Survey, European Report 3, The Effects of Strategic Bombing on the German War Economy, pp. 11, 107.

28 Richard Overy, Why the Allies Won (London: W. W. Norton & Company Ltd., 1995), p. 131.

29 Max Hastings, Bomber Command (New York: Dial Press/James Wade, 1979), p. 241.

30 Richard Overy, The Bombers and the Bombed, Allied Air War over Europe, 1940–1945 (New York: Penguin Group, 2013), p. 228.

31 Overy, Why the Allies Won, pp. 129, 131.

32 All shipping losses due to Allied bombing come from ADM 199/2447, German Ships: Losses and Damage in NW European Waters, 1939–1945 with additions from other sources. The merchant losses sunk include 12 minor vessels of unknown, but presumably limited tonnage.

33 British Bombing Survey Unit, The Effects of Strategic Bombing on the Production of German U-boats, Table 9, p. 24.

34 ADM 199/2447, German Ships: Losses and Damage in NW European Waters, 1939–1945 and Rohwer, Allied Submarine Attacks of World War Two, European Theatre of Operations 1939–1945, pp. 63–70.

35 ADM 199/2447, German Ships: Losses and Damage in NW European Waters, 1939–1945. This includes minor tonnage differences taken from other sources.

36 Ibid. with minor tonnage differences from other sources.

37 The term principal warship refers to major combat vessels ranging from battleships to large, purpose-built minesweepers. A more complete breakdown of the 12 warship classes comprising this designation is found in Chapter 11.

38 ADM 199/2447, German Ships: Losses and Damage in NW European Waters, 1939–1945.

39 Ibid. with additions from other sources. Included in this number are 14 minor vessels of unknown, but presumably limited tonnage.

40 AIR 40/2588, British Bombing Survey Unit: Sea Communications Panel; Report on Air Action against German Merchant Shipping, Appendix E.

41 Ibid.

42 Ibid., Appendix B.

43 Ibid., part III, p. 4.

44 AIR 41/48, The RAF in the Maritime War, Volume IV: The Atlantic and Home Waters; The Offensive Phase, February 1943 – May 1944, Appendix XVI.

45 Imperial War Museum, Speer Collection, Interrogation Reports, 3063/49. File 4, Report 35, Supplement II, 21 November 1945, pp. 3–4.

46 Goulter, A Forgotten Offensive, Royal Air Force Coastal Command's Anti–Shipping Campaign, 1940–1945, p. 314.

47 AIR 40/2588, British Bombing Survey Unit: Sea Communications Panel; Report on Air Action against German Merchant Shipping, part V, p. 3.

48 AIR 41/48, The RAF in the Maritime War, Volume IV: The Atlantic and Home Waters; The Offensive Phase, February 1943–May 1944, p. 445.

49 Ibid., p. 452.

50 United States Strategic Bombing Survey, European Report 3, The Effects of Strategic Bombing on the German War Economy, p. 284.

51 ADM 199/2447, German Ships: Losses and Damage in NW European Waters, 1939–1945 with additions and some tonnage differences taken from other sources.

Chapter 9: Operation *Neptune* and the Battle for Northwest Europe

1   Although Canadian led and predominately staffed, a sizable portion of the Canadian First Army's combat strength came from British sources. In fact, there would be times when there were more British soldiers in the Canadian First Army than Canadians.

2   L. F. Ellis, *Victory in the West, Volume I: The Battle of Normandy* (London: Her Majesty's Stationery Office, 1962), p. 28.

3   Robert W. Coakley and Richard M. Leighton, *The United States Army in World War II, The War Department, Global Logistics and Strategy, Volume II: 1943–1945* (Washington: Office of the Chief of Military History, United States Army, 1968), pp. 369–370.

4   Ellis, *Victory in the West, Volume I*, p. 29.

5   Depending upon the source, there is minor disagreement on the total number of ships assigned to the invasion. The official British history of the campaign lists a total of 6,939 ships while a related Admiralty battle summary puts this figure at 7,016. This disagreement centres overwhelmingly upon the number of ancillary and merchant ships employed since the force levels for combatant warships and landing/assault vessels are almost identical. See Ellis, *Victory in the West, Volume I*, p. 507 and ADM 234/366, Battle Summaries, No. 39, Volume I: Landings in Normandy (Operation *Neptune*) June 1944, p. 38.

6   Ellis, *Victory in the West, Volume I*, pp. 508–509.

7   For a general listing of the British and Allied ships assigned to Operation *Neptune* see ADM 234/367, Battle Summaries, No. 39, Volume II: Landings in Normandy (Operation *Neptune*) June 1944: Appendices, Appendixes A(1) and C.

8   Ibid., Appendixes A2 and B2.

9   Ellis, *Victory in the West, Volume I*, p. 510 and ADM 234/366, Battle Summaries, No. 39, Volume I: Landings in Normandy (Operation *Neptune*) June 1944, p. 38.

10   Ellis, *Victory in the West, Volume I*, pp. 501–502, 508–509.

11   Ibid., pp. 504–506, 508.

12   Ibid., p. 80.

13   Ibid., pp. 89–90.

14   Roskill, *The War at Sea 1939–1945, Volume III, Part II*, pp. 27–28.

15   Ibid., p. 29.

16   Ellis, *Victory in the West, Volume I*, pp. 72–73.

17   Included in No 19 Group's order of battle were four FAA squadrons and four attached USN squadrons.

18   Roskill, *The War at Sea 1939–1945, Volume III, Part II*, p. 16.

19   Matthew Cooper, *The German Air Force 1933–1945, An Anatomy of Failure* (London: Jane's Publishing Company Limited, 1981), p. 333.

20   Ellis, *Victory in the West, Volume I*, p. 567.

21   Ibid., p. 117.

22   Hilary St. George Saunders, *Royal Air Force 1939–1945, Volume III: The Fight is Won* (London: Her Majesty's Stationery Office, 1954), p. 89.

23   Overy, *The Bombers and the Bombed, Allied Air War over Europe, 1940–1945*, p. 393.

24   Terraine, *The Right of the Line, The Royal Air Force in the European War 1939–1945*, p. 632.

25   Ellis, *Victory in the West, Volume I*, p. 217.

26   Ibid., p. 194.

27   Ibid., p. 223.

28   Ibid., pp. 222–223.

29   ADM 234/366, Battle Summaries, No. 39, Volume I: Landings in Normandy (Operation *Neptune*) June 1944, p. 107.

30 Ellis, *Victory in the West, Volume I*, p 212 and ADM 199/2447, German Ships: Losses and Damage in NW European Waters, 1939–1945.

31 Ellis, *Victory in the West, Volume I*, p. 245.

32 The vessels *PA1*, *PA2* and *PA3* were captured French versions of the British Flower-class corvette. In 1939 France ordered 18 'Flowers' of which six were to be built at the Chantiers de la Loire shipyard in St. Nazaire. When Germany overran France in 1940 they took possession of four of these incomplete vessels. In the years that followed the Germans completed *PA1*, *PA2* and *PA3* with some modifications and assigned them to the 15th Patrol Boat Flotilla in Le Havre where they served as convoy escorts. These vessels weighed in at 930 tons and were armed with one 4.1-inch gun, heavy anti-aircraft armament and two depth charge throwers.

33 ADM 199/2447, German Ships: Losses and Damage in NW European Waters, 1939–1945.

34 The first U-boat, *U955*, was not actually part of the anti-invasion effort, but was rather returning from an Atlantic patrol when it was sunk by a British Sunderland aircraft in the Bay of Biscay on 7 June.

35 This takes into account the two Biscay-based snorkel boats that were lost thus giving a net gain of four.

36 These loss totals exclude landing craft and other miscellaneous small craft. See Ellis, *Victory in the West, Volume I*, p 295.

37 Ibid., p. 274.

38 Roskill, *The War at Sea 1939–1945, Volume III, Part II*, p. 66.

39 ADM 234/367, Battle Summaries, No. 39, Volume II: Landings in Normandy (Operation *Neptune*) June 1944: Appendices, Appendix H(2).

40 Ibid., Appendix H(3).

41 Zetterling, *Normandy 1944, German Military Organization, Combat Power and Organizational Effectiveness*, pp. 396–398.

42 Ronald Lewin, *Montgomery as Military Commander* (London: B. T. Batsford Limited, 1971), p. 207.

43 Robin Neillands, *The Battle of Normandy 1944* (London: Cassell, 2002), p. 175.

44 SHAEF G1 Document dated 8 March 1945 Showing Prisoners of War Captured by Month. See WO 299/7/1, Enemy Prisoners of War: Statistical Reports and Information.

45 Roskill, *The War at Sea 1939–1945, Volume III, Part II*, p. 66.

46 Ellis, *Victory in the West, Volume I*, p. 480.

47 Roskill, *The War at Sea 1939–1945, Volume III, Part II*, p. 70.

48 ADM 234/366, Battle Summaries, No. 39, Volume I: Landings in Normandy (Operation *Neptune*) June 1944, p. 141.

49 ADM 234/363, Battle Summaries, No. 49: Campaign in North-West Europe June 1944–May 1945, p. 12.

50 Ellis, *Victory in the West, Volume I*, p. 478.

51 Major British and British-affiliated formations that saw service during the Normandy Campaign (6 June 1944–31 August 1944) include:

> Armies: British Second and Canadian First.
>
> Corps: British I, VIII, XII and XXX and Canadian II.
>
> Divisions: British 7th, 11th, 79th and Guards Armoured; 6th Airborne; 3rd, 15th, 43rd, 49th, 50th, 51st, 53rd and 59th Infantry; Canadian 4th Armuored, 2nd and 3rd Infantry; Polish 1st Armoured.
>
> Independent Brigades: British 4th, 8th, 27th and 33rd Armoured; 31st, 34th and 6th Tank; 56th Infantry; 1st and 4th Special Service (Commandos); Canadian 2nd Armoured; 1st Belgian Infantry and Royal Netherlands Motorized Infantry.

52 This estimate only includes personnel from the army, Waffen-SS and Luftwaffe units earmarked for ground fighting. It does not include personnel associated with naval units, Luftwaffe air and anti-aircraft units and their support organisations. See Zetterling, *Normandy 1944, German Military Organization, Combat Power and Organizational Effectiveness*, p. 34.

53 Ellis, *Victory in the West, Volume I*, p. 306.

54 Roskill, *The War at Sea 1939–1945, Volume III, Part II*, p. 135.

55 The breakdown of competing forces on the various fronts as of midnight on 24 July 1944 is as follows:

> British Second Army:
> British 7th, 11th and Guards Armoured; 6th Airborne; 3rd, 15th, 43rd, 49th, 50th, 51st, 53rd and 59th Infantry Divisions; Canadian 2nd and 3rd Infantry Divisions.
> German Divisions Confronting the British Second Army:
> 2nd, 21st and 116th Panzer; 1st, 9th, 10th and 12th SS Panzer; 271st, 272nd, 276th, 277th, 326th and 346th Infantry Divisions.
> American First Army:
> 2nd, 3rd, 4th and 6th Armoured; 1st, 2nd, 4th, 5th, 8th, 9th, 28th, 29th, 30th, 35th, 79th, 83rd and 90th Infantry Divisions.
> German Divisions Confronting the American First Army:
> Panzer Lehr and 2nd SS Panzer; 17th SS Panzer Grenadier; 3rd and 5th Parachute; 91st, 243rd, 352nd and 353rd Infantry Divisions.

56 These figures are for the period of 6 June through 23 July and only include losses and replacements for German ground units. See Zetterling, *Normandy 1944, German Military Organization, Combat Power and Organizational Effectiveness*, pp. 30, 78.

57 By 27 July German materiel losses from the Normandy fighting included 381 tanks, 60 assault guns and 45 self–propelled anti-tank guns that were total write–offs. A few days later German authorities reported 406 tanks and 75 assault guns irretrievably lost and 353 tanks and 117 assault guns in workshops. See Zetterling, *Normandy 1944, German Military Organization, Combat Power and Organizational Effectiveness*, p. 82.

58 Martin Blumenson, *The US Army in World War II: European Theater of Operations, Breakout and Pursuit* (Washington D.C.: Office of the Chief of Military History, Department of the Army, 1961), p. 331.

59 SHAEF G1 Document dated 8 March 1945 Showing Prisoners of War Captured by Month. See WO 299/7/1, Enemy Prisoners of War: Statistical Reports and Information.

60 WO 219/1531, Casualty Reports: British, Canadian and U.S. Forces Daily Summaries, including Enemy Prisoners Taken.

61 These losses are primarily compiled from ADM 199/2447, German Ships: Losses and Damage in NW European Waters, 1939–1945 and AIR 41/79, RAF in the Maritime War, Volume VIII: Statistics with additions and minor changes taken from other sources.

62 ADM 186/796, Battle Summaries, No. 43: Invasion of the South of France, Operation *Dragoon*, 15 August 1944, Appendix A.

63 Rohwer and Hummelchen, *Chronology of the War At Sea 1939–1945*, p. 298.

64 ADM 199/2447, German Ships: Losses and Damage in NW European Waters, 1939–1945 with additions and minor changes taken from other sources.

65 Ibid.

66 Ibid.

67 Ibid.

68 Ellis, *Victory in the West, Volume I*, pp. 447–448.

69 WO 219/1531, Casualty Reports: British, Canadian and U.S. Forces Daily Summaries, including Enemy Prisoners Taken.

70 Blumenson, *The US Army in World War II: European Theater of Operations, Breakout and Pursuit*, p. 558.

71 Ellis, *Victory in the West, Volume I*, p. 448.

72 Blumenson, *The US Army in World War II: European Theater of Operations, Breakout and Pursuit*, p. 577.

73 Nigel Hamilton, *Master of the Battlefield, Monty's War Years 1942–1944* (New York: McGraw–Hill Book, 1983), p. 832.

74 SHAEF G1 Document dated 8 March 1945 Showing Prisoners of War Captured by Month. See WO 299/7/1, Enemy Prisoners of War: Statistical Reports and Information.

75 Zetterling, *Normandy 1944, German Military Organization, Combat Power and Organizational Effectiveness*, p. 77.

76 Neillands, *The Battle of Normandy 1944*, p. 411.

77 Ellis, *Victory in the West, Volume I*, p. 491.

78 These losses are primarily compiled from ADM 199/2447, German Ships: Losses and Damage in NW European Waters, 1939–1945 with additions and minor changes taken from other sources.

79 Ellis, *Victory in the West, Volume I*, p. 493.

80 Ibid., p. 488.

81 AIR 41/74 The RAF in the Maritime War, Volume V: Atlantic and Home Waters; The Victory Phase, June 1944–May 1945, p. 52.

Chapter 10: Victory in Europe

1 Philip Graves, *The Record of the War–The Twentieth Quarter: July 1, 1944–September 30, 1944* (Hutchinson and Company, Inc., 1946), p. 50.

2 Message from SHAEF MAIN to G–1 European Theater of Operations, REF No S–60136. See WO 229/47, Prisoners of War.

3 Ibid.

4 SHAEF G1 Report of Enemy Prisoners of War Dated 1 October 1944. See WO 229/47/4, Prisoners of War: Allied Prisoner of War Responsibilities.

5 L. F. Ellis, *Victory in the West, Volume II: The Defeat of Germany* (London: Her Majesty's Stationery Office, 1968), p. 2.

6 The West Wall was a defensive line constructed by the Germans prior to the beginning of the war. Stretching 390 miles along Germany's western border, the West Wall possessed numerous fortifications including some 3,000 bunkers and pillboxes as well as extensive minefields and anti-tank obstacles. Allied forces often referred to the West Wall as the Siegfried Line.

7 Cornelius Ryan, *A Bridge Too Far* (New York: Popular Library Edition, 1974), p. 599.

8 German records are incomplete for this period, and it is thus impossible to make a firm accounting of German casualties during Operation *Market-Garden*. A number commonly reported in many historical accounts is that the Germans suffered 3,300 casualties including 1,300 dead in the fighting around Arnhem and Oosterbeek, but this only covers a portion of the battle. In assessing the total cost, historian Cornelius Ryan estimates German losses at between 7,500 and 10,000 while Robert Kershaw puts these figures at 6,315 to 8,925 based upon an acknowledged incomplete accounting of the participating German units. Meanwhile, Stephen Badsey puts German losses at 2,000 dead and 6,000 wounded with no mention of prisoners taken.

9 Patrick Delaforce, *Smashing the Atlantic Wall, The Destruction of Hitler's Coastal Fortress* (London: Cassell & Co., 2001), p. 106.

10 C. P. Stacey, *Official History of the Canadian Army in the Second World War, Volume III: The Victory Campaign, The Operations in North-West Europe 1944–1945* (Ottawa: Queen's Printer and Controller of Stationery, 1966), pp. 336, 343, 352, 354.

11 This daily receipt of supplies included 7,000 tons at Dieppe, 5,000 tons at Le Havre, 11,000 tons at Boulogne and 5,000 tons at Ostend. See Delaforce, *Smashing the Atlantic Wall, The Destruction of Hitler's Coastal Fortress*, p. 217.

12 ADM 234/363, Battle Summaries, No. 49: Campaign in North-West Europe June 1944–May 1945, pp. 47, 48.

13 This included 40 landing craft assault, 20 landing vehicle tracked (Buffaloes) and 26 Weasel amphibious vehicles. See Delaforce, *Smashing the Atlantic Wall, The Destruction of Hitler's Coastal Fortress*, p. 191.

14 This proved to be *Warspite*'s final operation in an illustrious career that had begun 28 years earlier at the battle of Jutland and earned the great warship more battle honours than any other ship in Royal Navy history. During World War II *Warspite*'s many accomplishments included its key participation during the naval battles of Second Narvik, Calabria and Cape Matapan and the more than a dozen shore bombardments it conducted against targets in Norway, Albania, North Africa, Sicily, Italy and Northwest Europe.

15 These losses broke down into ten landing craft assaults, four landing craft tanks, four landing craft guns, three landing craft supports (fire support), two landing craft flaks (anti-aircraft), two landing craft personnels and one landing craft infantry. See Rohwer and Hummelchen, *Chronology of the War At Sea 1939–1945*, p. 314.

16 ADM 234/363, Battle Summaries, No. 49: Campaign in North-West Europe June 1944–May 1945, p. 54.

17 Roland G. Ruppenthal, *The US Army in World War II: European Theater of Operations, Logistical Support of the Armies, Volume II: September 1944–May 1945* (Washington D.C.: Office of the Chief of Military History, Department of the Army, 1959), p. 124.

18 Stacey, *Official History of the Canadian Army in the Second World War, Volume III: The Victory Campaign, The Operations in North-West Europe 1944–1945*, p. 424.

19 SHAEF G1 Report of Enemy Prisoners of War dated 7 December 1944. See WO 229/7/1, Enemy Prisoners of War: Statistical Reports and Information.

20 Charles B. MacDonald, *The US Army in World War II: European Theater of Operations, The Siegfried Line Campaign* (Washington D.C.: Office of the Chief of Military History, Department of the Army, 1963), p. 617 and Hugh M. Cole, *The US Army in World War II: European Theater of Operations, The Lorraine Campaign* (Washington D.C.: Office of the Chief of Military History, Department of the Army, 1950), p. 593.

21 Ellis, *Victory in the West, Volume II*, p. 195.

22 Charles B. MacDonald, *The US Army in World War II: European Theater of Operations, The Last Offensive* (Washington D.C.: Office of the Chief of Military History, Department of the Army, 1973), pp. 5, 14.

23 Dönitz, *Memoirs: Ten Years and Twenty Days*, p. 426.

24 Roskill, *The War at Sea 1939–1945, Volume III, Part II*, p. 477.

25 Ibid., p. 185.

26 The loss of *U247* is also recorded in Chapter 9.

27 Roskill, *The War at Sea 1939–1945, Volume III, Part II*, pp. 477–478 and Rohwer and Hummelchen, *Chronology of the War At Sea 1939–1945*, pp. 306, 315, 321.

28 ADM 199/2447, German Ships: Losses and Damage in NW European Waters, 1939–1945 and Roskill, *The War at Sea 1939–1945, Volume III, Part II*, p. 153.

29 Roskill, *The War at Sea 1939–1945, Volume III, Part II*, p. 479.

30 ADM 234/578, Naval Staff History: Defeat of the Enemy Attack on Shipping, 1939–1945: A Study of Policy and Operations, Volume IA (Text and Appendices), Appendix 6.

31 The American total is taken from Blair, *Hitler's U-boat War, the Hunted, 1942–1945*, p. 708 and the British total is taken from The Central Statistical Office, *Statistical Digest of the War*, p. 135.

32   The Central Statistical Office, *Statistical Digest of the War*, p. 184.

33   Roskill, *The War at Sea 1939–1945, Volume III, Part II*, pp. 286–287.

34   Ibid., pp. 301, 477.

35   The destruction of *U864* represented an amazing accomplishment in that for the first time in naval warfare one submarine successfully engaged another while both submarines were submerged. This was done through the use of hydrophone and Asdic detection as the primary means to acquire and track *U864*'s location and course.

36   Ellis, *Victory in the West, Volume II*, p. 233; Tarrant, *The Last Year of the Kriegsmarine, May 1944–May 1945*, pp. 212–221 and ADM 199/2447, German Ships: Losses and Damage in NW European Waters, 1939–1945.

37   AIR 40/2588, British Bombing Survey Unit: Sea Communications Panel; Report on Air Action against German Merchant Shipping, part II, p. 10.

38   Ibid., part II, p. 9.

39   Ibid., Appendix B1.

40   Ibid., part II, p. 9.

41   Ibid., Appendix E.

42   Tarrant, *The Last Year of the Kriegsmarine, May 1944–May 1945*, p. 225.

43   ADM 199/2447, German Ships: Losses and Damage in NW European Waters, 1939–1945. This includes a handful of tonnage differences taken from other sources relating specifically to the warship losses.

44   Roskill, *The War at Sea 1939–1945, Volume III, Part II*, pp. 139, 142.

45   These losses are primarily compiled from ADM 199/2447, German Ships: Losses and Damage in NW European Waters, 1939–1945 with additions and minor changes taken from other sources. This applies to all further listings of German surface shipping losses unless stated otherwise.

46   *M266* had been previously sunk by RAF bombers in August 1944. It had been raised and was under repairs when it was sunk again by USAAF bombers.

47   During the course of the war Swordfish aircraft sank or played a principal role in destroying the battleships *Conte di Cavour* (Italian) and *Bismarck*, the heavy cruiser *Pola* (Italian), ten assorted destroyers/torpedo boats, 16 submarines, one armed merchant cruiser and more than 150,000 tons of Axis merchant shipping.

48   The breakdown of these losses include at least nine ships worth 18,251 tons that were sunk by submarine-laid mines and nine ships worth 7,038 tons that were sunk in direct attacks. An additional five vessels worth 1,454 tons were listed in the official British records as sunk by submarine-laid or naval mines (and are counted as such here), but may in fact have been sunk by aerial mines or other means. See ADM 199/2447, German Ships: Losses and Damage in NW European Waters, 1939–1945 and Rohwer, *Allied Submarine Attacks of World War Two, European Theatre of Operations 1939–1945*, pp. 71–73.

49   AIR 40/2588, British Bombing Survey Unit: Sea Communications Panel; Report on Air Action against German Merchant Shipping, Appendix B1.

50   The breakdown of divisions that participated in the battle is as follows:
       Canadian First Army:
       2nd, 3rd and 4th (Armoured) Canadian Divisions; 3rd, 11th (Armoured), Guards (Armoured), 15th, 43rd, 51st, 52nd and 53rd British Divisions. Also present in a supporting role were elements of the British 79th Armoured Division.
       German First Parachute Army:
       2nd Parachute, 6th Parachute, 7th Parachute, 8th Parachute, 84th, 180th, 190th, 346th, 15th Panzer Grenadier, 116th Panzer and Panzer Lehr Divisions.

51   Stacey, *Official History of the Canadian Army in the Second World War, Volume III: The Victory Campaign, The Operations in North-West Europe 1944–1945*, p. 522.

52 Ibid., p. 524.

53 PW Supplement to HQ 21 Army Group "A" SITREP No. 287. See WO 219/1547, Casualty Reports: 21 Army Group Daily Reports, including Reinforcements and Enemy Prisoners Taken.

54 Ellis, *Victory in the West, Volume II*, p. 294.

55 MacDonald, *The US Army in World War II: European Theater of Operations, The Last Offensive*, p. 372.

56 Ellis, *Victory in the West, Volume II*, p. 312.

57 The breakdown of British and British–affiliated divisions participating in this final offensive phase is as follows:

> British Second Army:
> 7th, 11th and Guards Armoured; 6th Airborne; 3rd, 5th, 15th, 43rd, 51st, 52nd and 53rd Infantry Divisions (all British).
> Canadian First Army:
> 4th and 5th Canadian Armoured; 1st Polish Armoured; 1st, 2nd and 3rd Canadian Infantry and 49th British Infantry Divisions.
> 21st Army Group: 79th British Armoured Division.
> Note: The British 5th and Canadian 1st and 5th Divisions were all recent transfers from the Mediterranean theatre. The former did not become active until the middle of April. At the end of April the British 3rd Division came under the authority of the Canadian First Army.

58 Stacey, *Official History of the Canadian Army in the Second World War, Volume III: The Victory Campaign, The Operations in North-West Europe 1944–1945*, pp. 556, 557, 587, 614.

59 Of these losses, U-boats accounted for 16 merchant ships and the two warships while mines accounted for six merchant ships. See Roskill, *The War at Sea 1939–1945, Volume III, Part II*, pp. 444, 446, 477, 478.

60 ADM 199/2447, German Ships: Losses and Damage in NW European Waters, 1939–1945 and Tarrant, *The Last Year of the Kriegsmarine, May 1944–May 1945*, p. 222.

61 In the case of *Z43*, the destroyer was severely damaged by a mine strike in April and subsequently scuttled in early May.

62 PW Supplement to HQ 21 Army Group "A" SITREP No. 322. See WO 219/1547, Casualty Reports: 21 Army Group Daily Reports, including Reinforcements and Enemy Prisoners Taken.

63 Tarrant, *The Last Year of the Kriegsmarine, May 1944–May 1945*, pp. 230–236 and Rohwer and Hummelchen, *Chronology of the War At Sea 1939–1945*, p. 351.

64 PW Supplement to HQ 21 Army Group "A" SITREP No. 322 through SITREP No. 331. See WO 219/1547, Casualty Reports: 21 Army Group Daily Reports, including Reinforcements and Enemy Prisoners Taken.

65 ADM 234/369, Battle Summaries, No. 22: Arctic Convoys 1941–1945, Appendix A, Sections I, II and III.

66 Paul Kemp, *Convoy, Drama in Arctic Waters* (London: Brockhampton Press, 1999), p. 235.

67 Ian Campbell and Donald Macintyre, *The Kola Run, A Record of Arctic Convoys, 1941–1945* (London: Frederick Muller, 1958), p. 189.

68 ADM 234/369, Battle Summaries, No. 22: Arctic Convoys 1941–1945, Appendix A, Sections V and VII.

69 Ibid., p. 129.

70 The breakdown of German prisoners collected in these areas as of the middle of May was: the Wilhelmshaven-Emden peninsula – 60,000, Western Holland – 120,000, the Cuxhaven peninsula – 260,000, Denmark – 160,000, north Schleswig–Holstein – 250,000, south Schleswig-Holstein – 134,000, east Prussia – 75,000, Wismar Cushion – 360,000. See Francis De Guingand, *Operation Victory* (New York: Charles Scribner's Son, 1947), p. 458.

71 MacDonald, *The US Army in World War II: European Theater of Operations, The Last Offensive*, p. 478.
72 Ellis, *Victory in the West, Volume II*, p. 407.
73 This includes a handful of vessels that were sunk from June through August 1945 following Germany's surrender. See Roskill, *The War at Sea 1939–1945, Volume III, Part II*, p. 479.
74 Author's tally taken from a variety of sources.
75 This tally is primarily compiled from ADM 199/2447, German Ships: Losses and Damage in NW European Waters, 1939–1945 and AIR 41/79, RAF in the Maritime War, Volume VIII: Statistics with additions and minor changes taken from other sources.
76 Ibid.
77 These totals include 524 vessels of unknown but presumably minimal tonnage. See AIR 41/79, RAF in the Maritime War, Volume VIII: Statistics.
78 These principal warship losses consisted of seized Italian, French and other Allied vessels that came under German control during the course of the war.
79 Merchant losses compiled primarily from Jordan, *The World's Merchant Fleets 1939, The Particulars and Wartime Fates of 6,000 ships*. Affiliated losses consist of Italian, Vichy French, Finnish and Romanian ships that were seized or sunk in these outer areas.

Chapter 11: The Reckoning

1 David M. Glantz, *The Soviet-German War 1941–1945: Myths and Realities: A Survey Essay*, (A Paper Presented as the 20th Anniversary Distinguished Lecture at the Strom Thurmond Institute of Government and Public Affairs, Clemson University, October 11, 2001), pp. 9, 14.
2 Zetterling, *Normandy 1944, German Military Organization, Combat Power and Organizational Effectiveness*, p. 95.
3 Glantz, *The Soviet-German War 1941–1945: Myths and Realities: A Survey Essay*, p. 106.
4 This conclusion is clearly demonstrated by an analysis of aerial attrition that assesses the total number of Axis aircraft lost in operations confronting the Western Allies in Europe and the Middle East at well over 40,000 compared to just 11,000 lost on the Eastern Front. See Robert S. Ehlers, Jr., *The Mediterranean Air War, Airpower and the Allied Victory in World War II* (Lawrence: University Press of Kansas, 2015), pp. 402–403.
5 Ellis, *Victory in the West, Volume II*, pp. 406, 408.
6 The surrendered vessels include one light cruiser, three destroyers and one escort destroyer that proceeded to Spanish territory and were interned. These vessels eventually came under Allied control. The German-inflicted losses include several new warships that were seized while under construction. I used a launch date of 1943 or before as the delineating factor determining inclusion in this calculation. This also includes several Yugoslav and French warships that were under direct Italian control at the time of their capture.
7 The total Axis tally consists of 2,895 principal warships including Vichy French and Persian vessels sunk or seized by the Allies as well as the combined losses of Germany, Italy and Japan.
8 Roskill, *The War at Sea 1939–1945, Volume III, Part II*, p. 367.
9 Dear and Foot, *The Oxford Companion to World War II*, p. 629.
10 Ruge, *Der Seekrieg, The German Navy's Story, 1939–1945*, p. 259.
11 Author's calculation based upon data compiled from a number of sources.
12 These loss figures come primarily from The Joint Army-Navy Assessment Committee, *Japanese Naval and Merchant Losses During World War II By all Causes* (Washington: US Government Printing Office, 1947) with some additions or adjustments taken from other sources.

Index

Index of Warships

Index of U-boats

Index of Operations

Index of Convoys

Main Index